INVESTMENT ETHICS

D0814153

INVESTMENT ETHICS

SARAH W. PECK, Ph.D.

Associate Professor and Chair
Department of Finance
College of Business Administration
Marquette University

WILEY

JOHN WILEY & SONS, INC.

VP & Publisher	George Hoffman
Acquisitions Editor	Lacey Vitetta
Project Editor	Jennifer Manias
Senior Editorial Assistant	Emily McGee
Assistant Marketing Manager	Diane Mars
Media Editor	Greg Chaput
Production Manager	Janis Soo
Assistant Production Editor	Yee Lyn Song
Cover Designer	Wendy Lai

This book was set in 10/12 Minion by Laserwords Private Limited, and printed and bound by R.R. Donnelley. The cover was printed by R.R. Donnelley.

This book is printed on acid free paper. ∞

Founded in 1807, John Wiley & Sons, Inc. has been a valued source of knowledge and understanding for more than 200 years, helping people around the world meet their needs and fulfill their aspirations. Our company is built on a foundation of principles that include responsibility to the communities we serve and where we live and work. In 2008, we launched a Corporate Citizenship Initiative, a global effort to address the environmental, social, economic, and ethical challenges we face in our business. Among the issues we are addressing are carbon impact, paper specifications and procurement, ethical conduct within our business and among our vendors, and community and charitable support. For more information, please visit our website: www.wiley.com/go/citizenship.

Copyright © 2011 John Wiley & Sons, Inc. All rights reserved. No part of this publication may be reproduced, stored in a retrieval system or transmitted in any form or by any means, electronic, mechanical, photocopying, recording, scanning or otherwise, except as permitted under Sections 107 or 108 of the 1976 United States Copyright Act, without either the prior written permission of the Publisher, or authorization through payment of the appropriate per-copy fee to the Copyright Clearance Center, Inc. 222 Rosewood Drive, Danvers, MA 01923, website www.copyright.com. Requests to the Publisher for permission should be addressed to the Permissions Department, John Wiley & Sons, Inc., 111 River Street, Hoboken, NJ 07030-5774, (201)748-6011, fax (201)748-6008, website http://www.wiley.com/go/permissions.

Evaluation copies are provided to qualified academics and professionals for review purposes only, for use in their courses during the next academic year. These copies are licensed and may not be sold or transferred to a third party. Upon completion of the review period, please return the evaluation copy to Wiley. Return instructions and a free of charge return shipping label are available at www.wiley.com/go/returnlabel. Outside of the United States, please contact your local representative.

Library of Congress Cataloging-in-Publication Data

Peck, Sarah W., 1958-
  Investment ethics / Sarah Peck.
       p. cm.
  Includes bibliographical references and index.
  ISBN 978-0-470-43453-6 (pbk. : acid-free paper)
1. Finance–Moral and ethical aspects. 2. Investment advisors–Moral and ethical aspects. 3. Investments–Moral and ethical aspects. 4. Financial services industry–Moral and ethical aspects. 5. Business ethics. I. Title.
  HG103.P43 2011
  174–dc22
                              2010032744

Printed in The United States of America
10 9 8 7 6 5 4 3 2 1

Brief Contents

Contents

Chapter   2

FIDUCIARY DUTY OF INVESTMENT PROFESSIONALS: THE ETHICAL TREATMENT OF THE CLIENT   26

Chapter   3

ETHICAL REPORTING OF INVESTMENT PERFORMANCE   54

Chapter   6

INVESTING IN COMPANIES WITH ETHICAL ACCOUNTING PRACTICES   136

Chapter 7

INVESTING IN COMPANIES WITH GOOD CORPORATE GOVERNANCE PRACTICES 160

Preface

Investment Ethics

The Need for Ethical Education

When talking about investment ethics, the typical response is, "Isn't that an oxymoron?" This old joke may be . . . well, old, but it also highlights the importance of teaching ethics along with the nuts and bolts of investments and financial analysis. The need for ethical education is as long-standing as the history of scandals that plague the industry. There were the insider trading scandals of the 1980s, the accounting scandals of the late 1990s, and most recently the financial crisis that began in the fall of 2008, fraught with excessive risk taking and an explosion of ever-larger Ponzi schemes. The recent crisis further underscores the importance of ethics to ensure the long-run health of our financial markets. Educators are at the forefront of instilling ethical values in investment professionals.

Unethical behavior occurs for two reasons. First, the raison d'être of the investment business is to make money: returns. There is nothing inherently unethical about the profit motive, but it can blur the lines between when you are *fairly* making money for yourself and your firm and when you are *unfairly* making money by taking advantage of others. Second, finance is a technical and quantitative world not immediately comprehensible to everyone. This creates both opportunities for unethical behavior and a natural suspicion of investment professionals.

Ethical education and standards are critical in protecting students entering into the profession from ethical pitfalls that can ruin their careers. Some have argued that ethics cannot be taught. That may be true. There will always be individuals who have no conscience. Yet, the profit motive coupled with technological complexity can create conditions where even well-intentioned individuals are corrupted.

Practical knowledge about ethical issues in investments can ameliorate the incidence of bad behavior. In turn, ethical professionals maintain the integrity of the business, which generates more interest and trust in financial markets for the average person on Main Street. This book provides students entering the investment industry with an applied and practical understanding of ethics.

ORGANIZATION AND PEDAGOGICAL FEATURES

Chapter 1, The Case for Investment Ethics, sets the stage with a brief overview of the investment industry, regulations, and a history of scandals. In this chapter, we establish four fundamental principles of investment ethics, to guide the remaining chapters. We cite these four principles throughout the book as a wider platform to delve deeper into more specific and practical ethical issues.

The rest of the book tackles two roles that finance professionals play in investments. Chapters 2 through 5 address interactions and business dealings with various groups: clients, traders, employers, analysts, and other market participants. These chapters cover the laws, professional codes of conduct, and other guidelines for the behavior of investment professionals. It might seem simple to teach students to be ethical by reminding them to follow the Golden Rule—treat others as you would like to be treated—or the rule that says you shouldn't do anything that you wouldn't want to show up on the front page of the *Wall Street Journal*. But applying these rules in different situations can be confusing for new professionals who are trying to balance integrity and fairness with pressures to make money for both themselves and their firms. Further investments are complicated. These chapters provide practical

---

FUNDAMENTAL PRINCIPLES OF INVESTMENT ETHICS FOR PROFESSIONALS

Principle 1: ETHICAL UNDERSTANDING

Because investments are complicated, *you have an obligation not to knowingly engage in an investment transaction that either you or others do not sufficiently understand. This includes knowing the underlying source of returns or fees charged.*

Principle 2: ETHICAL USE OF INFORMATION

Because investments are information driven, *you have an obligation to ensure that you and others have access to relevant information and that you or others do not misuse or distort information in the investment transaction.*

Principle 3: RESPONSIBLE INVESTING

Because investments provide financial resources to others, *you have an obligation to ensure that you do not knowingly make or recommend investments that support activities that harm others.*

Principle 4: TRUST AND FAIRNESS

Because you are dealing with others' money either directly or indirectly, *you have an obligation not to abuse the trust that all others have either explicitly or implicitly placed in you to treat them fairly.*

guides that will help students navigate the ethical challenges they will face in their professional careers.

- Chapter 2, Fiduciary Duty of Investment Professionals: The Ethical Treatment of the Client
- Chapter 3, Ethical Reporting of Investment Performance
- Chapter 4, Ethical Use of Information
- Chapter 5, Analyst Integrity

Chapters 6 through 8 address the role that analysts play in making investment decisions and recommendations. The material in these chapters can help supplement the standard fundamental analysis taught in an investments or security analysis class. To be ethical, analysts need to consider the ethical practices of the companies and organizations they recommend: accounting practices, corporate governance, and social responsibility. These factors have recently been captured under the abbreviation ESG (environmental, social, and governance). The ability to analyze companies' practices in these areas can lead to better investment decisions. Analysts who can distinguish between true economic and sustainable earnings and those created by accounting gimmicks are likely to make investments in stocks that sustain strong returns. Similarly, firms with healthy corporate governance practices, such as boards that effectively monitor the top executive team and provide incentive compensation for the CEO and other top executives, are also likely to do well. Firms that are socially responsible are less likely to be the subject of scandal, lawsuits, and regulatory and legal fines and sanctions. In addition, there is a growing market for investors who care about social responsibility; these chapters will help prepare students to meet these clients' needs. But beyond earning good returns and keeping clients happy, these chapters can help students think about their larger role in society in evaluating the business practices of firms and directing capital toward those whose practices are beneficial to society overall.

- Chapter 6, Investing in Companies with Ethical Accounting Practices
- Chapter 7, Investing in Companies with Good Corporate Governance Practices
- Chapter 8, Socially Responsible Investing

Each chapter includes these features:

- Learning Objectives
- Chapter Outline
- Terms
- Review Questions
- Critical Thinking Questions
- Applied Student Project

- Recommended Cases
- References and Suggested Reading

The Learning Objectives give students a set of goals or specific tasks they should be able to accomplish after reading the chapter. With the chapter outline, these objectives help set up the chapter for them. All of the terms highlighted in the text are listed at the end of the chapter. Terms also help students acquire the common "language" of finance useful for their professional development. Review questions are designed to test students' most rudimentary comprehension of the chapter material. Critical thinking questions provide more thought-provoking questions. The applied student projects in almost all chapters incorporate ethics into more traditional investment exercises and security analysis. Additionally, these projects require students use the Internet for research and data collection. Chapter 3 has a project that asks students to construct a portfolio and manipulate various measures of risk and return relative to benchmark performance. Chapter 4 includes an event study. In Chapter 5, students are asked to develop earnings forecasts. Chapters 6, 7, and 8 each feature fundamental security analysis projects using a firm's quality of earnings and indications of earnings manipulation, corporate governance practices, and social responsibility. These projects are designed for students to apply investment theory and analysis; but they also integrate ethical considerations, which will become a very real part of their jobs as they move out of the classroom and into the workforce. All of the examples and projects use data from www.finance.yahoo.com. This website was chosen because it has a large amount of downloadable data; it's easy to use, and free. Related cases from Chapter 9 are also listed at the end of most chapters, and these cases can be used to spark class discussion and more thoughtful analysis of the issues raised in the chapter. In addition, each chapter provides a list of references and suggested reading.

We also include appendixes that review basics in investments and accounting that most students should have covered in other courses. These appendixes ensure that students have access to the most pertinent basics, so that they can understand each chapter on a stand-alone basis.

Chapter 9 comprises 30 "mini" cases. Each case begins with a brief factual overview, followed by four discussion questions. These cases can be used to supplement the material in the chapters or can serve as a spark for short discussions. The cases feature a mix of well-known companies and individuals as well as some that are more obscure. Finally, Chapter 9 can serve as a set of cautionary tales for students who don't adhere to the ethical guidelines provided in the earlier chapters!

This book is designed to supplement material in a standard investments or security analysis course. As an instructor, you could assign chapters in this book along with chapters from a standard investment text. You could then allow a 15-minute discussion about a particular case that is recommended in a chapter. The applied projects can be easily integrated with other hands-on assignments that students complete. Thus the material in this book is designed to be easily integrated into an investments course; it will enhance rather than detract from the standard material covered. This book can also be used to complement professional codes of ethics by providing a broader context for specific material related to codes of conduct, such as those dictated by the CFA®, CFP®, and FINRA organizations. The following table presents suggestions for how you can use chapters from this book with topics covered in a standard investments class.

Investment Topic	Investment Ethics Chapter
Introduction to Financial Instruments and Markets	Chapter 1, Introduction: The Case for Investment Ethics
How Securities Are Traded	Chapter 2, Fiduciary Duty of Investment Professionals: The Ethical Treatment of the Client
	Chapter 4, Ethical Use of Information
Portfolio Theory, Portfolio Performance Evaluation	Chapter 3, Ethical Reporting of Investment Performance
Portfolio Management	Chapter 2, Fiduciary Duty of Investment Professionals: The Ethical Treatment of the Client
Active Portfolio Management	Chapter 2, Fiduciary Duty of Investment Professionals: The Ethical Treatment of the Client
	Chapter 3, Ethical Reporting of Investment Performance
Market Efficiency	Chapter 4, Ethical Use of Information
Mutual Funds	Chapter 3, Ethical Reporting of Investment Performance
	Chapter 4, Ethical Use of Information
Security Analysis	Chapter 5, Analyst Integrity
	Chapter 6, Investing in Companies with Ethical Accounting Practices
	Chapter 7, Investing in Companies with Good Corporate Governance Practices
	Chapter 8, Socially Responsible Investing
Financial Statement Analysis	Chapter 5, Analyst Integrity
	Chapter 6, Investing in Companies with Ethical Accounting Practices

ACKNOWLEDGMENTS

Many people helped make this book possible—I thank them all. Marquette University, with its value-based mission, allowed me to create the course on which this book is based. The CFA Institute provided support and encouragement by recognizing the course syllabus as an example of best practices of CFA Program Partners as part of its overall commitment to ethics. The CFA Institute also suggested writing a textbook and gave me the opportunity to write ethics cases for them. I am grateful to my many students over the years, who let me "try out" most of the material used in this textbook in the classroom. They participated earnestly in debates about what is ethical and what is not and in discussions about the motives and consequences of the actions of various individuals involved in different cases. Margaret E. Monahan-Pashall did an excellent job proofreading the last draft. I appreciate my publisher, Wiley, and all the reviewers who have given me invaluable feedback.

O. Felix Ayadi, Texas State University

Paramita Bandyopadhyay, California State University

Kristine L. Beck, University of Wisconsin, Oshkosh

Earl Benson, Western Washington University

Ali M. Kutan, Southern Illinois University

Nikiforos Laopodis, Fairfield University

Adam Y.C. Lei, Midwestern State University

Tom C. Nelson, University of Colorado

Devendra Prasad, University of Massachusetts

Lina Zhou, Augustana College

Finally, I am deeply indebted to my family—Tom, Lauren, and Martha—who are an everlasting source of support and inspiration.

About the Author

Sarah W. Peck, Ph.D., is Associate Professor and Chair of the Finance department at Marquette University. She earned her bachelor's degree in Psychology from Yale University and a M.A. in applied economics and a Ph.D. in finance and accounting from University of Rochester. Her research interests are in the area of ownership structure, leveraged buyouts, board of directors, and other topics in corporate governance. She has published in the *Journal of Financial Economics, Journal of Corporate Finance, Journal of Forensic Accounting*, among other finance journals. She has also written ethics cases for the Chartered Financial Analysts (CFA) Institute and is a member of the CFA Institute. Dr. Peck has close to twenty years of teaching experience, including "Investment Management, Ethics, and Society," a course in Marquette's Applied Investment Management (AIM) program, the first undergraduate program named as an educational partner with the CFA Institute. Dr. Peck also serves as a trustee for the Milwaukee County Pension Board and is Chair of the Investment Committee.

1

Introduction: The Case for Investment Ethics

Learning Objectives

After reading this chapter, students should be able to:

- Describe some of the significant scandals in the history of investments.
- Explain the history and basic function of financial regulatory agencies.
- Identify key SEC filings and forms.
- Discuss the features of the investment industry that create opportunities for unethical professionals.
- List and discuss the four fundamental principles of investment ethics.
- Recognize and understand the importance of developing an ethical consciousness.

CHAPTER OUTLINE

- Introduction: The Investment Industry—A Legacy of Scandals and a Need for Ethics
- A Brief Overview of the Investment Industry
- Securities Laws and Regulations
- Investment Ethics Are Easier Said than Done
- Ethics Basics
- Four Fundamental Principles of Investment Ethics
- Costs and Benefits of Being Unethical
- Conclusion: Developing an Ethical Consciousness
- Appendix: Financial Market Regulatory Agencies

INTRODUCTION: THE INVESTMENT INDUSTRY—A LEGACY OF SCANDALS AND A NEED FOR ETHICS

The financial crisis of 2008, and the misconduct it exposed, is only the most recent scandal in a long line of disgraces that speaks to the need for more education in investment ethics. Consequently, in this chapter we develop basic principles of investment ethics in the context of the history of financial scandals, the structure of the investments industry, and its laws and regulations. This sets the stage for a deeper exploration of the applications of investment ethics in the remainder of the book.

Like most people, you probably believe *investment ethics* is a contradiction in terms. Why is it that the investment industry is plagued by the image of greedy shysters preying on naïve investors? A long history of scandals fosters this image and suggests it may be well deserved. Financial scandals are as old as the industry itself. One of the earliest-known schemes was undertaken by William Duer in 1792. At that time, Wall Street was the location of a fledgling investment industry. Besides commodities, such as tobacco, corn, and sugar, shares in the Bank of the United States and the Bank of New York were offered to the public and could be traded. Duer, a Caribbean plantation owner, teamed up with Alexander Macomb, an Irish land speculator, to form the Six Percent Club. These investors conspired to secretly acquire 6 percent of the bank shares. The idea was that the 6 percent purchases, spread across the market, would create an interest in these securities and drive up their prices. The Six Percent Club would then sell at the top of the market and make a nice profit. Unfortunately, Duer borrowed heavily to make his purchases. When the economy began to decline and the banks slowed down in making loans and profits, Duer's scheme fell apart, contributing to a market panic and decline.

Sound familiar? It should. Fast-forward more than two hundred years to the financial crisis of 2008. Industry professionals, regulators, and academics are still trying to sort out the causes of the most recent crisis. But it is generally agreed upon that a bubble in housing prices spurred by low interest rates and rampant subprime borrowing caused overconfidence in the markets and an underestimation of default risk. Some investors borrowed heavily, seeking even higher returns on credit-based investments, which drove prices even higher. For example, Bear Stearns advised clients to borrow to invest in **mortgage-backed securities (MBSs)**. MBSs are securities that are created from a portfolio or a pool of mortgages. The investor receives income from the securities from the interest and principal repayments on the underlying mortgages. As long as default rates are negligible, these are securities with minimal risks. In 2007, when default rates increased as housing prices started to fall, the value of these securities declined rapidly. The firm itself used its own funds to engage in a similar strategy as its clients—eventually reaching a leverage ratio of over 30 to 1.

Mortgage-backed securities (MBSs) securities that are created from a portfolio or a pool of mortgages; investor receives income from the securities from the interest and principal repayments on the underlying mortgages.

Remember that a leverage ratio represents how much debt is used relative to the equity investment; a 30:1 ratio means the firm is borrowing *a lot*. When the market began to decline, these investments lost over $1.5 billion, Bear Stearns collapsed, and JPMorgan Chase bought the firm. Duer could have been a cautionary tale to Bear Stearns about the use of leverage in the quest for profits. But would anyone listen? Before we answer this question, let's look at another example of history repeating itself.

Bernard L. Madoff's Ponzi scheme is perhaps the most outrageous scandal exposed during the recent financial crisis. Madoff's scheme is believed to have lasted over a decade and defrauded investors of over $65 billion. He claimed to be earning fabulous returns for investors but actually was using some of his investors' money to pay off other investors—the essence of a Ponzi scheme. Yet Ponzi schemes are nothing new. In fact, the scheme is named after Charles Ponzi, who perpetuated such a scheme in the 1920s. A **Ponzi scheme**, also known as a pyramid scheme, is when money raised from new investors is used to pay off old investors, thus creating the illusion that the crook is making profitable investments. Despite the tremendous growth in the size and number of innovations in the investment industry, the same

Ponzi scheme a fraudulent scheme whereby old investors' returns are paid out of funds raised by new investors.

TABLE	1.1	A SAMPLING OF FINANCIAL SCANDALS

1986	***Mike Milken and Insider Trading in the 1980s:*** Dennis Levine, Ivan Boesky, Mike Milken, and Martin Siegel devised a scheme to trade on inside information on investment banking deals. Many of these deals were leveraged buyouts arranged by Mike Milken, the "junk bond king," of Drexel Burnham Lambert. Drexel Burnham Lambert filed for Chapter 11 bankruptcy protection in the wake of the scandal.
1995	***Rogue Trader, Nick Leeson, and Barings Bank:*** Nick Leeson fraudulently covered up over $1 billion in trading losses. These staggering losses led to the downfall of Barings Bank.
2001	***Enron:*** Top executives at Enron engaged in a variety of unethical and deceptive activities to increase the profits and stock price of the company. Jeffrey Skilling, the COO and for a short time CEO, and Andy Fastow, the CFO, employed fraudulent accounting practices to hide debt and inflate profits. Timothy Belden, the head of Enron Energy Services, oversaw trading abuses in energy markets. All of these activities occurred under the auspices of the firm's founder, CEO, and Chairman, Kenneth Lay. Enron and its stock collapsed when the market learned that the company's profits were fictitious.
2002	***WorldCom:*** The CFO of WorldCom, Scott Sullivan, with the knowledge of the CEO, Bernie Ebbers, engaged in accounting fraud to inflate the earnings of the company. Jack Grubman, an analyst for Salomon Brothers and then Citigroup, reported favorable ratings on many telecom stocks, including WorldCom, to help win lucrative investment banking business. Faced with massive earnings restatements, WorldCom filed for bankruptcy.
2007	***Rogue Trader, Jérôme Kerviel, and Société Générale:*** Jérôme Kerviel overextended his trading authority at French bank Société Générale. His risky positions led to over $7 billion in losses.
2008	***Madoff Ponzi Scheme:*** Bernie Madoff was discovered to have run a Ponzi scheme believed to be almost $65 billion in size.

old scheme duped and hurt many investors. Table 1.1 briefly describes other major scandals that have tarnished the history of financial markets. All of the individuals identified in the table at one point enjoyed generous compensation, were well thought of, or held prestigious job titles. Ethical lapses turned their success into fines, jail time, and humiliation. Madoff went from being well respected in the industry (he even served as chairman of the board of directors of the National Association of Securities Dealers) to receiving death threats and a sentence of 150 years in jail.

That scandals are so deeply intertwined with the history of financial markets speaks volumes for the need to understand ethical principles and applications that are *specific* to investments. The schemes perpetrated by Duer and Charles Ponzi

---

MINI APPLICATION 1.1
PONZI SCHEMES ARE NOTHING NEW

1920—Charles Ponzi

Charles Ponzi perpetrated a scheme so large that it was soon named after him. In a Ponzi scheme, the operator promises good returns by making what seem to be profitable investments. But no investments are made. Instead, the scammer pays off early investors with fresh funds from new investors; and, of course, the perpetrator pockets some of the funds. Charles Ponzi got the idea for his scheme when a friend from Spain sent him a letter containing a reply coupon that cost one cent in Spain but could be redeemed for a six-cent stamp in the United States. Ponzi recognized the arbitrage opportunity. Arbitrage involves taking advantage of different prices for the same commodity in different markets. Ponzi realized he could purchase reply coupons for one cent in Spain and redeem them for a six-cent stamp in the United States and make five cents. Based on this opportunity, he promised a 50 percent return to investors in 45 days. The demand for coupons quickly outstripped supply, however, and Ponzi stopped investing in the redemption coupons. Instead, he paid off the early investors with funds from new investors, while at the same time skimming off money to support his lavish lifestyle. In a few months, he had over $20 million. A journalist, Clarence Barron (yes, that's the same Barron that founded *Barron's*, a well-known financial weekly), exposed the scheme.

2008—Bernard L. Madoff

In 2009, Bernard L. Madoff was sentenced to 150 years in prison for running one of the largest Ponzi schemes in history; its scope was believed to be over $65 billion. Bernie Madoff was a successful market maker and former chairman of NASDAQ (National Association of Securities Dealers Automated Quotations). He was well known and respected in the securities industry and began an investment advisory firm for a modest group of clients—at first. His firm provided consistent, high returns, and against all the odds seemingly continued to do so for many years. Much of investors' funds were solicited through so-called feeder funds. Firms such as the Fairfield Greenwich Group offered hedge fund products to investors, who in turn invested the money in Madoff's funds. Managers of feeder funds earned high fees for providing fresh investors for Madoff. In addition, Madoff's funds were always reported to be "closed" but opened to a new investor as a "special exception." Madoff's return history, the exclusivity of his funds, and his feeder funds all worked to continually attract new investors. Further, early investors kept their money with Bernie believing they were earning superb returns—on paper. The scam grew. Then, as securities markets declined in early 2008, investors' redemptions outstripped new funds. Madoff, realizing that the scheme would quickly be exposed, turned himself in.

MINI APPLICATION 1.2

MORAL HAZARD AND THE FINANCIAL CRISIS OF 2008

Moral hazard occurs when parties do not fully bear the costs of their risk-taking behavior. As a result, they take more risks than they would otherwise.

Moral hazard occurs when parties do not fully bear the costs of their risk-taking behavior. As a result, they take more risks than they would otherwise. Moral hazard became an important topic during the financial crisis of 2008. Many financial institutions got into trouble by loading up on complex, derivative debt instruments (i.e., mortgage-backed securities) without fully understanding their underlying risks. To make matters worse, they used excessive amounts of leverage to fund their operations. When housing prices collapsed, so did these firms. The Federal Reserve Board provided emergency financing to stave off a systemic market collapse. Some argued the bailout created moral hazard.

were repeated many years later by Bear Stearns and Bernie Madoff, but with more dire consequences (see Mini Application 1.1). Not only did the individuals involve suffer as they fell from grace, they took others with them. Their actions contributed to the recent collapse of the financial markets that, in turn, almost brought the broader economy to the brink of disaster. As financial markets become larger and more complex, the industry will need more professionals with an ethical conscience—those willing to question their own behavior as well as that of others. Suppose someone at Bear Stearns had questioned either the investments in MBS or the use of leverage (see Mini Application 1.2 which discusses the concept of moral hazard and this type of risk taking). The outcome may have been very different for Bear Stearns' employees, investors, and other market participants.

To be clear, this book is not meant to be a history lesson. But the investment industry's more infamous scandals over the years provide insights into needed ethical safeguards, and cases based on these scandals are an integral part of this text. The purpose of this book is to provide a practical ethical guide for students about to embark in a career in investments. These principles are developed from an amalgamation of past cases, laws and regulations, professional codes of conduct, and ethical theory. To start, let's briefly review the investment industry to better understand why it might be vulnerable to unscrupulous practitioners.

A BRIEF OVERVIEW OF THE INVESTMENT INDUSTRY

What is the essential function of the investment industry? Investors provide capital—money—to institutions, either for-profit or nonprofit, so that they have financial resources to support their activities. In exchange for this capital, investors are offered a return. Investments can take the form of different types of securities: bonds, stocks, and anything in between.

The investment industry serves to facilitate the exchange of capital for returns. Sounds simple, doesn't it? But as the financial markets have grown to trillions of dollars, the investment industry has become more complicated and features an ever-growing number of players with different roles in facilitating exchanges.

Issuers corporations or other entities that issue securities in exchange for capital.

- **Issuers:** These are entities that need to raise capital. Consider these examples: a manufacturing corporation that issues stock to build a new plant and expand; the U.S. government that issues treasury notes to finance the activities of the federal government; municipalities that issue bonds to build roads and schools; and nonprofit organizations that issue bonds to help with community development projects.

Investors parties who seek to invest money or capital in order to earn a return.

- **Investors:** Investors provide capital to the issuers and seek returns in exchange. Investors can be individuals who purchase securities on their own or via a fund vehicle, for example, a mutual fund. Investors can be pension funds—either public or private—designed to meet the needs of a specific group of retirees, for instance, city and state workers (a public fund) or General Motors retired workers (a private fund). Endowments are the investments of non-charitable organizations or foundations and universities. Your university has an endowment, and the returns earned by the endowment supplement your tuition to support the cost of your education.

Intermediaries firms or individuals who act to bring other parties (i.e., issuers and investors) together in an investment transaction.

- **Intermediaries:** This vast group constitutes what we think of when we say "the investment industry." For fees and commissions, intermediaries facilitate the trade of capital for returns between issuers and investors. Investment banks help issuers raise capital. Market exchanges provide liquidity, the ability to execute a transaction immediately. Brokers and traders help investors and funds buy and sell securities. Analysts aid portfolio managers and investors in deciding which securities to buy and which to sell. Portfolio managers help decide which securities to hold within a portfolio to meet risk and return objectives. Investment consultants work with pension funds, foundations, and universities in selecting portfolio managers and designing the asset allocation—for example, the mix of bonds and equities—for the entire fund. Mutual funds, index funds, actively managed funds, and hedge funds (to name a few) provide other types of security and portfolio products to investors. Financial planners recommend different investment products to individuals in the context of tax and retirement planning. Compliance officers make sure everybody is following the rules and regulations.

Let's look closer at an example of the many different players involved in making an investment—in this case, a public pension fund. A public pension fund is on the investor side in Figure 1.1. The fund takes taxpayer money and invests it to earn a return to pay benefits for retired public employees. Pension funds are overseen by a board of trustees who are appointed or elected. The board, in turn, usually hires an investment consultant. The investment consultant helps the board formulate investment policy, select fund managers, and report the performance of the fund; the consultant also provides advice on operational procedures. Should the fund invest in 70 percent equities and 30 percent bonds? How about a 60–40 split? Should the fund invest in small cap equities or large cap? Both? What about bonds? High yield or investment grade? Should Loomis Sayles be chosen for the high yield investment, or PIMCO? Once the investment fund managers are selected by the pension fund board, the managers are responsible for hiring portfolio

| FIGURE | 1.1 | **THE INVESTMENT INDUSTRY** |

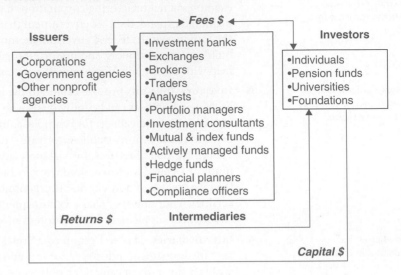

managers. The portfolio managers select different securities and include them in the fund to meet risk and return goals. The portfolio managers, in turn, rely on the research provided by analysts. Is the stock of JCPenney a better investment than that of Sears? Once an investment decision has been made, portfolio managers rely on traders to execute trades at the best price. On the issuer side in Figure 1.1 are corporations—like JCPenney and Sears—that issue stocks and bonds that are selected by the different investment funds. Investment bankers help these corporations issue and place the stocks and bonds. When all works as it should, these corporations are profitable and provide a good return to their investors. . .and the retirees get their checks!

The underlying transaction, in making an investment, is between the taxpayers and the corporations. The taxpayers provide capital to the corporations in exchange for a return. These returns ultimately allow the pension benefits to be paid. Yet, as you can see from Figure 1.2, many players help make a transaction possible (of course the actuaries, accountants, information technology specialists, lawyers, banks providing custodial services, and administrators in the background are no less critical for the transaction to occur). See Mini Application 1.3 for another example of the many intermediaries who can be involved in an investment transaction. All of these players are the intermediaries who are smack dab in the middle of Figure 1.1. They bring together the taxpayers and the corporations to make the underlying transaction come off. And they participate in the transaction for a fee.

This transaction involves a lot of money changing a lot of hands. Not just once, but several times and over a long period of time that starts when the first taxpayer dollar is invested and lasts until the retired public employee receives his or her last pension check. It's complicated! And it's the complexity that allows for ethical lapses to occur. Of course, laws and regulations are designed to protect investors. Let's review them next. Then we will turn to ethics—promise!

FIGURE	1.2	A PUBLIC PENSION FUND INVESTS IN STOCK AND BONDS

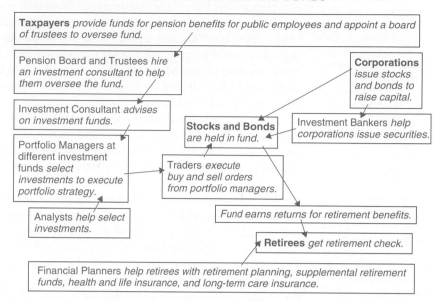

MINI APPLICATION 1.3

TEST YOURSELF

City, state, and county governments often issue what are known as municipal bonds to help finance public works. Investment banks typically have a public finance division that helps place these bonds, typically in "muni" bond funds or portfolios. Municipal bonds, in contrast to corporate bonds, provide tax-exempt income (usually semiannual interest payments) to holders of the bonds. Identify the issuer and the investors in the muni bond market. How many intermediaries can you list?

SECURITIES LAWS AND REGULATIONS

Securities Exchange Acts of 1933 and 1934 established the Securities and Exchange Commission (SEC), new securities laws regulating markets, and filing disclosures including audited financial statements.

THE SECURITIES AND EXCHANGE COMMISSION

Securities laws and regulations have evolved in response to widespread financial scandals and the public outrage that inevitably follows. The most important set of laws, the **Securities Exchange Acts of 1933 and 1934**, grew out of the Pecora Commission hearings in the wake of the 1929 stock market crash. These were Senate Banking Committee congressional hearings overseen by Ferdinand Pecora, the committee's chief counsel. Pecora's investigation exposed rampant stock manipulation and fraud. Joseph P. Kennedy was appointed the first chairman of the committee and helped draft many of the SEC's rules and regulations. Some claim that this was like asking the fox to guard the chicken coop; Kennedy had made a fortune on Wall Street and, rumor had it, through many of the stock manipulation and insider trading schemes that under his watch the SEC made illegal.

Investor Advisors Act and the Investment Company Act of 1940 under these acts, firms or individual professionals who seek to be compensated for advising on investments and in aggregate manage $25 million or more are required to register with the SEC and provide information about the nature of their business, their business and education and criminal background, and financial statements of the sole proprietorship or firm; advisors and investment companies must follow rules regarding record keeping and custody of client accounts and funds, disclosure of fees and commissions, and advertising.

Rule 10b-5 rule preventing the manipulation of markets either through deceitful trading or use of information (i.e., rumors or inside information).

Information disclosure information that is disclosed to investors in various required filings by the Securities and Exchange Commission.

Later, the SEC undertook a comprehensive study showing that market abuses continued—this time it was investment advisors taking advantage of naïve investors. The **Investor Advisors Act and the Investment Company Act of 1940** were passed. Under these acts, advisors and investment companies are held to stringent rules regarding record keeping and custody of client accounts and funds, disclosure of fees and commissions, and advertising. Firms or individual professionals who seek to be compensated for advising on investments and in aggregate manage $25 million or more are required to register with the SEC. In registering, the SEC requires investment advisors to provide information about the nature of their business, their professional and education background, and financial statements of the sole proprietorship or firm for which they work. Prior criminal behavior must also be disclosed. This act also specifies penalties for advisors who defraud investors. These are all ways to protect naïve investors from giving their money to a fly-by-night operation. Later, in 1942, the SEC adopted **Rule 10b-5**, designed to close loopholes in the original prohibitions on insider trading. Rule 10b-5 provides that anyone who has inside information, not just a company insider, must either publicly disclose it or refrain from trading.

The most important reforms the SEC enacted involved **information disclosure**. Disclosure occurs by requiring the different players in the financial markets to file different forms. The SEC—to the extent that it has staff resources—reviews these forms and investigates questionable information and may even bring an enforcement action (like a lawsuit) when there is misrepresentation by the filers. The threat of fines and other sanctions can help keep the players in line. There are over one hundred forms. Here are a few of the key forms and filings:

- Forms for the registration of publicly issued securities—Form S-1
- Filings of audited financial statements—Form 10-K (annual), Form 10-Q (quarterly), Form 8-K (material change)
- Disclosure of holdings and changes in holdings of "insiders"—Forms 3, 4, and 5
- Disclosure of holdings by "outsiders," institutional holders, and money managers—Forms 13D, G, and F
- Proxy statement issuances that disclose executive compensation, background, and composition of a board of directors, and allow shareholders to vote on the board and other corporate matters—DEF 14A
- Registration as an investment advisor—Form ADV

You should be aware of these filings in your investment career as you research different companies' securities and investigate the backgrounds of various investment companies. As an interesting note, Bernie Madoff never registered as an investment advisor. While this allowed him to escape scrutiny by the SEC, it also should have served as a red flag to more sophisticated investors.

SARBANES-OXLEY ACT

In the following 60 years, the SEC and Congress continued to make and amend rules regulating the investment industry. Not until 2002 was the next significant legislation

Sarbanes-Oxley Act of 2002 (SOX) this act (also known as SOX, and as the **Public Company Accounting Reform and Investor Protection Act of 2002**) was designed to enforce greater accountability for corporate executives for financial statements, more fully disclose compensation contracts and other payments made to executives, and eliminate conflicts of interest between accounting firms and the corporations that they audited. It also established the Public Company Accounting Oversight Board (PCAOB) to oversee and enforce new laws imposed on auditors.

Public Company Accounting Oversight Board (PCAOB) governmental body established by the Sarbanes-Oxley Act of 2002 to oversee and enforce new laws imposed on auditors.

passed—the Sarbanes-Oxley Act of 2002 (SOX) also known as the **Public Company Accounting Reform and Investor Protection Act of 2002**). Like the securities acts of 1933 and 1934, this legislation occurred after a large decline in the stock market and the revelation of financial scandals. During the 1990s, the stock market rose rapidly in the wake of telecommunications deregulation and the Internet boom. Rapid growth in the earnings of telecom and dot-com companies and their stock contributed to an overall rise in the market. Later the earnings of many large companies were exposed as fictitious. Companies engaged in accounting fraud so that they could continue to post earnings that met or exceeded analysts' expectations. Auditors failed to detect large-scale fraud. CEOs were found to have benefited from timely sales of stock and stock option grants. Boards forgave substantial personal loans for executives and footed the bill for top executives' extravagant lifestyles, including trips, luxury homes, and valuable artwork. The abuses perpetrated by executives at WorldCom and Enron are the most notorious cases.

Again, Congress responded to public outrage with new legislation. SOX was passed and designed to enforce greater accountability by corporate executives for financial statements. In addition, SOX required firms to more fully disclose compensation contracts and other payments made to executives. Further, SOX eliminated the most egregious conflicts of interest between accounting firms and the corporations that they audited. Before the passage of SOX, accounting firms earned lucrative consulting contracts from firms they audited, thus compromising their independence as auditors. Just as the Securities Exchange Act of 1934 created the SEC to oversee and enforce new securities laws, SOX created the **Public Company Accounting Oversight Board (PCAOB)** to oversee and enforce new laws imposed on auditors. See Mini Application 1.4. (A list of financial regulators is included in the appendix to this chapter.)

History shows that large-scale fraud and financial crises lead to cries for reforms and greater protections for investors. Figure 1.3 shows a history of market bubbles and crashes and the new major regulations adopted in the wake of each market collapse. As of this writing, Congress is considering reforms in response to the financial crisis of 2008. The financial crisis revealed excessive use of leverage and risk taking, questioned the independence of credit-rating agencies, and exposed many Ponzi schemes. It is likely that new reforms will address many of these ethical lapses.

As this brief history of legislation and regulation shows, however, new rules and regulations are always enacted *after* the wrongdoing. An understanding of ethical principles and how to apply them in your professional career should help you act ethically *before* a law is passed that forces you to do so.

INVESTMENT ETHICS ARE EASIER SAID THAN DONE

Acting ethically might seem a simple matter of just "doing the right thing." That's easier said than done. All participants in the investment industry have one thing in common, and that is the desire to make money. Issuers want to make money on the capital they raise from the market; investors want to make money—returns—on their investments; and intermediaries want to be compensated for the services they provide. When does economic self-interest devolve into greed? When does providing

---

MINI APPLICATION 1.4
KEY ELEMENTS OF SOX

Here are some key elements of SOX, which was designed to minimize conflicts of interest and create greater accountability for financial reporting for senior executives and management:

- The accounting firm is restricted from providing any "non-audit" services to the company during the time of the audit.
- The primary auditors are required to rotate on and off of the audit every five years.
- The accounting firm is required to report any accounting discrepancies that are used to alter financial statements within generally accepted accounting principles (GAAP).
- Top executive positions—such as the chief executive officer (CEO), chief financial officer (CFO), and others—cannot have been on the auditing committee for one year before employment.
- Each employee of the audit committee should be a member of the board of directors of the company they are auditing. The audit committee is responsible for the oversight of the accounting firm that the company has hired. The CEO and CFO are required to issue a statement certifying "financial statements fairly present in all material respects the financial condition and results of operations of the company" (*Source*: William H. Donaldson, "Testimony Concerning Implementation of the Sarbanes-Oxley Act of 2002," 9 September 2003, www.sec.gov/news/testimony/090903tswhd.htm#P108_26802
- If a company has to restate financial information, the CEO and CFO are required to reimburse the company any bonus and/or cash incentives during the year following one year after the filing.
- Buying or selling of stock by executives and directors is restricted during times of blackouts. Blackouts occur when the employee participants of the company's 401(k) plan are prohibited from selling their shares. If the person earns profits, the company has the option to recover those profits. If the company fails to recover the profits, then shareholders are free to file for reimbursement.
- It is illegal for any company to lend to executives and extend any kind of credit lines.

---

a valuable service become an exploitation of a naïve investor? When does charging fees and commissions become gouging? When does an information advantage become unfair? When does shrewd market timing become market manipulation? When is the responsibility of making risky investments the investor's or the professional's? The balance between profitability and treatment of others can at times become difficult to maintain, because investments themselves are not simple.

INVESTMENTS ARE COMPLICATED

Fundamentally, investments are payments made today for uncertain cash flows made in the future. Money changes hands today, money changes hands tomorrow, and money can change hands at any time in between as intermediaries take their fees and commissions. Investments are technically difficult to grasp. They require an understanding of numbers, contractual details, economic incentives, financial theory, and statistics. Investors can hand over their money and not get it back for many years. Or they may never get it back—was it because a risky investment went bad, or because of an unethical advisor? Or maybe they are happy with the amount

| FIGURE | 1.3 | ADJUSTED DAILY CLOSE DOW JONES INDUSTRIAL AVERAGE (OCT. 1, 1922 TO JUNE 26, 2009) |

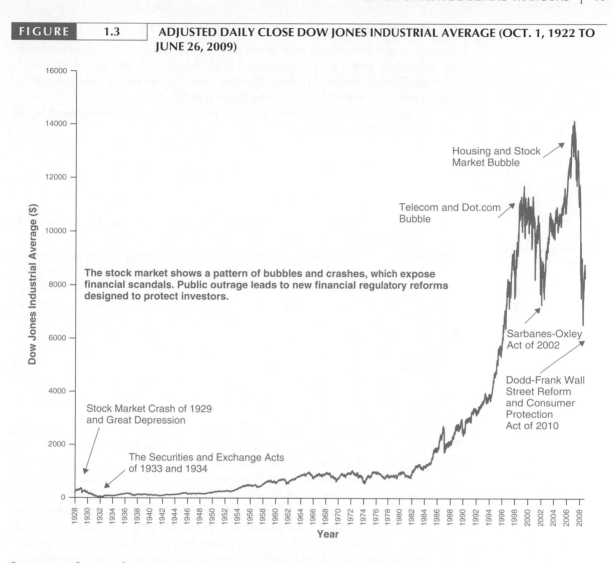

Source: www.finance.yahoo.com.

they get back, but never know that it could have been even greater if someone along the way wasn't unscrupulously helping her- or himself to some of their returns.

INVESTMENTS ARE ABOUT INFORMATION

Participants who acquire more accurate information than others have an advantage in predicting future cash flows. A vast amount of information is available to investors to use in decision making. Who is better at analyzing this information? Who receives this information first? Is information available to some investors and not available to others? What drives availability—money? Personal access? But isn't the business world about having a competitive advantage and profiting from it? When is an information advantage fair? When is it unfair?

INVESTMENTS ARE ABOUT RESOURCES

Remember that investments exist to provide financial resources to support activities. For example, by purchasing corporate stocks and bonds, investors provide support to a corporation's activities. Are these activities ethical? Does the corporation pollute? Create harmful products? Treat its employees poorly?

It's easy to become lost trying to participate ethically in the investment world. This book provides a road map.

ETHICS BASICS

Ethics standards for determining right or wrong behavior toward others in a particular context.

What does it mean to be ethical? **Ethics** are standards for determining what is right and wrong in a particular context. Ethics are not religion, morals, laws, or what is considered acceptable behavior in society. Different religions can all support the same ethical principles. For example, most religions do not condone countless forms of cheating. Morals are absolute rules of behavior of people toward others: we agree that murder is immoral; in comparison, annualizing six-month returns in performance reports is unethical but *not* likely to be considered immoral (see Chapter 3 to learn why reporting these returns is unethical). Laws determine only which specific types of unethical behaviors are illegal, but they don't necessarily make *all* unethical behavior illegal. For instance, fraudulently presenting past return performance to attract new investors is both unethical and illegal. Excluding terminated accounts in past return performance, though unethical, is *not* illegal. Finally, just because "everybody cheats," doesn't make cheating ethical.

The study of any type of applied ethics starts with philosophical ethical theories. Aristotle, one of the early Greek philosophers in the 300s BCE, described *ethics* as "good actions and virtues." Virtue ethics are based on different virtues: integrity, courage, compassion, and so forth. Virtues lie not only within actions, but within intentions as well, which means that character is important. John Locke, a classic philosopher in the 1600s, advocated the idea of rights. Humans have certain rights, and ethical behavior revolves around respecting those rights. Immanuel Kant, who wrote in the 1700s, argued that both consequences and intent were important. He believed that ethics were based on universal principles (i.e., no "exceptions"). Further, he posited that people should never be treated as a means to an end. John Stuart Mill, from the 1800s, espoused utilitarianism—the belief that behavior is considered ethical as long as it increases the overall utility or happiness of the most people in society. Do you remember the term *utility* from your economics classes? Here individuals can be used as a means to an end, as long as the end leaves more people better off (i.e., you have maximized utility for society as a whole). Feminist philosophy adds a twentieth-century perspective with the "ethics of care." Behavior is ethical when each individual is valued and cared for within any relationship. So what are all of these philosophers getting at? *Ethics is about how you treat others*; it involves your *direct* behavior toward others as well as the *indirect* impact your behavior has on others. Ethics provide moral standards of behavior that guide the right and wrong treatment of others.

The Golden Rule—"Do unto others as you would have them do unto you"—would seem to be all we need to know to behave ethically in the investments profession. However, remember that as a customer, you might want to receive investment services for free; but as someone who needs a paycheck, you want to be paid. So again, we are back to the tension between making a reasonable profit and taking advantage. How is this conflict resolved?

FOUR FUNDAMENTAL PRINCIPLES OF INVESTMENT ETHICS

Let's step back a minute. Remember that ethical lapses can occur in investments because they involve money, are complicated, are information driven, and provide financial resources for different activities. Ethical principles in investments can be tied to each of these four points and can be thought of as *obligations to others*.

ETHICAL UNDERSTANDING

In dealing with others, you have an obligation to make sure that *others* understand the transaction. Not all investors have the same level of financial sophistication. For example, suppose that to inform a client about the relative risk of an investment, you decide to report the investment's beta (its market risk) among other statistical measures of risk. If this investor is a private wealth advisor working for Morgan Stanley, you can be pretty sure that this client understands what *beta* means and can effectively use it in deciding whether the risk of the investment is appropriate for his or her needs. Now suppose your client is an artist who has recently become both wealthy and famous. Is reporting the beta sufficient to ensure this investor understands the risk of investment? If the artist directs you to invest all of his or her money in the investment with the highest historical return (which also happens to have the highest beta), are you off the hook? No. Clearly, you have an ethical obligation to ensure that you understand the artist's investment goals and can translate them into investments with the appropriate risk and beta. The anonymity of the markets makes it more than likely that at some point, you will be transacting with a naïve investor. That's okay. You are not *knowingly* taking advantage of someone who doesn't understand the transaction. Finally, because investment transactions are complicated, it is possible that unfair fees can be hidden. This is unethical. You have an obligation to make sure all parties understand what they are paying for and how.

You also have an obligation to ensure that *you* understand the activities *you* are involved in. You should not recommend an investment that you do not fully

---

PRINCIPLE 1: ETHICAL UNDERSTANDING

Because investments are complicated, *you have an obligation not to knowingly engage in an investment transaction that either you or others do not sufficiently understand. This includes the underlying source of returns or fees charged.*

comprehend. For example, if you do not understand a complex derivative instrument, you should not recommend it. Nor should you give the false impression that you *do* understand it but are recommending against the investment. It could be a fabulous opportunity for your client or firm! Instead, you should acknowledge your lack of expertise and recommend that your client or firm seek other expert advice.

The most recent financial crisis provides many examples of investment professionals acting without full understanding of the transactions they were conducting. Collateralized debt obligations (CDOs) were complicated derivative securities; they were built out of bundling and repackaging debt obligations—sometimes as many as one hundred debt contracts were repackaged in making one CDO. Understanding a CDO's payment structure and default risk required a sophisticated knowledge of financial models. Nonetheless, many of these securities were recommended to investors by professionals who didn't fully comprehend them or their risks. There has been some suggestion that the analysts rating these securities, many of whom rated CDOs at investment grade, didn't understand what they were rating. The ethical response should have been, "Stop! I don't understand this security, and thus I cannot rate, recommend, or invest in it."

Chapters 2 and 3 discuss in more detail the ethical issues related to understanding investments.

ETHICAL USE OF INFORMATION

This principle relates to the most widely known ethical (and legal) lapses in investments—insider trading and market manipulation. Inside information is important information ("material" information, in legal terms) that is not publicly available at the time of a trade. This doesn't include other important information provided via subscription-based data bases, at a price. *Public* doesn't mean free. But it does mean accessible. It also doesn't mean knowledge that is acquired through better analysis of public information. Investors shouldn't be allowed to benefit for free from the talent, education, and hard work of others. Of course, these talented analysts are free to sell their information.

As an investment professional, you also have an obligation to ensure that you are informed about all relevant information. For a stock investment, relevant information would include such things as earnings growth, sales, industry conditions, and the like. Recommending a stock purchase simply because you like the name of the company without any other research is neither sufficient nor ethical.

Market manipulation occurs when participants try to convey false information to the market via trading. Remember, this is what Duer and the Six Percent Club

---

PRINCIPLE 2: ETHICAL USE OF INFORMATION

Because investments are information driven, *you have an obligation to ensure that you and others have access to relevant information and that you and others do not misuse or distort information in the investment transaction.*

tried to do back in 1792. Buying securities to create the illusion of widespread market interests to push up prices distorts market information. This is not ethical. There is much more to say about the use and misuse of information in investments. Chapters 4 through 7 provide this coverage.

RESPONSIBLE INVESTING

Most often, investments take the form of buying corporate securities, and these security purchases provide financial capital for the company. Investors hope that the company earns a healthy profit, which in turn will translate into a good return on their investment. Is it ethical to profit from another's misery? No, of course not. But rarely do corporations that issue publicly traded stock advertise their wrongdoing—certainly none of them are named "Misery-R-Us, Inc." Let's look at a hypothetical example. Suppose an overseas company (one that is not subject to product safety laws) makes and sells baby food. The company uses cheap fillers that have no nutritional value. This information is not readily apparent on the labels. Because its costs are lower, the company earns a better profit margin and yields a higher return to its investors than its competitors do. However, babies fed on this company's product become malnourished. You figure this out. Would buying the stock of this company be an ethical investment? No! Remember that the underlying principle of all ethical behavior (whether in investments or not) is fair treatment of others. This company sells a product that hurts babies! This is not just a hypothetical example. In 2008, it was discovered that the Sunlu Group, a producer of infant formula in China, had been substituting an industrial chemical (melamine) in the formula it produced. Melamine caused the formula, when tested, to show it had sufficient protein content for sale. Melamine was used as a cheaper alternative to nutritional protein. The melamine-contaminated infant formula led to infant illnesses and deaths. Here profits were more important than the danger and harm the product posed to others. Unethical? Yes!

Corporations are not perfect. Almost all are likely to have hurt someone in some way at some time. Unfair hiring practices, pollution, and unsafe products are but a few possible complaints against a company. Yet, among claims that a company's practices were harmful, some people may have found them beneficial. It can be difficult to assess the overall ethical behavior of companies and an investment in their securities. Chapter 8 discusses these difficulties.

TRUST AND FAIRNESS

Fiduciary duty a duty that is owed to others when placed in a position of trust.

This final principle captures the notion of fiduciary duty, an idea that is widely understood by the investment industry. **Fiduciary duty** means that professionals are

---

PRINCIPLE 3: RESPONSIBLE INVESTING

Because investments provide financial resources to others, *you have an obligation to ensure that you do not knowingly make or recommend investments that support activities that harm others.*

Because you are dealing with others' money either directly or indirectly, *you have an obligation not to abuse the trust placed in you that all others have either explicitly or implicitly placed in you to treat them fairly.*

---

held to a higher standard of behavior and loyalty because of the confidence and trust their client places in them.

We cover fiduciary duty more fully in Chapter 2. But this final principle really encompasses *all* behavior. You can violate Principle 4 in a myriad of ways. For example, you could trade stocks in your client's account on insider information. While this behavior might benefit your client, you are hurting the other investors who trade with you and implicitly *trust* their trading partners not to violate insider trading laws. Another example is investing your client's money in the stock of the corporation with the unsafe baby food described above. Your client may be happy with the great returns the investments are earning, but the consumers who bought the unsafe baby food are not. The consumers may have implicitly *trusted* that the financial markets would not provide capital to such a corporation.

In the remainder of this text, we take these principles and apply them to specific cases and practices in the investment industry. Because Principle 4 is an overriding principle, as you read all of the chapters, for each specific issue ask yourself, "Who is hurt?" and "Whose trust is violated?"

COSTS AND BENEFITS OF BEING UNETHICAL

Because making investments is a business-based discipline, we are obligated to provide a cost-benefit analysis of being unethical. The benefits of being unethical are simple: unethical behavior can benefit you *if and only if you don't get caught.* *Greed* is one reason people are unethical. Remember, the investments industry is centered on money, and money always creates temptations. *Ego* is another reason. Some individuals act unethically to cover up poor performance; these individuals would rather act unethically than acknowledge failure. *Arrogance* or *hubris* is a related cause for ethical lapses, for instance, the inability to entertain failure or admit to the flaw in an investment strategy. This blindness can hurt others.

What are the costs? First, and foremost, is the cost of living with a guilty conscience. It's hard to feel good about yourself when you know that you have harmed someone else by your actions. Second, there is the cost of being fired for unethical actions—and worse yet, of going to jail. Third, there is the loss of reputation in an industry that depends critically on professional integrity. A single poor decision made in an instant can ruin your career forever. Fourth, there is the cost to your company and the industry. When ordinary people believe that the industry is rife with swindlers, they are unlikely to invest. The lack of investment capital hurts the economy and society as a whole. While it's not possible to quantify this cost-benefit analysis, reasonably you could conclude that the costs of being unethical exceed the benefits.

Further, you must take personal responsibility for acting ethically. It is not sufficient to rely on laws, professional codes of conduct, or compliance officers to ensure that you behave ethically. Laws, professional codes, and compliance, by necessity, work to prevent the future repeat of past wrongdoing. You should have been convinced of that as we reviewed the history of scandals and regulations in this chapter. But the finance industry is both innovative and technical. New products and business models create unique opportunities for unethical actions, and not all of them can be anticipated. Let's look at a recent example.

Credit default swap (CDS) a security that provides for insurance against a bond default.

American International Group Inc.'s London unit, known as AIG Financial Products (AIGFP), had become very profitable by issuing credit default swaps (CDSs). A **Credit default swap (CDS)** is insurance on a bond. Suppose Investor A purchases a bond that has a promised repayment of $1 million and matures in 10 years. Investor A can purchase a CDS from Firm B. Firm B promises to pay Investor A $1 million if the issuer of the bond defaults. For this insurance, Investor A must pay a premium to Firm B as long as Investor A owns the bond. Suppose the premium is 2 percent, and Investor A pays the firm $20,000 each year. If the bond never defaults, Firm B owes Investor A nothing and has made all the premiums, $200,000, that Investor A has paid over the life of the bond. If the bond defaults, however, Firm B will owe Investor A $1 million and will lose money.

In the early 2000s, the market for CDSs was small and not heavily regulated. AIGFP found a way to make profits in this market. An investor who had purchased bonds and other debt securities could also purchase credit default swaps to insure against the default of credit securities. If default occurred, the investor could recover her losses from AIG (technically AIGFP, but often called just AIG). This is like buying homeowner's insurance to protect against property damage. If your house burns down, you can recover your costs from your insurer. Regulators require insurers to maintain collateral against the policies they write. That way, if your house burns down, you can be sure that your insurance company has sufficient cash on hand to pay your claim. AIG was in effect acting as an insurer to protect against default. However, unlike other insurers, AIG did not have to post collateral as long as the value of its securities did not decline. Credit default swaps were not viewed as insurance policies, which are subject to insurance regulations, but as securities. Further, because AIG didn't have to come up with collateral against these credit default swaps, issuing them was even more profitable. AIG's holdings of such securities increased to over $500 billion by 2007. The London unit was earning hundreds of millions of dollars every year by issuing these securities. Why stop?

When default risk increased in the credit markets, the value of AIG's holdings fell. Because the company didn't have sufficient collateral, its trading partners—other investment firms that counted on the credit default swaps to provide insurance against just this type of decline in the value of their bond holdings—were also threatened with losses. In the fall of 2008, the U.S. government provided $85 billion to rescue AIG and the financial system from collapse. Should AIG have increased its collateral as it issued more CDS securities? In hindsight, the answer is yes. Was the company legally required to? There is likely to be future debate about whether any laws were broken, but it seems clear that the many people involved in the business didn't believe that they were violating any laws or regulations; even so, new regulations are now being proposed to prevent future abuses. Was their behavior unethical? Most likely, the answer to this question is yes. If greed compromised their ability to assess risk and their collateral needs to the detriment of others, then they acted unethically. Of course, arguments can be made that they diligently and honestly assessed risk and were blindsided by an unexpected change in the market. Only those individuals involved will really know whether their actions were unethical. Who didn't listen to that little voice inside that said, "Maybe this isn't right?"

CONCLUSION: DEVELOPING AN ETHICAL CONSCIOUSNESS

That little voice inside leads us to the final point. Ethical behavior depends critically on your internal thought process *before* you take any action. Stop and think about what you are considering before you act. Are you trying to justify your actions? If so, that should be a red flag. Only unethical actions need to be justified. Nor should you be tempted to look at regulations and codes and find "clever" ways to circumvent them. Many cases throughout this book involve individuals who thought they were

FUNDAMENTAL PRINCIPLES OF INVESTMENT ETHICS FOR PROFESSIONALS

Principle 1: ETHICAL UNDERSTANDING

Because investments are complicated, *you have an obligation not to knowingly engage in an investment transaction that either you or others do not sufficiently understand. This includes knowing the underlying source of returns or fees charged.*

Principle 2: ETHICAL USE OF INFORMATION

Because investments are information driven, *you have an obligation to ensure that you and others have access to relevant information and that you and others do not misuse or distort information in the investment transaction.*

Principle 3: RESPONSIBLE INVESTING

Because investments provide financial resources to others, *you have an obligation to ensure that you do not knowingly make or recommend investments that support activities that harm others.*

Principle 4: TRUST AND FAIRNESS

Because you are dealing with others' money either directly or indirectly, *you have an obligation not to abuse the trust all others have either explicitly or implicitly placed in you to treat them fairly.*

smart in exploiting loopholes in the rules. In the end, their behavior was deemed at best unethical and at worst illegal. Do you think about whether your actions will go undetected? Do thoughts such as "who will know?" "they won't understand," or "nobody will notice" go through your head? Only unethical actions need to be hidden.

When you find yourself thinking about hiding your actions, you can further check whether your actions are unethical by applying the four Fundamental Principles of Investment Ethics. If you think any of your actions violate these four principles, there is a good chance they are unethical.

To be ethical, you must develop a higher level of consciousness about your actions and their consequences for both you and others. It's important to listen to that "little voice inside" and pay attention to that "feeling in your stomach." Reading this book will raise that level of consciousness. On to the next chapter!

TERMS

mortgage-backed security (MBS)

Ponzi scheme

issuers

investors

intermediaries

Securities Exchange Acts of 1933 and 1934

Investor Advisors Act

Investment Company Act of 1940

moral hazard

Rule 10b-5

information disclosure

Sarbanes-Oxley Act of 2002 (SOX; also known as the Public

Company Accounting Reform and Investor Protection Act)

Public Company Accounting Oversight Board (PCAOB)

ethics

fiduciary duty

credit default swap (CDS)

REVIEW QUESTIONS

1. Give one example of history repeating itself in the legacy of financial scandals. Why do you think investors continue to be duped by old schemes?

2. Identify the three types of players in the investment industry, and describe each of their roles.

3. What financial crisis led to the creation of the SEC?

4. What financial crisis led to the passage of SOX?

5. What are three characteristics of the investment industry that make it easy for ethical lapses to occur?

6. Explain how high returns make it easier for unethical investment professionals to go undetected.

7. Why do market declines expose financial scandals?

8. Why does the SEC have a strong emphasis on information disclosure?

9. What is a form ADV?

10. What ethical lapses do you think occurred at AIG that may have contributed to its downfall?

11. How would you describe the essential nature of ethical behavior?

12. What are the four basic principles of investment ethics? How does each of these tie to a specific feature of the investment industry?

13. What is a benefit to unethical behavior?

14. What are some costs to unethical behavior?

15. Identify one way that you can increase your propensity to be an ethical investment professional.

CRITICAL THINKING QUESTIONS

1. If you are like most students, unfortunately you have encountered some type of student cheating. Make a list of some ways that students can cheat—including things students do to gain an advantage in earning a grade in a course, but that not everyone considers cheating. Next, explain why each item you listed should be considered cheating, and why it should *not*. In your explanations, identify who is potentially hurt by each type of cheating.

2. As discussed in the chapter, pervasive ethical lapses are often revealed following the collapse of a market bubble. What different types of pressures could exist during a bubble that could lead normally ethical professionals to act unethically?

3. Think about the difference between unethical and illegal behavior. Most behavior that is illegal is also unethical, for example, stealing. Could there ever be a situation where illegal behavior is ethical? (Your example doesn't have to involve investments.)

4. Some have argued that regulations stifle free markets and innovation. Sometimes "smart" investment professionals can devise ways to get around the rules, and in doing so, exploit profitable opportunities. One example discussed in the chapter is AIG. Can you think of other examples? When is "getting around the rules" ethical and when is it not?

5. Virtually all investment firms have compliance officers who typically are lawyers. These officers ensure that employees comply with all securities laws and regulations. They provide training in compliance for new employees and maintain reporting systems to monitor employee behavior. Is a compliance department sufficient to ensure that a firm conducts business ethically? Why or why not?

APPLIED STUDENT PROJECT: SELF-REFLECTION ON ETHICS

Write a self-reflective essay that considers the following questions. What do you think motivates you? Greed? Ego? Being creative or innovative? Being intellectually challenged? Helping others? What would you do if you saw someone else engaging in unethical behavior? Do you recall an incident in the past where you may have acted unethically or seen someone treated unethically? (The incident doesn't need to involve investments.) What did you do? What did you think? How did you feel about it?

REFERENCES AND SUGGESTED READING

Benson, Sandra S. "Recognizing the Red Flags of a Ponzi Scheme." *CPA Journal* 79 (June 2009): 6.

Boatright, John R. *Ethics in Finance* 2nd ed. New York: Wiley-Blackwell, 2007.

Boyd, Roddy. "The Last Days of Bear Stearns." *Fortune*, 14 April 2008, 86.

Bradsher, Keith. "China Begins Inquiry into Tainted Baby Formula." *New York Times*, 13 September 2008, 10.

Chernow, Ron. "Where Is Our Ferdinand Pecora?" *New York Times*, 6 January 2009, 25.

Coffee, John C. Jr. "What Caused Enron? A Capsule Social and Economic History of the 1990's." Columbia Law School. European Corporate Governance Institute (ECGI); American Academy of Arts & Sciences (January 30, 2003), Columbia Law and Economics Working Paper No. 214, http://papers.ssrn.com/sol3/papers.cfm?abstract_id=373581.

Cohan, William D. *House of Cards: A Tale of Hubris and Wretched Excess on Wall Street*. New York: Doubleday, 2009.

Cooper, Cynthia. *Extraordinary Circumstances: The Journal of a Corporate Whistleblower*. Hoboken, NJ: Wiley, 2008.

Gremilion, Lee Louis. *Mutual Fund Industry Handbook*. Hoboken, NJ: Wiley, 2005.

"House of Cards." www.cnbc.com/id/28892719/.

Karp, Richard. "Ponzi Lives!" *Barron's*, 16 September 1996, 16–17.

Kessler, Ronald. *The Sins of the Father: Joseph P. Kennedy and the Dynasty He Founded*. New York: Warner Books, 1996.

Leeson, Nick, with Edward Whitley. *Rogue Trader: How I Brought Down Barings Bank and Shook the Financial World*. New York: Little, Brown, 1996.

MacDonald, Scott B., and Jane E. Hughes. *Separating Fools from Their Money: A History of American Financial Scandals*. Piscataway, NJ: Transaction Publishers, 2007.

McEachern, Christina. "The New SEC: Creating a Regulator for the 21st Century." *Wall Street & Technology*, 1 March 2009, 36.

McLean, Bethany, and Peter Elkind. *The Smartest Guys in the Room: The Amazing Rise and Scandalous Fall of Enron*. New York: Penguin Group, 2003.

Morgenson, Gretchen. "Behind Biggest Insurer's Crisis, Blind Eye to a Web of Risk." *New York Times*, 28 September 2008, 1.

Rashbaum, William K., and Zachery Kouwe. "Madoff Will Plead Guilty; Faces Life for Vast Swindle," *New York Times*, 11 March 2009, A1.

Soderlind, Sterling E. "Clarence Barron, Wall Street Pepys." *Barron's*, 7 March 1994, 10.

Stewart, James. *Den of Thieves*. New York: Simon & Schuster, 1991.

Zwick, Steve. "Rogue Trader Hits Société Générale." *Futures*, March 2008, 3.

APPENDIX: FINANCIAL MARKET REGULATORY AGENCIES

SEC—THE SECURITIES AND EXCHANGE COMMISSION

The SEC protects investors and maintains the integrity of financial markets. The commission was created by the Securities Exchange Act of 1934. Website: www.sec.gov.

FINRA—FINANCIAL INDUSTRY REGULATORY AUTHORITY

FINRA protects investors and maintains integrity of financial markets by enforcing federal and state securities laws for broker members. This nonprofit organization was created in 2007 in a consolidation of the National Association of Securities Dealers (NASD) and regulatory functions of the New York Stock Exchange (NYSE). Website: www.finra.org.

THE FED—THE FEDERAL RESERVE

The Fed is the central banking system and establishes monetary policy. It was created by the Federal Reserve Act in 1913. Website: www.federalreserve.gov.

FDIC—THE FEDERAL DEPOSIT INSURANCE CORPORATION

The FDIC protects against the loss of deposits if an FDIC-insured bank or savings association fails. The FDIC was created by the Glass-Steagall Act of 1933. Website: www.fdic.gov.

CFTC—COMMODITIES FUTURES TRADING COMMISSION

The CFTC protects the public against fraudulent use of futures contracts. The CFTC was created by the Commodity Futures Trading Commission Act in 1974. Website: www.cftc.gov.

OCC—OFFICE OF THE COMPTROLLER OF THE CURRENCY

The OCC charters, regulates, and supervises all national banks. It was established by the National Currency Act of 1863. Website: www.occ.treas.gov.

OTS—OFFICE OF THRIFT SUPERVISION

The OTS supervises national thrift and savings associations and protects consumers. It was created by the Financial Institutions Reform, Recovery, and Enforcement Act of 1989. Website: www.ots.treas.gov.

NCUA—NATIONAL CREDIT UNION AGENCY

The NCUA charters and supervises federal credit unions. The NCUA was created by the Federal Credit Union Act in 1934. Website: www.ncua.gov.

2

Fiduciary Duty of Investment Professionals: The Ethical Treatment of the Client

Learning Objectives

After reading this chapter, students should be able to:

- Describe the role of a fiduciary and its importance in the investment profession.
- Distinguish between a fiduciary and an agency relationship.
- Identify and understand fiduciary obligations and potential conflicts in the areas of confidentiality, suitable investments, best execution, and the use of soft dollars.
- Comprehend the importance of identifying the client and ensuring fair treatment of all clients.

CHAPTER OUTLINE

- Introduction: What Is a Fiduciary?
- Agency versus Fiduciary Relationships
- The Role of Laws, Regulations, and Professional Standards
- The Importance of Confidentiality
- Conflicts in Finding the Right Investments
- Conflicts in Trade Management: Best Execution
- Conflicts in Trade Management: Soft Dollars
- Identification and Fair Treatment of Clients
- Conclusion: Disclose! Disclose! Disclose!
- Appendix: Professional Codes of Ethics

Introduction: What Is a Fiduciary?

Ethics at the most fundamental level provide standards on how to treat others. Investment professionals are held to ethical standards because they have a fiduciary duty toward their clients. What is a **fiduciary**? A fiduciary is a person who is entrusted to act in the interests of another. Many professions have a fiduciary duty. Take for example medicine and law. Doctors take the Hippocratic oath to "do no harm" when treating their patients. Lawyers must always act in the best interests of their clients, even if this means defending a guilty person.

An investment professional is a fiduciary entrusted to act in the interests of his or her client when providing investment advice and services. Research analysts, portfolio or money managers, financial planners, consultants, and brokers all have a fiduciary relationship with their clients. The investment professional must place the client's interests above his own and even his employer's interests. But this is tricky. Investment professionals *do* have their own interests. Like any other businessperson, these professionals provide services to earn a profit. *And therein lies the rub.*

The profit motive can make it difficult to fulfill fiduciary obligations. Further, other aspects of the investment business make it easier for the profit motive to overshadow fiduciary obligation. As we discussed in Chapter 1, *finance is complicated*. The complicated world of investing can mask substandard, pricey, or even fraudulent investment services. See Mini Application 2.1 for an example. An unscrupulous investment professional can invest a client's money in unsuitable securities, overcharge for trading commissions, charge the client's account for inappropriate fees, and the like. A trusting client who has little knowledge of investments can be easily convinced that the investments and charges are reasonable. Moreover, investment professionals and clients may have *different time horizons*. Investment professionals might have short-term interests in benefiting from a client's business, but a client may be investing for the long run. Poor investment advice to a client may not be apparent for many years and potentially long after the advisor is out of the picture. Jonathan Knee, an investment banker and author, coined the phrase **IBG YBG**, which means "I'll be gone; you'll be gone." In the recent financial crisis, this phrase was used to characterize excessive risk taking. Professionals continued to enter into transactions with excessive risk because of the fees they and their companies earned. These included not only subprime mortgages but also collateralized debt obligations and credit default swaps. Subprime mortgages are loans made to riskier borrowers who don't qualify for conventional loans. Despite the excessive risk, those involved in these transactions knew that the housing and stock market couldn't keep going up forever; but they assumed that by the time the market turned against them, they would be "gone." Thus they would share no adverse effects from making the risky investments but would have pocketed the fees while the market was strong. Who would suffer the adverse impacts? The investors who invested in the securities lost millions of dollars when the market declined.

Fiduciary a person who is entrusted to act in the interests of another.

IBG YBG "I'll be gone; you'll be gone." a phrase used to characterize the lack of accountability of parties to financial transactions.

MINI APPLICATION 2.1

PONZI SCHEMES: UNETHICAL BEHAVIOR CAN GO UNDETECTED FOR YEARS

Bayou Management LLC was a Connecticut-based hedge fund firm that collapsed in 2005, awash in allegations of fraud by its principal partners, Samuel Israel III and Daniel Marino. From 1997 to 2004 they raised more than $300 million from investors seeking the high returns that hedge funds offered. During this period, the partners falsely reported gains even as the fund lost money. They were able to prolong this fraud, via a typical Ponzi scheme: investors seeking redemptions were paid out of funds raised by new investors. Eventually the scheme collapsed, and Israel and Marino closed the fund in 2005. The fund lost money every year for *six* years before investors caught on. Bernie Madoff (see Chapter 1) is considered to have perpetuated the longest-running Ponzi scheme, which lasted more than 25 years!

Return uncertainty the uncertainty of the future return or price of a security.

Market timing strategy relies on the ability to predict whether different asset markets, i.e., the stock or the bond market, will do better and then reallocate investments across these markets.

Hedge funds an investment fund open only to financial qualified investors that may invest in nontraditional investments and proprietary trading strategies, some of which might seek to hedge risks.

Efficient markets hypothesis a hypothesis that on average all securities prices reflect all relevant publicly available information.

Return uncertainty can also hide unethical behavior. Return uncertainty is the deviation between expected risk-adjusted returns and actual returns. Actual returns will never *exactly equal* expected returns. Financial markets are inherently volatile. The value of a client's portfolio can vary from day to day. An investment advisor could disguise poor investment advice or unreasonable fees as part of the normal periodic declines in the market or in particular investments. For example, suppose an advisor recommends that a client invest $10,000 in a complicated investment vehicle. This vehicle could be presented as a portfolio of different securities or as a sophisticated **market timing strategy**. There are many different definitions of market timing strategies, but the most common one relates to stock and bond markets. This strategy relies on the ability to predict whether the stock or the bond will do better and then reallocate investments across these markets. For example, if you think the bond market is going to perform better than the stock market over the next six months, you would sell your stock investments and put the proceeds in the bond market. Or you could be following some other investment strategy that is "complicated" and difficult for the average investor to understand. The investment advisor also tells the investor that the investment strategy poses some risks, but she downplays them. The investment is made, but later only $5,000 is returned. The dishonest advisor can hide either her poor investment advice or even the possibility that the $5,000 has been pocketed behind the excuse of "risk." A naïve investor may never know otherwise.

The hedge fund industry has been particularly susceptible to claims of unethical practices and lack of transparency. **Hedge funds** earn higher returns but do so using proprietary investment strategies. Recall the **efficient markets hypothesis**, which holds that all relevant public information is immediately and completely reflected in securities prices, thus eliminating the opportunity to earn an economic profit from public information. Economic profit is the extra return that is earned above the risk-adjusted return. If hedge funds made their investment strategies public, everyone could do it, and that in turn would eliminate the profit

MINI APPLICATION 2.2
THE TECH BUBBLE AND A "SURE THING"

During the tech bubble in the late 1990s, many financial advisors recommended that their clients sacrifice diversification and invest all their money in tech stocks. After the bubble burst, investors incurred significant losses. Further, even when tech stocks were declining, many advisors still recommended that clients continue to hold these stocks, in the hope of a price rebound. Many sued their advisors, but most did not fully recover their losses. Below you can see the stock price of Cisco. Note that before 2001, this looked like a stock that could go nowhere but up. Investors who put the bulk of their savings into Cisco stock while the price was rising would have lost a significant portion of their portfolio as the price declined.

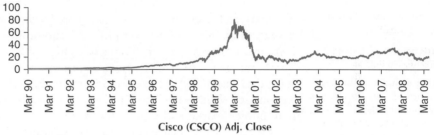

Cisco (CSCO) Adj. Close

Source: www.finance.yahoo.com.

opportunity. Ethical hedge fund managers earn better than risk-adjusted returns for their investors; unethical hedge fund managers hide behind "secret" or proprietary trading strategies.

Ironically, the complicated nature of investments that can mask unethical behavior is the very reason clients turn to the professional in the first place. In turn, this creates the need for a higher level of trust. Clients need to trust that the investment advisor is providing them with the best advice, even if they don't fully understand it. Because they are entrusting their money to the professional, they are inviting this person to have a significant impact on their lives—not just today but long into the future. Good investment advice can lead to a comfortable retirement and tuition for children's college education. Poor investment advice can lead to loss of security, opportunity, and maybe even one's home. Clients need to be secure in the knowledge that a decline in the value of their portfolios is from the risks inherent in financial investing and not because of incompetent advice or excessive fees charged by their investment advisor. Mini Application 2.2 shows how poor investing advice during the "tech bubble" hurt clients. Managing investments is not just about the numbers. It is also about people and relationships. Clients must be able to trust the professionals who manage their money.

AGENCY VERSUS FIDUCIARY RELATIONSHIPS

Agency theory this is a theory that explains the incentives and contractual solutions when a principal hires an agent to act on his or her behalf, and the agent's incentives are not perfectly aligned with the principal's.

Principal a party who hires another party, the agent, to work on her or his behalf.

Agent someone who is hired to work on behalf of another (the principal).

Basis point (bp) 1/100th of a percentage point.

Active managers managers who actively pick and choose investments within a particular investment strategy and seek to offer a better return relative to a prespecified benchmark.

Passive managers investment managers who do not seek to actively trade investments or select superior investments to save transactions costs.

Assets under management the total dollar amount invested by all clients by an investment management firm.

Monitor to watch over or oversee.

The closest idea in economics that captures the concept of the fiduciary relationship between an investment professional and a client is **agency theory**. In agency theory, the **principal** hires an **agent** to act on his or her behalf. However, the agent's incentives are not perfectly aligned with those of the principal. A contract between the principal and the agent is thus written to align both parties' incentives. For example, the money manager is paid a fee based on the return earned on the client's portfolio. This provides an incentive for the manager to maximize the returns for the client. Yet, this contract doesn't perfectly align the agent/manager and the principal/client's incentives.

Let's look at what happens in the case of money management. Most investment managers charge a fee based on the dollar value of the portfolio. For example, management fees may be 80 basis points. A **basis point (bp)** is 1/100th of a percent, or 0.0001, and *basis point* is a commonly used term in the financial industry. **Active managers** are hired to actively pick and choose investments within a particular investment strategy (i.e., small cap stocks, high-yield debt, or international equity). These managers seek to offer a better return relative to a prespecified benchmark. As such, they charge higher fees—from 50 to 200 bps. These are the types of managers we think of when we say "stock pickers." **Passive managers** seek to provide returns that mimic a market-based index for the lowest cost, for example, the S&P 500 and Russell 2000. These managers charge considerably lower fees—from 5 to 25 bps. Total fees earned by these firms are based on **assets under management**, the total dollar amount invested for all their clients. (See Mini Application 2.3 that provides an opportunity for you to think about what you cost your firm as an entry level analyst.) Both types of managers owe a fiduciary duty to their clients, but agency theory tells us that the economic incentives of managers will not be perfectly aligned.

Suppose, for example, that the investment professional is paid 20 percent of the return earned on the client's portfolio of $100,000. The investment professional can expend a reasonable amount of time researching investment options and then make investments that earn his or her client a 12 percent return. Yet, to earn a 13 percent return would require much more time trying to find undervalued securities. The investment professional hopes to earn only an extra $200 (20 percent $\times$ 1 percent $\times$ $100,000) for his or her efforts, while the client earns $800. The agent is unlikely to spend the extra time, and so the client will not receive the extra $800. See Mini Application 2.4 that discusses how the size of assets under management influences money managers' incentives to find extra returns for their clients.

There are costs to writing incentive contracts. First, there is the monitoring cost borne by the principal. The principal/client must **monitor** or watch over the agent/investment professional to ensure he is fulfilling his end of the contract. It can

---

MINI APPLICATION 2.3
TEST YOURSELF

Do you know what you cost? Suppose that the going rate (salary plus benefits) for a junior analyst is $80,000. If a firm charges 80 bps for its management fees, how much does assets under management have to increase to just break even on you?

MINI APPLICATION 2.4
MANAGEMENT FEES, INCENTIVES, PORTFOLIO SIZE, AND ASSETS UNDER MANAGEMENT

Portfolio size can influence how hard a money manager works to find additional returns. Suppose the size of the portfolio is $1 million and management fees are 80 bps. The manager earns only $80 to find an extra 1 percent in returns; the client earns $10,000. If it takes another 25 hours to find this excess return, the money manager will earn less than the minimum wage for this work.

But what happens if the portfolio is $100 million instead of $1 million? Now, the money manager earns $8,000 more for the additional 25 hours of work—well worth it.

Notice that the additional time spent finding an extra 1 percent of returns doesn't change with the portfolio size, but the manager's compensation does. What does this tell you? Investment strategies to find excess returns are scalable—that is, you can grow your business without adding more research analysts and portfolio managers. Thus managers often try to find excess returns when the sizes of their portfolios are small, so as to attract more business even if initially it may not be worthwhile (as described above). Managers seek to increase the number and size of client portfolios, or what's known as assets under management. However, there is a limit to growth. As a portfolio becomes larger, it becomes more difficult to exploit opportunities from market mispricing. The market can be tipped off with large trades, thus erasing any potential gains.

Bond economic incentive to ensure that an agent will work on the principal's behalf.

Residual loss the loss that occurs because of the inability to enforce all contracts perfectly.

be difficult for clients to monitor investment professionals because of the complexity of their investments. Second, there is the cost borne by the agent to bond himself to the principal. The **bond** is something of value to the agent that could be lost if the agent doesn't act in the interest of the principal. The bond acts as a credible promise. Education costs and professional certifications can act as a bond. The investment professional will waste his investment in education and certification if he poorly executes investment services for his clients. Poor investment services can hurt his reputation, leading to the eventual loss of clients and profits. Finally, the principal bears a **residual loss** because it's impossible to create a contract that perfectly aligns the agent's and principal's incentives.

Economics tells us that in the long run, or on average, investment professionals have sufficient incentives to provide quality services for their clients. That is certainly true. What about in the short run? What about the individual case that is a deviation from the average? It is cold comfort to the individual client who discovers that his portfolio has disappeared because of poor investment advice that "on average, investment professionals have incentives to behave ethically." A fiduciary relationship involves not just incentives, but trust. And trust occurs when behavior is governed by the highest ethical standards.

Ethical guidelines ensure that investment professionals uphold their fiduciary duty in each and every one of their client relationships. Not just on average. Clearly, some individuals in the investment profession are ruthlessly seeking to steal their clients' money. Bernie Madoff is one notorious example. But the vast majority of investment professionals are well-intentioned individuals. Yet, because they are in a relationship where they seek to profit from their clients (this is the rub), they need a road map to navigate ethical areas that at first blush appear gray. Is it okay to charge my client for this service? How much effort do I need to expend in getting the lowest fees or investments that earn the highest risk-adjusted returns for my client? How do I determine the most rewarding investments for my client in financial markets that are inherently fraught with uncertainty and risk? The remainder of this chapter provides the answers to these questions.

The Role of Laws, Regulations, and Professional Standards

Financial Industry Regulatory Authority (FINRA) a nonprofit organization with the legal authority to enforce securities rules and regulations among its members, who are primarily brokers and traders.

Chartered Financial Analyst (CFA) Institute a designation oriented toward analysts, portfolio, and active money managers. Certification as a CFA® is encouraged to indicate ethical standards and competence among the members.

Certified Financial Planner (CFP) a designation oriented toward financial planners. Certification as a CFP® is encouraged to indicate ethical standards and competence among the members.

Professional standards, regulations, and laws provide rules to ensure that investment professionals fulfill their fiduciary obligations (see Chapter 1 for more discussion). The Securities and Exchange Commission (SEC) requires under Rule 204A-1 of the Investment Advisers Act of 1940 that registered advisors have a code of ethics. The **Financial Industry Regulatory Authority (FINRA)** is a nonprofit organization that has the legal authority to enforce securities rules and regulations on its members, which are primarily brokers and traders. It also promotes investor education (remember, it is lack of understanding that creates opportunities for unscrupulous investment professionals) and ethical standards. The SEC also promotes investor education to protect against fraud.

The **Chartered Financial Analyst (CFA) Institute**, the **Certified Financial Planner (CFP)** Board of Standards, and the Financial Planning Standards Board (FPSB) Ltd. provide codes of ethics for investment professionals. The CFA designation is oriented toward analysts, portfolio, and active money managers. The CFP designation is oriented toward financial planners. These codes go beyond the legal requirements. Certification either through the CFA® or CFP® designation is encouraged to indicate ethical standards and competence on behalf of the members. The ethical codes for these organizations are included in the appendix to this chapter.

The remainder of the chapter discusses major areas that are problematic for professionals who are fiduciaries. These areas and their solutions are those that have been identified by securities regulators and professional organizations. This chapter offers but a brief overview. The SEC, FINRA, CFA Institute, and CFP Board of Standards all have much more detailed rules and regulations than can be covered in a single chapter. As students, you are encouraged to become more informed about these as your careers evolve.

Remember, however, that each of the more specific issues covered in this chapter relate to the fundamental principles of investment ethics introduced in Chapter 1.

The Importance of Confidentiality

One of the most important concerns of clients is confidentiality. You are, after all, talking about their money; and for most individuals, this is a very private matter. Confidentiality relates to Principle 4, Trust and Fairness. Clients need to trust you with some of their most sensitive and personal information.

FUNDAMENTAL PRINCIPLES OF INVESTMENT ETHICS FOR PROFESSIONALS

Principle 1: ETHICAL UNDERSTANDING

Because investments are complicated, *you have an obligation not to knowingly engage in an investment transaction that either you or others do not sufficiently understand. This includes knowing the underlying source of returns or fees charged.*

Principle 2: ETHICAL USE OF INFORMATION

Because investments are information driven, *you have an obligation to ensure that you and others have access to relevant information and that you or others do not misuse or distort information in the investment transaction.*

Principle 3: RESPONSIBLE INVESTING

Because investments provide financial resources to others, *you have an obligation to ensure that you do not knowingly make or recommend investments that support activities that harm others.*

Principle 4: TRUST AND FAIRNESS

Because you are dealing with others' money either directly or indirectly, *you have an obligation not to abuse the trust that all others have either explicitly or implicitly placed in you to treat them fairly.*

Many businesses build their customer base by using their current customers to attest to the quality of their product or service. This is difficult in the investment business, where you must keep the identity of your clients confidential. You cannot discuss the amounts that you have invested for them, nor can you say what investments you have made for them (i.e., stocks versus bonds). You cannot even identify them as customers.

These confidentiality requirements are similar to those in the medical profession. A doctor should neither discuss the health of her patients nor even identify who her patients are. Imagine if you knew that your neighbor was the patient of an oncologist, a doctor who treats cancer. You may be worried that your neighbor has cancer when he has simply seen the specialist for routine testing. In either case, this is a private matter for your neighbor to disclose, not his doctor.

Now imagine you learn, from your neighbor who works there, that your boss has investments with Alpha-Plus Hedge Fund. You also know that this fund has a minimum investment of $250,000. You now have learned some personal financial information about your boss. Simply by saying your boss is one of his clients, your neighbor has violated his confidentiality.

To ensure that you maintain your clients' confidentiality, do not tell anyone outside of work about your clients; also avoid discussing your clients with the people you work with. The more people learn about your clients' financial matters, the more likely there is to be a breach in confidentiality. Your colleagues should have information about your client accounts only to the extent that this knowledge helps your clients.

Once your client no longer works with you, may you reveal that he or she once was a client? No. The duty of confidentiality remains. This is similar to the medical profession. A doctor cannot talk about the health of his or her former patients. Again, by identifying your clients, you are revealing some type of information about their private financial matters. This is a violation of trust. Of course, if any of your current or past clients give you permission to use their names in soliciting business, you can do so.

CONFLICTS IN FINDING THE RIGHT INVESTMENTS

Besides keeping quiet about your client's investments, you also need to find the right investments for your client. This is one of the key responsibilities that an investment fiduciary has toward his client. Here is where the professional's expertise and knowledge become critical. Principle 1, Ethical Understanding, requires you to ensure that you understand your client's needs and that in turn your client understands your recommendations and the fees associated with your services and the investments.

RISK

First, the investment professional must assess the risk that a client is willing to accept. This can be one of the most challenging tasks in providing investment advice. Most of the time, you can't simply go to your client and ask what level of beta or market risk she is willing to bear. Nor can you ask what kind of portfolio standard deviation she had in mind. Unless this client has a background in finance, she is unlikely to have a clue about what you are asking.

But you can ask a series of questions that reveal how tolerant your clients will be toward short-term fluctuations in the value of their investments. Here are some other useful questions to consider when picking investments for your client:

- Holding horizon: How long are they thinking about holding their investments? Five years? Twenty years?
- Liquidity: Are there circumstances when they will need to liquidate their investments quickly?
- Income needs: Are they expecting to receive regular income (i.e., from dividends and interest), from their investments? How much? How often?
- Tax considerations: What is their tax bracket? Do they need tax-free investments?
- What does the rest of their portfolio look like? Do they have a large mortgage?
- Do they own real estate or have other investments? What is their annual income?

The concepts from your investment courses can help you construct the best portfolio for your clients based on the answers to these questions. So where do ethics come into play in this conversation?

DOCUMENTATION OF GOALS

Investment policy statement (IPS) written documentation of your client's investment goals as well as the compensation agreement between you and your client.

Agreement an arrangement formed between a client and financial advisor on investments and financial goals per CFP.

First, you have an obligation to be *diligent* in translating the client's wishes into an investment program. You need to be *competent* and knowledgeable about a wide range of investment products and have a good understanding of financial markets. Your investment in education is invaluable in fulfilling this duty.

Second, you should have a written **investment policy statement (IPS)** (per CFA Institute) or **agreement** (per the CFP Board of Standards) that you construct with your client and use as a basis for periodically reviewing your client's portfolio. It is particularly important for financial planners who are more likely to deal with small individual investors to ensure that their clients fully understand the recommendations. Written documentation of your client's investment goals as well as the compensation agreement between you and your client can help keep you honest. As a practical matter, it will also help eliminate any misunderstandings that may occur in the future. In the economist's terms, the IPS or agreement acts as bond put up by the investment professional. Deviation from the IPS or agreement can be legal grounds for contract violation.

COMMISSIONS

Commissions fees earned by making an investment or trade on behalf of a client.

You also need to be aware of how **commissions** or sales fees that you earn on different investment products can influence the advice you give your client. If you are able to earn higher commissions or sales fees on one type of product versus another, you may be tempted to recommend that your client invest in the product that earns you more money. If this product meets your client's investment goals, there is nothing wrong with recommending it. However, you may be tempted to convince yourself that it's okay to recommend an investment product that is *not* the best one for your client, because it is the best one for *you*. This is unethical because you are making yourself better off at your client's expense and violating his trust in you.

Annuity a constant or variable-period cash flow paid out for a fixed length of time.

Annuities are one type of product that can create conflicts between advisors and clients because of their commissions. Variable and fixed-rate annuities are available and are typically offered by insurance companies. Recall from your introductory finance course what an **annuity** is—a periodic payment. An annuity factor is determined by the time period and the interest rate. Suppose your client will have $500,000 when he or she retires. You anticipate that this amount can be held in an account that earns 8 percent a year for the next 30 years. Using the annuity factor of 11.2579, this would allow an annual income or annuity of $44,413 a year for your client over the next 30 years.

The investor pays into the annuity for a certain period of time, the accumulation phase. If the investor has purchased a variable annuity, the payments are invested into stocks and bonds and earn interest on a tax-deferred basis, the same as in a 401(k).

401(k) an account that allows investors to save and invest for retirement without having to pay taxes on a certain allowed portion of income invested or any returns earned by the investments until they withdraw the money during retirement.

A **401(k)** is an account that allows investors to save and invest for retirement. Investors do not need to pay taxes on a certain allowed portion of income invested or any returns earned by the investments until they withdraw the money during retirement.

The performance on the underlying investments then determines the annuity that is paid out during the payout phase. Some annuities also provide a death benefit, and this is why insurance companies often sell them. In addition, an annuity that pays lifetime benefits is attractive for people who are worried about outliving their assets. Annuities can also offer other benefits that are not available by investing in a tax-deferred retirement account, such as a 401(k) plan. However, there is a charge for these benefits. In addition, withdrawal from the account during the early years of the accumulation phase can lead to **surrender charges**. Surrender charges are often based on a percentage of the amount of the annuity and can be as much as 7 percent. Hence, the investor can pay a substantial penalty to get at her money. Charges, expenses, and poor underlying investments can rapidly reduce the value of the payout. Annuities can be appropriate if held as a long-term investment and along with other tax-deferred retirement assets such as a 401(k) plan.

Surrender charges charges for withdrawing from an account, usually with annuities.

The commissions earned by professionals selling annuities are high—typically from 6 to 8 percent of the value of the annuity. Sometimes they are as high as 14 percent. Hence, a $200,000 annuity can generate a $12,000 commission for the salesperson. As a result, the sale of annuities can be abused. Mini Application 2.5 discusses a firm that got in trouble while selling annuities.

FEES

Mutual fund a fund that invests in several securities and allows investors to purchase shares in the fund to achieve diversification at a low price.

As an investment professional, you need to be wary of sales fees earned on other investment products such as mutual funds. **Mutual fund** are securities that are created out of a large portfolio of securities. Each share of a mutual fund represents a share in a well-diversified portfolio. Mutual funds are attractive to investors because they allow smaller investors to get diversification without having to invest in a large portfolio. The value of each share of a mutual fund depends on the market value and the number of shares held of each security in the fund.

When you recommend a fund, you need to ask whether the fund is really appropriate for your client, or do you just earn a better sales fee on it than on

---

MINI APPLICATION 2.5

WADDELL & REED, INC. AND VARIABLE ANNUITIES

In early 2006 the state of Kansas issued a consent order against Waddell & Reed, Inc. and one of its employees who encouraged an elderly investor to purchase a variable annuity. Variable annuities often entail surrender fees during the first 5 to 7 years they are held. Seniors who need access to funds for retirement and health-care expenses during that time can incur surrender fees that reduce the overall value of their retirement assets. For these seniors, annuities are not appropriate investments.

other funds? It is fine to earn a sales commission, but not at your client's expense. Recall that any behavior that makes you better off while making someone else worse off is unethical. In this case, it is unethical to give your client poor and deceptive investment advice while steering him to a higher-commissioned product. Finally, if you recommend only products offered by your company, you need to ensure that your client understands that you are selling only those products and not offering more comprehensive investment advice. In 2004, Citigroup was accused of providing incentives to its sales force to push Citigroup mutual funds. Moreover, Citigroup did not disclose these incentives to investors.

Fees that should be disclosed to investors include a schedule of management fees, trailer fees, and 12b-1 fees (so called after the SEC rule that allows for such fees). These are usually stated as a percentage of the amount invested and are paid on an ongoing basis. Management fees on actively managed accounts intended to outperform the market are between 80 and 100 basis points. Hedge fund managers can charge even more. Trailer fees are paid to the salesperson or broker who sold the investor the fund for as long as the investor owns the fund. Mutual funds can charge 12b-1 fees for operational expenses, and they often are disclosed in the funds' expense ratio: annual operating expenses divided by the average assets under management during the year. Mutual funds can be load, no load, or back or deferred load. These terms all refer to one-time fees paid when either purchasing or redeeming shares in the fund. Expense ratios that are charged to accounts, wrap fees (typically flat fees charged on a quarterly or monthly basis), administrative fees, cash bonuses paid for setting up accounts, and other fees—all need to be disclosed. Trading costs and brokerage commissions that are charged to client accounts also need to be disclosed. These costs can be between two and five cents per share, but they can add up quickly. While disclosing these costs sounds simple, trading costs and brokerage commissions have some particularly thorny issues. We turn to these next.

CONFLICTS IN TRADE MANAGEMENT: BEST EXECUTION

Besides selecting the best investments, investment professionals also make trades on behalf of clients. These trades include the initial purchase of investments (e.g., stocks) as well as any subsequent sales and purchases. All of these trades cost money—your client's money. So as a fiduciary, you have an obligation to minimize the cost of trading. This obligation relates to Principle 1, Ethical Understanding, and Principle 4, Trust and Fairness. Your client trusts you to make cost-effective trades and not to take advantage of his relative lack of understanding of trading costs by overcharging him.

CHURNING

Churning occurs when a broker excessively buys and sells securities in a client's account to generate commissions for her- or himself.

One unethical practice in trading is **churning**. This occurs when a broker excessively buys and sells securities in a client's account just to generate commissions. Churning is not only unethical, but illegal. But what constitutes churning? There are no hard-and-fast rules, and whether you are churning or not depends on the client's IPS or agreement (see earlier discussion—remember written documentation might come in handy in eliminating misunderstandings). Supposing that your client's investments are in blue-chip stocks and he or she intends to hold these investments for 20 years, actively buying and selling every month would violate the IPS and constitute churning.

Suppose instead that you have a client who is willing to take on more risk. You in turn are offering an investment strategy that is opportunistic; that is, you take advantage of short-term mispricing in the market (and you are good at it—and you are doing so legally, which is to say you are not using inside information). Here it makes sense to do more buying and selling in your client's account. Presumably the return from the opportunities more than compensates your client for the additional transaction costs.

THE EFFECTIVE SPREAD

Best execution using the trading process to the overall benefit of your client.

Effective spread the difference between the price of the actual transaction and the amount halfway between the quoted spread.

Specialists professionals and/or companies with the role of fulfilling all orders for particular stocks that trade on the New York and American Stock Exchange. On the NASDAQ, these professionals are called market makers.

Market makers intermediaries in financial markets who act as middle men between buyers and sellers.

You also are required to seek **best execution** for trades you make on behalf of your client. What does this mean? You must use the trading process to your client's overall benefit. One dimension of best execution is to minimize the **effective spread** on securities transactions. When buying and selling securities, traders see price quotes—an ask price from them to buy securities and a bid price from them to sell. Traders might actually transact at these quoted prices, but they are more likely to transact at a price within the spread. The effective spread is then measured as the difference between the price of the actual transaction and halfway between the quoted spread. Figure 2.1 shows how the effective spread is measured. Investment professionals have an obligation to minimize the effective spread for their clients.

Brokers can fulfill orders in various ways. They can fulfill orders directly through an exchange that uses a specialist system. They can also fulfill orders through a third-party market maker, which is a firm that buys and sells securities. Or orders can go through a NASDAQ market maker for NASDAQ-listed securities. **Specialists**, on the New York and American Stock Exchange, and **market makers**, on NASDAQ, are in the business of fulfilling orders. As such, they have a large inventory of buy and sell orders that help them minimize spreads by matching up buy and sell orders.

FIGURE	2.1	BEST EXECUTION MINIMIZES EFFECTIVE SPREAD

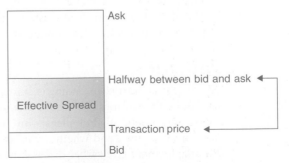

Electronic communications networks (ECN) networks that allow brokers to trade directly with each other—electronically—and eliminate the need for a market maker.

Internalization using the company's own trading desk to fulfill orders.

Limit order an order that specifies the price at which the trade can occur.

Market order an order that can be fulfilled at whatever price is available in the market.

Payment for order flow occurs when brokers reduce costs of trading to increase the number of trades.

Brokers can also use an **electronic communications networks (ECN)** to trade. These networks allow brokers to trade directly with each other electronically and eliminate the need for a market maker. Finally, investment professionals can use their own trading desk to fulfill orders. This is known as **internalization**.

Brokers will also aggregate orders to get the best price of execution no matter how they execute the trade. But the cost of trading delays created by aggregation must also be taken into account. If the market becomes fast moving (i.e., characterized by rapidly changing prices), waiting too long can eliminate the gains from trading. For example, suppose you are buying a stock on a client's behalf that looks like a good investment at its current market price of $10 per share. If this stock is rapidly increasing, waiting too long will cause the purchase to occur at a higher price. Making a trade a **limit order** can minimize the chances of buying too high or selling too low. A limit order specifies the price at which the trade can occur. If the broker is unable to get the limit price, the order is not fulfilled. This is in contrast to a **market order**, which is fulfilled at whatever price is available in the market.

Exchanges and market makers make money by processing trades. As a result, many of these firms engage in a practice known as **payment for order flow**—the exchanges pay brokers a per-share price for routing trades through their exchange. This is a way for brokers to make money and minimize the cost of trading to their investors. What are the ethical issues here? If firms are paid for order flow, they must disclose this to their investors. This disclosure is made to ensure that clients are fully informed of the trading costs incurred on their behalf. In addition, traders can attempt to influence brokers to route trades to them. One way they can do this is by providing gifts—in the form of tickets to sporting events, educational conferences, and the like. Educational conferences sound like they should benefit clients, but they are often held at resorts where there is a brief presentation and most of the participants' time is spent by the pool or at the golf course. These practices are against SEC regulations. Gifts can compromise a money manager's interest in seeking best execution and compromise her fiduciary duty to her client. Gifts should not exceed $100 per person per year. Nominal gifts such as pens and notebooks with the firm's

---

MINI APPLICATION 2.6
FIDELITY INVESTMENTS AND GIFTS FROM TRADERS

Fidelity Investments is a fund manager of many mutual funds, in aggregate representing billions of dollars. In early 2008, it was discovered that Fidelity employees were offered more than $1.6 million in travel, entertainment, and other gifts paid for by outside brokers courting the massive trading business. These gifts included private jet trips to such places as Bermuda, Mexico, and Las Vegas, and premium sports tickets to events including Wimbledon, the Super Bowl, and the Ryder Cup golf tournament. Acceptance of these gifts could compromise Fidelity employees' interest in seeking best execution for their clients. The SEC fined Fidelity $8 million for accepting these gifts. The SEC also imposed sanctions that included improving compliance systems to prevent future abuses.

logo are okay to both give and accept; an iPod with the firm's logo is not. See Mini Application 2.6 for other examples of gifts that are inappropriate.

As a practical matter, it is difficult to select a broker who will give you the smallest effective spread on a particular trade at a given point in time. Thousands of brokers execute trades; it is not feasible to get quotes from all of them in a timely way. Thus investment professionals need to select the broker traders that make the most sense to place client trades with regularly. In addition to information on effective spreads on past trades, you as an investment professional can also consider the price and size of trades executed, trading characteristics, financial condition, and research and services that brokers may provide to assist in the investment process. The purchasing of research and services from brokers is another area fraught with ethical pitfalls. We turn to this next.

CONFLICTS IN TRADE MANAGEMENT: SOFT DOLLARS

Soft dollars brokerage commissions generated that can be used for the purchase of services and equipment.

Soft dollars is a term that refers to research and other products and services that are paid for using trading commissions. The practice of soft dollars evolved prior to 1975, before commissions were deregulated. Until 1975, all commissions had to be charged at a fixed rate. This made it difficult for brokers to offer discounts to attract larger institutional customers. Remember that basic economics tells us that most businesses will offer a quantity discount to attract larger, more profitable customers.

Brokers created a way to get around the fixed-rate commissions by bundling research and other services into the commission rate. This became a way for them to offer a non-price concession or an in-kind rebate to attract customers. Customers that generated a minimum level of commissions through trading with a broker could then purchase research and services with these commissions, or "soft dollars." After commission rates were deregulated in 1975, there no longer seemed to be any reason to continue soft dollar practices, yet they persisted. Figure 2.2 shows how soft dollars work.

| FIGURE | 2.2 | THE MECHANICS OF SOFT DOLLARS |

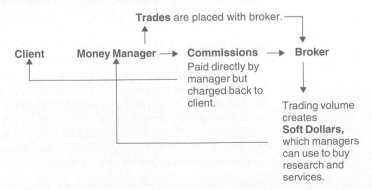

Two economic explanations are put forth for the continuation of soft dollar practices. First, research produced by brokers can act as a bond (see agency theory, above) that they will effectively execute trades. Brokers can generate valuable research by making an investment in third-party research, data, and analysts. Brokers can earn a return on these investments only by attracting clients willing to place trades with them. These clients, in turn, seek brokers that can provide quality execution of trades. One dimension of execution is the ability to effectively disguise informed trades. But in turn, brokers can disguise these trades only if they have sufficient trading volume or order flow to "bury" the trades. This is a case of the chicken or the egg! Providing good-quality research is one way that brokers can attract order flow. Figure 2.3 shows this circular relationship between research and trade execution.

A second rationale for using the soft dollar approach is that it allows clients and investment professionals to share the costs of research. Remember that investment professionals are seeking to provide excess risk-adjusted returns for their clients. They can achieve these excess returns ethically through hard work and research that identifies undervalued or overvalued securities. However, they share only a fraction of the excess returns that they earn through fees. Remember our earlier example (agency theory again)? If the cost of research exceeds the additional fees earned on the excess return, the investment manager will forgo the purchase of research. The clients, who earn a lion's share of the excess return, would find the cost worthwhile. Passing some of the cost of the research on to clients via commissions provides a mechanism whereby the investment professional and the client can share the cost to the client's benefit. Of course, having more clients and larger accounts allows the

| FIGURE | 2.3 | **AN ECONOMIC RATIONALE FOR SOFT DOLLARS** |

Source: Stephen M. Horan and D. Bruce Johnsen, "The Welfare Effects of Soft Dollar Brokerage: Law and Economics," CFA Institute, *Research Foundation Publications*, June 2000, 1–64.

investment professional to amortize the cost of research over a larger number of accounts, thus making the cost more economical.

USES OF SOFT DOLLARS

Most often, soft dollars are used to purchase either in-house proprietary research from a broker or third-party research provided by companies such as Standard & Poor's, Bloomberg, and Dow Jones. While the SEC allows the use of soft dollars for research purposes (and as long as there is full disclosure), and there might be good economic arguments for their use, some have argued that soft dollars create opportunities for abuse.

SOFT DOLLARS REGULATION

Starting in 1934—and again in 1998, 2004, and 2007—the SEC has issued rules, under section 28(e) of the Securities and Exchange Act of 1934, that regulate the use of soft dollars to ensure the balance between allowing clients to benefit from research and preventing the misuse of client commissions. Soft dollars have been used to pay for an employee's salary, marketing expenses, legal expenses, hotel and rental car costs, phone systems, personal travel, entertainment, limousines, interior design, and construction expenses. Here the investment professional is using commissions generated by clients' accounts to pay for business costs. These are costs that should be recovered through fees charged to clients, not trading commissions. Commissions are charged to clients' accounts. Using commissions to pay for these expenses hides from the clients the fact that they are bearing the business expenses of their investment advisor in addition to paying the advisor management fees and trading commissions. Further, managers might be tempted to use brokers who charge higher commissions but pay for their business expenses through soft dollars. Then those managers are also violating their duty to seek best execution.

Of course, clients expect that the management fees must be high enough to cover the manager's business or operating costs. This is how the manager stays in business. The problem is not in asking clients to cover operating costs. It's the way they are "asked," or more to the point, *not asked*. Here is where the complicated world of investments creates opportunities for unethical practices. Suppose clients are charged trading commissions. Clients accept that they should be charged for trades made on their behalf. But what if these commissions are artificially high because they are also paying for business expenses covered by soft dollars? How would the client know they are paying for both trades and business expenses? The use of soft dollars effectively allows the manager to charge the client twice for business expenses: once through the management fee and again through the trading commission. The abuse of soft dollars is a violation of Principle 4, Trust and Fairness, and especially of Principle 1, Ethical Understanding, when soft dollars obscure what fees are charged to clients and for what purpose.

The SEC requires that firms disclose their soft dollar practices in their client brochures when they register as an investment advisor by filing a Form ADV (see Chapter 1). This ensures that no business expenses are hidden in commissions. However, often soft dollars are used to purchase what are known as mixed-use services—those that provide both research and business benefits. An example is a computer system that provides research as well as the ability to track client accounts. In these cases, it is recommended that advisors attempt to make a reasonable allocation of the cost to client accounts and business accounts. Again, full disclosure of allocation can help prevent abuses. It's hard to be unethical when all the cards are on the table.

Directed brokerage occurs when clients direct their investment advisor to use a particular broker when making trades on behalf of their account.

Clients also have the ability to direct their advisor to use a particular broker when making trades on behalf of their accounts. This practice is known as **directed brokerage**. In these cases, the commissions and soft dollars generated by the account belong to the client. Research, services, or cash rebates may go directly from the broker to the client in these arrangements. The investment advisor has the obligation to ensure that the client is still receiving quality execution from the broker.

IDENTIFICATION AND FAIR TREATMENT OF CLIENTS

Another area that can be ethically ambiguous is the different treatment of clients. Again, what is common practice in most businesses can be unethical in the investment industry. Most businesses treat their larger and more profitable customers better. Better treatment means better terms—offering the same services for a lower price or providing valuable services that are not offered to other customers. Often the terms of transaction are negotiated with each party separately, leading to different terms for different customers. If one customer has a better deal than another, the business owner will not want to reveal that. Otherwise, the customer with the poorer deal is likely to demand better terms.

In the investment industry, the same fiduciary duty is owed to a client with a small account as to a client with a large account. It is okay to provide different services for different fees and to charge management fees that vary according to account size as long as there is full disclosure of these fee and service schedules to *all* clients regardless of the size of their account. Clients should know if larger accounts are charged less, and how much less, as well as whether additional services are provided either with larger accounts or for additional fees. These disclosures relate to Principle 4, Trust and Fairness.

Initial public offerings (IPOs) the first time that a firm's securities, usually stock, are offered to the investing public.

The allocation of **initial public offerings** (IPOs) is one area that can be problematic. An initial public offering is the first time that a corporation offers stock to the public markets. They are often associated with a large increase in price over the initial offer price within days of the offering. Mini Application 2.7 provides an example of a typical IPO. IPOs are highly sought-after investments. They also are in limited supply. Hence, investment professionals need to be careful when allocating them to client accounts. A firm could be tempted to allocate all of its limited supply of a "hot" IPO to a large and profitable client. However, *all* clients for which the IPO meets the investment objectives of the account (see the earlier discussion of the IPS/Agreement) should be given an opportunity to invest in the IPO. A fair way to distribute a limited amount of shares is on a **pro rata basis**. This is where each client account receives an amount in proportion to the size of the account. Example 2.1 shows how a pro rata allocation of an IPO across client accounts works.

Pro rata basis occurs when each client account receives an amount in proportion to the size of that account.

Sometimes clients attempt to get more profitable investments (i.e., via a greater share of IPO allocations), than other clients by offering investment advisors gifts or

MINI APPLICATION 2.7

INITIAL PUBLIC OFFERINGS (IPOS)

IPOs have been found to offer great returns in a short time when the investors can purchase them at the offer price. Below is the price history for an IPO, American Public Education, Inc., a company that provides online education for students in the Armed Forces. For those lucky enough to purchase some of the 15 million shares offered, this IPO earned investors a 60 percent return in the first day of trading.

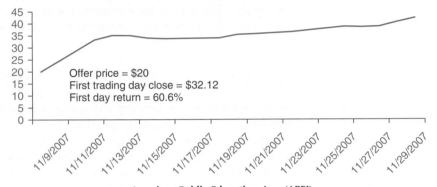

Offer price = $20
First trading day close = $32.12
First day return = 60.6%

American Public Education, Inc. (APEI)

Source: www.finance.yahoo.com.

suggesting extra compensation arrangements. This practice essentially allows clients to circumvent the published fee schedule and is unfair to the other clients. Of course it is common in the business world for happy customers to give those who provide them with good service a gift. At issue is the size of the gift. The SEC requires gifts beyond a certain nominal level (currently $100) to be disclosed.

Finally, investment advisors must ensure that new investment recommendations or changes in current investment recommendations to clients are disseminated to all clients simultaneously. It would be unfair to let some clients take advantage of a recommendation before others. E-mail is an effective way to ensure that all clients receive the same information at the same time. It is acceptable to discuss a recommendation with some clients in more depth than with others.

EXAMPLE 2.1

EXAMPLE OF PRO RATA IPO ALLOCATION

Suppose you are allocated 2,000 shares of Super Growth, Inc.'s IPO. You have three client accounts for which this investment is appropriate. These accounts are in the following amounts: $1 million, $9 million, and $10 million for a total of $20 million. The $1 million account would receive 1/20th, or 5 percent of the 2,000 allocation, or 100 shares. The $9 million account would receive 9/20ths, or 45 percent of the allocation, or 900 shares. The $10 million account would receive the lion's share: 10/20ths, or 50 percent of the allocation, or 1,000 shares.

MINI APPLICATION 2.8
PENSION FUND SCANDAL

Investment consultants or placement agents are often hired to help pension fund trustees select investment advisors. Due to the size of pension funds, winning this type of business (or mandates, for example a $100 million mandate for a large cap equity investment) can be very profitable for an investment firm. Remember, investment fees are usually a percentage of the assets under management. The New York State Pension fund has over $100 billion in assets. In 2009, it appeared that some investment advisors had paid a consultant to get access to the fund. This was a kickback scheme or "pay for play." Additionally, political contributions were made by some of these consultants to elected officials who could influence the direction of pension fund business. The scandal with the New York State Pension fund set off inquiries into other public pension funds practices. The trustees, investment managers, and consultants are all guilty of violating their fiduciary duty and, in some instances, state and federal laws.

Beneficiary individual who receives the benefit; beneficiaries are often retirees, employees (in an employee stock option plan, or ESOP), charitable recipients, and heirs.

Mandate amount of money to be invested in a particular asset class, fund, or firm.

Trustee a fiduciary who acts in the interest of the beneficiaries.

Investment advisors must also make sure that they have correctly identified their clients. A client or **beneficiary** is the individual(s) who has ownership of the assets and directly benefits from the returns earned on the portfolio. The dollar amount of the client/beneficiary account is known as a **mandate**. Most often, investment advisors communicate directly with their clients so there is no confusion over the identification of a client. More problematic are trusts, pensions, and endowments. In these instances the investment advisor is communicating with a trustee and not the ultimate beneficiary. A **trustee** is a fiduciary who acts in the interest of the beneficiaries. A trustee administers the trust, pension fund, or endowment. Trustees are often lawyers or investment professionals themselves. The beneficiaries can be retirees, employees (in an ESOP), charitable recipients, and heirs. As an investment professional, it can be easy to acquiesce to the interests of the trustee at the expense of the beneficiary. In part this is because the trustee usually has the authority to direct business to the investment advisor. In business it is natural to want to keep the customer happy. Trustees might wish the advisor to invest in funds and stocks of companies, or to use brokers where there is a direct benefit to the trustee but at the expense of the beneficiary. The investment advisor must always keep the beneficiary's interests front and center. Mini Application 2.8 is an example of practices in which the beneficiary was forgotten.

CONCLUSION: DISCLOSE! DISCLOSE! DISCLOSE!

At this point, you are aware of the multitude of potential conflicts between investment professionals and their clients. One way to ensure that investment professionals fulfill their fiduciary duties is to disclose all real or perceived conflicts. Disclosure serves two purposes. First, it keeps the investment professional honest. Disclosing a potential conflict makes it more difficult to use the conflict to benefit the professional at the client's expense (in agency-theory-speak, this lowers the client's or principal's monitoring costs). Second, disclosure alerts the client to potential areas in which he must remain vigilant. It makes it more difficult for the investment professional to act unethically if her behavior is more closely monitored in potentially problematic areas. Here are the things that should be disclosed:

- Fees charged for providing investment services
- Sales fees earned on different products
- Best execution practices
- Soft dollar practices
- Investment policy statement (IPS) or client agreement
- Treatment of clients: investment allocation policies; fee and service schedules

Finally, remember that ethical behavior is ultimately about how you treat other people. If you ever question your actions, try to put yourself in the other's shoes. If you were the client, would you perceive your behavior as ethical? If the answer is no, then the behavior is probably not ethical and you should refrain. Discussing the activity with your client, employer, or colleagues may possibly lead to resolution. These discussions can also help foster relationships and can create greater trust. Building relationships of trust also creates reputation capital, and ultimately economic success. Although that is undoubtedly true, ethical behavior should always be important in and of itself regardless of the profits it can create.

TERMS

fiduciary	assets under management	commission
I'll be gone; you'll be gone (IBG YBG)	monitor	annuity
	bond	401(k)
return uncertainty	residual loss	surrender charges
market timing strategies	Financial Industry Regulatory Authority (FINRA)	mutual fund
hedge funds		churning
efficient market hypothesis		best execution
	Chartered Financial Analyst (CFA) Institute	effective spread
agency theory		specialists
principal	Certified Financial Planner (CFP)	market makers
agent		electronic communications networks (ECN)
basis point (bp)	investment policy statement (IPS)	
active managers		internalization
passive managers	agreement	

limit order

market order

payment for order flow

soft dollars

directed brokerage

initial public offerings
   (IPOs)

pro rata basis

beneficiary

mandate

trustee

REVIEW QUESTIONS

1. Identify three reasons that fulfilling fiduciary duty can be difficult in the investment profession.
2. Explain the difference between a fiduciary and an agency relationship.
3. Why is confidentiality important in money management relationships?
4. Identify five questions a money manager should ask before recommending suitable investments for a client.
5. Why is holding horizon important in determining suitability of investments?
6. Define *churning*.
7. What is the goal of "best execution?"
8. Define *soft dollars*.
9. Identify one benefit that accrues to the client from soft dollar practices.
10. Identify one potential abuse of soft dollar practices.
11. Define directed brokerage.
12. Explain how soft dollars can align the interests of the client, the money manager, and the broker.
13. Define *pro rata*.
14. Given the following numbers, calculate the pro rata distribution of 20,000 shares of an IPO of a hypothetical company, NewCorp. Inc. (round to the nearest shares):

Dollar Size of Portfolios

Client A	$2,000,500
Client B	4,650,000
Client C	1,000,000
Client D	10,000,000

15. Is it ethical to exclude a client whose portfolio consists entirely of bonds from participation in an IPO allocation?

CRITICAL THINKING QUESTIONS

1. Fair treatment of clients requires that IPO shares are distributed on a pro rata basis—the number of shares allocated to the investment manager are allocated to appropriate client portfolios in proportion to the size of the client's portfolio. Client portfolios are deemed appropriate if the IPO fits the risk-return and other investment characteristics specified in each client's investment policy statement.

   An alternative allocation could be equal distribution. The following questions allow you to think about the ethical issues in allocating IPOs to client accounts.

Suppose a manager is allocated 4,000 shares of an IPO offered at $20 a share but closes at $25 a share on the first day of trading. The manager identifies three client accounts that are appropriate for the IPO allocation. These accounts are in the amount of $1 million, $5 million, and $10 million. The manager plans to take whatever amount is needed out of the account to provide the client with the IPO allocation at the IPO offer price. Assume that all of the assets remaining in all three accounts earn 10 percent. Calculate the return to each account depending on whether the shares are allocated equally or on a pro rata basis. Which method do you think is most equitable, and why?

2. Your finance professor has been appointed as a trustee of a large, nonprofit charitable endowment. A local money manager calls your professor and asks to make a pitch to the trustees of the endowment. In the same call, the money manager reminds the professor of the many finance students who have had internships with the company and landed full-time jobs at the firm. What are the ethical issues here? What should your professor do or say? Anything?

3. After graduation you started working for a small money management firm, taking advantage of the opportunity to grow your career along with the firm. It is now 10 years later. When you first started with the firm, the managers used soft dollars to help offset the cost of investment research, which in turn allowed them to keep their management fees low. This strategy, along with a successful track record of providing clients with excellent risk-adjusted returns (no doubt owing to hiring talented professionals such as you), allowed the company to aggressively grow its business and assets under management. Over time the company has been able to raise management fees but still continues to offset research costs with the use of soft dollars. Is the continued use of soft dollars ethical? Under what circumstances would it be unethical?

4. Fiduciary duty can suggest a paternalistic approach to providing investment advice. Does fiduciary duty negate a client's personal responsibility in deciding what to do with *his* money? What is the ethical division of responsibility between advisor and client in making investment choices?

5. You are trying to decide which fund to recommend to your client. The historical returns for Fund A and Fund B are below. For Fund A, you will be paid 25 basis points at the end of each quarter out of your client's account; for Fund B, you will earn 35 basis points. Assume that your client has $100 million to invest. Determine which account is likely to be better for your client and better for you by calculating (a) your client's account balance at the end of the eight quarters net of fees; (b) average return divided by standard deviation as a measure of the risk adjusted return; and (c) your total fees earned for each fund. Based on these calculations, which account will you recommend and why? Would there be a difference in the account recommended by an unethical versus ethical advisor?

Quarter	Fund A Returns	Fund B Returns
1	5	3
2	6.5	9
3	3	1
4	4.5	8
5	10	15
6	0.5	−2
7	4	9
8	3	5

APPLIED STUDENT PROJECT: CASE ANALYSIS

Using the Internet, identify and research a recent case of unethical behavior in the money management industry. Use the concepts in this chapter to analyze the ethical issues in the case.

RECOMMENDED CASES

1. Case 3—Fidelity Traders and Gifts from Jefferies: Soliciting Brokerage from Traders
2. Case 5—A. G. Edwards and Variable Annuities: An Inappropriate Investment
3. Case 7—Nicholas Cosmo and Agape World Inc.: A Ponzi Scheme
4. Case 21—Morgan Stanley: Brokerage Commissions and Brokerage Abuses
5. Case 25—Bernie Madoff: The Largest Ponzi Scheme in History?
6. Case 23—The Bayou Group: False Reporting

REFERENCES AND SUGGESTED READING

Battalio, Robert H., and Tim Loughran. "Does Payment for Order Flow to Your Broker Help or Hurt You?" *Journal of Business Ethics* 80, no. 1 (June 2008): 37–44.

Boatright, John R. *Ethics in Finance*, 2nd ed. New York: Wiley-Blackwell, 2007.

Certified Financial Planner Board of Standards, Inc. *CFP Board's Standards of Professional Conduct*, Washington, DC, March 2009.

CFA Institute, *Standards of Practice Handbook*, 9th ed. Charlottesville, VA, CFA Institute, 2005.

Fine, Jacob. "Mutual Funds: Citigroup Cited in Latest Suit Alleging Improper Compensation of Brokers." *Bond Buyer*, 7 June 2004, 7.

Friedman, Thomas L. "Why How Matters," *New York Times*, 15 October 2008, 35.

Gaber, Mohamed, Greg N. Gregoriou, and William Kelting. "Funds of Hedge Funds: Ethics of This Black Box Strategy." *Pensions: An International Journal* 9, no. 4 (June 2004): 328.

Goldfarb, Zachary A., and Tomoeh Murakami Tse. "Private-Equity Firms Under Scrutiny; U.S., N.Y. Probing Possible Pension-Fund Kickback Scheme." *Washington Post*, 15 April 2009, A13.

Horan, Stephen M., and D. Bruce Johnsen. "The Welfare Effects of Soft Dollar Brokerage: Law and Economics." CFA Institute, *Research Foundation Publications*, June 2000: 1–64.

Jacobius, Arleen. "Funds Scurrying to Cut Off Future Pay-to-Play Action." *Pensions & Investments*, 4 May 2009.

Jennings, Marianne M. "Come See the Harder Side of Soft Dollars." *Corporate Finance Review*, Jan.–Feb. 2007, 44–48.

Keim, Donald B., and Ananth Madhavan. "The Cost of Institutional Equity Trades." *Financial Analysts Journal* 54, no. 4 (July/Aug. 1998): 50–69.

Knee, Jonathan. *The Accidental Investment Banker: Inside the Decade That Transformed Wall Street*. New York: Oxford University Press, 2006.

Meckling, William H., and Michael C. Jensen. "Theory of the Firm: Managerial Behavior, Agency Costs and Ownership Structure." *The Journal of Financial Economics* 3, no. 4, 1976: 305–360.

National Association of Securities Dealers (NASD). Notice to Members 01-22, "NASD Regulation Reiterates Member Firm Best Execution Obligations and Provides Guidance to Members Concerning Compliance" (April 2001), www.finra.org.

Securities and Exchange Commission. 17 CFR Parts 270, 275 and 279, Release Nos. IA-2256, IC-26492; File No. S7-04-04. "Investment Adviser Codes of Ethics" (Aug. 31, 2004), www.sec.gov.

_____. 17 CFR Part 241, Release No. 34-52635; File No. S7-09-05. "Commission Guidance Regarding Client Commission Practices Under Section 28(e) of the Securities Exchange Act of 1934" (2007), www.sec.gov.

_____. The Office of Compliance, Inspections and Examinations. "Inspection Report on the Soft Dollar Practices of Broker-Dealers, Investment Advisers and Mutual Funds" (Sept. 22, 1998) www.sec.gov.

APPENDIX: PROFESSIONAL CODES OF ETHICS

TABLE 2.1.A	CFA® INSTITUTE: CODE OF ETHICS

Members of CFA Institute (including Chartered Financial Analyst® [CFA®] charter holders) and candidates for the CFA designation ("Members and Candidates") must:

- Act with integrity, competence, diligence, respect, and in an ethical manner with the public, clients, prospective clients, employers, employees, colleagues in the investment profession, and other participants in the global capital markets.

- Place the integrity of the investment profession and the interests of clients above their own personal interests.

- Use reasonable care and exercise independent professional judgment when conducting investment analysis, making investment recommendations, taking investment actions, and engaging in other professional activities.

- Practice and encourage others to practice in a professional and ethical manner that will reflect credit on themselves and the profession.

- Promote the integrity of, and uphold the rules governing, capital markets.

- Maintain and improve their professional competence and strive to maintain and improve the competence of other investment professionals.

Copyright 2005, CFA Institute, Reproduced with permission from CFA Institute. All rights reserved.

TABLE	2.2.A	**CFP® BOARD: CODE OF ETHICS**

These *Code Of Ethics* Principles express the profession's recognition of its responsibilities to the public, to clients, to colleagues and to employers. They apply to all CFP Board designees and provide guidance to them in the performance of their professional services.

Principle 1—Integrity *A CFP (Certified Financial Planner) Board designee shall offer and provide professional services with integrity.*

As discussed in "Composition and Scope," CFP Board designees may be placed by clients in positions of trust and confidence. The ultimate source of such public trust is the CFP Board designee's personal integrity. In deciding what is right and just, a CFP Board designee should rely on his or her integrity as the appropriate touchstone. Integrity demands honesty and candor which must not be subordinated to personal gain and advantage. Within the characteristic of integrity, allowance can be made for innocent error and legitimate difference of opinion; but integrity cannot co-exist with deceit or subordination of one's principles. Integrity requires a CFP Board designee to observe not only the letter but also the spirit of this *Code Of Ethics*.

Principle 2—Objectivity *A CFP Board designee shall be objective in providing professional services to clients.*

Objectivity requires intellectual honesty and impartiality. It is an essential quality for any professional. Regardless of the particular service rendered or the capacity in which a CFP Board designee functions, a CFP Board designee should protect the integrity of his or her work, maintain objectivity, and avoid subordination of his or her judgment that would be in violation of this *Code Of Ethics*.

Principle 3—Competence *A CFP Board designee shall provide services to clients competently and maintain the necessary knowledge and skill to continue to do so in those areas in which the CFP Board designee is engaged.*

One is competent only when he or she has attained and maintained an adequate level of knowledge and skill, and applies that knowledge effectively in providing services to clients. Competence also includes the wisdom to recognize the limitations of that knowledge and when consultation or client referral is appropriate. A CFP Board designee, by virtue of having earned the CFP® certification, is deemed to be qualified to practice financial planning. However, in addition to assimilating the common body of knowledge required and acquiring the necessary experience for certification, a CFP Board designee shall make a continuing commitment to learning and professional improvement.

Principle 4—Fairness *A CFP Board designee shall perform professional services in a manner that is fair and reasonable to clients, principals, partners and employers, and shall disclose conflict(s) of interest in providing such services.*

Fairness requires impartiality, intellectual honesty and disclosure of conflict(s) of interest. It involves a subordination of one's own feelings, prejudices and desires so as to achieve a proper balance of conflicting interests. Fairness is treating others in the same fashion that you would want to be treated and is an essential trait of any professional.

(continued)

TABLE	**2.2.A**	**CFP® BOARD: CODE OF ETHICS** (*continued*)

Principle 5—Confidentiality *A CFP Board designee shall not disclose any confidential client information without the specific consent of the client unless in response to proper legal process, to defend against charges of wrongdoing by the CFP Board designee or in connection with a civil dispute between the CFP Board designee and client.*

A client, by seeking the services of a CFP Board designee, may be interested in creating a relationship of personal trust and confidence with the CFP Board designee. This type of relationship can only be built upon the understanding that information supplied to the CFP Board designee will be confidential. In order to provide the contemplated services effectively and to protect the client's privacy, the CFP Board designee shall safeguard the confidentiality of such information.

Principle 6—Professionalism *A CFP Board designee's conduct in all matters shall reflect credit upon the profession.*

Because of the importance of the professional services rendered by CFP Board designees, there are attendant responsibilities to behave with dignity and courtesy to all those who use those services, fellow professionals, and those in related professions. A CFP Board designee also has an obligation to cooperate with fellow CFP Board designees to enhance and maintain the profession's public image and to work jointly with other CFP Board designees to improve the quality of services. It is only through the combined efforts of all CFP Board designees, in cooperation with other professionals, that this vision can be realized.

Principle 7—Diligence *A CFP Board designee shall act diligently in providing professional services.*

Diligence is the provision of services in a reasonably prompt and thorough manner. Diligence also includes proper planning for, and supervision of, the rendering of professional services.

CFP Board's Code of Ethics and Professional Responsibility Copyright © 2010, Certified Financial Planner Board of Standards, Inc. All rights reserved. Used with permission. Why Should I Choose a CFP® Professional Copyright ©2010, Certified Financial Planner Board of Standards, Inc. All rights reserved. Used with permission.

Ethical Reporting of Investment Performance

Learning Objectives

After reading this chapter, students should be able to:

- Understand the inherent uncertainty in predicting investment performance and how this can lead to unethical practices in reporting.
- Practice the ethical use of measures of return and risk.
- Identify specific practices that create misleading measures of performance.
- Recognize hidden sources of risk.
- Identify measurement issues with securities that do not trade.

CHAPTER OUTLINE

- Introduction: Ethics in Reporting Performance
- Calculating Return: Predicting Future Performance or Measuring Performance for Current Clients?
- Ethical Reporting of Risk Measures
- Time Periods Used to Estimate Historical Risk and Return Performance
- Other Ways to Distort Historical Performance
- Management Fees and Other Costs That Can Be Hidden
- Reporting Performance to Attract New Clients: Cherry-Picking Accounts
- Hidden Risks: Leverage, Short Selling, Liquidity

INTRODUCTION: ETHICS IN REPORTING PERFORMANCE

Broadly defined, **investment performance** is the risk-adjusted return earned by a particular investment or portfolio. Recall from Chapter 1 that ethical issues about reporting performance are rooted in the inherent risk or uncertainty of future returns. In the investing industry, we use statistics to capture uncertainty and measure risk. Statistics layered onto an activity that is already quantitative and technically complex creates even greater opportunities for an unscrupulous professional to distort the numbers. How? In the absence of fraud, aren't the numbers just the numbers? Let's look at a very simple example. Refer to Example 3.1. Suppose an investment manager decides *not* to report an unrealized capital loss to his or her client. The manager reasons that because the loss is unrealized, there is still an opportunity for prices to rebound and the client will never be the wiser. Ethical? No! But this example shows how uncertainty about returns (in this case, uncertainty about whether the unrealized capital loss will become realized) gives unethical managers wiggle room to hide poor returns or higher risks.

Investment performance various risk and return measures of an investment.

EXAMPLE 3.1

An investment manager decides to exclude an unrealized capital loss to improve reported performance. He rationalizes that since the loss is unrealized, it does not need to be included.

$Price_{t-1}$	1,000		$Price_{t-1}$	1,000
$Dividend_t$	30		$Dividend_t$	30
$Price_t$	900		$Price_t$	900
Investment Income	30		Investment Income	30
Unrealized Capital Loss	*−100*		*Unrealized Capital Loss Excluded*	*0*
Total Return$_t$	**−7%**		**Total Return**$_t$	**3%**

The SEC prosecutes investment managers who engage in outright fraud. Current clients become victims of fraud when advisors provide them with fictitious statements showing account balances that are nonexistent. Other types of fraud include understating the risk of an investment or showing past performance with very consistent returns or even going so far as to guarantee a return. One way that Bernie Madoff recruited new investors to his scheme was to show a history of unusually consistent returns (see Chapter 1 and Chapter 9, Case 25). These returns were fictitious. The SEC also prescribes how mutual funds report their performance to future clients in their prospectus via the required registration materials for investment advisors. Mutual funds may report past performance as long as they disclose how the performance was calculated. In addition, mutual funds must report, on a quarterly basis, fund expenses and portfolio holdings.

Professional organizations provide ethical guidelines for reporting performance beyond legal requirements. CFA Institute provides such guidelines: **Global Investment Performance Standards (GIPS)**. Active money managers (see Chapter 2), subject to verification, who are able to say they adhere to GIPS have the advantage of assuring investors that they are ethical managers. Another advantage of GIPS is that they provide an "apples-to-apples" comparison of different investment managers to potential investors choosing among managers. In this chapter, we explain the underlying ethical rationale for many of the GIPS and regulatory reporting requirements.

Most unethical behaviors involving reporting revolve around the use of ex post versus ex ante selection criteria. **Ex post** means "after the fact" and essentially allows managers the benefit of 20/20 hindsight. See Figure 3.1. **Ex ante** means "before the fact." Because returns are uncertain, there is an inherent bias in ex post reporting. You can always improve your performance by choosing after the fact *how* you report.

Global Investment Performance Standards (GIPS) guidelines for reporting performance developed by the Chartered Financial Accounting (CFA) Institute.

Ex post after the fact.

Ex ante before the fact.

FIGURE **3.1** **"SURE I CAN MAKE MONEY FOR YOU! LOOK AT MY TRACK RECORD!"**

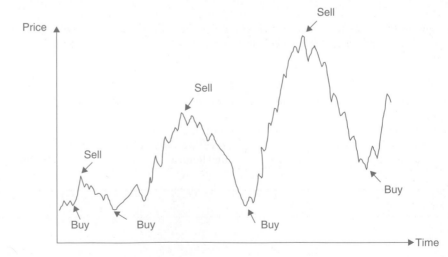

FUNDAMENTAL PRINCIPLES OF INVESTMENT ETHICS FOR PROFESSIONALS

As you read the rest of the chapter, think about how distortions of performance violate the fundamental principles of ethical understanding, use of information, and trust and fairness (see Chapter 1).

Principle 1: ETHICAL UNDERSTANDING

Because investments are complicated, *you have an obligation not to knowingly engage in an investment transaction that either you or others do not sufficiently understand. This includes knowing the underlying source of returns or fees charged.*

Principle 2: ETHICAL USE OF INFORMATION

Because investments are information driven, *you have an obligation to ensure that you and others have access to relevant information and that you or others do not misuse or distort information in the investment transaction.*

Principle 3: RESPONSIBLE INVESTING

Because investments provide financial resources to others, *you have an obligation to ensure that you do not knowingly make or recommend investments that support activities that harm others.*

Principle 4: TRUST AND FAIRNESS

Because you are dealing with others' money either directly or indirectly, *you have an obligation not to abuse the trust that all others have either explicitly or implicitly placed in you to treat them fairly.*

At that point you know the outcome, so you can pick the "how" that gives you the best results. For example, you select the client account that showcased your investment expertise or pick the benchmark that showed how much better you can do compared to another money manager or investment product. Ex post selection bias is cheating by peeking at the data or the "future." When an investor gives you her money, you can no longer peek at the future to generate the same type of performance for your client. The choice of an ex ante measure prevents managers from manipulating the game once they know the outcome and thus provides a better and more ethical means of reporting performance. It also creates a fair way for clients to evaluate the skills of different managers. This chapter discusses ways in which performance can be distorted and the ex ante guidelines that are designed to prevent such distortions.

Besides ex post selection bias, there are other ways that managers can make their results look better than they are. Deceitful managers can try to increase returns by taking additional risks that are not fully disclosed to the client. We also explore the problem of hidden risks in this chapter. Finally, we look at ethics surrounding performance reports for investments that don't trade on a regular basis. Without a regularly reported market price, managers have some leeway in assessing value. Unethical managers will take advantage of this leeway to improve performance. But before we go further, students who need a refresher on investment basics are encouraged to review the appendix at the end of this chapter.

Calculating Return: Predicting Future Performance or Measuring Performance for Current Clients?

Holding period return a holding period return is calculated by dividing the capital gain and any investment income earned during the period by the original investment amount.

Expected returns return that is most likely to occur; the average or mean return.

Average returns created by averaging past returns.

Portfolio managers have to measure return performance for two types of investors. First, they must report to their *current* clients how much they have earned for them. This means they must measure performance to date or *past performance*. The best measure for this purpose is a **holding period return**. A holding period return shows the client what he actually earned based on dollars invested and ending amounts. Second, the portfolio manager must report to *potential* clients **expected returns**. Expected returns are the best guess of future returns. Statistically, **average returns** provide the best measure of expected returns (see the Appendix to this chapter). Average return is the return calculated from the average of past returns. Average returns can be calculated with different weights—for example, equal weights or portfolio weights—depending on use.

As Example 3.2 shows, there is quite a difference in the performance reported depending on whether the manager uses a holding period return measure or an average return measure. The average return measure indicates that the return earned for the client has been, on average, 24,900.05 percent. Wow! While this is true, it belies the fact that the client has lost half of the original investment. The annual holding period return is *negative* 29 percent and provides a more accurate depiction of the manager's performance for his or her current client.

What about future clients? Statistics tell us the average return is the best measure of expected or future returns. Showing an average historical return of 24,900.05 percent to a future client *does* make sense, with a caveat. What is that caveat? Risk!

EXAMPLE 3.2	
DIFFERENT RESULTS FROM DIFFERENT FORMULAS	
Starting Investment	$ 1,000.00
Value at End of Year 1	$ 1.00
Value at End of Year 2	$ 500.00
Return for Year 1	− 99.90%
Return for Year 2	49,900.00%
Average Annual Return	*24,900.05%*
Total Return at End of Year 2	− 50.00%
Annualized Holding Period Return over Two Years	*− 29.00%*

ETHICAL REPORTING OF RISK MEASURES

Return on an investment cannot be measured without also measuring its risk. Risk, in its simplest form, measures the uncertainty of the return. Just looking at the example above, we can see that an investment that earns a huge average return also carries substantial risk. The year-to-year returns on this investment fluctuate wildly, from −99.90 percent (remember that a 100 percent loss means that you have lost everything and are out of the game) to +49,900 percent.

Beyond a simple measure of the range of returns, there are many more—standard deviation, beta, and VaR, to name a few commonly used measures (see the appendix to this chapter for definitions and examples). Because risk is a cost of investing (and return is the offsetting benefit), an unethical manager will minimize reported measures of risk. For example, suppose a portfolio strategy has a very low beta. An unethical advisor might use this point to suggest to a client that the strategy has low risk. However, if all of the client's money is invested in this portfolio, a low beta might not be sufficient to describe the risk. After all, if the economy and the stock market decline, so will the portfolio (although less so). The client might be more concerned about how much money she can potentially lose rather than her investment's covariance with the market (recall that covariance measures how two variables move together; a positive or negative covariance means the investment moves in the same or opposite direction as the market). Recall from your finance class that VaR is a risk measure that estimates the size of a loss for a given probability. For investors that are concerned about preserving capital, this would be an important risk measure to report. What are the ethical implications here? Managers should provide a wide range of risk measures as well as ensure that clients have sufficient understanding of these measures to make wise decisions.

Fixed-income investments have a different set of risks than those outlined above, which are more applicable to investments in the stock market. Some of these risks are interest rate risk, credit risk, and inflation risk. And just as with equities, returns must be reported along with the appropriate risk measures to both current and future clients.

TIME PERIODS USED TO ESTIMATE HISTORICAL RISK AND RETURN PERFORMANCE

An unethical money manager could choose the time period of historical data to underestimate risk and overestimate returns. In particular, it is important to use historical data that captures a full market cycle: "top to top" or "bottom to bottom." This way you have data that includes the market going both up and down. If a manager decided to use only historical data for a market that was going up—a bull market—and to ignore data from a period when the market was going down—a bear market—historical data could potentially show better returns and less risk. To illustrate, let's look at a hypothetical example.

Five years or 60 months is considered a period of time that is likely to capture a full market cycle. But if during a particular 60-month period there is a long bull

| **FIGURE** | **3.2** | **S&P 500 MONTHLY CLOSE AS OF MAY 1, 2007 (PRIOR 60 MONTHS BULL MARKET)** |

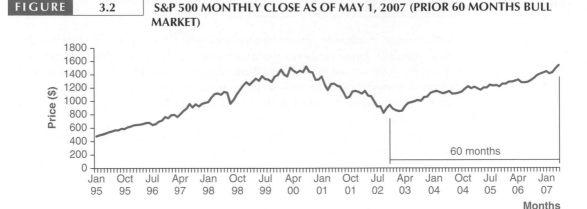

market, 60 months may not capture a full market cycle. (Refer to Figure 3.2.) Suppose that it is late spring of 2007. An investment professional might decide to measure risk and return using the last 60 months' worth of data, justifying that this period typically captures a full market cycle. But that's not true in this case. Using the last 60 months of data when the market was experiencing a prolonged bull run, the average monthly return is 0.80 percent and the standard deviation is 3.35 percent. There is a 5 percent probability that an investor with $1 million could lose $47, 269 within the month.

Suppose instead that returns back to the prior "top" of the market (early spring 2000) are used to ensure a full market cycle in performance estimates. Using this data, the average monthly return is only 0.10 percent and the standard deviation is 3.95 percent. There is a 5 percent probability that an investor with $1 million could lose $64, 094 within the month. This paints a very different picture! Ethical managers do not pick and choose time periods to measure past performances, but present their firm's investment products' entire past performance (usually up to 10 years) to show how they have performed in a variety of market conditions. See Mini Application 3.1 for another example of the misuse of historical data in calculating risk measures.

Another misuse of historical data came to light during the 2008 financial crisis. The general class of **structured investment vehicles (SIVs)** had grown dramatically

Structured investment vehicles (SIVs) a class of securities that are created out of pools or a portfolio of debt obligations, which are then sliced into different "pieces" or tranches of the promised cash flows in the portfolio and sold off.

MINI APPLICATION 3.1

VAR AND THE FINANCIAL CRISIS OF 2008

Until the financial collapse of Wall Street in 2008, VaR was a widely used measure that reassured Wall Street firms that risk was adequately controlled.

Some have claimed that the VaR that was calculated or used didn't capture extreme risks and thus lulled Wall Street firms into a sense of security and perhaps even encouraged more risk taking. Always remember that the underlying assumptions and the historical data used in calculating risk measures are as important as the risk measures themselves.

Source: Joe Nocera, "Risk Mismanagement," *New York Times*, 4 January 2009.

before the crisis. These include CDOs (collateralized debt obligations), ABS (asset-backed securities), and MBSs (mortgage-backed securities). These are securities that bundle different types of loans together and then sell pieces of the bundle (tranches). These tranches represent different cash flows (principal and interest repayments) and different levels of certainty of these cash flows. Some of the loans used in these securities are mortgage loans, subprime loans, corporate debt, leveraged bank loans, and credit card and auto loans. Mortgage-backed securities (MBSs) (see Chapter 1) are securities that are created from a portfolio or a pool of mortgages. The investor receives income from the securities that is generated from the interest and principal repayments on the underlying mortgages. **Collateralized debt obligations (CDOs)** are created from a portfolio of debt obligations. Different pieces or tranches of the promised cash flows in the portfolio are then sold off. The underlying collateral is corporate assets used in the original debt obligation. **Asset-backed securities (ABSs)** are pools of securities backed by other assets, for example, car loans.

While the economy was doing well, the credit risk on these securities was minimal and the market for them grew in the period before the financial crisis of 2008. However, not all investors fully understood these securities. Analysts and their use of historical data to provide credit ratings and values for SIVs played a critical role in lulling investors' concerns about their risks. Analysts for these securities create models of forecasted future cash flows based on default rates, changes in interest rates, prepayments, and changes in asset prices. When valuing MBSs, many analysts assumed that housing prices would continue to rise at a rate of 6–8 percent per year; these were current rates at the time, but much higher than the long-run average. When the increase in housing prices slowed down, these securities fell sharply in value. Assuming a high housing appreciation rate increased the value and demand for these securities, the securities in turn generated fees for professionals originating both mortgages and mortgage-backed securities. When profits cloud the objectivity and judgment of professionals, their behavior becomes unethical. An ethical investment professional should always question the use of historical data. Is it objective? Does it capture all possible market conditions? If the answer is no, you have an obligation to go back to the drawing board.

Collateralized debt obligations (CDOs) a security that is created from a portfolio of debt obligations. Different "pieces" or tranches of the promised cash flows in the portfolio are then sold off. The underlying collateral is corporate assets used in the original debt obligation.

Asset-backed securities (ABSs) pools of securities that are backed by assets such as auto loans or credit cards.

OTHER WAYS TO DISTORT HISTORICAL PERFORMANCE

Another way to distort performance is to take an investment or portfolio that is relatively new and has only a short period of returns (less than a year) and annualize the return. This method creates the impression that the performance is indicative of an entire year. But there is no way of knowing that. Hence, annualizing returns for less than a year is misleading and unethical.

Mutual funds are required to report their portfolio holdings on a quarterly basis. Sometimes mutual funds will wait until toward the end of the quarter to invest in stocks that have done particularly well during the quarter—that is, they invest only after the stocks have performed well. This can lead to the false perception that the mutual fund managers are adept at picking winners. This practice, called **window dressing**, is unethical.

Window dressing the practice by mutual funds of investing in stocks that have done particularly well during the quarter toward the end of the quarter; this is done to give the impression that managers can pick "winners."

Finally, if there is a significant change in the team managing the investment strategy, this can have an impact on the interpretation that prior return performance might be a good indicator of future performance. Investment skills reside in individuals. If those individuals leave the firm, there is no guarantee that the skills that generated past performance reside in the individuals hired to replace them. Both current and future clients need to know whenever there are changes in the investment professionals managing their money.

PICKING BENCHMARKS

Benchmark the measure against which the portfolio manager is compared.

Index fund a fund that actively trades during the day and is designed to mimic the returns of an index, for example, the S&P 500 index.

Exchange-traded fund (ETF) an investment fund that trades on an exchange throughout the day and usually tracks an index.

Another important issue in measuring risk-return performance for either current or potential clients is the choice of a **benchmark**. The benchmark provides a yardstick against which to measure performance. Active portfolio managers charge a fee to manage money, between 60 to 200 bps. Presumably they can generate better returns for a given level of risk versus investing in a passive investment vehicle that tracks a particular index. Passive investment vehicles are designed to mimic a chosen index and cost much less than actively managed investments—typically 20 bps. There are two types of common vehicles. **Index funds** are passively managed mutual funds that copy the holdings and performance of an index. Investors can buy into or sell their shares only once a day. **Exchange-traded fund** (ETF) track a specific index, for example, Standard & Poor's (S&P) 500, or MSCI EAFE. Unlike mutual funds, they can be bought and sold throughout the day. The choice of benchmark provides a return benchmark as well as a risk benchmark. Clients must be assured that returns are being earned at the level of risk they have agreed to take on (see Chapter 2).

The benchmark must be chosen ex ante. Otherwise, the unethical money manager might choose a benchmark ex post that makes his or her performance look better than it actually was. For example, suppose a manager earned only 5 percent by investing in a subset of S&P 500 stocks. During the same period the S&P 500 index earned 15 percent while Treasury bills earned 3 percent. Yes, the manager earned a better return than an investment in Treasury bills. But if the benchmark was the S&P 500, then the money manager has done poorly. Commonly used benchmarks for different asset classes are shown in Table 3.1.

Ethical reporting of performance measures includes *both* risk and return measures relative to the benchmark that has been chosen ex ante. Suppose the return performance beats the benchmark. But if the risk of the portfolio is substantially more than the benchmark, the manager is not necessarily earning better risk-adjusted returns for his or her client. Suppose the manager in the previous example was hired to use the S&P 500 as the benchmark. Let's say that during the past year, the S&P 500 earned a return of 13 percent and had a beta of roughly 1. The manager earns 17 percent on the portfolio. Did he or she beat the benchmark? It depends. If the beta was 2, the answer is no. If the beta was 1, the answer is yes. Thus ethical reporting requires managers to present a variety of risk and return measures such as the Sharpe ratio and the information ratio (see the appendix to this chapter for details). Managers are hired to find investments that earn greater returns than the risk that they impose on investors. Risk-return measures also prevent managers from reporting risk and return separately to a naïve client. "See how much return I earned for you (let's just ignore the huge risks)?" Or, "See what little risk your investments had (let's just ignore the meager returns)?"

TABLE 3.1	TYPICAL BENCHMARKS

Equity	Fixed Income	International	Others
S&P 500	Citigroup 3-Month T-Bill	MSCI EAFE	NCREIF Property
Russell 1000	Barclays Capital Int.	MSCI Emerging	Index
Value	Gov't/Credit	Markets	FTSE NAREIT
Russell 1000	Barclays Capital	Citigroup Non-US	Merrill Lynch Inv.
Growth	Gov't/Credit	Gov't Bond	Grade
Russell MidCap	Barclays Capital	Citigroup Non-US	Convertible
Russell MidCap	Aggregate	Gov't	Goldman Sachs
Value	Barclays Capital	Bond-Hedged	Commodity
Russell MidCap	Intermediate		Index
Growth	Government		
Russell 2000	Barclays Capital Long		
Russell 2000	Gov't/Credit		
Value	Barclays Capital		
Russell 2000	Mortgage-Backed		
Growth	Securities Index		
Russell 3000	Barclays Capital TIPS		
	Barclays Capital		
	Corporate High Yield		

MINI APPLICATION 3.2
TEST YOURSELF

Figures 3.3 and 3.4 provide the excess return to the benchmark and the tracking error. Calculate the information ratio and confirm why each benchmark is the best ex post one for the manager. If you need a review of how to calculate the information ratio, refer to the appendix at the end of this chapter.

Style drift this is when an investment manager selects securities that move away from the original investment strategy or "style" originally specified by the client.

Style boxes these boxes were developed by Morningstar, an independent investment research firm, to allow equity investors and managers to capture both a size (market capitalization) and value-growth continuum for equity investments.

Figures 3.3 and 3.4 show an example of the performance of a hypothetical portfolio compared to three benchmarks—the Dow Jones Industrial Average, the Russell 2000, and the S&P 500. According to whether the market is going up or down, one benchmark is better than another. This shows how ex post choices of benchmarks can change depending on ex post performance. See Mini Application 3.2 to figure out how much better you can do.

Another way to distort performance relative to a benchmark is through **style drift**. This occurs when managers advertise a particular style and then drift away from that, changing the risk-return characteristics of the investments. Morningstar, Inc., an independent securities research firm, created what are known as **style boxes**. They allow equity investors and managers to capture both a size (market capitalization) and value-growth continuum for equity investments. For example, a small cap value equity strategy would fall in the box indicated in Figure 3.5. Consider this: a client hires you to invest in a strategy that has similar risk and return characteristics of a

| FIGURE | 3.3 | BENCHMARK CHOICE IN AN UP MARKET (JULY 2004–DEC. 2006): THE DOW JONES IS THE BEST EX POST BENCHMARK |

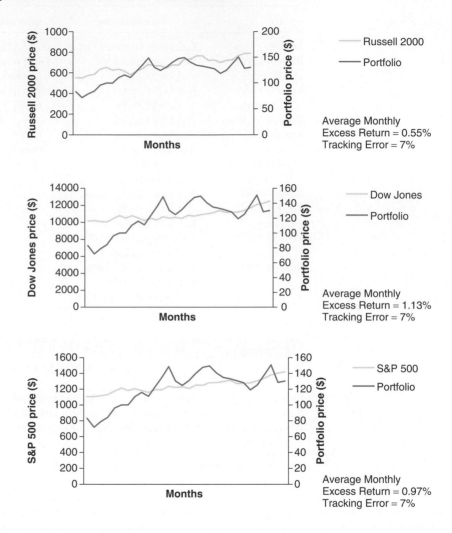

Source: www.finance.yahoo.com.

particular asset class and benchmark. But styles tend to go in and out of favor, or some styles can do better than others for certain periods of time. Figure 3.6 shows that in the late 1990s, large cap equity yielded higher returns; but then in the early 2000s, small cap performed better. Although your client hired you to invest in large cap equity, you might be drawn to smaller cap stocks as they perform better.

Managers might be tempted to invest in securities that offer higher returns but have characteristics that deviate significantly from the benchmark. For example, a

| FIGURE | 3.4 | **BENCHMARK CHOICE IN A DOWN MARKET (JAN. 2007–JUNE 2009): THE S&P 500 IS THE BEST EX POST BENCHMARK** |

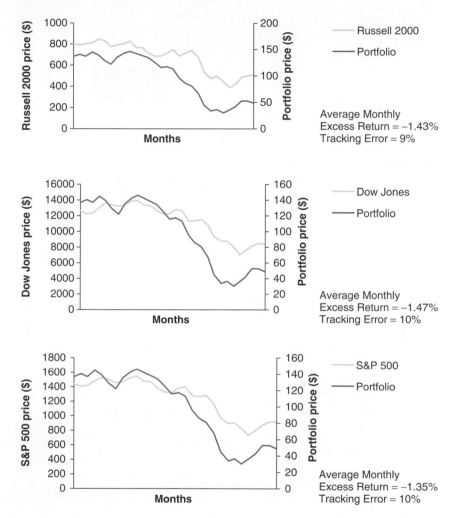

Source: www.finance.yahoo.com.

manager hired to manage a mid cap equity portfolio starts to invest in small cap stocks when small cap stocks do better than mid cap. The *mid cap range* is defined as stocks with a market capitalization of between $2 and $10 billion. Small cap stocks have a range of $300 million and $2 billion. Market capitalizations of portfolios can change as stock prices change. Ethical managers readjust their holdings to stay within their prespecified style box.

FIGURE	3.5	MORNINGSTAR STYLE BOX™

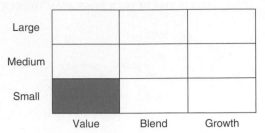

FIGURE	3.6	PERFORMANCE OF DIFFERENT MARKET CAPITALIZATIONS (MONTHLY JAN. 1989–JUNE 2009)

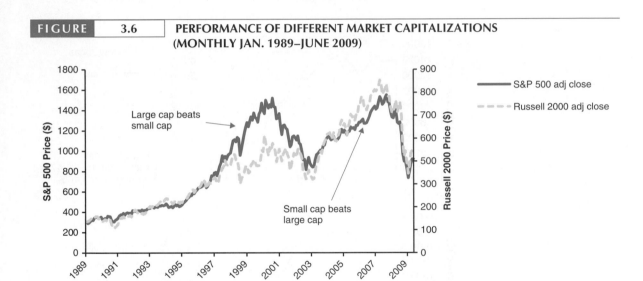

Source: www.finance.yahoo.com.

MANAGEMENT FEES AND OTHER COSTS THAT CAN BE HIDDEN

Gross of fees investment returns before management fees.

Net of fees investment returns minus management fees.

Even if historical performance is accurately portrayed, both past and future clients need to know the costs of that performance. It is important when reporting return performance that returns are designated either **gross of fees** or **net of fees**. Gross of fees means that returns are reported before taking out fees; net of fees means that returns are reported after fees have been subtracted. Suppose a money manager has beat the benchmark by 80 basis points (recall from Chapter 2 that a basis point or bps is 1/100th of a percent or 0.0001), but fees are 120 basis points. Gross of fees, the return above the benchmark is 80 bps; but net of fees, the return is 40 bps below the benchmark. Fees must be disclosed, and managers must provide net of fees measures to clients if requested.

Like management fees, trading costs must also be taken into account. Trading costs are the actual fees charged to trade securities, including brokerage commissions

FIGURE	3.7	**S&P MONTHLY CLOSE (JANUARY 2000–JUNE 2009)**

Source: www.finance.yahoo.com.

and spreads (see Chapter 2). Trading costs should be netted out from return measures. If a manager can beat the benchmark, but only by trading so much that these costs wipe out the excess return earned, then the manager is not earning an excess return for the client.

Ongoing fees such as wrap fees (see Chapter 2) are often netted out of mutual fund returns. This can make it difficult for investors to separate mutual fund performance and costs. Again, these fees need to be fully disclosed and disclosed in such a way that they are understandable to the average investor. Figure 3.7 shows how an annual fee of 50 bps can erode return performance over time.

REPORTING PERFORMANCE TO ATTRACT NEW CLIENTS: CHERRY-PICKING ACCOUNTS

Besides manipulating returns, benchmarks, choice of time periods, and fees, managers can also distort past performance of client accounts used to attract new clients. Suppose the client is searching for a large cap equity manager. The client finds two large cap equity managers and is trying to decide between the two. Example 3.3 shows the performance of two hypothetical managers using the types of risk and return measures that should be familiar to you from your investments class (see the appendix to this chapter for further details).

EXAMPLE 3.3
MANAGER PERFORMANCE

	Manager A	Manager B
Return	13%	14%
Beta	1.01	1
Standard deviation	4%	4.50%

But what's behind these numbers? This may seem relatively straightforward, but managers who have several large cap equity accounts over a period of time have some discretion about how they report performance. Let's look at some unethical choices.

Cherry-pick to use any selection process that selects the best accounts in creating the fund's composite reported performance.

Within a particular strategy, managers can pick and chose which accounts to include in reporting performance and how to aggregate performance. Managers can **cherry-pick** accounts by selecting the best accounts (ex post, of course). Managers can also decide to exclude terminated accounts. At first blush this might seem ethical. Why not just include active accounts? Well, it is likely that unhappy clients terminated accounts because performance was poor. Excluding these accounts can overstate performance. As Example 3.4 shows, excluding the weaker-performing, terminated accounts from a measure of historical performance improves the overall performance representation, in turn suggesting that the manager's track record is better than what it actually is. Ethical reporting includes terminated accounts.

Managers can come up with all sorts of other reasons to include or exclude client accounts. Size can be used to *exclude* accounts that can decrease aggregated performance. Managers can rationalize that the account is either too small or too big to be representative. All accounts of all sizes should be included as representative of managers' investment expertise in that strategy.

Stretching the definition of the investment strategy can be used to *include* accounts to increase aggregated performance. For example, managers might choose to

EXAMPLE 3.4							
REPORTING PAST PERFORMANCE: EXCLUDING TERMINATED ACCOUNTS							
Year	1	2	3	4	5	6	7	8
Returns								
Client A		10%	9%	11%	12%	10%	9%	11%
Client B		8%	8%	9%				
Client C		12%	10%	13%	15%	12%	10%	13%
End-of-period assets ($ millions)								
Client A	10	11	12	13	15	16	18	20
Client B	500	540	583	Account Terminated				
Client C	30	34	37	42	48	54	59	67
TOTAL	540	585	632	55	63	70	77	87
Number of portfolios	3	3	3	2	2	2	2	2
Asset-weighted composite return ***including*** terminated accounts		8.26%	8.13%	9.27%	14.28%	11.53%	9.77%	12.54%
Asset-weighted composite return *excluding* terminated accounts		11.50%	9.75%	12.51%	14.28%	11.53%	9.77%	12.54%

| MINI APPLICATION 3.3 |
| REPORTING MISLEADING PERFORMANCE: THE CASE OF VALICENTI |

In the 1990s, the SEC sanctioned Vincent R. Valicenti, the president and sole owner of an investment advisory firm, "for causing the firm to willfully misrepresent its historical investment record."

"In a chart prepared in 1991, VAS purported to show the rates of return realized by a composite of VAS discretionary accounts with a balanced objective over the five year period from 1987 through 1991. However, the SEC found that the composite:

■ consisted of only a few of the accounts that met the balanced criteria as set by the firm;
■ excluded accounts under a certain asset level without disclosing that fact; and
■ improperly included non-balanced accounts to boost investment results.

In addition, the SEC found that Valicenti engineered the narrow range of accounts to achieve better results by changing the accounts that made up the composite over time. Finally, Valicenti created a misleading comparison of the composite's distorted rates of return with the rates of other money managers, according to the SEC."

Source: "SEC Sanctions Investment Adviser for Presenting Misleading Investment Performance," *Standards Reporter* 4, no. 1 (January 1999): 7.

---

include accounts in a long-only (just "plain vanilla" buying) equity strategy that uses short selling or leverage to increase returns (more on hidden risks later in the chapter). If a potential client is not considering using leverage or short selling for his account, including accounts that do is deceptive. (See Mini Application 3.3 for another example of unethical reporting.) The SEC requires that if a fund uses a name with a type of investment (i.e., stocks), it must have 80 percent invested in stock. But this still allows the manager to invest 20 percent in something else—most likely a higher-risk investment designed to increase returns. While such inclusions are legal, they are unethical.

Managers can also try to distort their past performance by how they aggregate accounts. Should the manager present a simple average of the historical returns of all the accounts, or a weighted average? A weighted average return is more representative of performance because it includes size as a determinant of performance. The theory of market efficiency suggests that larger accounts are likely to generate smaller excess returns. It can be more difficult to find undervalued assets and take positions that go undetected by the market as the dollar amount of the position increases; in the same vein, smaller accounts are likely to have higher excess returns. If managers present a simple average, the larger accounts with lower performance will get less weight while the smaller account with the higher performance will get more weight. Example 3.5 illustrates what happens to reported performance as the way returns are aggregated change. Equally weighted aggregated performance suggests a better track record than the manager has achieved with the actual dollar amount of assets under management. This isn't illegal, but it is unethical.

Managers should also provide some measure of dispersion of performance over the different accounts they have managed. A potential client needs to know that

EXAMPLE 3.5
PAST PERFORMANCE: AGGREGATING CLIENT ACCOUNTS

Year	1	2	3	4	5	6	7	8
Returns								
Client A		10%	9%	11%	12%	10%	9%	11%
Client B		8%	8%	9%	9%	8%	8%	9%
Client C		12%	10%	13%	15%	12%	10%	13%
End-of-period assets ($ millions)								
Client A	10	11	12	13	15	16	18	20
Client B	500	540	583	636	693	748	808	881
Client C	30	34	37	42	48	54	59	67
TOTAL	540	585	632	691	756	819	885	968
Number of portfolios	3	3	3	3	3	3	3	3
Asset-weighted composite return		8.26%	8.13%	9.27%	9.42%	8.29%	8.15%	9.31%
Equally weighted dispersion around composite		1.38%	0.69%	1.37%	2.05%	1.36%	0.68%	1.36%
Equally weighted composite return		10%	9%	11%	12%	10%	9%	11%
Asset-weighted dispersion around composite return		0.95%	0.48%	0.97%	1.47%	1.00%	0.51%	1.03%

the aggregate measure of performance is not representative of all accounts. Here an equally weighted measure of dispersion gives a potential client an idea of the range in potential performance. An asset-weighted measure understates dispersion. Asset weighting gives greater weight to the larger accounts that deviate less from an asset-weighted average to begin with (because the composite is most like the largest "piece" or the account with the largest assets/size). Use of an asset-weighted measure would give clients the false impression that there is less deviation in account performance.

Managers should not present results from either back-tested strategies or simulated models to potential clients as representative of their investment performance. This is merely another form of using ex post selection bias to look good. Back testing is used to test hypothesized trading strategies and see how well they *would* have worked in the past. Rather than testing a strategy to see how well it would have done, unethical use would find a strategy that does well when back-tested to improve reported performance. This is like creating a strategy of "buying low and selling high" after you already know when prices were relatively low and high. You can't miss. But it is unlikely that you could duplicate this strategy for your clients in the future. Providing this information to a potential client as an indication of future performance is fraught with ethical pitfalls.

EXAMPLE 3.6					
INVESTING WITH LEVERAGE					

High Returns on Investment		Low Returns on Investment	
Client's investment	1,000,000	Client's investment	1,000,000
Amount borrowed	1,000,000	Amount borrowed	1,000,000
Total invested	2,000,000	Total invested	2,000,000
Borrowing rate	5%	Borrowing rate	5%
Investment return	50%	Investment return	0%
Total value of investment	3,000,000	Total value of investment	2,000,000
Amount repaid	1,050,000	Amount repaid	1,050,000
Amount returned to client	1,950,000	Amount returned to client	950,000
			−50,000
Return on client's investment with leverage	**95%**	Return on client's investment with leverage	**−5%**
Return on client's investment without using leverage	**50%**	Return on client's investment without using leverage	**0%**
Client gain with leverage	**450,000**	Client loss with leverage	**−50,000**
Management fees with leverage (100 bps)	19,500	Management fees with leverage (100 bps)	9,500
Management fees without leverage (100 bps)	15,000	Management fees without leverage (100 bps)	10,000
Difference in fees	4,500	Difference in fees	−500

HIDDEN RISKS: LEVERAGE, SHORT SELLING, LIQUIDITY

Investment professionals also need to disclose to their clients other types of risks that they take in investing their clients' money.

LEVERAGE

Leverage the borrowing of cash to increase the size of a client's portfolio; also, the use of debt.

One important source of risk is **leverage**. Leverage can take many forms. Its simplest form is borrowing. If a manager borrows (on the client's behalf) to increase the size of the client's investment beyond the original amount, then this increases the risk of the portfolio.

For example, suppose a manager borrows $1 million at 5 percent to combine with the client's $1 million to invest a total of $2 million in a risky investment. As Example 3.6 shows, whether borrowing or using leverage makes sense depends on the return the investment earns. If the investment earns a high return, say 50 percent, then the use of leverage increases the return to 95 percent. Great! But if the investment returns nothing, then the use of leverage yields a negative return of 5 percent instead of zero. The loan must still be paid back with interest even though the investment didn't earn anything. Leverage magnifies return performance and increases risk.

What are the ethical implications? Suppose a money manager uses leverage without a client's knowledge, betting that the investment will earn a great return and, in turn, a large fee for the manager. When the gamble doesn't pay off, the manager

MINI APPLICATION 3.4
LEVERAGE AND THE FINANCIAL CRISIS OF 2008

Many Wall Street firms took advantage of low interest rates and lower regulatory restraints on borrowing by taking on excessive amounts of leverage during the period leading up to the crisis. For example, Bear Stearns was leveraged 33 to 1. While markets were going up, the use of leverage allowed the firm to make record profits. However, when markets fell, leverage quickly brought the firm down and its investors down along with it. Bear Stearns was eventually bailed out by the U.S. government.

Source: Stephen Labaton, "Agency's '04 Rule Let Banks Pile Up New Debt, and Risk," *New York Times*, 3 October 2008.

EXAMPLE 3.7
RISK OF SHORT SELLING

Price Falls		Price Increases	
Price per share	100	Price per share	100
Number of shares	100	Number of shares	100
Change in price	50	Change in price	150
Profit	5,000	Profit	(5,000)

has lost even more money for the client. The manager also forfeits his or her fee, but this is small compared to the losses suffered by the client. As Example 3.6 shows, when the use of leverage doesn't work out, the client loses $50,000 but the manager still earns a positive fee, albeit one that is smaller by $500. The gamble is unethical not only because the manager took on risks not disclosed to the client but also because it put the manager's interests ahead of the client's. See Mini Application 3.4 for another example of the misuse of leverage.

SHORT SELLING

Short sale involves selling a stock you don't own by borrowing one from a broker in the hopes that stock price will decline.

Another way to create leverage in a portfolio is through **short sales**. Investors who short-sell stocks are betting that the price will decline. In a short sale, an investor borrows a share of stock from a broker and sells it. Later, the investor must buy a share of stock to repay the one that was borrowed (plus a fee or interest charge). If the price declines, the investor can profit from short selling. She can repay the loan by purchasing the stock at a lower price. However, if the price rises, the investor must now buy the stock at an even higher price to repay the loan (see Example 3.7). Thus, like any type of borrowing to make an investment, the use of leverage magnifies positive outcomes as well as negative outcomes. This is then a hidden source of risk that must be disclosed to clients.

Hedge fund managers can be particularly susceptible to making the gambles described above. First, the mystique associated with hedge funds revolves around proprietary trading strategies; these are kept secret for some very good reasons. Once the cat is out of the bag, all market participants can implement the strategy, thus eliminating the potential to earn excess returns (efficient markets theory again). However, the need for secrecy can also hide unethical investing—like the gambles described above.

Second, the typical structure of hedge fund management fees can exacerbate the gambling problem. Many hedge funds have what is known as a **two-and-twenty fee structure**. Managers receive a 2 percent fee for assets under management, but they receive 20 percent of any returns earned in excess of the benchmark. This fee structure gives ethical managers strong incentives to search for excess returns for their clients. However, it also gives poorly performing, unethical managers incentives to take excessive risks. As managers approach the end of a period with little prospect of earning the 20 percent, they might decide to go for broke and use leverage to improve performance—at the risk of losing a substantial amount of their client's assets. If the gamble doesn't pay off, the manager will lose both the fee and the client. But with the prospect of poor performance, the manager might reason he is likely to lose both anyway, so there is little to risk by taking the gamble—for him, but not the client.

Two-and-twenty fee structure this is a fee structure commonly used by hedge funds where management fees are two percent of the dollar amount in the client's account and twenty percent of returns earned in excess of a pre-specified benchmark.

LIQUIDITY

Liquidity the ability to freely buy and sell securities.

Another hidden risk is lack of **liquidity**, which is the ability to freely buy and sell securities. Illiquid investments are ethical as long as they offer a compensating extra return. Money managers also need to make sure that their clients are fully apprised of the liquidity of securities that don't trade on a regular basis. Investments in thinly traded securities can create similar problems. If an investor wants to sell, her position would drive the price down further and create additional loses for the client. Liquidity can dry up for securities that are declining in value, thus putting investors at even greater risk of loss.

SPECIAL CONSIDERATIONS WITH VALUING SECURITIES THAT DON'T TRADE

Some investments, such as private equity, real estate, and infrastructure funds, do not have active markets where recorded transaction prices are frequently observable. Most of these investments are held for a relatively long time. Private equity investments are typically made for about five years. Real estate and infrastructure investments can be held for longer periods, for example, up to 10 years. Returns are earned on these investments by the cash flows generated during the holding period and/or some type of exit price. For instance, investments in private equity generate a realized return only when the business goes public or is sold. Interim cash flows are usually reinvested into the company or used to pay down debt. Similarly, for real estate investments, cash flows from tenant leases are part of the return; but so is the sale of the buildings. Infrastructure funds are investments that allow for private investments in public assets such as bridges, tollways, and airports. An initial investment is made

Rating agencies these are agencies, for example, Moody's, that rate the investment safety of various securities, most often the credit safety of debt securities.

Rating agencies are paid by securities issuers to provide ratings. This creates a conflict of interest between investors and the rating agency. The security issuers want a high rating; the investor wants an accurate rating.

In the financial crisis of 2008, the role of the rating agency was particularly important in structured securities, where many risky assets were placed into bundles and the bundles were sliced into tranches. These securities were complex and inherently difficult to understand and value. Some rating agencies were accused of rating such securities investment grade despite the high credit risk of the underlying investments or of using analysts who didn't understand what they were rating. The argument is that the agencies were under pressure from investment banks that were issuing the securities because the rating agencies were paid by the banks.

to purchase the public asset. The investor agrees to service the public asset in exchange for the revenues generated by the asset. So, if an investor owns a highway, the investor is responsible for fixing the potholes but gets to keep the tolls collected.

Calculating periodic returns on these types of investments can be complicated. And when investments become more complicated, there are numerous opportunities for the unscrupulous investment professional to take advantage of less knowledgeable clients.

In these cases, a variety of valuation methods for the security must be provided. Some of these methods use comparative recent transactions (real estate), price to earnings or other multiples, discounted cash flow, and internal rate of return techniques. You should recall these last three techniques from your introductory finance class. Returns are often based on forecasted cash flows such as revenues and exit values. Ethical managers should be aware of inherent upward bias in management's cash-flow projections. Refinancing and leverage in these types of investments also need to be disclosed (see "Hidden Risks"). As always, transparency is vital. Events that are likely to cause a decline in value, for example a lawsuit, should be disclosed to clients.

As an investment professional, you should use the services of professionally certified appraisers when appropriate, for example, for real estate investments. If markets are declining, as in the recent decline in home prices, appraisals can quickly become stale and should be updated more frequently. Appraisers must be independent. Any potential conflicts should be disclosed.

You can also use rating agencies to rate the risk of securities. Rating agencies are often consulted on fixed-income investments (e.g., the credit risk of mortgages is rated, and corporate bonds are rated). Standard & Poor's, Moody's, and Fitch Rating, Inc. are some companies that rate securities. Rating agencies should be independent. However, care should be taken to disclose potential conflicts of interests with third-party consultants. These conflicts can cloud the judgment of these parties (see Mini Application 3.5).

CONCLUSION: THE CRYSTAL BALL

Because no one has a crystal ball and can predict future returns, historical returns serve as a best guess of the future. If no investment advisors have perfect foresight, they are not allowed to have hindsight either. That is, they can't go back and pick and choose the past that suits them best. Almost all of the rules surrounding ethical disclosure of investment performance are designed to prevent ex post selection of biased performance measures.

Both current and future clients also need to know that after fees, their managers are better than what they could get elsewhere, whether it is another active manager or a passive strategy. Thus fees must also be disclosed along with performance measures. This practice ensures that these fees are worth the skills of an investment professional, who should be more knowledgeable than his or her clients.

TERMS

investment performance

Global Investment
 Performance
 Standards (GIPS)

ex post

ex ante

holding period return

expected returns

average returns

structured investment
 vehicle (SIV)

collateralized debt
 obligation (CDO)

asset-backed security
 (ABS)

window dressing

benchmark

index funds

exchange-traded fund
 (ETF)

style drift

style boxes

gross of fees

net of fees

cherry-pick

leverage

short sales

two-and-twenty fee
 structure

liquidity

rating agencies

REVIEW QUESTIONS

1. Explain how uncertainty in returns creates ethical issues in reporting performance.
2. What are GIPS, and why are they important to well-functioning security markets?
3. When are annual holding period return and average return appropriate to use?
4. A money manager invests $1,000,000 for a client in the beginning of 2006. At the end of 2008, the value of the portfolio is $1,485,000. What is the annual holding period return that the manager has earned for the client?
5. A client's portfolio has had the following end-of-year values for the past four years: $750,000; $650,000, $825,000; $450,000. If $500,000 was the initial amount invested, what is the annual holding period return? What is the average return? What is the standard deviation? What return is appropriate to report to the current client? What return is appropriate to report to future clients?
6. Explain how choice of historical time period to measure performance can be used to distort future predictions of performance.

7. Suppose that a portfolio has an expected return of 15 percent and a standard deviation of 25 percent. If the value of the portfolio is $5 million and the returns on the portfolio are assumed to be normally distributed, what is the value at risk at a 5 percent probability (i.e., the VaR)?

8. You are given the following information about a managed portfolio. The average return has been 22 percent, and the standard deviation has been 38 percent. The beta is 1.3. The risk-free rate is 3 percent. What are the Treynor and Sharpe measures for this portfolio? What do they tell you about the risk-return performance of the portfolio? What are the ethical uses of these measures?

9. The tracking error on a managed portfolio is 200 bps, and the return on the portfolio gross of fees has been 29 percent. The benchmark return over the same period has been 26.5 percent. Fees are 80 bps. What is the information ratio gross of fees? What is it net of fees? What do these results tell you?

10. Identify three ways of cherry picking that an advisor could use to provide misleading measures of performance.

11. What is short selling? What are potential pitfalls for your client?

12. Explain how leverage can create a hidden risk in a portfolio.

13. Identify two sources of hidden risks in a portfolio.

14. Define *gross of fees* and *net of fees*. How does their use affect performance reporting?

15. Discuss the practices that you should use in valuing securities that don't trade to ensure fair representation of their value to clients.

CRITICAL THINKING QUESTIONS

1. Refer to the discussion in the chapter on style drift. Recall that a certain amount of style drift is inevitable as stocks fluctuate in value. At what point does style drift become a conscious decision to exploit the style currently in favor by the market to improve performance? What rules do you think portfolio managers can devise to discipline themselves? When would style drift hurt an investor? When would it help?

2. Suppose that you are working for an investment management firm has two products: Fund A and Fund B. The performance of these funds has been struggling lately. Your boss has visited all the firm's existing clients and pacified them but in addition has secured their permission to change the benchmark used in managing the different funds from Benchmark A to Benchmark B. Figures A through D show the data on both the funds and the benchmarks.

	Fund A	Fund B	Benchmark A	Benchmark B
Average Monthly Return	−0.41%	1.08%	0.67%	0.42%
Standard Deviation of Monthly Returns	8.59%	8.77%	4.82%	3.51%

Your boss has asked you to recalculate the performance for the firm's clients and prospective clients using the new benchmark, B. For the funds, calculate the return and the risk-return performance (calculated as average return divided by standard deviation) net of the benchmarks. What are the ethical issues here in changing the benchmark for both current and prospective clients?

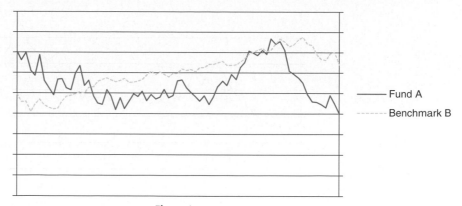

Figure A

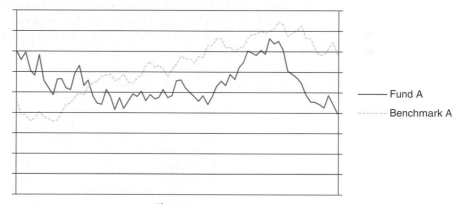

Figure B

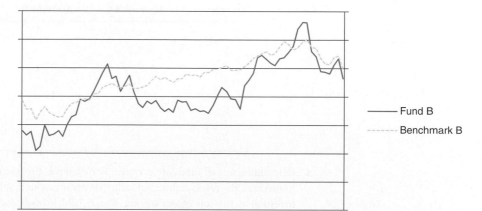

Figure C

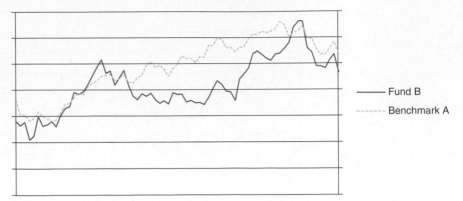

Figure D

3. You are working for a money management firm that primarily invests in domestic small cap equity. The company has been operating for two years, and you have three clients who started with you. One of your clients has given you permission to invest up to 30 percent in international small cap equity. You have invested up to 20 percent in the prior seven quarters; but just in the last quarter, you increased the client's account to the full 30 percent. You are preparing to summarize the performance of your fund to prospective clients. What numbers will you report? What are the ethical issues here?

	Beginning Investments
Account A	$100,000.00
Account B	$ 75,000.00
Account C	$ 50,000.00

Return to Accounts

Quarter	Account A	Account B	Account C
1	5	2	3
2	6.5	7	9
3	3	2	1
4	4.5	4	8
5	10	12	15
6	0.5	1	−2
7	4	5	9
8	3	4	5

4. Oftentimes, not all funds are invested. For example, the portfolio manager doesn't want to invest all the funds at once but rather slowly invest so that he or she doesn't get caught investing at the top of the market. Funds held as cash and included in performance measures will lower returns and are sometimes known as "cash drag." Should fund managers include or exclude cash from performance measures? What does excluding them measure? What does including them measure? What are the ethical issues here?

5. Beta for a given portfolio can be estimated in different ways, for example, using different measures for the market, different measures of excess returns, and different time periods. Try to create a list of the possible impacts that different ways of estimating beta can have on measuring the risk for different types of portfolios. Once you have created this list, discuss the ethical issues in choosing which beta estimate to report.

APPLIED STUDENT PROJECT: REPORTING PERFORMANCE

Collect data on stock and index prices (from www.finance.yahoo.com) and use these data to construct a portfolio of thirty or more stocks (so that it is reasonably well diversified). Using the different risk and return measures described in this chapter, estimate to the best of your ability the "true" risk and return performance of the portfolio to the index. Then find ways to use the data to improve and distort performance. You can present your distorted performance to your classmates as though they were a potential client. See if your classmates can figure out how you have distorted your performance.

RECOMMENDED CASES

1. Case 4—Heartland Advisors and Bond Funds: Misrepresentation of Bond Values
2. Case 7—Nicholas Cosmo and Agape World Inc.: A Ponzi Scheme
3. Case 9—Nick Leeson and Barings Bank: Rogue Trader
4. Case 12—Refco: Misrepresentation and Hidden Debt
5. Case 23—The Bayou Group: False Reporting
6. Case 25—Bernie Madoff: The Largest Ponzi Scheme in History?
7. Case 30—Infrastructure Funds: An SRI Investment?

REFERENCES AND SUGGESTED READING

Benninga, Simon, and Zvi Wiener. "Value-at-Risk (VaR)." *Mathematica in Education and Research* 7, no. 4 (1998): 1–8.

Bodie, Zvi, Alex Kane, and Alan J. Marcus. *Investments*, 7th ed. New York: McGraw-Hill Irwin, 2008.

CFA Institute. *Global Investment Performance Standards* (GIPS®). Charlottesville, VA: CFA Institute, 2005.

Cohan, William D. *House of Cards: A Tale of Hubris and Wretched Excess on Wall Street*. New York: Doubleday, 2009.

Elton, Edwin J., Martin J. Gruber, Stephen J. Brown, and William N. Goetzmann. *Modern Portfolio Theory and Investment Analysis*, 7th ed. New York: Wiley, 2007.

French, Kenneth. "The Cost of Active Investing." Working paper (April 2008). www.ssrn.com.

Gladwell, Malcolm. "Open Secrets: Enron, Intelligence and the Perils of Too Much Information." *New Yorker* (January 8, 2007).

"House of Cards." www.cnbc.com/id/28892719/.

Investment Company Institute. *2009 Investment Company Fact Book*, 49th ed. www.icifactbook.org.

Jacobius, Arleen. "Bye-bye Buyout; Hello Infrastructure." *Pensions & Investments* 37, no. 11 (1 June 2008): 2–3.

Jones, Charles P. *Investments: Analysis and Management*, 10th ed. Hoboken, NJ: Wiley, 2007.

Labaton, Stephen. "Agency's '04 Rule Let Banks Pile Up New Debt, and Risk." *New York Times*, 3 October 3, 2008.

Malkiel, Burton G. "Returns from Investing in Equity Mutual Funds 1971 to 1991." *Journal of Finance* 50, no. 2 (1995): 549–72.

Morgenson, Gretchen. "House Panel Scrutinizes Rating Firms." *New York Times*, 23 October 2008.

Nocera, Joe. "Risk Mismanagement." *New York Times*, 4 January 2009.

Securities and Exchange Commission. "Seniors: Protect Yourself Against Investment Fraud." Version 3, October 25, 2007.

_____. "Investment Adviser Codes of Ethics." 17 CFR Parts 270, 275 and 279, Release Nos. IA-2256, IC-26492; File No. S7-04-04 (August 31, 2004). www.sec.gov.

_____. "Shareholder Reports and Quarterly Portfolio Disclosure of Registered Management Investment Companies; Final Rule, Part VI." 17 CFR Parts 210, 239, et al. (March 9, 2004). www.sec.gov.

_____. "Implications of the Growth of Hedge Funds: Staff Report." (September 2003). www.sec.gov.

_____. "SEC Sanctions Investment Adviser for Presenting Misleading Investment Performance." *Standards Reporter* 4, no. 1 (January 1999): 7–7.

Stallings, Alex. "Toll Roads and Bridges for Sale." *National Real Estate Investor* (January 2009), 15.

Taleb, Nassim. *Fooled by Randomness: The Hidden Role of Chance in Life and in the Markets*. New York: Random House Trade Paperbacks, 2005.

Thorne, Charlotte. "Infrastructure's Era of Bumper Returns Over." *Financial Times* (July 21, 2008), 6.

Valle, Josephine B. "Special Report: Fourth Quarter Banking Report; Collateralized Debt Obligations: A Complex Game of Risk Relay," *BusinessWorld* (February 19, 2008).

APPENDIX: REVIEW OF INVESTMENT BASICS

MEASURING RETURNS

Returns are the heart of investments. Recall from your introductory finance course how to measure returns.

$$\textbf{Total return}_t = \frac{\text{Capital gain}_t + \text{Investment income}_t}{\text{Price}_{t-1}}$$

Capital gain is the price change of the security; this can be a realized or unrealized capital gain. It is realized when the security is sold.

Investment income is dividends or interest that are either paid or accrued.

Accrued interest is the amount that has been earned or accumulated while holding the security.

Total return for *n* years $= [(\text{Value at end of year } t + n)/(\text{Starting investment at year } t)] - 1$

Annualized holding period return $= [(1 + \text{Total return})^{1/n}] - 1$

Average return $= (\text{Return for year } 1 + \text{Return for year } 2 + \cdots + \text{Return for year } n)/n$

$t = \text{time period}$

RETURN DISTRIBUTIONS

Returns are commonly assumed to be normally distributed; that is, they follow a bell-shaped curve. An exception is stock returns distributions, which have "fat" tails, or more extreme outcomes than would be seen in a normal distribution. Moreover, returns can never fall below 100 percent (you can't lose more than your original investment), although the sky's the limit on the other end of the distribution. Nonetheless, the assumption of normality is commonly used to generate risk measures for stocks. Below are characteristics of **normal distributions** that are useful in characterizing expected risk and returns.

The **average** or the **mean** is the best estimate of the expected value. This is the summation of all the observations divided by the number of observations (*n*).

$$\text{Average} = E(R_i) = \left[\sum_{i=0 \text{ to } n} R_i\right]/n$$

The **variance** measures dispersion from the mean. This is the sum of all the squared deviations from the mean divided by the number of observations minus one. This gives us a measure that is in squared units.

$$\text{Variance} = \text{var}(R_i) = \left[\sum_{i=0 \text{ to } n} (R_i - E(R_i))^2\right]/(n-1)$$

The standard deviation is the square root of the variance; an easier measure to work with.

$$\text{Standard deviation} = \text{std dev}(R_i) = [\text{var}(R_i)]^{1/2}$$

68 percent of expected outcomes fall between ± 1 standard deviation;

95 percent of expected outcomes fall between ± 2 standard deviations;

99 percent of expected outcomes fall between ± 3 standard deviations.

RISK MEASURES

Assuming that returns are normally distributed is convenient in characterizing risk. As shown in Figure A3.1, a normal distribution has some properties that make it relatively easy and straightforward to measure the uncertainty of future returns. **Standard deviation** is the most basic measure of risk. It measures the total volatility

| FIGURE | A3.1 | MONTHLY RETURNS ON S&P 500 (1950–2008) |

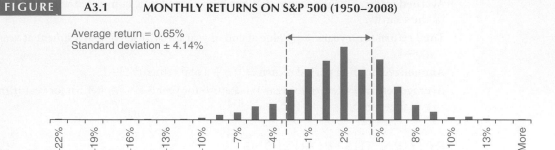

Average return = 0.65%
Standard deviation ± 4.14%

Source: www.finance.yahoo.com.

or likely fluctuations of a security or a portfolio. For example, a portfolio's standard deviation might be 10 percent. When securities are normally distributed, 68 percent of the outcomes for a security's or a portfolio's return will occur within plus or minus 1 standard deviation. However, returns are close to being normally distributed but not quite. Returns can never go below −100 percent; that is, you can never lose more than your original investment. But there is no limit to the upside. You can double or triple your money—that is, earn 200 percent or 300 percent.

Figure A3.1 shows the distribution of monthly returns for the S&P 500. The figure shows that investors can expect to earn about 0.65 percent each month and that about 68 percent of the time, returns will be between −3.49 percent (0.65% − 4.14%) and 4.79 percent (0.65% + 4.14%). Figure A3.1 also shows how risky investments in the stock market can be. The standard deviation is almost 6 1/2 times the expected return!

Beta is another commonly used measure of risk. It measures how an individual security or portfolio moves with the market. It also shows how variation in returns of either a security or a portfolio contributes to the overall risk in the market. A beta of 1 means that the security or portfolio bears the same risk as the market. You can think of beta as being like a correlation coefficient. Remember that when something is perfectly correlated with something else, it has a correlation of one. Beta also measures what is known as undiversified risk. This is the risk that cannot be reduced through diversifying, because all investments are affected by macro or global economic conditions to some degree. Investments with low betas are affected less; investments with high betas are affected more.

Beta = β = Covariance(return on market with portfolio or security)/

Total variance in the market

What's the difference between beta and standard deviation? Standard deviation is a good measure of risk when you are looking at the risk of all of your client's wealth or his entire portfolio. Beta is a valid measure of risk when you are looking at how adding an additional security or a different type of portfolio will affect your client's total wealth.

Value at risk (VaR) tells investors the dollar amount they can lose during any given period for a given probability. In its simplest form, this measure uses the historical average return and standard deviation to estimate a normal distribution much like that in Figure A3.1. The standard deviation and return can be used to estimate the probability of a loss of a certain amount. Let's look at the return data for the S&P 500 above to see how this works. Ninety-five percent of all outcomes occur within plus or minus 2 standard deviations. This means 5 percent of outcomes occur outside of this range. Half of the outcomes occur in the lower range and half the outcomes occur in the upper range. We're not worried about the upside. So there is a 2 1/2 percent probability of a return of 2 standard deviations below the mean. In any given month, an investor might earn a negative return of 7.63 percent (0.65%−2 × 4.14%). Suppose an investor had $1 million invested in the S&P 500 at the beginning of the month. Then the investor faces a 2 1/2 percent probability of losing $76,300 in that month. Most often, in practice, the VaR is measured at a 5 percent probability of a loss that is 1.65 standard deviations below the mean.

Tracking error is a measure of how well a manager is tracking the benchmark. It measures the standard deviation between the return on the portfolio and the return on the benchmark. Suppose the benchmark is the S&P 500. If the manager's portfolio tracks the benchmark *perfectly*, then the tracking error will be zero. Generally, actively managed portfolios do not have zero tracking error. This is not a bad thing. If your manager always tracks the S&P 500 perfectly, then why pay this manager more than using a passive index investment? Usually tracking error ranges between 200 and 800 bps. However, a positive tracking error is good only insofar as the manager does in fact generate return performance that is better than the benchmark. The information ratio (see below) captures both tracking error and performance relative to the benchmark.

$$\text{Tracking error} = \text{TE} = \Sigma[\text{var}_{i\,=\,1\text{ to }n}(R_P - R_B)^2/(n-1)]^{1/2}$$

where
   R_P = return on the managed portfolio
   R_B = return on the benchmark
   n = the number of observations

RISK-RETURN MEASURES

Risk-return measures allow investors to "price risk." This allows you to see how much return you are getting per unit of risk that you bear, and thus these measures are expressed as ratios. Below are common measures and their uses:

Sharpe Measure

$$S_p = (R_p - R_f)/\text{standard deviation } R_p$$

Use: This measure is useful for a well-diversified portfolio.

Treynor Measure

For a portfolio:

$$T_p = (R_p - R_f)/\beta_p$$

where
  p = portfolio
  β_p = beta of portfolio
  R_f = risk-free rate

Or for an individual security, i:

$$T_i = (R_i - R_f)/\beta_i$$

Use: For an individual security or a portfolio that is well diversified but included with other portfolios in an investment strategy.

Information Ratio

$$I_p = (R_p - R_B)/\text{TE}_p$$

Use: This measure allows an investor to see how much return in excess of the benchmark was earned relative to the portfolio's tracking error.

Jensen's Alpha

$$R_p - R_f = \beta_p + \beta_p(R_m - R_f)$$

Use: Alpha is a direct measure of how much return is earned in excess of the risk-adjusted market return. It is estimated in a regression and requires many observations. This measure is useful for evaluating longer-term performance of a portfolio.

4

Ethical Use of Information

Learning Objectives

After reading this chapter, students should be able to:

- Understand the role of information in generating excess risk-adjusted returns.
- Discuss how information can be misused to unethically generate excess returns.
- Differentiate between talent and the unethical information access and/or distortion in generating alpha.
- Define *insider trading* and cite generic examples.
- Define *market manipulation* and provide generic examples.

CHAPTER OUTLINE

- Introduction: Information and the Search for Alpha
- Information Asymmetry
- Trading on Insider Information
- Private Information: Talent
- Trading on Trading by Insiders
- Influential Publications
- Direct Communication with Corporations
- Investment Banking and Chinese Walls
- Mosaic Theory

- Front Running

- High-Speed Flash Trading

- Mutual Funds and Information Advantages from Stale Prices

- Market Manipulation

- Conclusion: Information and Fairness

INTRODUCTION: INFORMATION AND THE SEARCH FOR ALPHA

Investors make money in the stock market by buying "low" and selling "high." What is low and what is high? Low or high is determined by the intrinsic value of the security relative to its market value. The informed investor has better information than the market about intrinsic value. Securities have an intrinsic or true value and a market price. Sometimes these are the same, but often they are not. An investor who has superior information about true prices is called an **informed investor**. Such an investor can profit from buying (selling) securities when their market price is below (above) their true price. Remember the old adage, "buy low, sell high?" Here the low (high) is when the market price is below (above) the true price.

Bear in mind that that a security's price is the discounted value of future earnings or cash flows to investors. Presumably, the informed investor predicts cash flows more accurately than the market. As these cash flows are realized (i.e., through earnings reports), the market will "learn" that it was wrong in its forecast and adjust the security's price so that it is more closely aligned with that of the investor's. Voilà! The investor's prediction is realized, and he or she can then earn a "good" return (we will define what *good* is in a minute). Figure 4.1 shows how this might work.

What is a good return? First, let's define a **normal return**. A normal return is what you expect to earn given the risk of the investment. A pricing model describes the "normal" relation between risk and return; as risk increases, return must increase to compensate for the higher risk. Many different models are used to describe the normal relation between risks and return (see Example 4.1). If we assume that the **capital asset pricing model** (CAPM) is the correct model for describing the risk-return relation, then a normal return can be described as

$$E(R_i) = R_f + \beta_i[E(R_m) - R_f]$$

An **abnormal return** is the extra return beyond what is described in the normal return relation. This extra return is the economic profit (economic profit earned

Informed investor investor who has better information than other investors, whether it involves illegal inside information or superior analysis.

Normal return a return that is what you would expect to earn, given the risk of an investment.

Capital asset pricing model (CAPM) describes the risk-return relation: $R_{p \text{ or } i} = R_f \beta_{p \text{ or } i} \times (R_m - R_f)$, where R = return on a portfolio, p, or individual security, i; R_m = return on the market; R_f = risk-free return; and β is beta, the risk measure for the portfolio, p, or individual security, i.

Abnormal return the extra return beyond the expected risk-adjusted market return.

| FIGURE | 4.1 | BUYING LOW: INVESTOR A BELIEVES THAT THE INTRINSIC VALUE OF STOCK XYZ IS $35 |

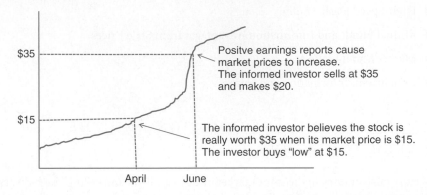

beyond marginal cost pricing) from investing. Again, using the CAPM as an example, the abnormal return is depicted as **alpha** in the following equation:

$$E(R_i) = \alpha_i + R_f + \beta_i[E(R_m) - R_f]$$

The alpha term can be added to any model to represent the extra return that is earned beyond the risk-adjusted return. We continue to use the designation of "expected" return to indicate that this alpha is generated systematically and not the result of dumb luck. See Mini Application 4.1.

Alpha extra return that is the economic profit from investing; often depicted as alpha in the following equation:

$$E(R_i) = \alpha_i + R_f$$
$$+ \beta_i[E(R_m) - R_f]$$

.

EXAMPLE 4.1
COMMON RISK-RETURN PRICING MODELS

The Capital Asset Pricing Model (CAPM)

$$E(R_i) = R_f + \beta_i[E(R_m) - R_f]$$
$$E(R_i) = \text{expected return on security}$$
$$R_m = \text{return on market}$$
$$R_f = \text{risk-free rate}$$

The Arbitrage Pricing Theory (APT) Model

$$E(R_i) = R_f + \beta_{ij}\Sigma_{j=1 \text{ to } n} F_j$$

$F_j =$ the jth factor, usually macroeconomic measures, such as change in GDP and inflation

The Fama-French Three-Factor Model (FF)

$E(R_i) = R_f + \beta_i[E(R_m) - R_f] + s_i$ (relative book-to-market measure) $+ h_i$ (relative market capitalization measure)

MINI APPLICATION 4.1
TEST YOURSELF

A friend of yours says, "Efficient markets! Nonsense! I know tons of people who have made money in the stock market!" What do you say to him?

When markets are efficient, alpha will be zero. This means that all market participants in their search for profits have squeezed any profits out of the market. Market efficiency is an "on average" concept. On average, markets are efficient; but this doesn't mean that there aren't instances of mispricing here and there. In fact, the opportunity to make money on mispricing is what keeps markets efficient. If a stock is priced too low, investors will continue to buy the stock, driving the price upward until it is correctly priced—making money all along the way. Active investment managers must have a superior strategy that selects mispriced securities and generates alpha to justify the fees they charge their clients (see Chapter 2). How can you generate alpha? Superior information! Is it ethical? Read on!

When managers or other investors purchase what they believe to be mispriced securities, are they being ethical in these transactions? It depends. Are they trading because they have a different belief about what public information implies about future cash flows? Or do they know something that other investors don't? Transactions based on different *beliefs* about the pricing implications of information are not the same as transactions based on *access* to different types of information or *distortion* of information.

Ethical use of information is determined by these two basic concerns: accessibility and distortion. Ethical access means that all market participants have access to the same information at the same time. If we think of this information as a theatrical production, then everybody gets to see the same show at the same time. No one is allowed to peek behind the curtain. No one is kept out of the show or has an obstructed view. However, there can be services that use public information to produce proprietary research, databases, analytical software, and the like. These are resources that cost money to produce. Think of them as opera glasses that the theatergoers purchase and bring on their own to the show. There is nothing wrong with charging the public for opera glasses, or analysis, or organization of public information. Access becomes unethical when the only way we can get at the information is by knowing "a friend of a friend" (e.g., insider information).

Some have argued that there is nothing unethical about trading on insider information. They say that trading on insider information gets information impounded into stock prices faster and makes the market more efficient. Efficiency is beneficial for society—so insider trading should be allowed. There is no doubt that the economics behind this argument are solid. But it ignores an ethical perspective that any behavior that hurts another is unethical. When insiders trade, they are taking unfair advantage of the party on the other side of the deal. Further, the advantage is unfair because the other party does not have access to the information even at a price—whether the price is writing a check for proprietary research or the cost of education to be a more

---

FUNDAMENTAL PRINCIPLES OF INVESTMENT ETHICS FOR PROFESSIONALS

Principle 1: ETHICAL UNDERSTANDING

Because investments are complicated, *you have an obligation not to knowingly engage in an investment transaction that either you or others do not sufficiently understand. This includes the underlying source of returns or fees charged.*

Principle 2: ETHICAL USE OF INFORMATION

Because investments are information driven, *you have an obligation to ensure that you and others have access to relevant information and that you or others do not misuse or distort information in the investment transaction.*

Principle 3: RESPONSIBLE INVESTING

Because investments provide financial resources to others, *you have an obligation to ensure that you do not knowingly make or recommend investments that support activities that harm others.*

Principle 4: TRUST AND FAIRNESS

Because you are dealing with others' money either directly or indirectly, *you have an obligation not to abuse the trust that all others have either explicitly or implicitly placed in you to treat them fairly.*

---

sophisticated investor. Nor is the type of information based on individual talent in finding alpha. Ethical theory tells us, however, that we also must respect individual rights. Along these same lines, talent, as in a talented stock picker, can be privately owned and does not need to be subject to public access. Ethical use of information also means you don't distort information, for example, by spreading false rumors about a stock.

To help you understand better, think about how you might feel, as a student, if there wasn't fair access to information that would affect your grade. Suppose some students were told about an extra-credit opportunity but others weren't? What if some students started a false rumor that the instructor said the final wasn't going to cumulative, but in fact it was? Probably, you would be pretty steamed. Now you know how someone who trades with an insider feels. What if members of fraternities or sororities got access to old exams that the instructor didn't make available to all students? Fair? What if instead, your college made *all* old exams for *all* old courses available to *all* students at a price? This is like some investors paying for research reports. As a student, you may not be happy about having to pay for these exams (or for your textbook, for that matter), but it's likely you wouldn't feel that you are being treated unfairly compared to other students. The same goes for investors not willing to pay for research.

The bottom line is that it is unethical to fool people, whether you are participating in the stock market or any other activity. The Securities and Exchange Commission (SEC) sets the stage for the fair use of information in designing securities laws and regulations. CFA(Chartered Financial Analysts) Institute also provides further guidelines for the ethical use of information in investments (see Chapter 2). The accompanying box lists the fundamental principles of investment ethics. Principle 2, Ethical Use of Information, is the focus of this chapter. The rest of the chapter fleshes out the details. But first, underpinning the fair use of information—whether access or distortions—relies on understanding the notion of information asymmetry.

INFORMATION ASYMMETRY

Information asymmetry occurs when one party has better information than another.

Information asymmetry is an important concept in market efficiency. Information asymmetry occurs whenever one party has better information than another. Without information asymmetry, it wouldn't be possible to profit—that is, earn alpha—from information-based trades. Remember Investor A from Figure 4.1? She believes that she has better information about Stock XYZ's intrinsic value ($35 per share) than other market participants who in aggregate have priced the stock at $15. If Investor A turns out to be right (and lucky Investor A does get it right in this example), she can make money by buying the stock at $15. If all market participants have the same information about the stock's intrinsic value, it would be priced at $35 today and there would be no reason to trade.

What is the definition of "better" information? In the above example we have depicted it as a belief, but this is an oversimplification. There are all sorts of ways that investors can have better information. Some are ethical and some are unethical.

TRADING ON INSIDER INFORMATION

Insider trading insiders as well as others that trade on insider information.

Insider information confidential information that, if made public, is likely to have a material impact on the securities value.

Insider trading is probably the best-known source of information asymmetry in the market. Insider trading refers to insiders who trade as well as to those who trade on inside information. Insiders are fiduciaries—individuals placed in a position of trust, such as the firm's officers and directors, employees, lawyers, accountants, and bankers. Trading on **insider information** occurs when insiders or others trade on "material" nonpublic information. *Material* means that this information is likely to have an impact on prices. Learning that the CEO is getting a new desk for his or her office is not material, but hearing that the company's next-quarter earnings are higher than analysts' forecasts is. Insiders, such as officers and directors, can trade their company's shares but must do so openly. They are required to file with the SEC–Forms 3, 4, and 5 (see Chapter 1).

What makes this kind of trading unethical? It is information that is gained through an unfair advantage. An example is insider information obtained from a fiduciary to the shareholders. Suppose an investment manager personally knows a CEO who tips him off that his or her firm in a week is going to announce

| FIGURE | 4.2 | **ILLEGAL INSIDER TRADING IN ADVANCE OF PUBLIC ANNOUNCEMENT** |

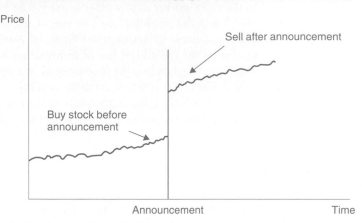

better-than-expected quarterly earnings. This is not information that is made available to all investors. If the investment manager buys the stock, he is taking unfair advantage of the investor who sells the stock to him. See Figure 4.2.

An infamous case of insiders taking advantage of other investors is Enron. Jeff Skilling, the CFO, told his employees and the public to continue to invest in Enron stock even though he was selling millions of his shares. As revealed in the aftermath of Enron's collapse, Skilling had fraudulently manipulated accounting earnings to continually beat analysts' expectations so as to prop up the stock price. He knew at some point they couldn't keep covering up poor performance and tried to liquidate his personal holdings before the stock price declined. He made millions on his stock sales, while many employees and investors who believed Skilling and Enron's inflated earnings hung onto their stock and lost their life savings. Skilling was convicted of insider trading along with accounting fraud.

Tippees can also be charged with insider trading. A friend, acquaintance, or anybody else who gets the information from a corporate fiduciary is known as a **tippee**. A tippee can also receive the information "nth" hand. For example, the spouse of a CEO tips off a friend to an upcoming merger, who in turn tells another friend, who trades on the tip. As long as the second friend knows that the information is coming from a reliable source, that friend is a tippee. This trading is illegal because the information was learned in a fiduciary context (i.e., duty to shareholders) and thus misappropriated or stolen when used to benefit the trader or the tippee.

Another example of a tippee involves the Internet. In 1997, John Freeman, James Cooper, and Benton Erskine met in an Internet-based chat room dedicated to a stock where all three had lost money. There they colluded to trade on inside information. John Freeman worked for a temporary agency that placed him at various investment banking firms; one of these was Goldman Sachs. While at these firms, he had access to insider information on impending mergers and acquisitions. (Mini Application 4.2 discusses why information about mergers and acquisitions are so attractive to insider traders.) He used the information on these deals to tip off Cooper and Erskine.

Tippee friend, acquaintance, or anybody else who gets inside information from a corporate fiduciary or another reliable source.

MINI APPLICATION 4.2
MERGERS & ACQUISITIONS AND TAKEOVERS

Takeovers occur when one firm offers to buy the shares of another firm in an attempt to take over the firm. The firm doing the buying is known as the bidder. The firm being sought after is known as the target. Typically a bidder firm offers to buy up to 50 percent of the target (to get majority control) and offers a 50 percent premium over market price for the shares. When the announcement is made, the target stock price increases dramatically. Trading on insider information about impending tender offers can be very profitable but is illegal as well as unethical.

The circle of Freeman's tippees grew to waiters and waitresses he worked with, other coworkers at temporary jobs, his neighbors, and then to a wider circle of tippees—friends of the first group of tippees. Figure 4.3 shows how tippees grew in this case. Freeman was paid in cash, gift cards, and cases of wine. In all, 18 tippees were prosecuted by the SEC for illegally trading with insider information in 20 stocks. The scheme lasted almost four years. Freeman, Cooper, and Erskine never did meet face-to-face.

| FIGURE | 4.3 | INSIDER TRADING AND "NTH" TIPPEES |

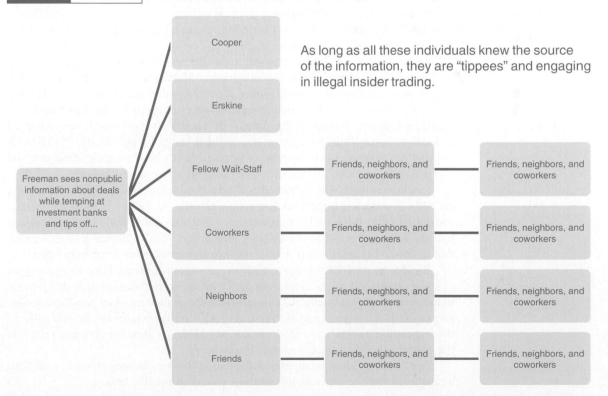

A more recent example of a tippee ring is that centered on Raj Rajaratnam, founder of a hedge fund, the Galleon Group. Rajaratnam was arrested in October 2009 in an ongoing criminal investigation. Rajaratnam had a career in Silicon Valley before joining Wall Street. His fund focused on, among other things, technology stocks. He used his contacts in both Wall Street firms and technology companies to trade ahead of earnings announcements. Besides Rajaratnam, others have been implicated in the scheme and the investigation continues to identify an ever-widening circle of tippees.

Another famous case of insider trading involves a well-known television personality, Martha Stewart. In 2002, Sam Waksal, CEO of ImClone Systems, Inc., learned that the Food and Drug Administration (FDA) was not going to approve its drug Erbitux for cancer treatment (ironically, eventually the drug *was* approved). Waksal knew of the adverse consequences that the announcement would have on the share price. He called his broker, Peter Bacanovic, to tell him to instruct his family and friends to sell their ImClone shares in advance of the FDA announcement. Martha Stewart was both a friend and shareholder. Douglas Faneuil (Bacanovic's assistant) called Martha and told her that Sam Waksal and his daughter were selling all of their shares and advised her to do the same. She did and avoided losing $45,673 on her stock. On the day of the FDA announcement, share value fell 16 percent. Later Stewart told the SEC that she had not traded on the inside information but rather had a standing order with Bacanovic to sell the stock if it fell below $60 a share (this is known as a **stop-loss order**, which is when investors instruct their brokers to sell their shares at a prespecified price; it is meant to limit losses when prices are falling). Ultimately Stewart was convicted for lying to law enforcement officials about the stop-loss order and not for insider trading.

There are two striking things about the Stewart case. First, before becoming founder and CEO of her very successful company, Martha Stewart Living Omnimedia, Inc., Stewart had worked as a stockbroker. More than other individuals caught trading on inside information, she should have known better given her background in the securities industry. Second, at the time of the scandal, her net worth was estimated at $650 million. While the amount she avoided losing by her actions ($45,673) is nothing to sneeze at, in the context of her wealth, it's hard to understand why she was willing to break the law for such a relatively small amount of money.

Her behavior certainly exhibited both greed and arrogance. Greed because saving the $45,673 was more important than acting ethically. Arrogance because it appeared she thought that she would not get caught or that she could "fool" law enforcement that the sale was related to the $60 stop-loss order. Recall Chapter 1 when we said that unethical behavior is driven by arrogance and greed. Here is a case in point.

Besides advance knowledge of a corporate announcement, there are other types of insider trading. Trading in advance of *any* information dissemination that is likely to move the market is unethical. This information is called material (see Table 4.1 for some examples). A good rule of thumb is to ask, "If the investor on the other side of the transaction had the same information, would she go ahead at the same price?" If the answer is no, then the transaction is unethical.

Are there *any* kinds of superior information that you cannot access but are both legal and ethical? Yes! Private information—we examine this next.

Stop-loss order a trade order that specifies a price below (sell) or above (buy) which the order is not to be executed.

| TABLE | 4.1 | EXAMPLES OF MATERIAL INFORMATION |

- Earnings;
- Mergers, acquisitions, tender offers, or joint ventures;
- Changes in assets;
- Innovative products, processes, or discoveries;
- New licenses, patents, registered trademarks, regulatory approval/rejection of a product;
- Developments regarding customers or suppliers (e.g., the acquisition or loss of a contract);
- Changes in management;
- Change in auditor notification or that issuer may no longer rely on auditor's report or a qualified opinion;
- Events regarding the issuer's securities (e.g., defaults on senior securities, calls of securities for redemption, repurchase plans, stock splits, changes in dividends, changes to the rights of security holders, public or private sales of additional securities, and changes in credit ratings);
- Bankruptcies;
- Significant legal disputes;
- Government reports of economic trends (employment, housing starts, currency information, etc.);
- Orders for large trades before they are executed.

Source: Copyright 2005, CFA Institute, Reproduced with permission from CFA Institute. All rights reserved.

PRIVATE INFORMATION: TALENT

Private information the superior ability to interpret information or the ability to formulate a "better" belief about the pricing implications of the information.

Private information is the superior ability to interpret information or the ability to formulate a "better" belief about the pricing implications of the information. In other words, the superior analyst has the *same* public information—or raw data—as other investors but is better at analyzing it and predicting changes in prices. This analysis generates alpha. The investor's superior analysis then becomes valuable information itself. It is material and nonpublic. Because this type of information doesn't fit the definition of insider information that is factual in basis, it is sometimes known as private information. Warren Buffet is an investor who illustrates the concept of superior private information (see Mini Application 4.3). Whatever advantages the superior analyst earns represents a "normal" return based on his or her superior talent as an analyst.

Is it ethical to trade on private information? Your talent is not a public good, and you have an individual right to it. It follows, then, that it is ethical to use your talents to profitably trade for yourself and your clients. It is also ethical to sell your talent, for example, in the form of proprietary research reports.

MINI APPLICATION 4.3

WARREN BUFFET: A "SUPER ANALYST"

Warren Buffett is famed for his long-running success in investing. He began investing during the fifties and has amassed wealth in the billions of dollars. He is known for "value" investing. He selects investments of firms he believes have strong prospects for long-run profitability. He has been consistently right.

Star analysts analysts that are top rated by various financial publications and have the ability to move stock prices with their investment recommendations.

There is a caveat. When you make your analysis public, the game changes. One thing analysts do is forecast earnings from quarter to quarter. The other thing they do is make investment recommendations: buy, sell, or hold. Analysts who are right more times than not come to be known as **star analysts**. More important, their pronouncements can also move prices. Thus their forecasts and recommendations are valuable information before they are made public. Trading in advance of the public dissemination of this information can be profitable. It is also illegal and unethical.

What about unequal resources? Along with proprietary research reports, some investors have access to better electronic information (i.e., Bloomberg Terminals) than other investors. Is this somehow unfair or unethical? No. First, creation of data sets and manipulation of raw data is similar to analysis of publicly available information. As long as Bloomberg isn't providing its users with insider information, the company can ethically charge for a subscription. Second, anyone can purchase a Bloomberg Terminal *if* he or she is willing to bear the cost. The barrier is the cost, or capital resources. Access to capital to generate profits is common to all types of business. Ethical doesn't mean equal.

TRADING ON TRADING BY INSIDERS

Now that we have established the distinction between trading on insider information and talent, let's look at some other types of insider trading. Suppose an individual who is likely to have inside information tells you of an upcoming trade. But you don't know the reason for the trade. What would you do? Well, you could easily infer that if the insider is buying, then he or she likely knows that "good news" about the company. If the insider is selling, then you infer the opposite. He or she is likely to have "bad news." You do not need to know what the insider knows specifically—only that he or she is an insider, and the direction of the trade.

Because insider trades convey important information, the SEC requires that insiders disclose their trades (buys and sells) in a Form 4 filing within two business days of trading. If you trade on the basis of an insider's trades that have not yet been publicly disclosed, then you are guilty of insider trading. It is both illegal and unethical.

INFLUENTIAL PUBLICATIONS

The ethical issues with influential publications are similar to those with star analysts. "Heard on the Street" is a column in the *Wall Street Journal* that regularly features a specific real-world firm and can move the prices of securities of companies discussed. Why? This might be the revelation of valuable "private" information that we discussed above. Using inside information to trade on these securities before the information is published is a violation. In the 1980s, R. Foster Winans contributed to this column. He conspired with others to trade in advance of the column and was convicted of insider trading. Journalists at other influential publications such as *Forbes, Fortune,* and *Business Week* could also have the same private information. The publication of their columns could move stock prices. Trading in advance of public distributions of these publications is both illegal and unethical. Why unethical? Won't the public get the information anyway? Yes, but before these publications hit the newsstands (and this includes posting of online versions), access to them is restricted. While eventually the information is sold for a price (the cost of the magazine, newspaper, or online subscription), the companies producing the information are not making a general offer to the public to get the magazine or whatever other vehicle (and its valuable information) early for a higher price.

Economists often use the example of hardcover versus paperback books to demonstrate that some consumers are willing to pay more to get content (in this case, the book) earlier. Hardcover books are more expensive than paperback books. Why would anyone pay more for the hardcover (ignoring for the moment those who are true bibliophiles) when the paperback is so much cheaper? You get the hardcover sooner. If you can't wait, you will pay more for the hardcover. Or if you *really* can't wait, you can purchase a Kindle or some other handheld electronic reading device for $250 and download the e-book in 60 seconds. Is this ethical? Yes, everyone can purchase the hardcover or the e-book. But the *Wall Street Journal* is not offering a more expensive advance version of its column before public dissemination. Access is gained only by an insider working for the *Journal*. Because access is limited, it is both unfair and unethical.

DIRECT COMMUNICATION WITH CORPORATIONS

Analysts can have direct communication with executives of corporations that issue the securities they follow. Until 2000, analysts were allowed to participate in conference calls with corporate executives, and these calls were not open to the public. During these calls, analysts could acquire valuable information; for instance, that a large customer canceled a contract or that preliminary estimates of last month's sales were higher than expected. The unethical analyst could then profitably trade on this information to the disadvantage of the investing public. In 2000, the SEC adopted what is called **Regulation Fair Disclosure (FD)** (known as Regulation FD). This rule requires that conference calls be made publicly available. Again, the adoption of this

Regulation Fair Disclosure (FD) a rule requiring that conference calls be made publicly available.

regulation reflects the underlying ethical principle that all investors have equal access to information that eventually becomes public.

Phone conversations are now publicly available; however, information gathered during site visits is not. Analysts often visit the companies that issue the securities they analyze. During these visits, they can possibly become privy to nonpublic information. Is this ethical? Does the public have equal access to a site visit? While a public investor can call to visit and meet with top executives, he or she is unlikely to be granted the same access as a professional analyst. It is not feasible to run a company and open the gates to everyone who wants a tour and a conversation with senior management. So an ethical analyst should refrain from trading on any information gleaned from a site visit. Alternatively, the analyst could make this information public by disseminating it in a public report.

INVESTMENT BANKING AND CHINESE WALLS

Chinese wall or **firewall** firm policies and procedures to prevent sharing of information between the investment banking and investment management division of the same firm.

Another source of inside information about corporations is the investment banking division of an investment firm. Investment banks work directly with corporate clients to place securities, facilitate mergers and acquisitions, and complete a myriad of other transactions. All of these transactions have substantial implications for share prices. For example, when a hostile tender offer is announced, the targeted stock increases, on average, by 40 percent. Advance knowledge of this announcement can be very profitable. Advance trading on this knowledge is also illegal and unethical. A **Chinese wall**, or **firewall** (see Mini Application 4.4), prevents sharing of information between the investment banking and investment management division of the same firm. These so-called walls are also used to prevent analysts from losing their objectivity when rating the securities of corporations that are the clients of the investment banking division (more about this in Chapter 5). Firms often create lists of corporations and securities that they are actively involved with in an investment banking deal. These lists are then circulated to the money management division, and the firm's employees are told they cannot trade on those securities.

MINI APPLICATION 4.4

WHERE DO THE TERMS CHINESE WALL AND FIREWALL COME FROM?

Chinese wall refers to the Great Wall of China, which was built long ago to protect the Chinese empire. For some people, the wall also symbolizes the cultural divide between Mongolian and Manchurian tribes; thus, this term can be offensive to the Chinese and shouldn't be used. Nonetheless, Wall Street firms commonly use this term; you should be familiar with it, but discourage its use.

A *firewall* is a wall made of fire-resistant material and designed to stop the spread of fire from one part of a building to another. In Wall Street firms, the firewall stops the spread of information from different divisions.

Mike Milken and Ivan Boesky are the most infamous practitioners of insider trading on investment banking deals. Mike Milken was an executive at Drexel Burnham and Company during the takeover mania of the 1980s. Milken was famous before he became infamous. He is largely credited with pioneering the junk bond market, which allowed for many large firms to become private through **leveraged buyout (LBO)**. An acquisition of a public company by a management group, an investor group, or another company can be structured as a leveraged buyout. In these deals, 100 percent of the shares are sought. The firm is taken private and the deal is financed with large amounts of newly issued debt, known as junk bonds. Typically, premiums for buyouts range from 20 to 40 percent. When the premiums are announced, stock price increases dramatically. Purchasing stock in an LBO target before its announcement can be profitable, but it is also illegal and unethical. Ivan Boesky was the head of an arbitrage firm. Milken conspired with Ivan Boesky, among others, to trade on inside information about the many leveraged buyout and takeover deals occurring at both his firm and other ones. He and Ivan Boesky were convicted of insider trading. Their story is the basis for Oliver Stone's movie, *Wall Street*, which made Boesky's speech at the University of California–Berkeley in 1986 ("Greed Is Good") infamous.

> **Leveraged buyout (LBO)** a transaction financed with high amounts of debt or leverage whereby all of the public shareholders are bought out.

MOSAIC THEORY

> **Mosaic theory** the idea that securities researchers can take pieces of public information and, through analysis, assemble the pieces to reveal an accurate forecast of future value.

In art, a mosaic is a collection of small, indistinct pieces that together reveal a picture. **Mosaic theory** is the idea that securities researchers can take pieces of public information and, through analysis, assemble the pieces to reveal an accurate forecast of future value. This is another example of distinguishing between insider information and talent. What if an investment professional is especially adept at trading in securities that subsequently have announcements that substantially affect price? Will this investor be subject to prosecution by the SEC for insider trading? Not necessarily. If the investor can show how he made his prediction using publicly available information, he is "in the clear" (i.e., he can demonstrate how he created the mosaic). For example, suppose an investor creates a model predicting takeover targets. Inputs into this model could be declining stock price and earnings (indicative of mismanagement), high cash balances (available to finance a takeover), low holdings by corporate executives (so that they aren't able to effectively fight a takeover), and so on. A sophisticated model could justify a good track record by such an investor and not necessarily imply either illegal or unethical use of information.

Risk or merger arbitrage is another legal and ethical trading strategy that involves takeover contests. The price of the target often trades below the offer price until the deal is completed. This is because there is a risk that the deal won't go through (lack of financing or due diligence reveals impairment of the target value, such as a lawsuit pending against the target company). An arbitrager buys the target stock and then holds to completion.

Another form of arbitrage occurs in stock-for-stock transactions. The arbitrager buys the target stock and shorts the bidder stock. The bidder stock often declines in value for stock transactions because of "dilution" when more stock is issued to complete the deal. When the deal is completed, the arbitrager takes the target stock—which is now bidder stock—to close out the short position on the bidder stock. If you engage in these strategies, make sure you keep good records to support your recommendations.

FRONT RUNNING

Front running the practice of placing an order ahead of the trade of another investor.

Front running is the practice of trading ahead of the trade of another investor. Usually this occurs when a broker gets an order from an institutional customer, such as a pension fund or mutual fund. Front running is an illegal practice that unfairly uses information from the trade itself. A substantial trade occurs because there is either a large investment or divestiture from the fund. The manager may have changed her assessment (private information) of the expected returns of the holding. Or the fund may have a large enough position that trading in the security can influence the price. Due to the size of the order or the identity of the customer, the broker reasonably predicts that the order will move prices. The broker then places a trade before the customer's trade and takes advantage of the predictable change in prices from the customer's order. See Mini Application 4.5.

Who does front running hurt? It could potentially hurt the customer that you are trading in front of, if the front-running trade adversely changes the price that the customer trades at, say, a buy order executed at a higher price or a sell order at a lower one. The broker is also hurting the party on the other side of the trade. The broker has an unfair information advantage about an impending change in price that is likely to occur when she places her customer's order. In fact, the only way to make a profit from the trade is through an information advantage. There is no talent involved in front running.

HIGH-SPEED FLASH TRADING

High-speed flash trading the ability to "flash" customer orders to traders for a few seconds before they are distributed to the market.

A practice that is related to front running is **high-speed flash trading**. Flash trading is the result of the establishment of electronic communications networks (ECNs—see Chapter 2), which use computers to match and execute trades more accurately and faster. Flash-trading firms electronically collect and aggregate orders and delay the

---

MINI APPLICATION 4.5
HEDGE FUNDS AND FRONT RUNNING

In 2007 the SEC launched an investigation into front running by hedge funds. Traders at desks at large Wall Street banks would "tip off" hedge fund managers about forthcoming large trades by mutual funds. Because hedge funds do a large amount of trading, some speculated that this was an attempt by investment firms to curry favor with the manager of these funds and earn brokerage commissions.

orders for a second or so before making them available to all traders. During the delay, they "flash" the orders to proprietary traders. This allows traders to take advantage of the slower traders. Often the slower traders are institutional investors or traders, such as those for mutual funds. Just as in front running, a flash trader can see, for example, that a mutual fund has placed a buy order. The flash trader then buys up shares to sell to the slower trader at a higher price. The profit is usually only pennies on each trade, but by using computer algorithms for high-frequency trading, a flash trader can execute trading over millions of shares all day long.

What are the ethical issues here? Only select traders have access to the data feed that provides these 1-second flashes, by virtue of paying exchanges a fee to have powerful computer servers located on exchange floors. Colocation allows for additional time, even though it is only milliseconds, ahead of other traders. The information in flash trades is not publicly available, nor is it possible to give everyone space on the exchange floor for a computer server. Further, they are raw data—that is, the data have not been subject to processing or manipulation. There can be no claim that access to these data is related to talent. Thus it gives traders an unfair information advantage over the rest of investors and is unethical. The counterargument is similar to those made by proponents of insider trading. Flash trading allows information to be impounded into prices faster, thus reducing volatility. By executing trades more quickly, it also creates greater liquidity. As of the writing of this text, the SEC was considering enacting new regulations to limit this practice.

MUTUAL FUNDS AND INFORMATION ADVANTAGES FROM STALE PRICES

Net asset value (NAV) price of mutual fund shares determined by taking the total market value of securities in the fund minus the total liabilities of the fund divided by the number of shares.

Recall from Chapter 2 that mutual funds are securities that are created out of a large portfolio of securities. The value of each share of a mutual fund depends on the market value of the securities in the fund. In addition, fund managers deduct the cost of running the fund, such as salaries of fund managers, accountants, trading costs, and so forth. The total market value of securities in the fund minus the total liabilities of the fund divided by the number of shares in the fund yields the **net asset value (NAV)**. NAV is the price at which mutual fund investors can trade their shares. Example 4.2 shows how a NAV is calculated.

There are two types of mutual funds. Open-end funds allow investors to redeem or buy shares at the NAV. Closed-end funds do not redeem or issue new shares. Investors in closed-end funds who wish to sell their shares must sell to other investors interested in the funds. Most mutual funds are open-end funds. Mutual funds are different from most other types of securities because their transaction value is determined only *once* per day. At the end of trading, fund accountants determine the closing market price of all the securities within the fund and, on that basis, determine the NAV.

While pricing is determined only once a day, information that affects the value of the underlying securities occurs all day long. As a result, prices and information become disconnected, and prices become stale. For example, suppose that during the

EXAMPLE 4.2
ARITHMETIC BEHIND MUTUAL FUNDS: DIVERSIFICATION AT AN AFFORDABLE PRICE

Number of Shares	Price per Share	Total Value	Percentage of Portfolio
1,000,000	50	50,000,000	20%
2,000,000	30	60,000,000	24%
350,000	100	35,000,000	14%
4,000,000	25	100,000,000	40%
75,000	80	6,000,000	2%
	Total value of fund's assets	251,000,000	100%
	Fund's liabilities	10,000,000	
	Net assets	241,000,000	
	Total shares in mutual fund	10,000,000	
	Net asset value (NAV) of each mutual fund share	$24.10	

trading day some of the firms that have stock in the fund announce positive earnings, and the stock price increases almost immediately. The NAV of the mutual fund will still reflect the stale NAV from the day before; that is, it will be too low relative to the new information that has been released during the day. After the markets have closed, the NAV will increase to reflect the new information and prices. There are two practices that allow investors to take advantage of these stale prices—late trading and market timing.

LATE TRADING

Late trading the practice of allowing investors to purchase a share of a mutual fund at that day's net asset value (NAV) after the market has closed but before markets have opened the next day.

Late trading lets investors purchase a share of a mutual fund at that day's NAV after the market has closed but before markets have opened the next day. Often corporations release information that is likely to have an impact on share price after trading hours. Investors can profit from this information by "squeezing" in at the old price but before the new price is calculated. For example, suppose a corporation released positive information after the market closed. An investor could purchase the fund at the current NAV. The next day, when markets open, share prices will increase, reflecting information released the day before. The investor could then sell the share at the higher NAV and make a profit. The SEC prohibits late trading. Besides being illegal, it is also unethical because not all investors are able to take advantage of late trading. In 2003, several mutual funds that engaged in late-trading practices got in trouble with the SEC. Why would mutual fund managers allow some investors to take advantage of late trading? Many mutual funds also serve as brokers. Some institutional investors and hedge funds were allowed to engage in late trading in exchange for brokerage.

Who is hurt by late trading? Other investors in the fund, that's who. When the late traders are able to transact at favorable prices, they dilute the value of the fund. Example 4.3 shows how. Here the late traders take advantage of positive information after the market closes. The current NAV is too low; but the next day, after market prices adjust to the new information, the NAV will increase. The late traders are able to buy into the fund at "too low" a price, causing the total value of the fund to be too low relative to the new number of shares. This in turn dilutes the per share value of the fund.

Late traders able to buy in at the stale NAV of $10.00 are able to sell the next day at the new NAV of $10.17 and make 17 cents per share. At the time of the late trade, the NAV should be $10.20, but *only if* it was calculated to reflect the new information. If the late traders had to pay in $10.20 to the fund instead of $10.00, next day the NAV would be $10.20. But it's not—it's $10.17 a share. Thus the other investors in the fund have lost 3 cents per share.

As Example 4.3 shows, late trading costs other investors only pennies. For this reason, some have argued that late trading is inconsequential. However, from an ethical perspective, these are the investors' pennies—not others' pennies. There is no justification for stealing *any* amount in this way, no matter how small.

EXAMPLE 4.3
HOW LATE TRADING HURTS OTHER INVESTORS IN THE FUND

Number of shares	10,000,000
NAV	$10.00
Total value	$100,000,000
Return from information after market closes	2%
Total value next day	$102,000,000
NAV next day	$10.20
Late Trading Allowed	
Number of new shares purchased	2,000,000
Purchase price per share "stale price"	$10.00
Total value of shares	$122,000,000.00
Total number of shares	12,000,000
New price per share	$10.17
No Late Trading Allowed	
Number of new shares purchased	2,000,000
Purchase price per share at NAV next day	$10.20
Total value of shares	$122,400,000
Total number of shares	12,000,000
New price per share	$10.20
Investors' Loss per Share from Late Trading	**−$0.03**

MARKET TIMING

Market timing trading in or out of a mutual fund at the previous day's net asset value (NAV) to take advantage of the difference in timing of public announcements across different markets and the calculation of NAV.

Like late trading, **market timing** exploits a disconnection between NAV and more current market prices. Market timing takes advantage of the difference in timing of public announcements across different markets and the calculation of NAV. The most common occurrence is in international funds. Recall that international funds invest in stocks that trade on foreign exchanges. Foreign markets close before United States markets, so an after-hours news release for a stock on a foreign exchange can have an impact upon stock valuations that will not be reflected in the NAV until the next day. The ability to move in and out of the fund at the stale NAV can generate profits for those allowed to do so.

Refer to Figure 4.4. Suppose there is an international mutual fund that includes the stock of Rolls Royce Group. Rolls Royce stock trades on the London Stock exchange. When the London market closes at 4:30 p.m. Greenwich mean time (GMT), it is only 11:30 a.m. eastern standard time (EST) in New York. The NAV for the fund from yesterday's (Monday's) close is $50. After the London Stock exchange closes on Tuesday, Rolls Royce reports unexpected increase in earnings. The next day, Wednesday, the price of Rolls Royce's stock increases from the prior close of $25 to $40 at the close on the London Exchange. As a result, the international mutual fund's NAV will be higher at close on the New York Stock Exchange—three and one-half hours later.

If Rolls Royce stock constitutes 10 percent of the mutual fund's holdings, then the NAV will increase by 10 percent × (40 − 25), or $1.50 a share (keeping constant the values of all other holdings in the fund) on Wednesday. But current NAV in New York at noon EST on Tuesday doesn't reflect that. It is still at $50, even though the value from Roll's Royce's good news will place it at $51.50. On Tuesday, at the London close and the New York close, Rolls Royce's closing stock price is still $25. If you could engage in market timing, what would you do? You can purchase at the

FIGURE	4.4	MARKET TIMING IN INTERNATIONAL FUNDS

New York Exchange Close at 4:00 pm EST	NAV = $50	NAV = $50 Reflects Rolls Royce's closing price of $25. **Market timer buys at $50**	NAV = $51.50 Reflects Rolls Royce's closing price of $40.	
		After London close, Rolls Royce announces unexpected increase in earnings.		
London Exchange Close at 11:30 am EST		Rolls Royce stock closes at $25/share.	Rolls Royce stock closes at $40/share.	**Market timer sells at $51.50**
	Monday	Tuesday	Wednesday	Thursday

stale NAV of $50.00 on Tuesday and then, in the next few days, sell out at the new higher NAV of $51.50. Just as with late trading, the profits come from collecting pennies from all the other investors as their share value becomes diluted.

Unlike late trading, market timing is not illegal; but it is unethical. While market timers are trading on public information available to all investors, they are engaging in short-term trading that dilutes the value of long-term investors. Funds that explicitly state they don't allow market timing in their prospectuses and then allow preferred investors to do so are subject to regulatory action. Market timing was another practice that mutual funds got in trouble with in 2003. Richard Strong was founder and CEO of Strong Capital Management. Strong Capital Management was one of the mutual funds investigated by New York State Attorney General Eliot L. Spitzer, and later by the SEC, for trading abuses. The investigation revealed that Richard Strong engaged in market timing for both his account and those of friends in funds that claimed in their prospectuses that they prohibited such practices. Strong publicly apologized to investors (a rare event at the time) and made restitution to the funds.

MARKET MANIPULATION

Market manipulation the use of trading or rumors to mislead other market participants about the value of a security.

Market manipulation occurs when investors trade to give the illusion of *false* information. For example, an investor can buy a stock and then disseminate positive false information. The stock price will then rise. The unethical investor then sells the stock at the higher price before the market realizes that it has been duped.

Pump-and-dump schemes a tactic designed to artificially increase the price of the stock before selling it.

There are many ways in which false information can be created in the markets. **Pump-and-dump schemes** are designed to artificially increase the price of a stock. The criminal behind such activity purchases the stock and then disseminates false information designed to increase buying interest and increase the price in the stock (the "pump"). Once the stock has increased in price, the criminal sells and makes a profit (the "dump"). Internet chat rooms and e-mail blasts are designed to encourage naïve investors to purchase a stock. Criminals also tend to employ pump-and-dump schemes for securities that are thinly traded. **Thinly traded** securities are those whose trading volume is minimal. Hence, a small increase in transactions can have a big impact on price. See Mini Application 4.6.

Thinly traded describes securities for which there is not much trading volume.

MINI APPLICATION 4.6
PUMP AND DUMP AND THE SOPRANOS

The Sopranos was a popular cable TV series about an organized crime family. In one season, the family engaged in a pump-and-dump scheme. They bought stocks and then, through their brokerage firm, encouraged naïve investors (mostly senior citizens) to buy the stock. This buying in turn increased the stock's price. The mobsters and their friends then sold the stock at a tidy, but illegal, profit.

Another way to create false information is to buy and sell a thinly traded stock between accounts. This makes it appear as though more than one party is interested in the stock. It also increases trading volume. Recall that trading volume is the number of shares that changes hands during the day for a stock. Market participants often use volume as a gauge for interest in a stock. As volume surges, the market infers that there is some hidden positive information about the stock and others begin buying the stock. Buying pressure in turn increases the price of the stock.

How does the trading scheme work? Suppose a stock's typical daily trading volume is 40,000 shares. The crook sets up an account at brokerage firm A and another account at brokerage firm B. He buys 10,000 shares via his broker at firm A and then sells these while at the same time buying back 10,000 shares via his broker at firm B. Really only one transaction has occurred—the original purchase of the 10,000 shares. But trading volume will be 20,000 shares because of the second transaction between the two accounts in firms A and B. The market knows only that trading volume has increased from 40,000 to 60,000 shares—or a 50 percent increase. The inference is that buying interest in the stock has increased. What's behind this interest? Maybe somebody knows some favorable news about the stock that hasn't been released yet. Speculation drives up the market price. The crook now closes out his scheme by selling his shares at a profit.

Another way to create false information is to exaggerate earnings forecasts. The investor buys (or short-sells) the stock and then disseminates an earnings forecast that exaggerates an increase (or decrease) in EPS. The stock price rises (or falls), and the investor closes out his or her position. Again, these types of strategies work best in markets that have less volume and are not as frequently followed by reputable analysts, such as penny stocks (stocks that trade for less than $5 over the counter on the Over the Counter Bulletin Board (OTCBB). Under these circumstances, it is easier to push prices around with false information and increases in trading activity.

CONCLUSION: INFORMATION AND FAIRNESS

Information is the name of the game in being able to make money in the stock markets—the information that allows investors to buy low and sell high, or make alpha. Fair and ethical use of information occurs when all investors have access to the same information: raw data on which to apply their skills as analysts. Talented analysts have the right to keep their analysis private and profit from it. Use of information that others don't have access to (insider information) or the creation of false information (market manipulation) is both unfair and unethical. It's not ethical either to "trick" another person or to take advantage of his or her ignorance. In the case of the mutual fund industry, it is unfair and unethical to allow investors to use information to trade on while barring other investors from making the same trades.

Regulation plays an important role in ensuring that use of information is both fair and ethical. When investors perceive that markets are not fair—that is, the deck is stacked against them—they will not participate. This in turn excludes an important source of capital from the economy.

Beyond following the law, you as an investment professional must ensure that your use of information is ethical. Because information is so valuable in trading, analysts constantly need to ask themselves whether their investments are based on analysis of public information or exploitation of nonpublic information. As an analyst, your ethical duty is always to shy away from the latter, no matter how tempting that information may be.

TERMS

informed investor

normal return

capital asset pricing model (CAPM)

abnormal return

alpha

arbitrage pricing theory (APT)

Fama-French three-factor model

information asymmetry

insider trading

insider information

tippee

stop-loss order

private information

star analysts

Regulation Fair Disclosure (Regulation FD)

Chinese wall (firewall)

leveraged buyout (LBO)

mosaic theory

front running

high-speed flash trading

net asset value (NAV)

late trading

market timing

market manipulation

pump-and-dump scheme

thinly traded

REVIEW QUESTIONS

1. How do investors make money in investments? How is this measured with a model of expected returns?

2. What is information asymmetry? Give an example.

3. What is the difference between insider information and private information? When does private information become insider information?

4. Some investors have the ability to purchase resources such as software and proprietary research. Is it unethical or unfair to allow some investors to have resources that others don't? How is this practice different from having access to inside information?

5. What is a tippee? Give an example.

6. What is material information? Why is it important in insider trading?

7. Why would influential publications or star analysts be able to move prices? When is it ethical to trade on talent?

8. What is mosaic theory, and why is it important in countering accusations of insider trading?

9. If an analyst learns some nonpublic material information on a site visit to a company, should he or she trade on it?

10. Define *front running*. Explain why this practice is considered to be trading on inside information.

11. What is a Chinese wall or a firewall? Why is it important in the investment business?

12. What is pump and dump? Why does this practice work well in thinly traded markets?

13. What is late trading? What is market timing? Why would a mutual fund allow these practices in the funds it manages?

14. How are other investors hurt by late trading? Why is this unfair?

15. Suppose a mutual fund has 5 million shares with a NAV of $20 a share. After markets close, the NAV is expected to increase by 5 percent. If an investor is allowed to purchase 500,000 shares at the stale NAV of $20 in late trading, what will the per share cost be for the other investors in the fund?

CRITICAL THINKING QUESTIONS

1. Refer to Critical Thinking Question 1 in Chapter 1. Student cheating can also be thought of as unequal access to information, for example, getting the exam questions the night before the exam. Can you think of other types of cheating that also depend on information? In what ways can faculty eliminate unfair use of information in accessing student performance? What are the parallels in the unfair use of information in securities markets?

2. Refer to the discussion of Regulation FD in this chapter. Unlike equity analysts, bond analysts who work for rating agencies are not subject to Regulation FD. These analysts are paid by the corporations rating their bonds and are subject to confidentiality agreements. Should these analysts be viewed as insiders? What if an analyst did not trade a corporation's bonds but did trade the stock? Is this behavior ethical? Why or why not?

3. There are many ways investors might seek to gain an information advantage. Suppose your friend removes trash for a select number of publicly traded companies. You ask her to bring the trash to you rather than the dump site. You and your team of "researchers" regularly go through the trash (although it's a "dirty" job) and occasionally find corporate memorandums that contain material inside information. You are able to trade profitably on this information. Can the information be considered no longer proprietary once the corporate personnel has discarded it in the trash? Are the profits you make simply a normal return to your willingness to dig through garbage? Is this use of information ethical?

4. As a student, on your own, you try your hand at analyzing and picking stocks. As you are developing your skills as an analyst, you also participate in a variety of investor blogs and Internet chat rooms, sharing your opinions about various stocks. It turns out that you are more often right than wrong about your calls, and your investment acumen has not gone unnoticed. You have developed a following, and eventually your opinions are moving stock prices as soon as they are posted. Realizing this, you invest more heavily in your stocks before posting your opinions. Is this ethical? What are the issues?

5. You are working as a health-care analyst at Excellent Investment Management, LLC. A new acquaintance of yours works at Excellent Health Care, Corp. (EHCC), one of the largest health-care providers in the market. One night at a party, you overhear this acquaintance complaining about working ever-longer hours. On Monday morning you investigate EHCC's financials, and they appear solid. They even look poised for higher earnings. On a hunch, you include them in your stock recommendations to the portfolio managers. The following quarter, EHCC announces earnings that beat the consensus forecast and the stock price surges. Your boss is pleased. Soon you find yourself more interested in social acquaintances who work in the health-care industry. Finally, someone mentions that EHCC is going to acquire a smaller health-care company, Pretty Good Health Care Corp.

(PGHCC), which is publicly traded. Again, first thing Monday morning, you dig into PGHCC's financials. You even go a step further and develop a simple takeover probability model showing that PGHCC is a candidate. You show the results of your model to the portfolio manager who, because of your successful track record, takes a position in the stock. The next weekend, you run into a lawyer at another party (because you are a party animal). She says, "You work on Wall Street, right? Well, I have a tip for you: PGHCC is going to announce that it's being acquired next week. I know because I'm working on the deal. Take my advice, buy the stock!" First thing Monday morning, you tell the portfolio manager to buy more PGHCC stock. Is this ethical? What about the other trades? Why or why not? If you believe that some are ethical, where do you draw the line?

APPLIED STUDENT PROJECT: EVENT STUDY

You can do a classic event study to investigate the importance of information in trading. Select an event from Table 4.1, "Examples of Material Information," for a particular stock using a web search. Estimate a CAPM model of expected returns using 60 months' worth of data *three months before* the event. Use the beta from this regression to measure expected *daily* returns during the three months before the event. Also collect data on daily volume. You can collect data on stock prices and market indexes from various electronic sources (i.e., from www.finance.yahoo.com).

Using the model expected returns, measure the abnormal return and cumulative returns during the three months before the event. Based on your results, assess the market's reaction to the announcement as well as whether you think any leakage or information trading occurred before the official announcement. Depending on the nature of the event, speculate on what type of investors might have access to inside information and trade on it. Also speculate on what types of investors might be using superior analysis to predict the event and how they might trade to take advantage of their information. Present your analysis in a professionally written report of two to three pages.

RECOMMENDED CASES

1. Case 1—UBS and Morgan Stanley: An Elaborate Insider Trading Scheme
2. Case 2—Emulex and Mark Jakob: Market Manipulation with False Information
3. Case 10—Kellogg's "Matched" and "Washed" Trades: Tax Avoidance or Market Manipulation?
4. Case 13—Salomon Brothers and Treasuries: Cornering the Market
5. Case 15—John Mangan and Short Selling: Insider Trading
6. Case 17—Canary Capital Partners LLC: Mutual Fund Abuses
7. Case 20—The Squawk Box: Front Running
8. Case 22—Brian Hunter and Amaranth Advisors: Market Manipulation of Natural Gas?

REFERENCES AND SUGGESTED READING

Avery, Helen. "Front-Running: Is Wall Street Tipping Off HFs?" *Euromoney* (March 2007).

Block, Stanley. "Merger Arbitrage Hedge Funds." *Journal of Applied Finance* 16, no. 1 (2006): 88–96.

Bodie, Zvi, Alex Kane, and Alan J. Marcus. *Investments*, 7th ed. New York: McGraw-Hill Irwin, 2008.

CFA Institute. *Standards of Practice Handbook*, 9th ed. Charlottesville, VA: CFA Institute, 2005.

Chung, Joanna, Stacey-Marie Ishmael, and Sam Jones. "Insider Trading Net Entangles Further Suspects." *Financial Times* (November 7, 2009), 9.

Cohan, William D. *House of Cards: A Tale of Hubris and Wretched Excess on Wall Street*. New York: Doubleday, 2009.

Duhigg, Charles. "U.S. Regulator Pushes to Ban 'Flash' Trading; Technique Allows Traders to Peek at Others' Orders Before They Hit Market." *International Herald Tribune*, 6 August 2009.

Elton, Edwin J., Martin J. Gruber, Stephen J. Brown, and William N. Goetzmann. *Modern Portfolio Theory and Investment Analysis*, 7th ed. New York: Wiley, 2007.

Frankel, Tamar, and Lawrence A. Cunningham. "The Mysterious Ways of Mutual Funds: Market Timing." *Annual Review of Banking and Financial Law* 25, no. 1 (2006): 235–293.

Gillis, John G., and Glenn J. Ciotti. "Insider Trading Update." *Financial Analysts Journal* 48, no. 6 (1992): 46–51.

Hemand, Desai, Bing Liang, and Ajai K. Singh. "Do All-stars Shine? Evaluation of Analyst Recommendations." *Financial Analysts Journal* 56, no. 3 (2000): 20–29.

Jones, Charles P. *Investments: Analysis and Management*, 10th ed. Hoboken, NJ: Wiley, 2007.

Irvine, Paul, Marc Lipson, and Andy Puckett. "Tipping." *Review of Financial Studies* 20, no. 3 (2007): 741–68.

Lewis, Michael. *Liar's Poker*. New York: Penguin Books, 1989.

Moulin, Herve, and John Roemer. "Public Ownership of the External World and Private Ownership of Self." *Journal of Political Economy* 97, no. 2 (1989): 347–67.

Pu, Liu, Stanley D. Smith, and Azma A. Syed. "Stock Price Reactions to the *Wall Street Journal*'s Securities Recommendations." *Journal of Financial and Quantitative Analysis* 25, no. 3 (1990): 399–410.

Review & Outlook (Editorial). "We Were Robbed." *Wall Street Journal*, 17 November 1987, 1.

Securities and Exchange Commission. "RE John Freeman, et al." (March 14, 2000). www.sec.gov.

————. "Litigation Release No. 18169/Securities and Exchange Commission v. Martha Stewart and Peter Bacanovic." 03-CIV-4070 (NRB)(S.D.N.Y.), June 4, 2003. www.sec.gov

Sivanithy, R. "Should High-Speed Trading Be Regulated?" *Business Times Singapore*, 29 July 2009.

Statman, Meir. "Fair Trading." *Journal of Portfolio Management* 32, no. 1 (2004): 76–86.

Stewart, James B. *Den of Thieves*. Simon & Schuster Paperbacks, 1992.

Sullivan, Daniel. "Big Boys and Chinese Walls." *University of Chicago Law Review* 75, no. 1 (Winter 2008): 533–68.

Winans, R. Foster. "Let Everyone Use What Wall Street Knows." *New York Times*, 13 March 2007. www.nytimes.com.

Zuckerman, Gregory. "U.S. News: Trader Is Known for Speed, Smarts," *Wall Street Journal*, 17 October 2009, A.2.

5

Analyst Integrity

Learning Objectives

After reading this chapter, students should be able to:

- Describe the role that analysts play in an efficient market.
- Identify different conflicts and pressures that can compromise an analyst's integrity.
- Articulate the difference between buy-side and sell-side analysts.
- Recognize the pressures that investment banking relationships create for analysts.
- Have a basic understanding of how analysts do research and be familiar with different types of research: fundamental, quantitative, hybrid, and third party.

CHAPTER OUTLINE

- Introduction: Analysts and Their Ethical Obligations
- Investment Recommendations: Pickers
- Forecasters
- Buy-Side and Sell-Side Analysts: Who Pays for the Research?
- Behavioral Finance and Analyst Ethics
- Originality of Ideas
- Other Analyst Conflicts
- Conflicts with Employers
- Conclusion: Be Aware!

INTRODUCTION: ANALYSTS AND THEIR ETHICAL OBLIGATIONS

What do analysts do? Equity analysts sift through the vast amount of publicly valuable information to help investors decide which stocks to buy or sell. Bond analysts evaluate the credit risk of debt-based securities. Analysts have an ethical obligation to be *competent, diligent*, and *unbiased*. And investors have to *trust* that analysts are all three of those things when relying on their research. A *competent* analyst has the appropriate educational background and/or professional certifications—that is, CFA® (Chartered Financial Analyst). Ethical analysts not only have the right background, but they do not mislead investors about their qualifications. Suppose an analyst—let's call him Joe Analyst—claims to have been educated at Wharton, a university with a prestigious finance program. He makes this claim based on a three-day conference that he attended there. Before attending the conference, he had never taken a finance course and found much of the conference to be way over his head. Even so, he advertises his "Wharton" background on his website, where he makes stock recommendations (he earns advertising revenue from the site). His recommendations are mostly wrong, and investors who take his advice lose money. These investors are hurt by Joe's incompetence.

A *diligent* analyst is one who has done his or her homework. Investors who rely on sloppy or incomplete research will make poor decisions. For instance, Joe Analyst recommends buying Widget, Inc. stock, based on strong quarter-to-quarter revenue growth. Joe Analyst just looks at the revenue growth and doesn't do additional research to find out how the company can achieve such spectacular results. Joe simply does not want to spend the extra time. If he had dug a bit deeper into the firm's financial statements, he would have discovered that revenue growth was made possible only by incurring high marketing expenses and selling the product far below manufacturing costs. With no plan in place to get costs under control, the firm appears headed for bankruptcy. And within a year, that is exactly what happens. Investors who purchased Widget, Inc. stock on Joe's recommendation lose their money. Joe has betrayed the trust of investors that his recommendations were based on diligent research. The analyst has hurt these investors.

Investors relying on *biased* or misleading analysis can also make poor investment decisions. Suppose Joe Analyst is now both diligent and competent—he has done enough research to know that Widget, Inc.'s business model is seriously flawed. But his company, Wall Street, Inc., is courting Widget's CFO to complete an equity offering (Widget is in serious need of a cash injection because its business model "bleeds" cash). Wall Street, Inc. stands to earn large fees from the equity offering. Not only does Wall Street, Inc. want to avoid losing Widget's business by issuing a negative research report, but it wants to ensure the success of the offering by issuing a "strong buy" or "bullish" stock recommendation. Joe Analyst acquiesces to his employers' wishes. Wall Street, Inc. gets the financing deal and earns lucrative fees. But once again, and this time despite the cash infusion from the equity issuance, Widget, Inc. files for bankruptcy within a year. Investors who purchased Widget stock based on Joe's recommendations now own shares that are worthless. That analyst's biased and misleading report harmed these investors.

You may be saying to yourself, "Couldn't these investors have done their own homework and learned that Widget, Inc. did not have a viable business plan? Don't they have only themselves to blame for blindly following Joe Analyst's recommendations?" Remember (from Chapter 1) that *finance is complicated*. Not everyone has the background that allows them to understand financial statements and assess the business model and stock value for a company. This creates a demand for analysts in the first place, which is good for students of investments because it creates an industry for your services. Investors *rely* on the recommendations of analysts. Analysts who betray that trust by issuing either careless or biased reports are unethical.

In other professions—for example, auto repair, home construction and repairs, and medical care—individuals also must rely on professionals to provide expert advice as well as good and fairly priced services. If your car breaks down, you trust that your mechanic is both correctly fixing the problem and fairly charging you for parts and labor. However, unlike handling a car problem, investing in stocks involves more uncertainty about returns. The impact of investment uncertainty on being an ethical analyst is similar to its impact on other issues, such as reporting performance, fees, trading costs, and use of information in earning the excess risk-adjusted returns that we discussed in earlier chapters. Uncertainty can camouflage countless unethical behaviors in the investment profession. A client can find it difficult to determine whether an investment loss is the result of an analyst's biased and sloppy recommendation or the inherent risks of investing. Uncertainty drives a wedge between ex ante (before the fact) expectations of returns and ex post (after the fact) results. Here, uncertainty in stock prices makes the need for high ethical standards an imperative; unethical analysts can hide ex ante biased and careless analysis behind ex post poor results.

Look back at the fundamental principles of investments we established in Chapter 1. By virtue of Principles 1 and 2, analysts must be competent and diligent; they need to gather all relevant information and make sure they thoroughly understand an investment by completing a comprehensive analysis. By virtue of Principle 4, analysts must be fair in delivering analyses; that is, they cannot be biased. We can place analysts in two loosely defined categories: "pickers" and "forecasters." The importance of being competent, diligent, and unbiased is important for both of these types of analysts (see Chapter 2 for a discussion of the difference between active and passive management; active managers rely heavily on analysts' expertise to beat benchmarks). Let's briefly review the roles of each type of analyst before discussing the ethical issues for analysts in more detail.

FUNDAMENTAL PRINCIPLES OF INVESTMENT ETHICS FOR PROFESSIONALS

Principle 1: ETHICAL UNDERSTANDING

Because investments are complicated, *you have an obligation not to knowingly engage in an investment transaction that either you or others do not sufficiently understand. This includes the underlying source of returns or fees charged.*

Principle 2: ETHICAL USE OF INFORMATION

Because investments are information driven, *you have an obligation to ensure that you and others have access to relevant information and that you or others do not misuse or distort information in the investment transaction.*

Principle 3: RESPONSIBLE INVESTING

Because investments provide financial resources to others, *you have an obligation to ensure that you do not knowingly make or recommend investments that support activities that harm others.*

Principle 4: TRUST AND FAIRNESS

Because you are dealing with others' money either directly or indirectly, *you have an obligation not to abuse the trust all others have either explicitly or implicitly placed in you to treat them fairly.*

INVESTMENT RECOMMENDATIONS: PICKERS

Pickers investment professionals who make investment recommendations, buy, sell, or hold, or "pick" stocks that will be "winners" or "losers."

Pickers are analysts who compare a stock's intrinsic value to the market value and then make investment recommendations. These analysts help investors "pick" stocks that will be winners. If the intrinsic value of the security is greater than the market value, the picker issues a buy recommendation; if it is less, he or she issues a sell recommendation. When the valuation is close to the market's, a hold recommendation is issued. Analysts' recommendations take the form of grades. Table 5.1 shows the common types of grades.

Pickers also regularly change their grades, and investment services that track these grades will note whether the analysts have upgraded or downgraded the stock. Example 5.1 shows the analysts' opinions about investing in the stock of Whole Foods Markets, Inc.

As Example 5.1 shows, there is a wide difference in opinion about the merits of investing in Whole Foods Markets, Inc. Five analysts have upgraded the stock while four have downgraded it. Analysts who downgraded the stock might have been reacting to downturn in the economy and the belief that consumers would shift away from more expensive organic food to cheaper, more basic groceries.

TABLE	5.1	COMMON INVESTMENT RECOMMENDATIONS AND GRADES

Investment Grade	Definition
Positive Ratings: Buy, accumulate, long-term buy, strong buy, outperform, overweight	All these ratings suggest that investors should invest or *buy* more in the stock or *overweight* it in a portfolio, because it is expected to *outperform* the market.
Negative Ratings: Sell, strong sell, underweight, underperform	All these ratings suggest that investors should invest less or *sell* the stock or *underweight* it in a portfolio, because it is expected to *underperform* the market.
Neutral Ratings: Hold, market perform	All of these ratings suggest that if you own some of the stock you shouldn't sell it; but if you don't own it already, you shouldn't buy it either.

Analysts who upgraded the stock may have believed that the economic downturn would also influence consumer spending habits but play out for Whole Foods differently. They may have believed that consumers would shift away from more high-priced luxuries such as vacations to lower-priced luxuries such as more expensive groceries. And with aging baby boomers dominating the consumer landscape, these

EXAMPLE 5.1
ANALYSTS' INVESTMENT RECOMMENDATIONS

Analysts' opinion for Whole Foods Markets, Inc. Ticker Symbol: WFMI

Date	Research Firm	Action	From	To
11-Aug-09	Deutsche Securities	Initiated		**Hold**
5-Aug-09	Argus	Upgrade	Sell	**Hold**
1-Jun-09	RBC Capital Mkts	Upgrade	Sector Perform	**Outperform**
27-Apr-09	UBS	Downgrade	Neutral	**Sell**
3-Apr-09	Jefferies & Co	Downgrade	Buy	**Hold**
16-Mar-09	FBR Capital Markets	Upgrade	Underperform	**Mkt Perform**
19-Feb-09	Jefferies & Co	Upgrade	Hold	**Buy**
19-Feb-09	Pali Research	Upgrade	Sell	**Buy**
16-Dec-08	JP Morgan	Downgrade	Overweight	**Underweight**
24-Nov-08	William Blair	Downgrade	Outperform	**Mkt Perform**

Source: http://finance.yahoo.com/q/ao?s=WFMI+Analyst+Opinion, accessed April 20, 2010
Note: Analysts' opinions have evolved from the simple, buy, sell, and hold. Performance is now evaluated relative to the market or industry sector (outperform, perform, underperform), and analysts also recommend weights relative to market capitalization weights (equal weight, underweight, overweight).

health-conscious consumers would choose expensive organic foods. The divergence in grades reflects the inherent uncertainty in stock prices. Further, there is no *one* way to pin down intrinsic value. Let's review analysts' different approaches.

FUNDAMENTAL ANALYSTS

Fundamental analysts analysts who research companies' financial statements within an industry and look at economic trends to help forecast trends that affect the future profitability of a company.

Fundamental analysts dig through financial statements and seek to understand how a firm generates profits. Fundamental analysts also rely on industry- and economy-wide reports to help forecast trends that affect the future profitability of the company. Often analysts are experts in an industry sector, which helps the analysts learn not only about the company they are covering, but also about competitors. For example, *Morningstar*, an independent research firm, has 12 sectors:

1. Software
2. Hardware
3. Media
4. Telecommunications
5. Health care
6. Consumer services
7. Business services
8. Financial services
9. Consumer goods
10. Industrial materials
11. Energy
12. Utilities

Fundamental analysts need to have strong backgrounds in accounting and economics as well as investments.

QUANTITATIVE ANALYSTS

Quantitative analysts analysts who use statistical and mathematical techniques applied to large data sets in looking for systematic mispricing of securities.

Quantitative analysts use statistical and mathematical techniques applied to large data sets, looking for systematic mispricing of securities. Quantitative analysts often have PhDs in statistics or engineering. One goal of quantitative analysis is to remove the human judgment that plays a role in fundamental analysis. Mini Application 5.1 discusses a case where quantitative analysts got into trouble.

HYBRID ANALYSIS

Hybrid analysis the practice of using a combination of both statistical analysis and fundamental analysis.

Often analysts take a **hybrid analysis** approach. They use statistical analysis on large samples of securities to screen for different characteristics. For example, ranges of P/E ratios, market capitalizations, earnings and sales growth, and dividend yields can be used to create a smaller set of stocks for further fundamental analysis. Finally, analysts need to continually update their valuations—no matter what method they use—to take into account new information.

No one approach is more ethical than another. This in some ways makes the ethical issues involved with diligence in analysis thorny. First, it's not possible to

---

MINI APPLICATION 5.1

QUANTITATIVE ANALYSIS AND LONG TERM CAPITAL MANAGEMENT

Long Term Capital Management was one of the early hedge funds that used quantitative analysis to find mispriced securities. The firm was started in the 1990s by Wall Street professionals and academics with PhDs in finance.

The firm used statistical models to find small mispricings in the market, or arbitrage opportunities.

The firm eventually failed when its models did not take into account statistically unexpected events and as the heads of the firm, in retrospect, became heady with their success and used too much leverage to take positions in the market. Does this sound reminiscent of the financial crisis of 2008?

No matter what type of analyst you become, remember not to let success go to your head!

---

prespecify the correct model for determining intrinsic value. If it were, there would be no reason to find undervalued securities and search for alpha, the excess risk-adjusted return (see Chapter 4). Second, because of volatility in stock prices, it can be difficult to fully assess diligence ex post. If an analyst makes the wrong call, is this due to a lack of diligence or to the inherent uncertainty in stock prices? It's hard to chase a moving target. Even the best analysts are likely to be wrong at least some of the time.

FORECASTERS

Forecasters analysts who forecast earnings.

Forecasters are another type of analyst. They forecast quarterly and annual earnings along with other accounting components of earnings, for example, sales. Earnings are important in assessing the "true" value of a security. Recall that in a basic stock price model, the true price would be considered to be discounted future earnings per share (EPS)—as EPS changes, so does price. To help refresh your memory, let's look at the following model:

$$P_{0,i} = E(\text{EPS}_{1,i})/E(R_i) + \text{PVGO}$$

where

$$P_{0,i} = \text{price today of security } i$$
$$E(\text{EPS}_{1,i}) = \text{Expected earnings per share in the next period}$$
$$E(R_i) = \text{Expected risk-adjusted return of security } i$$
$$\text{PVGO} = \text{present value of growth opportunities created by}$$
management taking +NPV projects (recall from your introductory finance course, that +NPV projects are those that earn returns higher than the cost of capital)

Present value of growth opportunities (PVGO) this is present value of all positive net present projects (those that earn a return higher than the cost of capital) that is reflected in the stock price today.

You can see that as the forecasted EPS on the right-hand side of the equation increases, the price on the left-hand side of the equation also increases. Thus forecasting earnings is important to forecasting prices and, in turn, to making investment recommendations. Firms issue earnings results quarterly in 8-K filings and annually in 10-K filings made with the SEC (see Chapter 1). Let's review some basics of forecasting.

Quarterly forecasts are based on seasonality in earnings. For example, retail firms that have fiscal year-ends in December often record their best earnings in the fourth quarter because of holiday shopping. Analysts would begin their forecasts with earnings from the fourth quarter from the *prior* year. Further understanding about the company's business model, along with additional information from company, competitive forces, and overall economic conditions, would modify these forecasts. Forecasts are made both long term and short term. Analysts revise their forecasts as new and relevant information is released before the release of final earnings numbers. Analysts can forecast different types of earnings: earnings before or after extraordinary items, earnings on continuing operations or including discontinued operations, basic (just shares outstanding,) or fully diluted (assuming all options are exercised and convertible securities are converted).

FORECAST ERRORS

Forecast errors the difference between actual earnings and forecasted earnings.

When earnings are released, they can be better or worse than expected. The differences between actual earnings and expected earnings are known as **forecast errors**. If analysts are *really* good at forecasting, then forecast errors would be zero. However, because we don't expect analysts to forecast *perfectly* (the inherent uncertainty in stock prices means uncertainty in earnings as well), forecast errors are standardized by an error term. These are known as **standardized unexpected earnings surprises** (SUES). Expected earnings can be generated from different types of models. A simple one is a time series model in which forecasted earnings are based on the earnings in the same quarter of the previous year plus a trend or "drift" term. Other models might be based on the consensus of analysts' forecasts. The difference between the actual results and earnings forecasted by the model is the "surprise." The surprise is then standardized by the standard deviation of the error term in the predictive model (we don't expect earnings to be *exactly* what is predicted). Finally, EPS forecasts and errors are scaled by stock price. A one-cent error means more when the stock price is $5 than when it is $200 per share. Several factors can influence the amount of "noise," or fluctuations, in earnings forecast models. Market capitalization, extent of analyst following, industry, and firm age are just a few factors that can affect earnings' volatility.

Standardized unexpected earnings surprises (SUES) the difference between actual and forecasted earnings divided by a standard error term from the forecasting model.

Standardized means that the forecast error is divided by the standard deviation of the error term from the model. A SUES of two or more means roughly that the surprise was two standard deviations greater than what we would expect, given a natural amount of noise in earnings from period to period. Recall that in a normal distribution, 2 standard deviations plus or minus the mean accounts for 95 percent of all outcomes (see the appendix in Chapter 3 if you need a refresher). So something outside this range is pretty unexpected, or statistically significant. A significant increase (or decrease) in earnings means that the company is doing better (or worse) than forecasted. It could also mean that management is manipulating earnings and

EXAMPLE 5.2

COMMON CALCULATION OF QUARTERLY SUES

$$E(\text{QEPS}_{i,t}) = \text{QEPS}_{i,t-4} + \delta_i$$

where δ_i is the estimated "drift" term.

The SUE for firm i in quarter t is then calculated as follows:

$$\text{SUE}_{i,q} = [\text{QEPS}_{i,t} - E(\text{QEPS}_{i,t})]/\sigma$$

where σ is the standard deviation of the forecast error.

The model would be estimated using historical data. For example:

$$\text{Fourth-quarter EPS} = \text{Previous year's fourth-quarter EPS} + \text{Drift}$$

The drift term is $0.05. This means that fourth-quarter EPS year-over-year growth is at about 5 cents. The previous year's fourth-quarter EPS is $0.32. Then

$$E(\text{EPS}) = \$0.32 + 0.05 = \$0.38$$

And suppose the standard deviation of the forecast error is 0.10.

If actual earnings are $0.40, then the SUES is $(0.40 - 0.38)/0.10 = 0.20$, or 0.20 standard deviations from an expected mean of 0 (zero means the forecast is dead on and there is no error).

certainly is something that a good analyst needs to be aware of. Ethical accounting practices are the subject of Chapter 6. Example 5.2 takes you through the steps of calculating a SUES.

Putting aside the consideration that management might be engaging in some funny business with earnings, for the most part, earnings *do* indicate that something has changed in the firm's underlying economic fortunes. As a result, the stock market reacts in systematic ways to these SUESs. When SUES are positive (or negative), the stock market reaction is positive (or negative) on the magnitude of 2 to 3 percent (or negative 2 to 3 percent) above (or below) the risk-adjusted return. A 2 to 3 percent return earned over a *few days* of earnings announcements is significant given that the typical return on the S&P 500 earned over *a year* is about 12 to 14 percent. Figure 5.1 shows how a SUES might affect stock price.

REPORTING SERVICES

Several services report earnings forecasts. Institutional Brokers' Estimate System (I/B/E/S), Zack's, Standard & Poor's (S&P), and First Call are some well-known services that report analysts' forecasts. With quarterly forecasts, analysts are routinely held to the test every three months as their forecasts are compared with actual results. Example 5.3 shows how well analysts did for Whole Foods in late 2009.

Biased forecast occurs when an earnings forecast systematically inflates the earnings upward or downward.

Ethical forecasts are both unbiased and accurate. **Biased forecasts** are those that either artificially inflate or underestimate earnings. Bias is important because it can cause market prices to deviate from true values. Intentional bias is a form

FIGURE 5.1 HOW A SUES MIGHT WORK

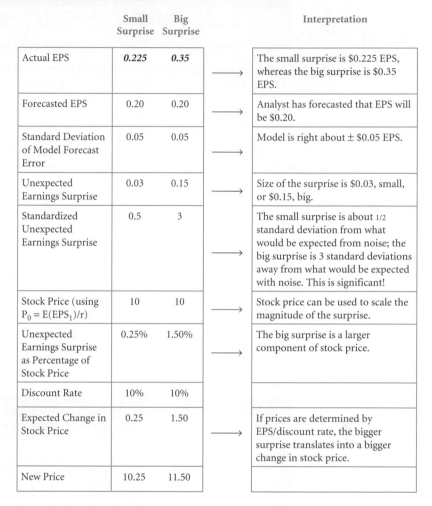

	Small Surprise	Big Surprise		Interpretation
Actual EPS	*0.225*	*0.35*	⟶	The small surprise is $0.225 EPS, whereas the big surprise is $0.35 EPS.
Forecasted EPS	0.20	0.20	⟶	Analyst has forecasted that EPS will be $0.20.
Standard Deviation of Model Forecast Error	0.05	0.05	⟶	Model is right about ± $0.05 EPS.
Unexpected Earnings Surprise	0.03	0.15	⟶	Size of the surprise is $0.03, small, or $0.15, big.
Standardized Unexpected Earnings Surprise	0.5	3	⟶	The small surprise is about 1/2 standard deviation from what would be expected from noise; the big surprise is 3 standard deviations away from what would be expected with noise. This is significant!
Stock Price (using $P_0 = E(EPS_1)/r$)	10	10	⟶	Stock price can be used to scale the magnitude of the surprise.
Unexpected Earnings Surprise as Percentage of Stock Price	0.25%	1.50%	⟶	The big surprise is a larger component of stock price.
Discount Rate	10%	10%		
Expected Change in Stock Price	0.25	1.50	⟶	If prices are determined by EPS/discount rate, the bigger surprise translates into a bigger change in stock price.
New Price	10.25	11.50		

of market manipulation (see Chapter 4). Overly optimistic earnings forecasts can cause investors to buy stocks and push prices upward. Pessimistic forecasts can cause selling and price declines. Bias is measured by both the sign and the magnitude of the forecast errors.

Earnings accuracy a measure of how accurate forecasted earnings are relative to actual reported earnings.

Earnings accuracy is measured by looking at the absolute value of the magnitude of deviation between the analysts' forecast and the actual earnings numbers. Thus the accuracy number is just like the bias number without the sign. Example 5.4 demonstrates how to calculate accuracy and bias. Analysts have an ethical duty to provide meaningful forecasts and not just noise. Research has shown that, on average, analysts' forecast errors are about 2 percent of stock price measured about 10 days before the forecast is released (remember that the forecast itself can affect stock

EXAMPLE 5.3
ANALYSTS' EARNINGS FORECASTS

Analysts' Forecasts for Whole Foods Markets, Inc. Ticker Symbol: WFMI

Earnings History	Mar 09	Jun 09	Sep 09	Dec 09
EPS Est	0.18	0.20	0.18	0.26
EPS Actual	0.19	0.25	0.20	0.32
Difference	0.01	0.05	0.02	0.06
Surprise %	5.60%	25.00%	11.10%	23.10%

Earnings Est	Current Qtr. Mar 10	Next Qtr. Jun 10	Current Year Sep 10	Next Year Sep 11
Avg. Estimate	0	0	1	1
No. of Analysts	17	16	19	18
Low Estimate	0	0	1	1
High Estimate	0	0	1	2
Year Ago EPS	0	0	1	1

Source: http://finance.yahoo.com/q/ae?s=WFMI+Analyst+Estimates, accessed April 20, 2010.

EXAMPLE 5.4
ACCURACY AND BIAS

Stock Price 10 Days Prior ($)	Actual EPS	Forecasted EPS	Forecast Error	Error as a Percentage of Stock Price
50	0.33	0.36	−0.03	−0.06%
55	0.34	0.36	−0.02	−0.04%
54	0.32	0.31	0.01	0.02%
57	0.33	0.37	−0.04	−0.07%
			Average Bias	**−0.04%**
			Accuracy	**0.04%**

price). Analysts who have forecast errors that are consistently greater than those of their peers should work harder, or find another profession!

Researchers have also found that, on average, analysts have a positive bias. Estimates suggest that about 60 to 85 percent of forecasts have a positive bias. Now let's delve deeper into the possible reasons for this bias.

BUY-SIDE AND SELL-SIDE ANALYSTS: WHO PAYS FOR THE RESEARCH?

Buy-side analysts describes analysts who provide their recommendations to portfolio managers.

Sell-side analysts describes analysts who work for companies with investment banking business.

Analysts often face conflicts between their obligation to be independent and the pressure to create revenue streams out of which they are paid. There are two sides to the investment management business—the buy side and the sell side. The buy side makes investments and manages portfolios for institutional clients (e.g., public pension funds), retail investors (e.g., mutual funds), and wealthy individuals. **Buy-side analysts** provide their recommendations to portfolio managers. Their research pays for itself when portfolio managers profitably trade on it.

The sell side of the investment business provides investment banking and brokerage services. Investment banking clients are typically corporations that are seeking to raise capital by selling securities. Hence the term *sell side*. A **sell-side analysts** works for a sell-side firm. Unlike buy-side, sell-side analysis is not used internally to generate profitable picks for the firm's portfolio managers. What is analysis used for, and who pays for it? Sell-side firms disseminate their analysts' research to institutional and retail investors. The wide distribution of this research throughout the market effectively makes it public. Once the analysis is public, its informational value for trading mispriced securities declines. Consequently, investors do not pay for the full cost of generating this research.

There are two indirect sources of revenue for sell-side research. First, the public posting of the analyst's recommendations and forecasts can increase interest and trading volume of the security. Increased trading volume means increased brokerage commissions for the sell-side firm. Second, the agreement to provide analysts following, or "coverage," for a firms' stock can help secure investment banking business, particularly for clients doing an initial public offering (IPO). An IPO is available when a private firm goes public for the first time by offering securities to the investing public. The issuer stock is listed on an exchange, such as the New York Stock Exchange. Firms enlist the help of investment bankers to navigate them through the process. Investment banks charge high fees for this service. Firms value coverage because it can generate interest in their securities and in turn increase order flow and liquidity. Positive coverage (i.e., buy recommendations), can increase stock price.

Investment banking relations create inherent conflicts with sell-side analysts. Investment banking clients want favorable investment recommendations for their securities. They can implicitly threaten to withhold investment banking business when coverage fails to be positive. Because sell-side firms cannot charge for the full cost of producing the research, investment banking business becomes a valuable source of income and can compromise the independence of the research.

The Internet and telecom boom of the late 1990s was marked by a period of many new and quickly growing firms. These firms needed financing, which investment bankers were only too happy to provide. Investment bankers sought to keep IPO clients happy so that they could win add-on deals with additional issuances of stock or debt placements for these fast-growing and cash-hungry firms. These clients had the potential to create a steady stream of lucrative banking fees. One way to keep them satisfied was to provide positive coverage by analysts. The Enron case illustrates the pressures analysts faced during this period. Enron was a fast-growing energy company that disappeared in an explosion of scandals in 2001. Before Enron's bankruptcy, John Olson, an energy analyst with Merrill Lynch, downgraded Enron. Enron executives threatened to exclude Merrill from a $750 million stock offering because of the downgrade. Two Merrill Lynch investment bankers eager to win Enron's business urged Merrill's president to replace Olson. Olson was fired and replaced with Donato Eassey, who quickly upgraded Enron. Merrill Lynch got the Enron business. Some firms threaten to withdraw not only potential investment banking business but also the management of employee 401(k) accounts, unless analysts provide positive coverage.

Analysts can also face direct pressure from the management of the firms they cover. One incident involves Digital River, Inc., a company that provides e-commerce solutions. The CEO sent a bullying e-mail message to an analyst who had expressed negative views: "I expect we'll be seeing you in the papers under the heading 'white collar criminal.'" Another incident involves Overstock.com, an Internet retailer. The firm filed a lawsuit against an independent research firm, Gradient Analytics, alleging that the analysts conspired with a short seller to drive down the stock price. However, Overstock had consistently missed earnings estimates.

The crash of the Internet and telecom bubble in the early 2000s revealed not only massive accounting fraud at several firms but also the duplicity of analysts that followed these companies and recommended their stock to investors. In 2003 Eliot Spitzer, attorney general for New York State, won a $1.4 billion settlement as well as new procedures from ten Wall Street firms to ensure independence of research. Investment firms responded by erecting a Chinese wall or firewall (see Chapter 4) between analysts and bankers. Contact between these two groups is limited, and analysts' compensation is not tied to investment banking revenues. A firm is required to disclose investment banking relationships with the issuers its analysts cover. An ethical analyst should vet a firm's policies with respect to ensuring that banking business doesn't compromise analysts' independence. You don't want to find yourself in a situation where your boss is asking you to compromise your integrity. A biased report can hurt your professional reputation.

Analysts can also outright sell their recommendations to firms. Here an analyst may fraudulently convey that she is independent, but in fact is paid by the firms she covers. An early case occurred in 1998. Barrow Street was a company that produced an investor newsletter with investment recommendations. It advertised itself as an independent research firm. However, it routinely received cash from issuers in exchange for stock recommendations on its website. The SEC obtained imposed an injunction and fine on Barrow Street. Another case occurred during 2002. Dutton Associates was a business that published paid-for stock analysis reports for issuers. However, the company did not disclose this to potential investors. Management stated that "anyone" could enroll a company for research coverage for a payment of $25,000 per year and that Dutton's reports were performed on behalf of the public and were not a service to any company. This was false. Of course, only the issuers were the "anyone's" who were willing to pay the fee of $25,000 a year to have coverage provided on their stock. The SEC put Dutton out of business.

Behavioral Finance and Analyst Ethics

Behavioral finance an area of finance that seeks to explain the behavior of markets via psychological principles.

Behavioral finance is a relatively new area of finance that integrates concepts of psychology with traditional ideas of economic rationality when describing market and investor behavior. It is important for ethical analysts to be aware of behavioral pitfalls that can lead them to make irrational judgments. Investors rely on professionals to be rational. When professionals succumb to cognitive biases and market psychology they can hurt investors, even though they may not intend to. The following sections discuss some of the ways these behaviors can conflict with analysts' ethical obligations.

STAR ANALYSTS: OVERCONFIDENCE AND REGRET AVERSION

Star analysts analysts who are top rated by various financial publications and have the ability to move stock prices with their investment recommendations.

In counterbalancing pressures from investment bankers and issuers, analysts also have incentives to be both accurate and unbiased (i.e., right more often than not), so that their skills as pickers and forecasters warrant generous compensation. Like professional athletes, rock stars, and movie stars, analysts can develop a reputation for having unique and valuable talents. Different publications rate analysts. *Morningstar*, *Institutional Investor*, *StarMine*, the *Dow Jones*, the *Wall Street Journal*, and *Zack's*, among others, all provide ratings. Analysts are rated by EPS accuracy and investment recommendations. The top-rated analysts are known as **star analysts**. What makes an analyst a star? He or she "gets it right" more often than not. After a while, the market begins to realize that star analysts' ratings provide valuable information, and stock prices react to their ratings. Meredith Adler is an example of a star analyst. As of early 2008, she was rated a star analyst by *StarMine*, in the Food & Staples Retailing Industry. Adler's recommendations earned an industry excess return of 5.7 percent (see www.finance.yahoo.com).

Overconfidence having an irrational belief in one's self and one's ability to make superior investment recommendations or earnings forecasts; displaying hubris, or arrogance.

Regret aversion taking actions to avoid losses or making mistakes.

All analysts want to be stars. In addition to higher compensation, there is professional recognition. The drive to "be right" makes analysts susceptible to hubris. Recall from Chapter 1 that hubris is **overconfidence** in oneself, or arrogance. Analysts may want to believe that the stocks they follow are from "good" companies. They can overestimate earnings—not intentionally, but because of their own cognitive biases. Researchers have also found that analysts are reluctant to change their ratings. No one likes to admit they were wrong; they have what behavioral economists characterize as **regret aversion**. Ethical analysts need to be aware that personal biases should not enter into their work. In Chapter 1, arrogance is defined as one motivation for unethical behavior. The investment industry attracts smart people. Smart people like to be right. Ethical analysts are aware that they can succumb to hubris. They question themselves and seek others to critique their work. High-quality investment research firms scrutinize their analysts' work via teams or investment committees.

What is the role of the analyst in an efficient market? This depends on the ability to be better than the market in either assessing price or forecasting earnings. If an analyst is good at either of these tasks, his analysis is valuable and can move prices. Before becoming public, the analysis is insider information. Star analysts who trade ahead of public dissemination of their forecasts or recommendations, or let others do so, are engaging in insider trading (see Chapter 4). It is extremely difficult to determine whether an analyst is tipping someone off about an impending research report. Diligent analysts talk to all sorts of market participants as part of their research and formulation of their recommendations. In 2003 the SEC began investigating Holly Becker, at the time a star analyst for Internet retail stocks at Lehman Brothers (now defunct), and her husband, Michael Zimmerman, a hedge fund trader formerly at Omega Advisors and then SAC Capital. Because Becker was a star analyst, her research reports affected the prices of stocks she wrote about. The SEC investigated whether Zimmerman was able to profit by having Becker's research reports in advance. The SEC dropped the investigation. Whether the SEC can make a case is unimportant to the ethical analyst. An ethical analyst knows when he or she has crossed the line from gathering market sentiment to tipping off a colleague.

HERDING: THE INFLUENCE OF OTHER ANALYSTS

Herding occurs when people "flock" together and mimic each others' behavior.

Herding occurs when people flock together and mimic each others' behavior. It is a natural human instinct to find safety in numbers. But is it ethical? Analysts herd when they coalesce around similar investment recommendations or earnings forecasts. Remember that investment is naturally a business fraught with uncertainty (see Chapter 1). Analysts can be reluctant to make a call that is out of step with other analysts, even if they have a strong conviction and reasonable basis for their call. What if they are wrong? Analysts have career concerns. Often analysts' performance is judged relative to other analysts. If you are wrong, it's not so bad if others are wrong as well. But if you are wrong and others are right, the consequences can be more severe. Researchers have found that older analysts are more willing to make their forecasts or recommendations ahead of other analysts. They are also more consistent than younger analysts. Older and more experienced analysts may have more conviction in their opinions and/or feel more secure in expressing them. Younger analysts have a longer career ahead of them and more to lose if they go out on the wrong limb.

All analysts, regardless of age, can be unsure of their own research. They can use the recommendations of other analysts to confirm or reject their results. As part of their research process, they also might use other analysts' recommendations as an additional source of information. Remember that these analysts, by virtue of their talent, can possess valuable private information. Herding because there is safety in numbers is different from using other analysts' research as an input in the research process.

Herding can also reflect a prevailing market sentiment. It is often said that markets are ruled by either greed or fear; they are either bullish or bearish. Again, given the uncertainty in future prices, analysts often can get caught up in the groupthink that sometimes characterizes markets. The telecom bubble of the 1990s exposed many analysts who were bullish on stocks with spectacular growth in revenues, but little or no earnings, who continued to be so despite no improvements in performance. The most recent financial crisis of 2008 reflects analysts who as a group believed housing prices could continue to increase at unprecedented growth rates despite growing evidence that aggregate personal income couldn't sustain such high rates. You may be someone who will join the ranks of young analysts. Make sure you can fully justify your forecasts and recommendations. Test your ideas with more experienced analysts. Do not just go with the crowd. You have a greater obligation to investors.

OTHER BEHAVIORAL PITFALLS

Anchoring occurs when analysts hold on to a past reference point, even though there is no longer any rational basis for that point.

Ethical analysts need to be wary of other behavioral pitfalls, all of which evolve out of shortcuts to careful and rational analysis. It may be part of human nature, not poor intentions, to take shortcuts; nonetheless, they can hurt investors who rely on the careful research of analysts well schooled in rational economic theory. Behavioral traps can be avoided as long as analysts remember their obligation to be diligent. One such trap is **anchoring**. Anchoring occurs when analysts hold onto a past reference point, even though there is no longer any rational basis for that point. For example, suppose the price of a stock has fallen dramatically from its previous high. Some analysts might recommend a buy simply because the stock appears to be so cheap *compared to its past high*. But the past higher price may no longer make sense for the stock, given the *new* information. In fact, given the new information, even at the lower price, the stock might be overvalued by the market. Diligent and ethical analysts continually update their stock recommendations and earnings forecasts based on new information, even if that information conflicts with their experience.

Overreaction an exaggerated reaction to an event; stock price that moves either too high or too low in response to new information.

A behavior related to anchoring is **overreaction**. Here an analyst overreacts to either good news or bad news. For example, a firm announces better-than-expected earnings for the quarter. The analyst overreacts and projects that the higher earnings will not only persist into the future, but are the harbinger for even higher earnings. It could be that the increase in earnings is only a one-time event. Again, a diligent analyst carefully assesses the good news and rationally adjusts his or her recommendations.

Heuristics rules of thumb.

A final ethical trap for analysts is the use of **heuristics,** or rules of thumb. The problem with using heuristics is that it applies general notions to specific situations without accounting for important differences between the two. For example, suppose that on average the P/E ratio for health-care stocks is 8. An analyst uses this average as a rule of thumb in picking which health-care stocks to recommend as a buy; health-care stocks with lower P/Es are considered undervalued by the market. This rule might work well for some stocks with low P/E ratios. But further research might show that for some stocks, a lower P/E ratio is warranted because of poor prospects for earnings growth. See Mini Application 5.2 for another example. This doesn't

---

MINI APPLICATION 5.2

TEST YOURSELF

Suppose you are an analyst who follows the stock of Fix It Up, Inc., a home improvement company. The average P/E ratio for both the stock and the industry has been around 20. The firm announces higher earnings but the stock price doesn't move, driving its P/E ratio downward to below both the industry average and the stock's historical average. You are considering changing your rating from a sell to a buy. Can you list all the cognitive biases that you might be susceptible to in thinking you should change your rating before doing any further research?

mean that an ethical analyst abandons rules of thumb completely. Rules of thumb can be useful in providing a stepping-off point for further research, for example, the quantitative screens discussed earlier in the chapter. But an ethical analyst does not solely rely on heuristics and completes the necessary additional research before making recommendations.

ORIGINALITY OF IDEAS

Besides providing unbiased research, analysts also have an ethical duty not to plagiarize others' research. Lazy or incompetent analysts can be tempted to look over someone else's shoulder for the "answer." Remember that good ideas help identify mispriced securities and create alpha, a measure of additional return beyond that which compensates for risk (see Chapter 4). Generation of alpha is the name of the game in investments. Ideas that generate profits in investment management research are considered proprietary.

Third-party research original research that can be purchased from companies such as Standard & Poor's, Bloomberg, or Dow Jones.

As we have discussed, analysts can also avail themselves of **third-party research**. Third-party research is that provided by brokerage houses (see the discussion of soft dollars in Chapter 2) or independent analysts. Sources of research need to be acknowledged. Purchased research also has the potential to be either biased or sloppy. Analysts also need to understand the source of data in third-party research, how different measures are calculated, and any assumptions used.

OTHER ANALYST CONFLICTS

Investment banking relationships are a major source of conflict for sell-side analysts. But analysts face a multitude of other conflicts as well. Analysts can encounter ownership conflicts. If they or the company they work for own stock of a company they are covering, they can be tempted to bias their forecasts upward. Analysts often serve on boards as directors. If they cover the stock for the same firm, they can face conflicts. They can receive stock as part of their compensation as a director. Stock ownership creates the usual conflicts: analysts may be tempted to provide a positive recommendation as loyalty to the company and its shareholders. A negative recommendation is not likely to get the analyst reappointed to the board. Ethical analysts will try to avoid situations where there may be conflict; but if they can't, they will disclose all ownership and other potential conflicts. This at least allows investors the opportunity to take the recommendations with a grain of salt.

Finally, analysts must be careful that their forecasts are not based on material, nonpublic information. Buy-side analysts can use this information to improve their investment recommendations and portfolio performance (see Chapter 4). Sell-side analysts can use insider information to improve the perception of their abilities. Further, sell-side analysts may have access to insider information from the investment banking division of their firms. They can learn about impending mergers, acquisitions, capital changes, and so on that can have a significant impact on stock price. Firms often have a firewall between the investment banking and their analysts to prevent the exchange of material insider information (see Chapter 4).

CONFLICTS WITH EMPLOYERS

Analysts have an ethical duty to their employers as well as to investors. For a buy-side firm, the assets of the firm are clients and proprietary research. If analysts take either, they are stealing the firms' assets. Of course, firms can't erase the memory and skills that analysts have acquired while employed at the firm. However, analysts can't download computer programs and client lists before leaving to join another firm or start up their own. Firms take stealing their assets—client lists and investment process—seriously. In May 2006, Robert W. Baird & Co. sued three former employees who left to form Red Granite LLC. Baird alleged the founders took information about Baird's investment performance, confidential client facts, or trade secrets. Subsequently both parties settled out of court.

FIGURE	5.2	ANALYSTS ARE SUBJECT TO MANY PRESSURES AND CONFLICTS

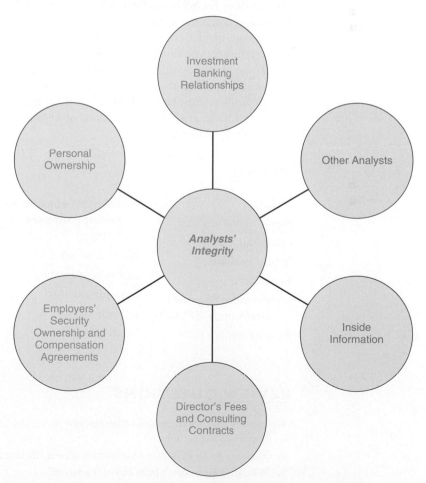

Firms that have proprietary quantitative research models often employ different analysts who use or "see" different parts of the model. This makes it more difficult for analysts to steal the model when they leave the firm. Only the principals have access to or see the entire model. The principals of the firm are those individuals who have ownership interests. They know that if they reveal the secrets of their research methods, their ownership interest will fall significantly in value.

CONCLUSION: BE AWARE!

Analysts are subject to all sorts of pressures—from their employers, issuers, investors, and peers. Employers can pressure analysts to change negative recommendations to positive ones to help solicit and keep investment banking clients. Issuers can threaten analysts who provide less-than-glowing forecasts or recommendations. Investors can pressure for recommendations from star analysts ahead of the market. Peer evaluation can cause analysts to use insider information in their analysis or change their recommendations because it feels safer to follow the crowd. Figure 5.2 shows all the pressures you can face as an analyst.

These pressures do not come with large signs attached to them. As an analyst, you need to be diligent and independent. Diligence is based on education and hard work. Conflicts must be disclosed to investors. But analysts also need to be aware of conflicts. Ethical analysts are conscious of hidden pressures as a means of keeping their professional integrity.

TERMS

pickers

fundamental analysts

quantitative analysts

hybrid analysis

forecasters

present value of growth
opportunities (PVGO)

forecast errors

standardized unexpected
earnings surprises
(SUES)

biased forecast

earnings accuracy

buy-side analysts

sell-side analysts

behavioral finance

star analysts

overconfidence

regret aversion

herding

anchoring

overreaction

heuristics

third-party research

REVIEW QUESTIONS

1. Identify three characteristics that describe an ethical analyst, and explain why they are important to investors.
2. Explain why analysts play an important role in efficient markets.
3. Who pays for research from buy-side analysts?

4. Who pays for research from sell-side analysts?

5. How can firms minimize pressures from investment banking relationships?

6. Besides investment banking relationships, list at least three other sources of potential conflicts that can compromise an analyst's independence.

7. Explain forecast bias and accuracy.

8. Describe the general process for forecasting quarterly earnings.

9. Explain how hubris can cause a positive bias in analysts' earnings forecasts.

10. What is a star analyst? What are the incentives for becoming a star analyst?

11. Define *herding*.

12. Identify the reasons that analysts might follow other analysts' recommendations and forecasts.

13. What is the difference between fundamental and quantitative research?

14. What conflicts do analysts have with their employers?

15. Why is plagiarism considered a particularly unethical analyst practice?

CRITICAL THINKING QUESTIONS

1. You are a sell-side analyst for a large firm. You are one of a team of three analysts who follow stocks in the consumer discretionary sector. Your team comes to a consensus before changing a rating on any stock. All three of you are evaluated on how often your team makes the right calls. You are in your fourth quarter, and so far your team has not had much luck. You and your colleagues are facing the prospect of a poor bonus. You know that one of your team members was counting on a good bonus to help pay for medical costs for a sick family member. One of your team members suggests changing the rating on Mediocre, Inc. from sell to a strong buy. Your colleague provides a rationale, but you feel it is weak. The third team member goes along with the recommendation, and your team changes its rating. In the following week, Market Dominator Corp. announces a takeover bid for Mediocre and its stock goes soaring. You know that Market Dominator is an investment banking client of the firm. You strongly suspect that your colleague somehow got wind of the takeover bid from the investment banking division. What should you do?

2. You are a small cap equity analyst following the stock of ABC Corporation. ABC announces its fourth-quarter earnings, and they have beat the consensus forecast by a considerable margin. Analysts begin posting revisions in their forecasts for the next year. Your boss is pressuring you to post your forecasts soon, so that the firm and its investors aren't left behind. You usually use both a model and further fundamental analysis when making changes to your forecasts. But because of the pressure you are under, you simply update the inputs into your model and post the output as your new earnings forecasts. Is this ethical? Why or why not?

3. Describe the circumstances under which it would be both ethical and rational to use other analysts' earnings forecasts and ratings in developing your own forecasts and ratings. Under what circumstances would it be unethical? How can you tell the difference between the two?

4. Suppose you are a buy-side analyst for a firm that actively manages different equity funds for individuals who have high net worth. Your firm has a lot of discretion in making investment decisions. Your boss, who also happens to be a portfolio manager, has taken a heavy sector bet by overweighting on stocks of financial service firms—largely based

on your analysis, because you are responsible for covering financial service firms. The stocks of these companies rose after the firm made its initial investment, but now they are declining. Your current analysis suggests that no recovery is in sight. On Monday, there is a firm meeting with analysts, portfolio managers, and the chief investment officer. Your boss comes to you the Friday before and subtly pressures you to tilt your analysis so that the firm will maintain its position. Your boss is hoping that these stocks will rebound and that her year-end performance will not suffer from a realized loss. What will you say in the meeting?

5. Some professionals have claimed that prohibitions against downloading and taking models or client lists to another firm or to start your own firm are not enforceable and therefore don't need to be adhered to. Remember that firms can't prevent you from taking any knowledge you gained while working for them; they can't "zap" your brain and erase your memory as you walk out the door. So, for example, if you remember the size of a client's account and his phone number, there is nothing wrong in soliciting this client after you start at your new firm (providing you aren't breaking any legally enforceable contract agreements). So why is it unethical to download this information into a computer and take it with you?

APPLIED STUDENT PROJECT: EARNINGS FORECASTS AND INVESTMENT RECOMMENDATIONS

You can create your own forecasts and stock recommendations as well as evaluate other analysts' research (www.finance.yahoo.com is one source for these data). Select a stock and collect both earnings forecasts and investment recommendations from different analysts. Evaluate each analyst's recommendations, and select the analyst you believe has the most accurate forecast. Create your own earnings forecasts using a time series model like the one described in this chapter if you have access to sufficient data. Otherwise, you can look at year-to-year trends in quarterly earnings. You can also develop your own valuation of a stock's intrinsic value by using any of the analytic approaches described in the chapter. Finally, revise the analysts' forecasts and recommendations throughout the class as new information is made available to the market. You should assess your own diligence and behavioral biases. For example, did you succumb to hubris?

RECOMMENDED CASES

1. Case 1—UBS and Morgan Stanley: An Elaborate Insider Trading Scheme
2. Case 6—Charles Hintz and Sanford Bernstein: Analysts' Conflicts with Personal Holdings
3. Case 11—Qwest Communications International: Accounting Fraud and Overstated Revenues
4. Case 14—Merrill Lynch and the Internet Boom: Analysts' Conflicts
5. Case 24—Morgan Stanley: Analyst's Coverage and Investment Banking Business
6. Case 19—WorldCom: Capitalizing Operating Expenses; an Unethical Accounting Practice
7. Case 26—Enron: A Case of Extreme Hubris

REFERENCES AND SUGGESTED READING

Abarbanell, Jeffrey S. "Do Analysts' Earnings Forecasts Incorporate Information in Prior Stock Price Changes?" *Journal of Accounting and Economics* 14 (1991): 147–65.

Agrawal, Anup, and Mark A. Chen. "Do Analyst Conflicts Matter? Evidence from Stock Recommendations." *Journal of Law and Economics* 51, no. 3 (2008): 503–37.

Alpert, Bill. "Tainted Good." *Barron's*, May 5, 2003, 12.

Bajari, Patrick, and John Krainer. "An Empirical Model of Stock Analysts' Recommendations: Market Fundamentals, Conflicts of Interest, and Peer Effects." NBER Working Paper Series, *National Bureau of Economic Research*, August 2004.

Barber, B., R. Lehavey, M. McNichols, and B. Trueman. "Reassessing the Returns to Analysts' Stock Recommendations." *Financial Analysts Journal* 59, no. 2 (2003): 88–96.

——————. "Can Investors Profit from the Prophets? Security Analyst Recommendations and Stock Returns." *Journal of Finance* 56 (2001): 531–63.

Bernard, V., and J. Thomas. "Post Earnings Announcement Drift: Delayed Price Response or Risk Premium?" *Journal of Accounting Research* 27 (1989, Supplement): 1–36.

——————. "Evidence that Stock Prices Do Not Fully Reflect the Implications of Current Earnings for Future Earnings." *Journal of Accounting and Economics* 13 (1990): 305–40.

Bliss, Richard T., and Mark Potter. "Corporate Decision-Making and Behavioral Finance." *Corporate Finance Review* 7, no. 6 (2003): 5–15.

Cohan, William D. *House of Cards: A Tale of Hubris and Wretched Excess on Wall Street*. New York: Doubleday, 2009.

Conrad, Jennifer, Bradford Cornell, Wayne R. Landsman, and Brian R. Roundtree. "How Do Analysts Recommendations Respond to Major News?" *Journal of Financial and Quantitative Analysis* 41, no. 1 (2006): 25–49.

Craig, Susanne. "The Breakup: When Brokerage Houses Attack; Suit by the 'Other' Purcell's Firm Shows What Wall Street Will Do to Keep Clients from Defecting." *Wall Street Journal*, 10 November 2006, C1.

——————. "U.S. Won't Charge Ex-Lehman Analyst, Spouse." *Wall Street Journal*, 11 October 2004, C4.

Dechow, Patricia, Amy Hutton, and Richard Sloan. "The Relation between Analysts' Forecasts of Long-Term Earnings Growth and Stock Price Performance Following Equity Offerings." *Contemporary Accounting Research* 17 (2000): 1–32.

Der Hovanesian, Mara. "How the Independents Fared." *Business Week*, July 25, 2004, 74.

Desai, Hemang, Biang Liang, and Ajai K. Singh. "Do All-Stars Shine? Evaluation of Analyst Recommendations." *Financial Analysts Journal* 56, no. 3 (2000): 20–29.

Francis, Jennifer, Qi Chen, Donna R. Philbrick, and Richard H. Willis. *Security Analysts Independence*. Charlottesville, VA: CFA Institute, 2004.

Frolet, Huber. "Behavioral Finance—Theory and Practical Application." *Business Economics* 36, no. 3 (2001): 63–69.

Goedhart, Marc H., Timothy M. Koller, and David Wessels. "What Really Drives the Market?" *MIT Sloan Management Review* 47, no. 1 (Fall 2005): 21–24.

Groysber, Boris, Paul Healy, and Craig Chapman. "Buy-Side vs. Sell-Side Analysts' Earnings Forecasts." *Financial Analysts Journal* 64, no. 4 (2008): 35–39.

Hong, Harrison, and Jeffrey D. Kubik. "Analyzing the Analysts: Career Concerns and Biased Earnings Forecasts." *Journal of Finance* 58, no. 1 (2003): 313–51.

Lerman, Alina, Joshua Livnat, and Richard R. Mendenhall. "Double Surprise into Higher Future Returns." *Financial Analysts Journal* 63, no. 4 (2007): 63–71.

Lim, Terence. "Rationality and Analysts' Forecast Bias." *Journal of Finance* LVI, no.1 (2001): 369–85.

Lin, H., and M. McNichols. "Underwriting Relationships, Analysts' Earnings Forecasts, and Investment Recommendations." *Journal of Accounting and Economics* 25 (1998): 1–34.

Lowentstein, Roger. *When Genius Failed*. New York: Random House, 2000.

McLean, Bethany. "The Real Culprit in the Analyst Scandal." *Fortune*, January 9, 2006. www.cnn.money.com.

Morgan, Mary. "How the Rankings Are Compiled." *Financial Times*, 15 May 2008, 8.

Nichols, Craig, D., and James M. Wahlen. "How Do Earnings Numbers Relate to Stock Returns? A Review of Classic Accounting Research with Updated Evidence." *Accounting Horizons* 18, no. 4: 263–86.

Pretzuk, Charles. "Blodget Pays Out Dollars 4m and Gets Life Ban." *Financial Times*, London (UK), 29 April 2003, 33.

Rizzi, Joseph V. "Behavioral Basis of the Financial Crisis." *Journal of Applied Finance* 18, no. 2 (2008): 84–96.

Securities and Exchange Commission. *Securities and Exchange Commission v. John D. Attalienti and Barrow Street Research, Inc.* Release No. 15957, October 27, 1998. www.sec.gov.

_____. *In the Matter of John M. Dutton*. Release No. 8524, January 19, 2005. www.sec.gov.

Spiegel, Peter. "Analyst Removal 'Linked to Enron Deal,'" *Financial Times*, 30 July 2002, 6.

Welch, Ivo. "Herding Among Security Analysts." *Journal of Financial Economics* 58, no. 3 (2000): 369–96.

Womack, K. "Do Brokerage Analyst Recommendations Have Investment Value?" *Journal of Finance* 51, no. 1 (1996): 137–67.

Investing in Companies with Ethical Accounting Practices

Learning Objectives

After reading this chapter, students should be able to:

- Describe how accrual accounting can create opportunities for unethical distortion of performance.
- Measure accruals.
- Differentiate between discretionary and nondiscretionary accruals.
- Discuss some of the incentives that managers have to manipulate earnings.
- Explain some of the common methods used to inflate earnings.
- Detect earnings management using several common methods.
- Understand the role ethical analysts play in detecting accounting distortions in protecting investors.

CHAPTER OUTLINE

- Introduction: Reported Accounting Performance—Healthy Cynicism
- The Source of Accounting Distortions: Accruals
- Discretionary and Nondiscretionary Accruals
- Managers' Incentives to Manage Earnings
- Cookie Jar Reserves and Big Baths
- Aggressive Revenue Recognition

- Special-Purpose Entities and Hidden Debt

- Quality of Earnings

- Earnings Smoothing: Is It Ethical?

- Conclusion: Cash versus Accruals—Be Skeptical!

INTRODUCTION: REPORTED ACCOUNTING PERFORMANCE—HEALTHY CYNICISM

Accounting is a system that provides financial information about a firm through the vehicles of the balance sheet, the statement of cash flows, and the income statement. Financial information is important for investors; they use this information to forecast future earnings, cash flows, and stock prices (see Chapter 5). Because the market relies on accounting information, it needs to be both accurate and unbiased. Ethical managers and accountants will ensure that it is. Investment analysts cannot be naïve. Managers *do* have incentives to report biased or inaccurate performance. Ethical analysts are cognizant of these incentives and can untangle true economic performance from possibly manipulated or distorted numbers. This chapter alerts aspiring analysts to unethical accounting practices.

Which of our four fundamental principles of investment ethics apply in this chapter (see Chapter 1)? Well. . .*all* of them. Investors *trust* that analysts fully *understand* the *information* contained in financial statements and that they do not recommend investments in firms where accounting fraud and mismanagement could potentially *hurt others*, costing investors and creditors millions and employees jobs when poor performance becomes unmasked, stock price crashes, and the firm files for bankruptcy. Admittedly, this is an extreme scenario, but you get the idea. Unmasked poor performance can be a bombshell to those who were fooled into believing everything was fine.

A bombshell was dropped in the recent financial crisis of 2008. When house prices and the stock market crashed, millions of people were hurt when they lost their homes through foreclosures, were laid off, and saw their stock-based savings disappear. Many parties who helped perpetuate the housing and stock market bubble held a short-run interest in the series of transactions that built the bubble. Mortgage origination brokers earned fees for mortgages they turned around and sold to investment banks, which created debt securities. Investment banks in turn earned fees when they were sold. Rating agencies earned fees from investment banks that paid to have debt securities sold. Many earned lucrative fees but had no long-run interests in these loans and securities. No one said, "Stop, something is not right!" (see "House of Cards," www.cnbc.com/id/28892719).

Accounting a system that provides financial information about a firm through the vehicles of the balance sheet, the statement of cash flows, and the income statement.

FUNDAMENTAL PRINCIPLES OF INVESTMENT ETHICS FOR PROFESSIONALS

Principle 1: ETHICAL UNDERSTANDING

Because investments are complicated, *you have an obligation not to knowingly engage in an investment transaction that either you or others do not sufficiently understand. This includes knowing the underlying source of returns or fees charged.*

Principle 2: ETHICAL USE OF INFORMATION

Because investments are information driven, *you have an obligation to ensure that you and others have access to relevant information and that you or others do not misuse or distort information in the investment transaction.*

Principle 3: RESPONSIBLE INVESTING

Because investments provide financial resources to others, *you have an obligation to ensure that you do not knowingly make or recommend investments that support activities that harm others.*

Principle 4: TRUST AND FAIRNESS

Because you are dealing with others' money either directly or indirectly, *you have an obligation not to abuse the trust that all others have either explicitly or implicitly placed in you to treat them fairly.*

How does this relate to ethics and accounting information? Managers can also have relatively short-run interests in inflating accounting earnings. CEOs typically are closer to the end of their careers than the beginning. Unethical managers can hope to keep earnings propped up just long enough to earn bonuses, cash out options, and the like. When they are gone, someone else can take the blame and deal with the mess that's left. What is your ethical obligation? You can be the one who says, "Stop, something is not right!" This chapter gives you the tools for spotting dubious accounting earnings and for protecting investors and others who can be hurt when the house of cards comes tumbling down.

How can managers inflate earnings and not be thrown in jail? Managers and accountants have discretion over accounting methods used to report performance. Generally accepted accounting principles (GAAP), applied correctly and ethically, should eliminate major differences between reported accounting income and true, underlying, economic income. Absent outright fraud, in the *long run* there are no gains to choosing one accounting method over another to inflate earnings. Differences in accounting methods can cause differences in the *timing* of revenue and expense accruals over time, but not in the *total* amount accrued (see the appendix at the end of this chapter). And the total amount accrued should reflect the economic substance of the transaction—earning revenues, incurring expenses, and investing in capital.

However, the accounting system has many moving parts. There is a multitude of accounting choices to be made over a multitude of transactions. Further, GAAP is not a specific set of rules, but principles that are applied and thus rely on the ethical interpretation and judgment of managers and their accountants. We need to look closer at how management can manipulate earnings as we develop a healthy suspicion of reported performance. Before we start, if you need a refresher on accounting basics, please review the appendix to this chapter.

THE SOURCE OF ACCOUNTING DISTORTIONS: ACCRUALS

Accruals accounting measure created to adjust for a mismatch between when the economic substance of the transaction has occurred and is recorded and when the cash changes hands.

Net income reported accounting earnings of a company or entity.

Accruals provide the means to distort earnings either within the confines of GAAP or fraudulently. Accruals are created when the revenues and expenses that generate income are not wholly cash. **Accruals** represent the reporting of amounts that have been accrued (hence the term)—revenues that have been earned and expenses that are incurred—but that have not been turned into cash on the balance sheet but do not show up on the income statement. Reported **net income** consists of both cash income and income that has accrued. Accounts receivables (noncash or credit sales) minus accounts payables (noncash or expenses not yet paid for) represents income, but not *cash* income. Because firms don't operate solely on a cash basis, all firms will always have a certain level of accruals as a product of GAAP.

$$\text{Net Income} = \text{Cash} + \text{Total Accruals}$$

Because net income consists of both cash income and accruals, increases in accruals can cause increases in income. Eventually these accruals should turn into cash, so they can provide investors with valuable information about the firm's *future* cash flows. Sometimes, however, accruals do *not* turn into cash. An unethical manager can use accruals to hide his inability to generate cash income for his shareholders. How can an analyst determine when accrual use is unethical?

Let's look at what's in the accrual portion of net income a little more closely. We can measure total accruals by either what is known as the balance sheet method or the cash-flow method.

Balance sheet method of measuring accruals the use of changes in various balance sheet amounts to measure the accrual component of net income.

Cash-flow method of measuring accruals the use of operating cash flows to measure the accrual component of net income.

Balance Sheet Method of Measuring Accruals:

$$\text{Total accruals} = [\Delta\text{Current assets} - \Delta\text{Cash}] - [\Delta\text{Current liabilities}]$$
$$- \text{Depreciation and amortization}$$

Cash-Flow Method of Measuring Accruals:

$$\text{Total accruals} = \text{Earnings before extraordinary items and}$$
$$\text{discontinued operations} - \text{Operating cash flow}$$
$$+ \text{Depreciation and amortization}$$

The cash-flow method measures the difference between reported income (adding back depreciation and amortization) and operating cash flow. Let's look a little closer at the balance sheet method for measuring accruals. This can give us some added insight into how managers might manipulate accounting income.

Revenues that are not cash based are accounts receivables and are included in current assets along with inventory, prepaid expenses, and other current assets. Because cash is also included in current assets, we want to net that item out. Offsetting noncash revenues are noncash expenses. Noncash expenses that are incurred but not yet paid are accounts payable and are included in current liabilities. Why do we look at changes in these amounts? Remember that net income is a "flow" measure—unlike the balance sheet, which is a "stock" measure. Thus looking at changes in balance sheet items turns these stock measures into flow measures. For example, suppose most sales were credit sales. Then the year-to-year change in accounts receivable would give us a good chunk of the amount of sales earned for the year to use in computing net income. Finally, depreciation and amortization expenses are always noncash items and deducted from net income.

Accruals are created by the choice of accounting methods that determine when revenue and expenses can be recognized. Accelerating revenue and/or delaying expense recognition can increase reported earnings. Auditors with management determine whether methods used to recognize noncash revenues and expenses are consistent with GAAP. Because there is discretion in applying GAAP principles, conflicts of interest can lead to unethical reporting where the limits of GAAP are strained (see Mini Application 6.1 for some common ways this is done).

Managers who test the limits of GAAP run the risk of a Securities and Exchange Commission (SEC) investigation into their reporting practices. An investigation can lead to restatements and penalties. It also hurts the firm's stock price. In 2005, the SEC investigated accounting practices at the Dana Corporation, an auto-parts supplier.

MINI APPLICATION 6.1

TEST YOURSELF

Below are some common methods of increasing earnings. Go through the list and see if you can briefly describe why each method increases earnings, violates GAAP, and is unethical.

- Recording revenue when future goods and services remain to be provided.
- Recording revenue when the customer is not obligated to pay.
- Recording revenues to affiliated third parties.
- Recording a one-time gain by selling assets with "low" book value.
- Delaying the recording of operating expenses by improperly capitalizing them.
- Amortizing expenses over "too long" a time period.
- Using "too low" an amount for uncollectible receivables.
- Delaying the recognition of impaired assets.
- Failing to recognize future liabilities.
- Reducing liabilities by changing accounting assumptions.
- Using mergers and acquisitions to hide re-valuation of assets and reserve pools.

Source: Howard Schilit, *Financial Shenanigans: How to Detect Accounting Gimmicks & Fraud in Financial Reports* (New York: McGraw-Hill, 2002).

During the prior year, Dana violated GAAP by using the combination of improper revenue recognition and failure to record expenses to increase reported earnings by 74 percent. When the fraud was revealed, stock price fell by over 50 percent. Ethical analysts need to steer clear of firms that are potentially SEC targets.

Accruals also provide an opportunity to either legally, but unethically, inflate earnings or to engage in outright fraud. Fictitious sales can be hidden in accounts receivable, or managers can prematurely recognize revenue before it is truly earned. Pushing current costs into future liability accounts can hide them. The accrual system accommodates a delay between the recording of these sales and expenses and the cash flows associated with them. Thus for a short period of time, fraud or a decline in earnings can go undetected. However, eventually accounts must turn over into cash earned by investors. When the cash dries up, the fraud or manipulation is exposed.

Firms often engage in earnings manipulation when performance has stalled. In the 1990s many firms that rode up the telecom and Internet bubble became mired in accounting fraud when they could no longer sustain high growth and continue to beat Wall Street's earnings expectations. WorldCom and Enron are the most infamous cases from that time (see Chapter 9). Thus analysts need to make sure they don't get too enthralled with a stock (see Chapter 5 and the discussion on hubris). Analysts who carefully scrutinize accounting practices will avoid the trap of recommending a once high-flying stock that becomes full of hot air.

DISCRETIONARY AND NONDISCRETIONARY ACCRUALS

Accruals are a natural part of the accounting system. When do accruals indicate that management is unethically attempting to cover up the true earnings performance? To answer this question, we need to understand how "normal" accruals are generated.

Accruals can increase as a firm grows. For example, as a firm sells more of its product or service and increases its profit margin, noncash working capital may increase because both accounts receivable and inventory net of current liabilities will grow. Offsetting the increase in the accruals is the addition of property, plant, and equipment (PP&E). These additions can increase depreciation and amortization expenses. Increases in depreciation and amortization expenses, in turn, are subtracted from accruals. Example 6.1 shows how accruals fluctuate with changes in revenues and PP&E.

Though we often think of accruals as positive, they can also be negative. Depreciation and amortization expense are noncash accruals that decrease net income. If a firm has a high level of PP&E, then depreciation expense will also be high, causing total accruals to be negative. This is perfectly normal for these types of firms (see Example 6.2).

Let's look at another example. Example 6.3 is a modification of Example 6.1. Here we have the same net income, revenues, and PP&E. What's different? We take some of the increases in cash and make them increases in current assets. How could this occur? A simple explanation could be relaxing credit terms for customers, causing accounts receivable to increase. Perhaps some of these accounts receivable should

EXAMPLE 6.1
ACCRUALS FLUCTUATE WITH CHANGES IN REVENUES AND PROPERTY, PLANT, AND EQUIPMENT

Test Yourself:
Do you get these numbers with the balance sheet method?

Fiscal Year End	Δ CA	Δ Cash	Δ CL	Depreciation & Amortization Expense	Total Accruals	NET INCOME	PP&E	Δ Revenues
12/31/2000	150	40	80	10	20	120	100	700
12/31/2001	170	50	95	12	13	130	130	950
12/31/2002	165	45	90	14	16	125	150	875

EXAMPLE 6.2
FIRMS WITH HIGH DEPRECIATION AND AMORTIZATION EXPENSE CAN HAVE NEGATIVE ACCRUALS

Test Yourself:
Do you get these numbers with the balance sheet method?

Fiscal Year End	Δ CA	Δ Cash	Δ CL	Depreciation & Amortization Expense	Total Accruals	NET INCOME	PP&E	Δ Revenues
12/31/2000	150	40	80	50	−20	120	500	700
12/31/2001	170	50	95	62	−37	130	600	950
12/31/2002	165	45	90	70	−40	125	750	875

be deemed uncollectible and written off. Maybe management is becoming more aggressive in recognizing sales. Despite changes in cash sales, net income remains the same. Thus the increase in total accruals suggests the manipulation of earnings to cover up a decline in sales. This is unethical. Good analysts spot this type of manipulation and steer clear of recommending the stock of these firms.

EXAMPLE 6.3

FIRM HAS HIGHER ACCRUALS INDICATING EARNINGS MANIPULATION

Test Yourself:
Do you get these numbers
with the balance sheet
method?

Fiscal Year End	Δ CA	Δ Cash	Δ CL	Depreciation & Amortization Expense	Total Accruals	NET INCOME	PP&E	Δ Revenues
12/31/2000	170	20	80	10	60	120	100	700
12/31/2001	195	25	95	12	63	130	130	950
12/31/2002	185	25	90	14	56	125	150	875

Normal accruals or **nondiscretionary accruals** or **expected accruals** accruals that occur due to past choices of accounting method coupled with the underlying economic activity of the firm and not due to the discretion of management.

How can we tell how much of the accruals number is from manipulation? We separate accruals into a "normal" and "abnormal" component. **Normal accruals** can be considered **nondiscretionary accruals**. In other words, these accruals occur because of past choices of accounting method coupled with the underlying economic activity of the firm. Management can't change these if they tried (absent fraud, of course). Some accruals are discretionary. These accruals occur because of new choices in accounting methods. For example, managers can choose either the LIFO ("last in, first out") or FIFO ("first in, first out") method to account for inventory. Suppose managers decide to switch from LIFO to FIFO. If costs are rising, the FIFO method will decrease reported cost of goods sold and increase reported earnings. Discretionary changes in accruals are also independent of the underlying economic activity. Unethical managers will turn discretionary accounting choices into opportunities to distort earnings.

If analysts can pin down a model for the normal or **expected accrual** generating process, they can measure how actual accruals deviate and, in turn, measure abnormal or unexpected accruals. This is the same idea as models of expected risk-adjusted returns and abnormal returns (see Chapters 3 and 4). Unexpected accruals are also known as **discretionary accruals** or **unexpected accruals**. These are accruals that may indicate management has manipulated earnings.

Discretionary accruals or **unexpected accruals** accounting accruals that occur because of the accounting choices made by management.

Researchers have proposed and tested a variety of models that best describe the normal accrual generating process. Analysts may not always develop a formal model based on historical data, but only look at year-to-year changes in accruals. Yet formal models can help frame the analysis of these changes. A model can help benchmark a company's normal accruals to the way the company has generated accruals in the past, or the way that other companies within the same industry generate accruals,

Jones (1991) model a widely known model of expected or normal accruals developed by Jennifer J. Jones and reported in an 1991 article in *Journal of Accounting Research*.

or some combination of the two. The **Jones (1991) model** is one that is widely known. This model includes changes in revenues and PP&E as independent variables that drive the level of normal accruals. As revenues increase, credit sales/accounts receivable and inventory are likely to increase under the firm's current accounting practices. The change is then "normal" and doesn't indicate manipulation. PP&E is included because it drives the level of depreciation and amortization expense. More property means more assets to depreciate. Finally, all of the variables are scaled by the beginning period of total assets. Total accrual is a dollar amount. Bigger firms have higher net income and higher total accruals. The total assets value controls for the size of the firm; as the firm grows, the total amount of accruals also grows. The specification for the Jones (1991) model is as follows:

Model of Expected Accruals:

$$TA_{i,t}/A_{i,t-1} = \alpha_1(1/A_{i,t-1}) + \alpha_2(\Delta REV_{i,t}/A_{i,t-1})$$
$$+ \alpha_3(PPE_{i,t}/A_{i,t-1}) + \varepsilon_{i,t}$$

where

$\quad A_{i,t-1} =$ total assets of firm i at the end of year $t-1$

$\quad \Delta REV_{i,t} =$ change in revenues for firm i from $t-1$ to t

$\quad PPE_{i,t} =$ gross property plant and equipment of firm i at the end of year t

$\quad \alpha_1, \alpha_2, \alpha_3 =$ firm-specific parameters

$\quad \varepsilon_{i,t} =$ error term for firm i in year t

Unexpected accruals = Actual accruals − Expected accruals:

$$UA_{i,p} = TA_{i,p}/A_{i,p-1} - [a_1(1/A_{i,p-1}) - a_2((\Delta REV_{i,p})/A_{i,p-1})$$
$$- a_3(PPE_{i,p}/A_{i,p-1})]$$

where

$\quad UA_{i,p} =$ unexpected accruals for firm i, in hypothesized manipulation year p

$\quad a_1, a_2, a_3 =$ estimated firm-specific parameters from the expected accruals model

The model is estimated using historical data that describe the normal accrual generating process for the firm given its size, recent changes in revenues, and PP&E. For example, the model might predict an expected accrual of *minus* $0.04 per asset dollar because revenues are declining. But actual accruals from reported earnings are only *minus* $0.01. This means there is an unexpected accrual of *positive* $0.03, indicating that management *may* be manipulating earnings upward to hide the slowdown. We say "may" because the change in accruals can mean that the underlying accrual generating process is changing as the underlying economic activity of the firm is changing. It's just that the historical data used to estimate the model is stale, not necessarily that management is fooling around with the numbers. A diligent analyst assesses an abnormal accrual in the context of other information about the firm's business model and industry. A diligent analyst also digs deeper to assess management's propensity to manipulate. To learn how to do this, read on.

MANAGERS' INCENTIVES TO MANAGE EARNINGS

Self-reversing when an accrual amount accrues more revenue (less expense) earlier it must accrue less revenue (more expense) later so that the total amount accrued doesn't exceed the total amount of the transaction.

Diligent analysts should interpret unexpected accruals in the context of management's incentives to manipulate earnings. Why does it matter? It could be that the firm's performance is, in fact, improving and investors should hold onto the stock. If management is manipulating earnings via discretionary accruals, then eventually, using accruals as a strategy to mask poor performance will run out of steam. Why? Because accruals are **self-reversing**, which means that an accounting method that accrues more revenue (less expense) earlier must accrue less revenue (more expense) later so that the total amount accrued doesn't exceed the total amount of the transaction (see the appendix to this chapter). Accrual manipulation will widen the gap between cash and net income. Accrued income is not cash income that can be used to pay creditors, suppliers, and employees. When the jig is up, stock prices will decline and the analyst who recommended the stock will lose the trust of investors.

Accounting-based bonus schemes create the most clear-cut incentives to manipulate earnings. If earnings increase, the bonus does as well, and more money goes into the managers' pockets. Managers also have stock-based incentive compensation, for example, stock awards and stock options (see Chapter 7). Stock-based compensation gives managers incentives to provide positive information to the stock market. Managers can give their stock price a boost by beating analysts' earnings expectations.

Managers also have incentives to manipulate accounting information to provide favorable terms in accounting-based contracts and transactions. Here are some examples:

- *Debt contracts.* When accounting ratios violate debt covenants, the firm is in default and debt holders have the upper hand. This can create difficulties for managers because they must acquiesce to the terms dictated by the debt holders. In the worst case, managers can lose their jobs. If managers suspect that they are close to contractual limits, they have incentives to manipulate earnings away from these limits.

- *Union contracts.* Higher earnings can serve as the basis for unions to demand higher wage concessions. Managers have incentives to manipulate earnings downward before entering union renegotiations so they can avoid making these concessions.

- *Buyout transactions.* Managers can have incentives to manipulate earnings downward before making an offer to buy out the public shareholders of the firm in order to take the firm private. Lower earnings can help justify a lower buyout premium.

An ethical analyst is mindful of all these scenarios when using earnings to make forecasts and investment recommendations. If you think management is likely to have incentives to manipulate earnings, besides dissecting accruals, you also need to be familiar with other accounting red flags to help you confirm or alleviate your suspicions. We turn to these next.

COOKIE JAR RESERVES AND BIG BATHS

One controversial accounting practice is the use of reserve accounts. Reserve accounts recognize future liabilities. On the one hand, these accounts are consistent with GAAP. Expenses should be recognized and recorded as soon as management is aware of them. On the other hand, they provide opportunities to manipulate earnings. Need lower expenses this period? Just reach into the cookie jar of reserves!

COOKIE JAR RESERVES

Cookie jar reserves reserve accounts created in anticipation of future liabilities and/or expenses.

How do these **cookie jar reserves** work? They are often created along with mergers and acquisitions or restructuring plans. For example, suppose a company plans to lay off 10,000 employees. After estimating severance pay and other costs associated with the restructuring, management creates a $1 million reserve account reflecting future liability. As it turns out, only 5,000 employees need to be let go. The actual costs are $500,000. The firm has to reverse the original charge, reducing future expenses and improving net income. Mergers and acquisitions create similar opportunities. Reserve accounts may be created to pay lawyers, accountants, and investment bankers down the road. If the actual amount turns out to be less, then future earnings are increased. Figure 6.1 shows how reserves can be used to change reported net income. In addition, reserve accounts or one-time charge-offs are taken after operating income. The assumption is that analysts will focus only on the operating income and ignore below-the-line nonrecurring charges. You of course, as an ethical analyst, know better.

Callaway Golf Company illustrates the misuse of a liability reserve account. Callaway got in a dispute with its auditor about the way it changed its estimate for a reserve account for future payments for warranties on its golf clubs. Callaway decided it overestimated the future liability of the warranties by about $17 million and went about reversing the charge. Management decided to reverse the liability by reducing selling expenses and increasing net revenues, which in turn increased gross margin and net income. The auditor believed that the liability should have been reversed as

| FIGURE | 6.1 | **HOW COOKIE JAR RESERVES ARE USED TO INCREASE NET INCOME** |

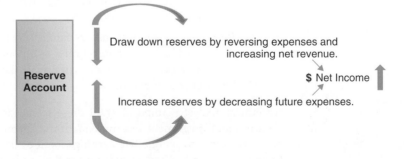

an accounting error and *prior* income should be restated. Current income should be left alone. Pulling the $17 million out of the liability reserve cookie jar *increased* net income by 19 percent. Without the reversal, net income would have *declined* by 10 percent. The use of the reserve masked poor performance.

BIG BATHS

Big bath occurs when firms make large write-downs or charge-offs to earnings.

Mergers and acquisitions also provide opportunities for managers to take a big bath. Here, managers write down assets to reflect impairment of value (usually impaired by the other management team). Inventory that is written down creates lower cost of goods sold in the future as it moves from the inventory account on the balance sheet to the income statement. Lower cost of goods sold means higher net income.

AGGRESSIVE REVENUE RECOGNITION

Channel stuffing practice whereby managers ship products they know will be returned so that they can book revenues.

Another way that managers make the numbers look better is by recognizing revenue before it is truly earned. One common method is known as channel stuffing. Managers ship products to distributors who can return unsold merchandise for full credit. In trying to make their numbers, managers knowingly ship product that will be returned in the next period. When the product is shipped, they book the revenue, thus making the firm look like it is doing better than it really is. Unethical.

Our golfing buddies at Callaway again provide an example. In a press release on March 29, 2001 the company announced that it would retroactively comply with SEC Staff Accounting Bulletin No. 101 ("SAB 101"). This bulletin directed companies to recognize revenue only when items were delivered, not just shipped. By *retroactively* complying with the SEC directive, Callaway took revenues out of the prior quarter's earnings (when they were shipped at an earlier date) and put them into the current quarter's earnings (the later date when they were delivered). This change allowed them to announce that earnings per share (EPS) had increased.

The SEC's investigation into Xerox illustrates another way firms can get too aggressive in reporting revenue. Xerox sold copiers and provided long-term service contracts with the sales of the machines. Machines were sold with financial leases. Under GAAP, the service revenue should have been recognized *over the life* of the lease. From 1997 through 2000, Xerox booked *all* the service revenue *at the time of the contract*. The accounting gimmick increased net income by about 30 percent. Furthermore, the accounting treatment of the service leases was not disclosed in footnotes or elsewhere in the financial statements, thus making it even more difficult for investors to figure out what the company was up to. In these cases, year-to-year comparisons of sales and service lease revenue may have indicated a change in treatment and raised a red flag. In 2002 the SEC imposed an unprecedented $10 million penalty on Xerox.

Special-Purpose Entities and Hidden Debt

Special-purpose entity (SPE) research and other products and services that are paid using trading commissions.

Firms also try to get debt off their balance sheets to make their financial shape look better than it is. One way is to set up a **special-purpose entity** (SPE), a subsidiary firm that is created for a specific project. The subsidiary can issue the debt, rather than the parent. As long as the parent's ownership in the subsidiary is less than 50 percent, the subsidiaries' financial statements are not consolidated with the parent's. Cash can be funneled back to the parent through its ownership interest. A SPE in effect takes debt off the parent's balance sheet and improves the firm's reported cash position. Figure 6.2 shows how SPEs work.

Enron (see Chapters 1, 5, and 9) once again provides the most egregious case of the misuse of SPEs. Andy Fastow, Enron's CFO, created a complex web of hundreds of SPEs known as "raptors" that allowed Enron to hide debt and Fastow to profit via his ownership interests in the SPEs. Enron used its own stock for capital investment in the SPEs (which turned out to be worthless). The profits of the SPEs were created through fictitious sales of assets (a Nigerian barge was bought and sold back to one SPE by an investment bank that had no business reason to buy the barge but did have an interest in the SPE and Enron's banking business) and increases in Enron's stock. While Fastow gave himself an ownership interest ostensibly (he was the third party) to avoid consolidation of the SPEs with Enron's financial statements, he in effect used his interest to funnel cash into his own pockets. It was not an arm's-length transaction. Fastow's boldness in proposing and running these SPEs is a good example of how arrogance can lead to unethical behavior (see Chapter 1).

Items such as the treatment of warranty liabilities and SPEs should be disclosed in footnotes to the financial statements. Analysts need to make sure they pay attention to footnotes. But in the case of Enron, even disclosure in a footnote would not have helped. Analysts have an ethical duty to ensure they understand where the numbers come from and how the company is able to make money before making a recommendation. Many analysts recommended Enron stock on the prior price

| FIGURE | 6.2 | **A SPECIAL-PURPOSE ENTITY CAN HIDE DEBT** |

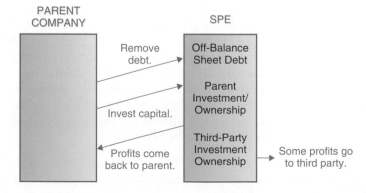

performance and the increase in EPS alone without fully understanding Enron's business model. These analysts betrayed the trust of investors who relied on their recommendations. When Enron collapsed, these investors were hurt.

QUALITY OF EARNINGS

Earnings informativeness the ability of earnings to convey information about the true economic profitability of a firm.

Earnings quality how informative earnings are.

Earnings persistence how long earnings are expected to persist in the future.

Accruals and other accounting practices can also make it more difficult for the market to ferret out the true earnings of a firm. The ability of earnings to convey information about the true profitability of the firm is called **earnings informativeness**. Earnings that either *normally* have higher levels of accruals or more one-time charges or gains are less informative. Earnings that are less informative are said to be of lower **earnings quality**. Analysts also need to be aware of the overall quality of the earnings they look at as well as the period-to-period changes that might indicate manipulation.

Related to earnings informativeness is **earnings persistence**. Earnings persistence measures how long earnings are expected to persist in the future. Earnings are more likely to be persistent when they are driven by sustainable sales growth and cost-cutting measures versus a one-time increase. Firms with higher-quality earnings have earnings changes that persist.

How do we measure earnings informativeness? We can look at how stock prices react to unexpected earnings. Remember that in an efficient market, stock prices react to information. If the unexpected earnings are positive and large *and* the market believes that this earning change is expected to last, the stock price reaction will be substantial. Here an earnings change provides a lot of information about future earnings to the market. Alternatively, suppose that the market discounts the same unexpected earnings number and underreacts. The market finds it difficult to evaluate the earnings and believes that the earnings are more likely to be transient (i.e., a one-shot deal).

THE EARNINGS RESPONSE COEFFICIENT

Earnings response coefficient (ERC) the estimate of regression coefficient between the unexpected stock price reaction to the earnings surprise.

We can look over time at how the market views a firm's earnings announcements. The **earnings response coefficient (ERC)** is the estimate of regression coefficient between the unexpected stock price reaction and the earnings surprise. The ERC is the estimated alpha in the regression: unexpected stock price reaction $= \alpha_i$(unexpected earnings).

The higher the number, the more information is conveyed by unexpected earnings and the more the change in earnings is expected to persist into the future. Analysts can estimate ERCs using historical data. This calculation can be a valuable tool for assessing a firm's earnings quality. Example 6.4 shows that the ERC captures how much of the earnings change the market believes is permanent; the higher the ERC, the higher the belief.

THE BENEISH (1999) MODEL

Beneish (1999) model a model developed by Messod D. Beneish to detect accounting earnings manipulation.

Other models can be used to capture earnings quality. A common one is the **Beneish (1999) model**. The components of the model try to detect a slowdown in sales and increases in expenses that may not be apparent by looking at earnings alone.

	EXAMPLE 6.4		
	DIFFERENT ERCS REFLECT DIFFERENT MARKET BELIEFS ABOUT EARNINGS CHANGES		
	Market Believes that *All* of Earnings Change Is Permanent	Market Believes that *Half* of Earnings Change Is Permanent	Market Believes that *Only 10%* of Earnings Change Is Permanent
Unexpected Earnings Surprise (EPS $)	0.03	0.03	0.03
Change in Future Expected Earnings (Δ EPS)	0.03	0.015	0.003
Discount Rate, r	10%	10%	10%
$\Delta P = \Delta$ EPS/r	0.3	0.15	0.03
Unexpected Change in Price ($)	0.3	0.15	0.03
ERC	10	5	1

Beneish includes measures that indicate accruals are becoming a larger portion of net income. For example, the Change in Days Receivable Index shows that receivables are growing relative to sales, suggesting that more generous credit terms are given to improve sales. Beneish also includes measures that are consistent with managements' incentives to manipulate earnings. For instance, managers are more likely to be tempted to manipulate earnings when earnings growth is slowing down. The Gross Margin Index captures whether margins and profitability are shrinking over time. Table 6.1 provides the complete list of accounting measures used in the model to signal earnings manipulation. The Beneish model also conveys the importance of carefully examining year-to-year changes in a firm's results. Changes can signal manipulation.

EARNINGS SMOOTHING: IS IT ETHICAL?

Earnings smoothing managing earnings via discretionary accruals to eliminate period-to-period volatility.

Some have argued that managers manipulate or manage earnings not to distort, but to "smooth" them. That is, they attempt to eliminate the natural volatility in earnings. Managers engage in **earnings smoothing** when they increase (or decrease) discretionary earnings to make up for a decrease (or increase) in income.

Is there any justification for smoothing? Remember that reporting earnings is how managers convey to the market information about the future prospects of the firm. If earnings are volatile, stock prices can become volatile in return. Higher volatility can increase the risk of the stock and in turn impose a cost on a firm's shareholders. Further, if earnings flip-flop, the market might view them as a noisy

TABLE	6.1	BENEISH (1999) ACCOUNTING MEASURES OF EARNINGS MANIPULATION

Accounting Measure	Likelihood of Earnings Management
Change in Days Receivables Index $$= \frac{\text{Receivables}_t/\text{Sales}_t}{\text{Receivables}_{t-1}/\text{Sales}_{t-1}}$$	Increase suggests revenue inflation.
Gross Margin Index $$= \frac{(\text{Sales}_{t-1} - \text{COGS}_{t-1})/\text{Sales}_{t-1}}{(\text{Sales}_t - \text{COGS}_t)/\text{Sales}_t}$$	Index greater than one suggests that gross margins are deteriorating, thus increasing propensity to manipulate earnings.
Asset Quality Index $$= \frac{(1 - \text{Current assets}_t + \text{PP\&E}_t)/\text{Total assets}_t}{(1 - \text{Current assets}_{t-1} + \text{PP\&E}_{t-1})/\text{Total assets}_{t-1}}$$	Index greater than one indicates a propensity to capitalize expenses.
Sales Growth Index $= \text{Sales}_t/\text{Sales}_{t-1}$	High sales growth puts pressure on managers to continue to achieve financial targets and increases likelihood of manipulation.
Depreciation Index $$= \frac{\text{Depreciation}_{t-1}/(\text{Depreciation}_{t-1} + \text{PP\&E}_{t-1})}{\text{Depreciation}_t/(\text{Depreciation}_t + \text{PP\&E}_t)}$$	Index greater than one indicates rate of depreciation has slowed. Slower deprecation can increase income.
Selling, General, and Administration Expense Index $$= \frac{\text{SG\&A}_t/\text{Sales}_t}{\text{SG\&A}_{t-1}/\text{Sales}_{t-1}}$$	A greater index suggests more aggressive pursuit of slowing sales and a greater propensity to manipulate.
Leverage Ratio $$= \frac{(\text{Long-term debt}_t + \text{Current liabilities}_t)/\text{Total assets}_t}{(\text{Long-term debt}_{t-1} + \text{Current liabilities}_{t-1})/\text{Total assets}_{t-1}}$$	Increase in leverage gives incentives to manipulate to avoid violation of debt covenants.
Total Accruals $= (\Delta\text{Current assets}_t - \Delta\text{Cash}_t - \Delta\text{Current liabilities}_t$ $-\text{Current maturities of debt}_t - \text{Income taxes payable}_t$ $-\text{Depreciation and amortization}_t)/\text{Total assets}_t$	Positive accruals are more likely to indicate earnings manipulation.

signal of the firm's true earnings. After a while, these earnings may be seen as not being informative.

Because of other conflicts, such reasons should be viewed with skepticism. Further, smoothing can distort the true economic volatility of earnings and the resulting stock risk. That is an unethical distortion. Additionally, the SEC takes a

FIGURE	6.3	MONTHLY STOCK PRICES WHILE MICROSOFT SMOOTHED EARNINGS, 1994–1998

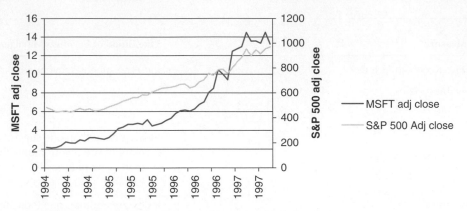

Monthly standard deviation as a percentage of average return:

MSFT   197%
S&P 500   215%

dim view of such behavior. From 1994 to 1998, Microsoft had set up several reserve accounts and would add to or take from them when it had excess revenue or not enough. Microsoft was not using the reserves to systematically inflate earnings, but rather to smooth them. In a settlement with the SEC, management agreed to stop. Although the SEC didn't impose any fines, the firm suffered from poor publicity evident in an almost 6 percent drop in the stock price during the month the investigation was announced. Figure 6.3 shows that during the smoothing period, Microsoft stock outperformed the market and had lower volatility. We can't say for sure whether the stock price movements were solely caused by smoothing. But nonetheless, smoothing could have misled investors. When the SEC told Microsoft to stop the smoothing practices, the stock price declined. Ethical analysts steer investors clear of stocks for which managers smooth earnings.

CONCLUSION: CASH VERSUS ACCRUALS—BE SKEPTICAL!

The opportunity for managers with their auditors to unethically manipulate earnings occurs because of the use of accruals inherent to accounting information. Cash is cash. Accruals are what managers want them to be. Sometimes accruals are fraudulent. Sometimes accruals are consistent with GAAP, but are nonetheless misleading.

An ethical analyst develops a healthy distrust of reported earnings and looks carefully at the accounting choices made by managers in financial reporting. Changes in accounting methods and accruals need to be carefully evaluated in light of the overall assessments of a firm's prospects and profitability along with the incentives of managers to manipulate earnings. There are no flashing signs that signal unethical practices before the damage is done. It is the analysts' responsibility to be skeptical and develop their own set of red flags as they seek to be diligent and ethical in fulfilling their fiduciary duties to their clients.

TERMS

accounting

accruals

net income

balance sheet method of
   measuring accruals

cash-flow method of
   measuring accruals

normal or
   nondiscretionary
   accruals

normal or expected
   accruals

unexpected or
   discretionary accruals

Jones (1991) model

self-reversing accruals

cookie jar reserves

big bath

channel stuffing

special-purpose entity
   (SPE)

earnings informativeness

earnings quality

earnings persistence

earnings response
   coefficient (ERC)

Beneish (1999) model

earnings smoothing

REVIEW QUESTIONS

1. Explain the difference between accrual- and cash-based accounting. How can accrual accounting create opportunities for unethical accounting practices?

2. Can earnings be consistent with GAAP, yet still be unethical? If so, how?

3. Explain the difference between discretionary and nondiscretionary accruals.

4. What does it mean to say accruals are "self-reversing?"

5. Identify and briefly explain the components of total accruals and how changes in each component affect reported net income.

6. Explain three reasons management would have incentives to manipulate earnings *upward*.

7. Explain one reason managers would have incentives to manipulate earnings *downward*.

8. Why are changes in revenues and property, plant, and equipment important variables in modeling expected or nondiscretionary accruals?

9. Explain one way that managers could inflate earnings by overstating revenues.

10. Explain how cookie jar reserves work.

11. Why should an ethical analyst be suspicious of reported earnings?

12. List and explain at least three measures in the Beneish (1999) model that can indicate possible earnings manipulation.

13. What does the ERC tell you about the markets assessment of earnings persistence?

14. Define *earnings quality*.

15. Explain why earnings smoothing can be considered ethical. Why is it unethical?

CRITICAL THINKING QUESTIONS

1. Below is the financial information for a firm for the past five years. The table shows that sales have steadily declined during this period. Net income also declined, but in the last year increased despite the continued decline in sales. Is this evidence of earnings manipulation? What else would you want to know? What other accounting data could you use to help you decide whether the increase in net income is bona fide?

Financial Information ($ millions)

	1/29/2005	1/28/2006	2/3/2007	2/2/2008	1/31/2009
Net sales	16,267	16,023	15,943	15,763	14,526
Net income	1,150	1,113	778	734	967

2. Retail stores often allow customers to purchase gift cards. Maybe you have gotten one of these. When the gift card is sold, the company receives cash and creates a liability for the future sale when the card is redeemed. Some of the cards sold are never redeemed; they are lost, forgotten, and so on. At some point, the company determines that the card is unlikely to be redeemed and will eliminate the liability from its books and recognize the income by reporting "other" income. If you are a retail analyst, how would you go about determining whether a company is being overly aggressive in recognizing the income from unredeemed gift cards? What other accounting or industry information would you like to have in making this determination? How would overall economic conditions (i.e., expansion versus recession) fit into your analysis?

3. The chapter discusses the use of models for measuring unexpected accruals. Some models look at the time series pattern of accruals for an individual firm. Others look at the cross-sectional pattern of accruals, benchmarking an individual firm's accrual pattern to similarly sized firms in the same industry. The telecom, Internet, and housing bubbles have all demonstrated that for brief periods, some industries can suffer from widespread aggressive reporting practices. This can make the job of ferreting out earnings manipulation more difficult. As an analyst, what steps would you take to help you avoid getting caught up in market excitement about a particular industry and avoid recommending stocks whose earnings are created by upward manipulation of accruals? Think about other information and analyses you might need in drawing a conclusion.

4. Below is some select financial data for two companies that operate in a similar industry. Use these data to calculate some of the Beneish (1999) accounting measures of earnings manipulation (Table 6.1). How would you argue that these measures show that ABC Corp. is manipulating earnings? What would you argue against this assertion? What else would you need to know?

ABC Corp.	2008	2007	2006	2005	2004
Receivables	38,083	30,638	29,276	27,060	26,879
Sales	279,552	234,816	229,754	203,637	205,010
Cost of goods sold	181,094	153,418	153,126	130,218	137,532
Selling, general, & administrative expenses	50,456	50,782	47,840	46,263	47,281
Net income	25,084	16,457	7,548	13,253	9,633

XYZ, Inc.	2008	2007	2006	2005	2004
Receivables	6,472,000	6,600,000	5,697,000	4,987,000	3,815,900
Sales	38,062,000	34,624,000	32,235,000	27,479,000	24,603,000
Cost of goods sold	32,536,000	29,548,000	27,815,000	23,997,000	21,325,200
Selling, general, & administrative expenses	3,231,000	2,514,000	2,395,000	1,599,000	1,298,600
Net income	979,000	1,252,000	1,028,000	909,000	817,500

5. One reason management might be tempted to manipulate earnings is to beat analysts' forecasts. The announcement of higher-than-expected earnings can cause an increase in stock price. As an analyst recommending investments, does it matter if management has indeed manipulated earnings, as long as the stock price goes up? Can you develop an investment strategy that involves investing in the stocks of companies where you think management has a propensity to manipulate earnings? Under what conditions would this work? What are the potential pitfalls of such a strategy?

APPLIED STUDENT PROJECT

You can do your own evaluation of a company's accounting practices. Select a company and collect financial data for a firm for 3 to 5 years, depending on data availability. Annual reports or 10-K filings are available from the SEC website at www.sec.gov. You can calculate changes in total accruals for this firm as well as the various accounting measures suggested by Beneish (1999) that are potential indicators of earnings manipulation. Based on these measures, make your own assessment of whether managers are engaging in earnings manipulation and how that would affect your investment recommendations. Present your assessment in a professionally written report of two pages.

RECOMMENDED CASES

1. Case 11—Qwest Communications International: Accounting Fraud and Overstated Revenues
2. Case 12—Refco: Misrepresentation and Hidden Debt
3. Case 19—WorldCom: Capitalizing Operating Expenses; an Unethical Accounting Practice
4. Case 26—Enron: A Case of Extreme Hubris

REFERENCES AND SUGGESTED READING

Ashbaugh-Skaife, Hollis, Daniel W. Collins, William R. Kinney Jr., and Ryan LaFond. "The Effect of SOX Internal Control Deficiencies and Their Remediation on Accrual Quality." *Accounting Review* 83, no. 1 (2008): 217–50.

Beneish, Messod D. "The Detection of Earnings Manipulation." *Financial Analysts Journal* 55, no. 5 (1999): 24–36.

Beneish, Messod D., and Eric Press. "Costs of Technical Violation of Accounting-Based Debt Covenants." *Accounting Review* 68, no. 2 (1993): 233–58.

Collins, Daniel W., and Paul Hribar. "Errors in Estimating Accruals: Implications for Empirical Research." *Journal of Accounting Research* 4, no. 2 (2002): 105–134.

Cooper, Cynthia. *Extraordinary Circumstances: The Journey of a Corporate Whistleblower.* Hoboken, NJ: Wiley & Sons.

Desai, Hemang, Shivram Rajgopal, and Mohan Venkatchalam. "Value-Glamour and Accruals Mispricing: One Anomaly or Two?" *Accounting Review* 79, no. 2 (2004): 355–85.

"House of Cards." www.cnbc.com/id/28892719/.

Huang, Pinghsun, Timothy J. Louwers, Jacquelyn Sue Moffitt, and Yan Zhang. "Ethical Management, Corporate Governance, and Abnormal Accruals." *Journal of Business Ethics* 83, no. 3 (2008): 469–88.

Jones, J. J. "Earnings Management during Import Relief Investigations." *Journal of Accounting Research* 29 (1991): 193–228.

Kerber, Ross. "Called to Account Companies Are Facing Heightened Scrutiny of Bookkeeping Tricks Amid the Fallout Over High-Profile Debacles." *Boston Globe*, 9 June 2002, C1.

Kothari, S. P., Andrew J. Leone, and Charles E. Wasley. "Performance Matched Discretionary Accrual Measures." *Journal of Accounting & Economics* 39, no. 1 (2005): 161–97.

McLean, Bethany, and Peter Elkind. *The Smartest Guys in the Room: The Amazing Rise and Scandalous Fall of Enron.* New York: Penguin Group, 2003.

Mehta, Stephanie N., and Ann Grimes. "Digits." *Wall Street Journal*, 14 January 1999, 1.

Morgenson, Gretchen. "When a Rosy Picture Should Raise a Red Flag." *New York Times*, 18 July 1999, 36.

Munterm, Paul. "SEC Sharply Criticizes 'Earnings Management' Accounting." *Journal of Corporate Accounting and Finance* (Winter 1999): 31–38.

Reed, Brad J., and Ena Rose-Green. "Cookie Jar Reserves: The Case of Callaway Golf Company." *Journal of the International Academy for Case Studies* 13, no. 13 (2007): 13–21.

Schilit, Howard. *Financial Shenanigans: How to Detect Accounting Gimmicks & Fraud in Financial Reports.* New York: McGraw-Hill, 2002.

Schipper, Katherine, and Linda Vincent. "Earnings Quality." *Accounting Horizons* 17 (2003): 97–110.

Securities and Exchange Commission. "Xerox Settles SEC Enforcement Action Charging Company with Fraud." SEC Release No. 2002-52, April 11, 2002. www.sec.gov.

————. "SEC Files Settled Accounting Fraud Case Against Four Former Employees of Dana Corporation; Dana Holding Corporation Settles to Cease-and-Desist Order for Reporting Violations." Litigation Release No. 21207, September 11, 2009. www.sec.gov.

Appendix: Accounting Methods: Review of the Basics

How is accounting information created? Remember that there are three statements. First, there is a balance sheet—a snapshot that tells investors what a firm's assets and liabilities are at any given time. Because the accounting equation is Assets = Liabilities + Owners' equity, this also provides a measure of net worth to investors. Second, there is an income statement—the amount of income earned over a period of time. Finally, there is a statement of cash flows that measures cash flows over a given period.

| FIGURE | A6.1 | **FINANCIAL STATEMENTS** |

Many items on financial statements are interrelated.
EBITDA(earnings before interest, taxes, depreciation, and amortization), sometimes
known as operating cash flow, is highlighted here.
EBITDA is chosen because it is often used in assessing the financial position of the firm.

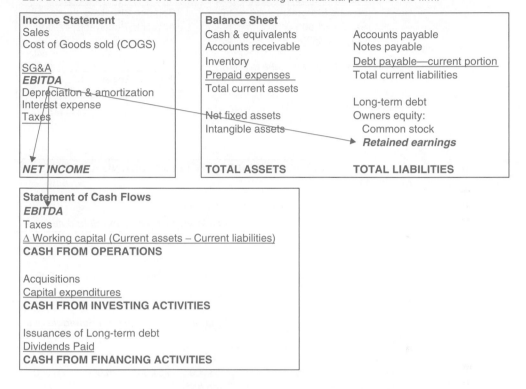

Sources of cash must equal uses of cash. All three statements—the balance sheet, the income statement, and the statement of cash flows—are interrelated because they reflect the same underlying economic activity (see Figure A6.1).

Accounting methods are designed to record economic transactions as they occur. One principle of accounting is that the balance sheet must balance. Accountants record transactions so that changes on one side of the balance sheet offset changes on the other. Another principle of accounting is matching. Transactions are recorded so that revenues are matched to expenses. **Accruals** occur when there is a mismatch between when the economic substance of the transaction has occurred and is recorded and when cash changes hands.

Look at Figure A6.2. Suppose a customer makes a purchase on a credit card. At the time of the transaction, revenue from the sale is recorded or recognized and matched with an expense. On the balance sheet, inventory declines as it is sold and an account receivable is created to reflect the credit sale. At a later date, when the customer pays off the credit, the accounts receivable will decline and cash will increase. The income from the transaction is recognized before the cash flows into the firm.

Accruals accounting measure created to adjust for a mismatch between when the economic substance of the transaction has occurred and is recorded and when the cash changes hands.

FIGURE	A6.2	**THE MISMATCH BETWEEN TIMING OF CASH FLOWS AND ECONOMIC ACTIVITY**

Sale is recognized in period 1, but cash is not received until period 2.

Period 1: Credit Sale of $1,000

Income Statement	Balance Sheet
Sales + $1,000	Accounts Receivable + 1,000
COGS + $500	Inventory – $500

Period 2: Credit Sale Is Paid

Balance Sheet
Cash + 1,000
Accounts Receivable – 1,000

FIGURE	A6.3	**ACCOUNTING METHOD CHOICE AFFECTS TIMING AND AMOUNTS OF ACCRUALS**

Capital expense to be depreciated: $100,000

Accelerated Depreciation Schedule

Year	1	2	3	4	5
Percent depreciated	33%	45%	15%	7%	-
Depreciation expense	33,000	45,000	15,000	7,000	-
Total depreciated	100,000				

Straight Line Depreciation Schedule over 5 Years

Year	1	2	3	4	5
Percent depreciated	25%	25%	25%	25%	0%
Depreciation expense	25,000	25,000	25,000	25,000	-
Total depreciated	100,000				

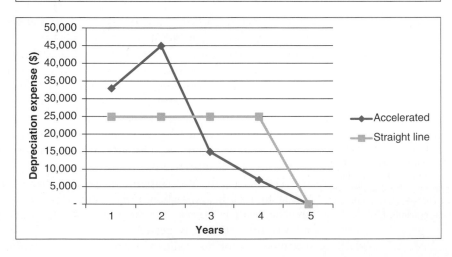

The magnitude and timing of recording accruals depends on the accounting method chosen. One example is depreciation expense. Suppose that a firm purchases a piece of capital equipment for $100,000. The firm has a choice between a straight-line and an accelerated method. Figure A6.3 shows the difference in the amount charged as depreciation expense each year under the two methods.

There are two things to note about this example. First, the total amount depreciated is the same under each method. Second, accruals are **self-reversing**. That is, under the accelerated method, depreciation expense is low relative to the straight-line method and then is higher. Suppose management decides to use the straight-line method over the accelerated method to report higher earnings. In the early years, this "works." Depreciation expense is lower, causing reported income to be higher. But what happens in later years? Now the accelerated method gives a lower depreciation expense number and higher reported earnings.

Self-reversing when an accrual amount accrues more revenue (less expense) earlier it must accrue less revenue (more expense) later so that the total amount accrued doesn't exceed the total amount of the transaction.

CHAPTER

7

Investing in Companies with Good Corporate Governance Practices

Learning Objectives

After reading this chapter, students should be able to:

- Describe how a board of directors is formed.
- Explain the function of the following board committees: compensation, audit, and nominating.
- Distinguish among inside, outside, and gray directors.
- Identify and understand the conflicts that nonexecutive directors face.
- Understand different ways in which shareholder rights can be strengthened or weakened.
- List and discuss the different components of executive compensation and the incentives they create.
- Indicate how the takeover market can discipline managers and how managers can insulate themselves from the takeover market.

CHAPTER OUTLINE

- Director Compensation and Shareholdings

- The Nominating Process, Voting Rights, and Potential Conflicts

- Executive Compensation: Structure and Incentives

- Option Grant Abuses

- Golden Parachutes, Golden Handcuffs, Golden Coffins

- Horizon Problems and a Firm's Long-Run Profitability

- Shareholders' Rights and the Takeover Market

- Conclusion: Shareholders' Rights and Conflicts

- Appendix: Review of Stock Options

INTRODUCTION: CORPORATE GOVERNANCE AND ITS IMPORTANCE TO ETHICAL ANALYSTS

Stockholders entrust a firm's directors and executives to maximize shareholder wealth. Yet as with all economic relationships, conflicts of interest exist (see Chapter 2 and the discussion of agency theory). **Corporate governance** is a set of internal mechanisms and policies designed to ensure that officers fulfill their fiduciary duty to shareholders. The board of directors is responsible for firing a poorly performing chief executive officer (CEO) and setting compensation to align the CEO's incentives with the shareholders' incentives. The takeover market is a mechanism of last resort when these mechanisms fail; the firm is acquired, and the board and CEO are kicked out. This chapter identifies and discusses the efficacies of these "carrot and stick" devices. It is important for analysts to understand how they affect stock prices. In fact, many analysts often identify corporate governance as a risk factor.

Ethical analysts evaluate firms' corporate governance practices along with standard financial measures so they can make better investment recommendations. While reading this chapter, keep in mind that, as with financial performance, analysts cannot make a right or wrong investment call based on a firm's corporate governance. For example, one analyst can argue that strong sales growth will continue and issue a buy recommendation. Another can have an equally valid justification for deciding that the firm cannot sustain strong sales and issue a sell. Similarly, two analysts can interpret the same set of corporate governance practices differently—one can see weak practices where another sees strong ones. No matter what the analyst concludes, the opinion should be based on diligent research and sound reasoning (see the discussion of analysts' ethical obligations in Chapter 5). This chapter is an amalgamation of the findings of academic studies that have examined the relation between corporate

Corporate governance a set of internal mechanisms and policies designed to ensure that officers fulfill their fiduciary duty to shareholders.

FUNDAMENTAL PRINCIPLES OF INVESTMENT ETHICS FOR PROFESSIONALS

Principle 1: ETHICAL UNDERSTANDING

Because investments are complicated, you *have an obligation not to knowingly engage in an investment transaction that either you or others do not sufficiently understand. This includes knowing the underlying source of returns or fees charged.*

Principle 2: ETHICAL USE OF INFORMATION

Because investments are information driven, *you have an obligation to ensure that you and others have access to relevant information and that you or others do not misuse or distort information in the investment transaction.*

Principle 3: RESPONSIBLE INVESTING

Because investments provide financial resources to others, *you have an obligation to ensure that you do not knowingly make or recommend investments that support activities that harm others.*

Principle 4: TRUST AND FAIRNESS

Because you are dealing with others' money either directly or indirectly, *you have an obligation not to abuse the trust all others have either explicitly or implicitly placed in you to treat them fairly.*

---

governance characteristics and financial performance. These studies are referenced at the end of the chapter for the interested student. Academic studies provide typical or average findings. You can interpret them as rules of thumb. But like most rules of thumb, they must be applied judiciously within a particular context. Good analysts do just that.

While an analyst's primary obligation is to investors, his or her evaluation of a firm's corporate governance practices can have a wider reach. It is easy to think of a firm as an anonymous entity. But *individuals* run the company. Individuals are subject to human frailties that can lead to ethical lapses (i.e., greed, ego, and arrogance, as we discussed in Chapter 1). Directors and top executives make decisions that affect not only the value of securities but also employees, suppliers, customers, and communities. When boards fail to replace poorly performing executives, companies can be forced to lay off employees, leave suppliers and customers hanging, and put creditors on the hook. Firms with weak corporate governance may have other unethical practices. Remember it is the same set of individuals at the top calling the shots. Analysts have a duty to alert both investors and the public to other questionable practices as they unearth them through diligent research. In doing so, the firm can be disciplined by the market and pressured to change before others are hurt. While investment professionals are neither charged nor obligated to serve as corporate watchdogs, they can by happenstance find themselves in this role. Yes, strong corporate governance practices that maximize security values will not always benefit other stakeholders in the firm (this thorny topic is discussed in Chapter 8); but *there can be* overlap, and ethical analysts are conscious of their larger role in society.

Thus all of the four fundamental principles of investment ethics (see Chapter 1) apply here. But let's briefly look at a case that will help illustrate these issues and set the stage for a deeper look into corporate governance for the rest of the chapter.

COUNTRYWIDE FINANCIAL CORPORATION: A CASE OF WEAK CORPORATE GOVERNANCE AND UNETHICAL BUSINESS PRACTICES

Countrywide was a company that rose and fell with the housing boom and bust. Its business was originating mortgage loans. When housing prices fell in 2006–2007, Countrywide was identified as one of the key culprits. The firm was accused of fueling the boom with subprime mortgages issued to unqualified borrowers, particularly in California, which experienced both the sharpest increase and decline in real estate values. Most financial scandals involve firms that ride the latest wave of boom to bust. Recall the discussion in Chapter 1 of Enron and the telecom and Internet stock market boom and bust in the late 1990s. Just as Enron was a notorious case from that era, Countrywide is one from the most recent financial crisis.

Countrywide saw a rapid increase in both earnings and stock price starting from the early 2000s. Stock price tripled from $15 in 2003 to a high of $45 in February 2007. In 2004 the company hit a bump in the road when earnings per share (EPS) fell from $4.18 to $3.63. EPS started climbing again to $4.11 in 2005 and to $4.30 in 2006. Management got the EPS and stock price back on track by altering the business strategy. The company increased its issuance of unconventional loans—adjustable rate mortgages and pay-option or negatively amortizing loans. These types of loans are both more profitable and *riskier*.

Conventional mortgages are typically for 15 or 30 years and have a fixed interest rate and a fixed payment of principal and interest. "Exotic" mortgages are different.

Adjustable rate mortgages (ARMs) refers to mortgages where the interest adjusts periodically over the life of the loan.

The interest rate on **adjustable rate mortgages (ARMs)** changes or is "adjusted" periodically over the life of the loan. The adjustments are pegged to market interest rates, for example, the London Interbank Offered Rate (LIBOR). Most ARMs initially offer a rate lower than a conventional fixed rate, thus making them attractive to borrowers. But when rates are adjusted, monthly payments can increase and borrowers may be unable to make their house payments. **Pay-option mortgages** allow borrowers to defer payments on principal and even some part of the interest.

Pay-option mortgages mortgages that allow borrowers to defer interest and principal payments by adding these deferred payments on to the principal already owed.

The deferred interest and principal payments are then added onto the total principal or the amount owed. Sometimes these are known as negative amortizing loans because rather than paying down the loan, borrowers *increase* the amount owed. But lenders usually cap the total amount of the loan, for example, to 115 percent of the appraised home. Borrowers who deferred interest on a house with a declining value can suddenly find themselves having to make higher mortgage payments—higher than they can afford.

Besides originating more of these "exotic" and riskier loans, Countrywide also began to *invest or hold* more of them. Managers raised the money for investing from two sources. First, they used payments made on mortgage services agreements. When a company services a mortgage, it collects the interest and principal payments from the borrower. Because many of these service agreements were made on risky loans, they were a risky source of funding. Second, Countrywide used short-term borrowing to make investments in mortgages. Short-term rates tend to be low, but firms need to ensure they have sufficient cash to pay back the loan quickly. Short-term funding can be risky if a firm runs into a cash crunch. As long as the potential risks of funding weren't a reality at Countrywide, the cost of funds to invest was low relative to the higher interest rates the firm earned on these "exotic" mortgages. The strategy increased earnings per share. But issuing and investing in these mortgages was risky for Countrywide's borrowers *as well as* its shareholders. Furthermore, the company's loan origination and loan investment business was increasingly concentrated in California. Geographical risks were not diversified.

Many people lost their homes when ARMs or pay-option loans were adjusted to monthly payments they could not afford. California was particularly hard-hit. As Figure 7.1 shows, Countrywide's financial performance took a nosedive, and the firm was sold to Bank of America in 2008 for about $7 a share. A year earlier, the stock was trading at around $45 a share. Both consumers and shareholders were hurt by doing business with Countrywide. As of this writing, the Department of Justice is investigating Countrywide for predatory lending practices. The Securities and Exchange Commission (SEC) charged top executives with financial fraud for failing to fully disclose all the company's risks to investors. In addition, the former CEO, Angelo Mozilo, was charged with insider trading (see Chapter 4) because he sold his shares—for a profit of $140 million—while knowing the company was headed toward disaster.

What was going on with corporate governance practices during this time? Who was "minding the store?" In the year prior to the company's downfall, the CEO and directors' compensation increased significantly. Incentive compensation was based largely on EPS and stock values; officers were rewarded for earnings but not penalized

| FIGURE | 7.1 | **COUNTRYWIDE FINANCIAL CORP. (CFC)** |

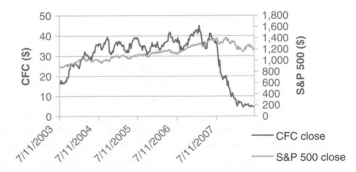

Source: Thomson ONE Banker.

for risk or unscrupulous business practices. In 2005, the board had 14 directors as well as 2 insiders. Over the next two years, they lost five directors. The CEO was chairman of the board, and the board was staggered. A **staggered board** divides the board into classes. Only one class of directors can go up for election in any given year. The ability to acquire board control by the voting process is effectively slowed down. For example, suppose the board consists of 9 directors and three classes of 3 directors each. Then it will take two years to elect and create a majority of new directors on the board—six of nine board seats. Countrywide had a staggered board with three classes of directors. In this chapter, you will learn why *all* of these were red flags for poor corporate governance practices. Of course, we have the benefit of 20/20 hindsight. But in the summer of 2007 Paul Kedrosky, an analyst and contributor to the "Seeking Alpha" website, noted that "four brave analysts already *had* (have) Countrywide at Sell." We hope that you become one of these brave analysts. Read on!

Staggered board refers to a board that is divided into classes, and only one class of directors is eligible for election in any given year.

THE ROLE OF THE BOARD: AN OVERVIEW

Shareholders of publicly held corporations elect directors to the board who in turn oversee or monitor the management of the firm. The board typically meets once a month. Its most important task is to hire, fire, and design compensation contracts for the firm's top executives (i.e., the CEO). Members also hire the independent auditor and oversee internal accounting controls for the firm. The board provides input on long-range strategic planning. Finally, the board brokers the terms of changes in control (i.e., mergers and acquisitions). The board is not involved in the day-to-day operations of the firm. Its principal role is to monitor the CEO to ensure that the firm is managed so as to maximize shareholder wealth. The directors serve as the primary means of giving shareholders a voice in how the company is run. Figure 7.2 shows how this system works.

The election of the board occurs each year at the annual shareholders' meeting. Typically this meeting is in the spring, following the firm's fiscal year-end in December. This way, shareholders can take into account the firm's financial performance when voting for the directors. Did the current set of directors do a good job in generating profits for the shareholders? Do they deserve to be reelected? Firms send shareholders materials on financial performance as well as biographical information about the directors who are nominated. Information about the top five executives' compensation is also included because determining compensation is a critical part of the directors' job. All this information is sent out in **proxy statements** or form 14A filings with the SEC. Most voting is done online by institutional investors (e.g., mutual fund and pension managers). Money managers have a fiduciary duty to vote the proxies on behalf of their investors and must disclose their voting policies (see Chapter 2). Often, money managers outsource proxy voting to a firm such as RiskMetrics Group. These firms evaluate directors' backgrounds and independence and make recommendations. Voting rights are usually one vote per one share of common stock, although variations exist as discussed later in this chapter.

The number of directors serving on the board can vary from, say, 6 (small) to 24 (large). Boards can include executives of the firm and almost always include the

Proxy statements materials sent to shareholders to disclose the financial performance, executive compensation, board composition, and major shareholder ownership as well as biographical information about the directors that are nominated by the firm and subject to a proxy vote by shareholders.

| FIGURE | 7.2 | **THE ROLE OF THE BOARD** |

Shareholders elect directors.

Directors hire CEO.

Electing board of directors gives shareholders a voice in wealth maximization.

Profits are distributed to shareholders.

CEO runs the firm to maximize profits.

Inside directors directors who are management or have obvious affiliations with management.

Outside directors directors who are nonexecutive and have no obvious affiliations with management.

Gray directors directors who are nonexecutives and might have ties to executives.

CEO. Directors who are not executives are typically those who have achieved some type of professional prominence. These can be CEOs, chief financial officers (CFOs), and executives from other firms. Directors can be ex-government officials, such as presidents and cabinet secretaries. They can be lawyers, accountants, and investment professionals. Sometimes ex-executives serve on the board of the company they retired from. Family members of founders also serve on boards. Directors who are currently part of the management team (i.e., the CEO) are called **inside directors**; directors who are independent of management are **outside directors**; and those who don't neatly fit in either category are called **gray directors**.

Table 7.1 shows who was nominated or on the board at Countrywide when the company was still doing well. You can see there were 14 board members in all, 2 of them executives. The nonexecutive board members were high-level executives and had varying degrees of ownership interest in the company. Let's look next at how an analyst can evaluate the information given about directors in the proxy statements.

WHAT MAKES A GOOD DIRECTOR?

Good directors are those who serve as alert watchdogs for shareholders. They need to be independent of management, have sufficient expertise in business decision making, and have enough time to devote to board matters. What are the economic forces that help them either fulfill or shirk these duties? In theory, a director's reputation as a good monitor should ensure that she will act in shareholders' interest; if she fails,

TABLE	7.1	COUNTRYWIDE FINANCIAL CORPORATION BOARD OF DIRECTORS, 2005–2006

Name	Age	Profession	Director Since	Stock Ownership
1. Kathleen Brown	60	Head of West Coast Municipal Finance at Goldman Sachs & Co.	2005	15,190
2. Henry G. Cisneros	58	Founder and chairman of CityView America, a joint venture to build affordable homes in metropolitan areas; secretary of Housing and Urban Development under President Clinton	2001	98,023
3. Jeffrey M. Cunningham	53	Chairman and chief executive officer of NewsMarkets LLC, publishers of *Directorship* magazine	1998	182,437
4. Robert J. Donato	66	President of Donato Financial Services	1993	391,103
5. Michael E. Dougherty	65	Founder and chairman of Dougherty Financial Group, LLC	1998	387,563
6. Stanford L. Kurland	53	President and chief operating officer of Countrywide	2000	6,173,930
7. Martin R. Melone	64	Retired partner of Ernst & Young LLP	2003	23,685
8. Angelo R. Mozilo	67	Chairman of board, chief executive officer, and cofounder of Countrywide	1969	11,450,584
9. Robert T. Parry	66	Retired president and chief executive officer of Federal Reserve Bank of San Francisco	2004	16,405
10. Oscar P. Robertson	67	President and chief executive officer of Oscar Robertson Solutions, LLC, a holding company, Orchem Corporation, a manufacturer of specialty chemicals, and OR Document Management Services, LLC, a document management provider	2000	176,089
11. Keith P. Russell	60	President and chief executive officer of Russell Financial, Inc.	2003	22,725
12. Harley W. Snyder	73	President of HSC, Inc., a real estate development company	1991	202,489
13. Ben M. Enis (retired in 2005)	64	Founder and chief executive officer of Enis Renewable Energy Systems, LLC	1984	771,226
14. Edwin Heller (retired in 2005)	76	Retired Partner, effective May 2004, of the law firm of Fried, Frank, Harris, Shriver & Jacobson	1993	254,386

Source: Countrywide Financial Corporation, Proxy Statements; Filing Dates June 14, 2006, and June 15, 2005. www.sec.gov.

| FIGURE | 7.3 | **WHAT MAKES A GOOD DIRECTOR? IT'S A BALANCING ACT** |

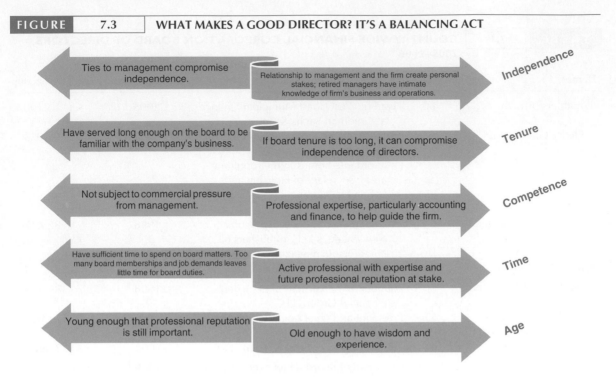

her reputation becomes tarnished. But that is not always so. Directors face conflict of interests, deal with competing demands on their time, and have varying degrees of professional expertise. All of these factors can compromise their fiduciary duty to shareholders. Figure 7.3 shows all the tensions between the different dimensions that shape the director's ability to be an effective voice for shareholders. Let's now discuss each of these issues in more detail.

RELATIONSHIPS

Ethical analysts need to carefully assess the relationships directors have with management. Can these relationships compromise their independence? Family members and executives who once worked for the firm and are now board members have personal ties to management. A director may be reluctant to fire the CEO if that CEO is his or her sister or brother. Directors who are engaged in current business dealings with the firm, or are planning for future business dealings, are not wholly independent because management decides who gets the business. This is known as commercial pressure. Lawyers, accountants, consultants, investment professionals, suppliers, and customers fall into this category. For example, an investment professional serving on the board may hope to manage the firm's pension fund. In turn, this director may be less critical of management (see Chapter 2 for further discussion on money managers and directorships).

TENURE

Board tenure is another dimension of independence. A certain level of board turnover is healthy. Directors who serve for many years can become entrenched. But too much turnover can make it difficult for the board to be effective. It can take a while for directors to get up to speed on board matters; if too many directors at once are still learning the basics of the firm, it can be difficult to identify problems that are less obvious. Countrywide had five directors who served for seven or more years; their tenure could have compromised their independence. Further, resignations of outside directors can be a sign of trouble. Three nonmanagement directors resigned in the year before the firm's collapse.

COMPETENCE

What about competence? Individuals who have backgrounds in finance or accounting tend to be more proficient directors. The management team is often judged by accounting performance and can have incentives to manipulate earnings (see Chapter 6). Directors who have sufficient expertise to see through management's manipulation are likely to be better monitors. Countrywide's nonmanagement directors were all top executives, many in the area of finance and real estate. On the one hand, their backgrounds suggest they had sufficient expertise to be good monitors. On the other hand, their current or potential business connections could have compromised their independence. For example, one of the directors worked for Goldman Sachs. Goldman earned fees by providing financing services to Countrywide. Directors also had mortgages and home equity lines arranged by Countrywide.

TIME LIMITATIONS

Professional directors individuals who have retired from their primary profession but are serving as board directors.

What about time? Nonmanagement directors are not full-time employees of the firm. The time they spend on board matters is limited. Individuals who have retired from their primary professions have more time to spend on board matters and can do a better job of monitoring. These are sometimes known as **professional directors**. Countrywide had two such directors. Similarly, individuals who serve on many boards make poor monitors. They may be overcommitted and stretched too thin. How many is too many? Three to four directorships is a lot. Countrywide limited its nonmanagement directors to serving on a maximum of four boards. Some of the directors were quite busy. Four served on three boards, including Countrywide's. Three served on four boards.

AGE

The director's age can also influence his effectiveness. A younger director in the prime of his career is likely to be more concerned about his reputation. On the one hand, a director with a reputation for cooperating with management may be nominated by management more often and earn lucrative board seats. On the other hand, a director who makes management toe the line is less likely to tarnish his reputation by serving on the board of a poorly performing company. An older director may be less concerned about his reputation but have more experience. Good analysts consider the director's age when evaluating his effectiveness.

EFFECTIVE BOARD STRUCTURE

Besides who is on the board, analysts should also evaluate the board's structure. Boards that are too small won't have enough directors to divvy up tasks or enough experts to provide advice and counsel to the management team. Boards that are too big also can be ineffective. In larger boards, individual board members are less likely to take responsibility. It also can be difficult to develop board consensus and efficient decision making. Boards of 6 to 8 directors appear to be associated with firms having higher firm values. Countrywide had 12 to 14 directors before its collapse. In retrospect, this seems too many. Boards that separate the chairman of the board position from that of the CEO can also be more independent. When the CEO is also the chairman of the board, he or she is more likely to dominate board deliberations. Following this line of reasoning, it is important for boards to sometimes meet without the CEO present. This can allow for freer discussions about the CEO's performance. Countrywide's CEO was chairman of the board.

Compensation committee a board committee that sets the compensation of the CEO and other top executives.

Audit committee a board committee charged with hiring the external auditor and overseeing the internal audit controls of the firm.

Nominating committee a board committee that nominates new directors to the board.

The board almost always has committees that consist of smaller subsets of the board. The **compensation committee** structures compensation contracts for the CEO. Typically, board members hire a consultant to help with this task. The **audit committee** hires the independent auditor, makes recommendations on non-audit services, and evaluates internal controls. The **nominating committee** makes recommendations for new directors to be elected to the board. Independent directors with relevant areas of expertise should be appointed to important committees. For instance, the audit committee should consist of all nonexecutive directors with sufficient backgrounds in finance and accounting. The CEO and other executives should not serve on the nominating and compensation committees. Executives have inherent conflicts in selecting directors hired to watch over them and structure their compensation. Figure 7.4 shows a typical board structure that is effective.

Table 7.2 shows the committees for Countrywide. Besides the usual committees, the company also had three others: Finance, Credit, and Operations and Public Policy. The Finance and Credit committees were responsible for overseeing the firm's credit exposure and financing. The Operations and Public Policy Committee oversaw the firm's operational risks and lending policies. The recent additions of the Credit and Operations and Public Policy committees suggest the board was aware of the risks the firm was facing. All of the company's committee members were nonmanagement directors. Most striking is the number of times the Compensation Committee met in 2006. It met more times than any other committee. Compensation for both officers and directors increased significantly that year. A cynic might claim the Compensation Committee was more interested in lucrative pay packages designed to enrich board members than in paying attention to the increasing risks the company was facing. Another interpretation could be that the committee was concerned that compensation was structured to ensure continued success of the company. What do you think? To help you decide, we look at the compensation package in more detail later in the chapter.

| FIGURE | 7.4 | EFFECTIVE BOARD STRUCTURE FOR MOST FIRMS |

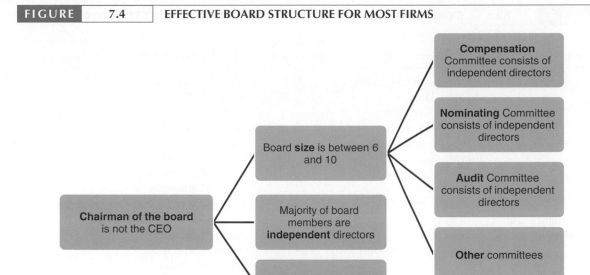

MINI APPLICATION 7.1

ENRON AND DIRECTOR COMPENSATION

Enron was a company in the 1990s that reported strong earnings growth and had a stock price that kept on increasing until massive fraud was discovered.

Before Enron's demise, nonexecutive directors earned $50,000 a year in deferred compensation. If they continued to serve on the board, they received the accumulated amount after five years: $250,000. One plausible reason for this type of compensation structure is to help retain stability in board composition. Another is that it could be used to buy directors' silence. If a director is not renominated, he loses his deferred compensation. An ethical analyst considers both reasons when evaluating a firm's corporate governance practices.

DIRECTOR COMPENSATION AND SHAREHOLDINGS

Analysts also need to evaluate directors' economic interests in serving on a board. On the one hand, directors should not receive compensation that makes them look—and more importantly, act—like executives. Oftentimes compensation is referred to as *nominal* because it is relatively small compared to executive compensation. On the other hand, directors are individuals with high time costs and may need to be compensated. Compensation is also important in aligning incentives. The average total compensation (including fees, equity awards, and other benefits) earned by Countrywide's nonmanagement directors ranged from $300,000 to $400,000 in the year before its failure. This is a lot. See Mini Application 7.1 for another example of questionable director compensation.

TABLE 7.2	COUNTRYWIDE FINANCIAL CORP. BOARD COMMITTEES, 2005–2006			
Committee	Members in 2005	Number of Meetings in 2005	Members in 2006	Number of Meetings in 2006
Audit and Ethics	Martin R. Melone (chair) Robert J. Donato Henry G. Cisneros Keith P. Russell	21	Martin R. Melone (chair) Robert T. Parry Henry G. Cisneros Keith P. Russell	14
Compensation	Harley W. Snyder (chair) Ben M. Enis Michael E. Dougherty Edwin Heller	8	Harley W. Snyder (chair) Robert J. Donato Michael E. Dougherty Oscar P. Robertson	29
Corporate Governance and Nominating	Michael E. Dougherty (chair) Edwin Heller Jeffrey M. Cunningham Harley W. Snyder	8	Michael E. Dougherty (chair) Robert J. Donato Henry G. Cisneros Harley W. Snyder	5
Credit (new in 2005)	Keith P. Russell (chair) Ben M. Enis Kathleen Brown Oscar P. Robertson Jeffrey M. Cunningham	2	Keith P. Russell (chair) Robert T. Parry Jeffrey M. Cunningham	5
Finance	Robert J. Donato (chair) Martin R. Melone Kathleen Brown Robert T. Parry	6	Robert J. Donato (chair) Martin R. Melone Oscar P. Robertson Keith P. Russell	10
Operations and Public Policy (new in 2005)	Robert T. Parry (chair) Jeffrey M.Cunningham Henry G. Cisneros Oscar P. Robertson	3	Robert T. Parry (chair) Jeffrey M.Cunningham Henry G. Cisneros Oscar P. Robertson	5

Source: Countrywide Financial Corporation, Proxy Statements; Filing Dates June 14, 2006, and June 13, 2007. www.sec.gov.

Annual retainer fee fee paid to nonexecutive directors of corporate boards.

Per meeting fees fees paid to nonexecutive directors for attendance at board or committee meetings.

Stock awards stock-based compensation essential to managers' incentives. There are many types of stock awards.

Stock option grants the right to buy a stock at a prespecified price, the exercise price, at a prespecified date, the exercise or maturity date, in the future.

Almost all directors earn an **annual retainer fee**. This amount can vary from $10,000 to $250,000. Directors can also earn **per meeting fees** for full board meetings, ranging from $1,000 to $5,000, and per meeting fees for committees or for participating in phone calls. These fees are usually somewhat less than full board meeting fees. When annual retainer fees and per meeting fees add up, directors can lose their independence. Countrywide reported that 2006 annual retainer fees were $70,000 a year, and per meeting fees were $1,500.

Stock awards and **stock option grants** for directors are less common but a more prevalent practice than a decade ago (see the appendix at the end of this chapter for a refresher on stock options). Stock awards and options grants can occur when directors join a board and as part of their annual compensation. Countrywide reported that in 2006, each nonmanagement director was given restricted stock awards worth $220,000. Directors were restricted from cashing in on their awards for one year. A director's stock ownership can range from a few thousand dollars to millions of dollars. Outside directors who own a large block of stock have stronger ownership interests in the firm and are more likely to act in shareholder interests. Proxy statements disclose the amount of stock beneficially owned by directors. Besides stock owned outright, **beneficially owned stock** often includes stock held by family members or trusts. Beneficially owned stock also includes stock options that are exercisable in 60 days. A diligent analyst carefully reads the footnotes to see what is included and excluded. In December 2006, when Countrywide's stock was $45 a share, nonmanagement directors held from $680,000 to over $34 million in the company's stock. Many sold their stock over the next year.

Beneficially owned stock stock in which the holder has either a direct or indirect ownership or voting interest.

THE NOMINATING PROCESS, VOTING RIGHTS, AND POTENTIAL CONFLICTS

Voting is a critical mechanism to ensure the right board is in place and looking out for shareholders' interests. As already noted, the nominating committee is usually charged with nominating directors to serve on the board. Analysts need to evaluate that committee's independence. In the absence of a nominating committee, the entire board may be involved in nominating the directors. Either way, the current set of both directors and executives have a heavy hand in selecting new directors. Is this a problem? It could be. Directors and executives can become **entrenched**. This means they become secure enough that they do not fear being replaced for doing a poor job, and/or they begin to stick their hands in the cookie jar (i.e., taking excessive compensation and perks). Analysts also must evaluate the power that shareholders exercise over nominations. Corporate charters and regulations dictate the election policies for firms. For example, the charter determines whether the board is staggered; a staggered board can entrench the current set of directors and executives. For most firms, the current board makes nominations and sends these out for a shareholder vote via the proxy statements.

Entrenched refers to directors and executives who become secure enough that they do not fear being replaced for doing a poor job.

Incumbents these are current nonmanagement directors and top executives that the current board nominates for re-election to the board.

Proxy fight a fight over the proxies to elect directors.

Dissident a shareholder or shareholder group that criticizes the current slate of director nominees and offers an alternative slate.

Activist shareholders shareholders who seek to increase investment returns by pressuring the firm to change its operating strategy and corporate governance practices.

What if shareholders disagree with management's nominees or the **incumbents**? They can put forth their own slate of nominees in a **proxy fight**. A proxy fight is just that—a fight over the proxies to elect directors. A **dissident** shareholder or shareholder group can take out ads in financial publications, such as the *Wall Street Journal*, criticizing the current slate of nominees and offering an alternative slate. The dissidents often seek legal means to access the list of shareholders eligible to vote in the election, which they use to contact and solicit votes for their nominees. Proxy fights aren't cheap.

Professional investors, known as **activist shareholders**, sometimes wage proxy fights as part of their investment strategy. These can be individuals such as Carl Icahn, an activist shareholder often in the news, or institutional investors such as the California Public Employees' Retirement System (CalPERS). They call for reforms ranging from how the board is constituted to how the CEO is compensated. Reforms can lead to increases in stock price and yield a nice return to the activists. These investors often acquire 5 percent or more of the firm's shares outstanding. Why 5 percent? This figure is in part driven by SEC disclosure requirements. The SEC requires all investors who acquire 5 percent or more to publicly disclose their holdings. If they seek to acquire or influence the control of the firm, they must

13D form SEC disclosure form required when an investor or an investor group acquires 5 percent or more of the firm's shares and intends to influence or change control of the firm.

13G form when an investor or an investor group acquires 5 percent or more of the firm's shares outstanding in the ordinary course of business, they must use this form to file quarterly with the SEC.

Blockholder an investor who has 5 percent or more ownership of the shares outstanding in a firm.

Superior voting rights a class of stock with more than one vote per share.

Cumulative voting a voting practice that allows shareholders to cast all their votes for one particular director nominee.

"Say on pay" amendments corporate charter amendments that allow shareholders to provide advisory voting on the approval of CEO compensation.

Vote with their feet occurs when institutional investors disagree with management proposals or director nominees; they sell their shares rather than vote no.

file a **13D form**. Otherwise, they can file a **13G form**. Because of the SEC filing requirements, **blockholder** are defined as investors who own 5 percent or more of the firm's shares outstanding. Blockholders not only wage proxy fights but also often acquire shares, to gain a toehold before making a takeover attempt. For any of these reasons, analysts need to keep an eye on blockholder activities because they are indications of changes in voting coalitions, control of the firm, and, ultimately, stock prices.

Voting rights for shareholders are most often one vote per one share of common stock. There can be differences created by the various classes of stock with different voting rights. For example, Stock A might have four votes per share while Stock B might have one vote per share. Stocks with **superior voting rights** are often held by management and affiliated investors. Such rights weaken public shareholders' rights.

In contrast, **cumulative voting** is a way to enhance rights. Cumulative voting allows shareholders to cast all their votes for one particular director nominee. Suppose there are 10 directors, and a shareholder owns 100 shares. The shareholder has 10 times 100, or 1,000 votes. The shareholder can cast 100 votes for the entire slate of director nominees or 1,000 votes for just one of the nominees. This allows shareholders to increase their voting power to ensure they get the director representation they want. Many shareholders do not vote their shares, so it is possible for a director to be elected with a small number of votes. Institutional shareholders have pushed for amendments to corporate charters to require that a director who does not receive a majority of the votes must resign, and another director be nominated. They have also proposed **"say on pay" amendments** that allow shareholders to provide advisory voting on CEO compensation. Advisory voting allows shareholders to say whether they agree with the compensation, but directors are not obligated to take the votes into account. However, ignoring shareholders' wishes can cost the directors the next election. Corporate charters can also require that voting is confidential. This helps alleviate commercial pressure on institutional investors. Otherwise, to avoid conflicts, institutional investors may **vote with their feet**, that is, sell their shares rather than vote against management.

Over the past years, the SEC has considered proposals to increase shareholders' voting power. In 2003, William Donaldson, then the SEC chairman, proposed that large shareholders be allowed to nominate directors as part of the proxy process if 35 percent of the firm's shareholders withheld votes from existing directors and management. The proposal was abandoned. Then in 2007 again, the SEC proposed allowing large shareholders greater access to the nominating process. That proposal also languished. As of this writing, the SEC once more is considering new voting proposals.

EXECUTIVE COMPENSATION: STRUCTURE AND INCENTIVES

How executives are compensated drives performance—not just how *much* they are paid, but *how* they are paid (i.e., the structure of their compensation package). Management's total compensation should be sensitive to changes in stock price so their incentives are aligned with shareholders' incentives. For example, the CEO's

MINI APPLICATION 7.2

HOME DEPOT AND ROBERT NARDELLI

In 2006, Robert Nardelli was fired as the CEO of Home Depot. Over the prior year, stock returns were down 13%. The board came under criticism when it was revealed that Nardelli was guaranteed at least a $3 million bonus each year and earned a total of $38 million in the year before he was fired. Ethical analysts understand the interplay between the board, executive compensation, and investment performance.

Source: www.businessweek.com.

Pay-performance sensitivity a measure of how total executive compensation changes with changes in shareholder wealth or stock value.

pay can change by $0.53 per $1,000 change in shareholder wealth. This relation is known as pay-performance sensitivity (Mini Application 7.2 shows one example where pay became disconnected to performance). Compensation packages are often complex. They can consist of salary, accounting bonuses, stock-based awards, and benefits, such as life and health insurance, pensions, and use of company assets such as corporate jets and real estate. Analysts need to look at these components closely and assess their impact on managerial decisions.

SALARY

Salary is an annual cash payment; it can range from a few hundred thousands of dollars to tens of millions of dollars. Salary is often renegotiated each year, but sometimes salary is guaranteed in a multiyear contract. Cost-of-living adjustments or built-in percentage raises can be part of these contracts. Salary renegotiations can give executives incentives to perform well. The threat of firing, which means no salary, can also provide positive incentives. However, salary renegotiation is not an incentive if CEOs are on the verge of retiring. In 2006, Countrywide's CEO, Angelo R. Mozilo (aged 58), earned a salary of $2,866,667.

Benefits are not related to performance. Some benefits make sense and others don't. Health insurance is not directly related to the CEO's performance, but the shareholders certainly want a healthy CEO. Benefits such as personal use of the company's jets, corporate-owned residences, expensive redecorating, family vacations to luxurious resorts, and so on are more questionable.

ACCOUNTING-BASED BONUSES

Accounting-based bonuses bonuses are tied to meeting ex ante goals of accounting performance—earnings, sales, return on assets, and so on.

Most CEOs earn accounting-based bonuses that are tied to meeting preset goals of accounting performance—earnings, sales, return on assets, and the like. Oftentimes performance measures are benchmarked to a preselected group of peer firms. Wal-Mart's performance might be compared to that of other discount retailers, for example, Target and Kmart. Suppose a firm's earnings are up for the year. Should the CEO earn a large bonus for improved earnings? It depends. If the increase in earnings is high relative to other peer companies, then the answer is yes. If the increase in earnings is low relative to peers, then the answer may be no. Additionally, many companies benchmark CEO compensation relative to a peer group to ensure that compensation is competitive. Mozilo earned a cash bonus of $20,461,473 in 2006.

TABLE	7.3	COUNTRYWIDE FINANCIAL CORPORATION BENCHMARK COMPANIES FOR EXECUTIVE COMPENSATION, 2006

- American Express Company
- Merrill Lynch & Co, Inc.
- Bank of America Corporation
- Morgan Stanley
- Bank of New York Company, Inc.
- National City Corporation
- BB&T Corporation
- The PNC Financial Services Group, Inc.
- Citigroup Inc.
- SLM Corporation
- Comerica, Incorporated

- SunTrust Banks, Inc.
- Fifth Third Bancorp
- U.S. Bancorp
- Golden West Financial Corporation
- Wachovia Corporation
- JPMorgan Chase & Co.
- Washington Mutual, Inc.
- Keycorp
- Wells Fargo & Company
- Lehman Brothers Holdings, Inc.
- MBNA Corporation

Source: Countrywide Financial Corporation, Proxy Statements; Filing Dates June 14, 2006 and June 15, 2005. www.sec.gov.

Table 7.3 shows Countrywide's peer group. Many of these disappeared during the financial crisis of 2008 along with Countrywide.

Why use accounting-based bonuses at all if shareholders care only about stock price? Stock price can be influenced by many factors outside of management's control. Overall market sentiment, information asymmetries between investors and managers, and macroeconomic factors affect stock prices, and the CEO cannot control them. Managers have greater control over accounting performance of the firm; it makes sense to create incentives to generate strong accounting performance. However, because managers have control over accounting methods used to report this performance, they can also manipulate them (see Chapter 6). One solution to discouraging earnings manipulation is to make bonuses part of **long-term incentive plans (LTIPs)**. Here accounting performance is taken into consideration not only for the current year, but for a longer time period—say, five years. This gives managers disincentives to manipulate accruals to improve the current year's performance at the expense of later years (see Chapter 6). In addition, many compensation contracts have **clawback provisions**. If earnings are restated, bonuses based on misstated higher earnings must be repaid. Analysts need to look at accounting-based bonuses along with earnings to assess how compensation contracts can influence reported earnings.

Long-term incentive plans (LTIPs) incentive plans that are based on comparative accounting performance beyond that in the current year.

Clawback provisions compensation that must be returned if it turns out it was based on faulty financial reports.

STOCK-BASED COMPENSATION

Stock-based compensation is essential to aligning managers' incentives with shareholders' interests. There are many types of stock awards. Firms can simply give managers stock. If managers turn around and sell it, they have lost their

Restricted stock stock that is awarded but whose transfer of ownership is restricted for a certain period of time.

Stock appreciation rights, or phantom stock rather than awarding stock, the firm agrees to pay out the difference in share value that has accumulated over a set period of time.

Stock options the right to buy a stock at a prespecified price, the exercise price, at a prespecified date, the exercise or maturity date, in the future.

Vesting the point at which granted benefits such as stock awards or contributions to retirement plans can be kept by the employees even after leaving the firm.

ownership interest in the firm. Often managers are granted **restricted stock**. The stock is awarded, but transfer of ownership is restricted for one to five years. To make money on these shares, managers better be sure the decisions they make will improve long-term share value. Managers can also be given **stock appreciation rights, or phantom stock**. Here the firm agrees to pay out the difference in share value that has accumulated over a set period of time. This compensation creates incentives for managers to improve share price, but after the payout, managers no longer have an ownership interest in the firm. **Stock options** are one of the most common forms of compensation. A stock option is the right to buy a stock at a prespecified price, the exercise price, at a prespecified date, the exercise or maturity date, in the future (see the appendix if you need a refresher on options). Stock options can also be the largest portion of total compensation. The grant usually is made annually, and the exercise price is set based on the stock price on the grant date. Under this system, managers have incentives to work hard to increase the stock price beyond the grant price.

Executive option grants are a bit different from options that trade on exchanges—that is, the Chicago Board of Options Exchange (CBOE). Standard contracts listed on the CBOE expire within less than a year. Usually executive options are exercisable over longer periods of time than exchange-traded options. This factor minimizes incentives to manipulate stock price for short-run increases at the expense of long-run profitability. Executive options can have maturities of up to ten years. Options are often granted but have a vesting schedule. **Vesting** means the CEO receives the options only if he or she stays with the firm for a certain period of time. But usually there are exceptions to vesting; often options vest when managers leave the firm, as long as they are not fired for cause. In addition, traded options are third-party agreements, and they are settled by using stock that the firm has already issued. Executive stock options are settled by using either newly issued or repurchased shares. Finally, if the stock price falls below the exercise price, boards often reprice the options. When the stock price falls below the exercise price, the options are said to be underwater. Boards argue that repricing is necessary to retain executive incentives. Critics of this practice argue that it nullifies the original incentive. Underwater options on the CBOE are not repriced.

Why give stock options and not just stock? The value of stock options increases not only with the stock price but also with increases in price volatility. Managers are usually more risk averse than shareholders. Remember that most shareholders hold the firm's stock in a well-diversified portfolio. In contrast, most managers have all of their eggs in one basket. If the firm does poorly, their performance-based compensation drops and they even may be out of a job. Managers who receive more stock options are encouraged to assume higher risk. Figure 7.5 shows how the unique payoff structure of options encourages risk taking. CEOs should not take on uncompensated or excessive risks, only those that increase stock price. Longer holding periods or exercise dates can discourage executives from taking risks that could increase stock price in the short term, but over a longer period could lead to declines in price. Mozilo was granted $1,103,745 in restricted stock awards and $23,047,104 worth of stock options the year before Countrywide's collapse. Because Mozilo had reached retirement age in 2006, his options and restricted stock awards

| FIGURE | 7.5 | **OPTION GRANTS INCREASE RISK TAKING** |

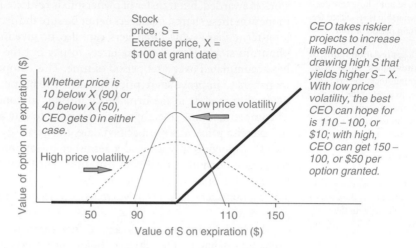

were fully vested. Mozilo made over $140 million when he sold his stock before its decline. The SEC subsequently charged him with insider trading.

OPTION GRANT ABUSES

Remember that the value of the option depends on the value of the exercise price relative to the stock price at the time of exercise (see the appendix to this chapter). The exercise price is set by the market price at the time of the grant. Abuses of options grants occur when the grant date and exercise price is chosen to maximize the difference in exercise price and future stock price. How can executives do this? They use hindsight to change the grant date and exercise price to be on the date of the lowest stock price of the year. Hindsight doesn't create forward-looking incentives.

OPTION BACKDATING

Option backdating use of hindsight to change the grant date or exercise price to be on the date of the lowest stock price of the year.

The difference between the exercise price and the current market price immediately creates value for the executive. This is known as **option backdating**. Figure 7.6 shows how this works. There is nothing wrong with backdating options, as long as the practice is fully disclosed to investors and all relevant taxes are paid. But most of the time, this is not what happens.

   In 2005–2006, more than 100 companies were caught in options backdating scandals. Apple, Inc. was one of these companies. A SEC investigation discovered that Apple had been involved in several instances of backdating options. For example, as Figure 7.7 shows, CEO Steve Jobs was given 10 million share options on January 18, 2000, but they were backdated to January 12 when Apple's stock price was $16.75 or 19 percent lower. Because the options were issued in the money (when the stock price

| FIGURE | 7.6 | **BACKDATING OPTIONS** |

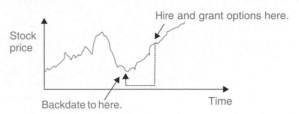

| FIGURE | 7.7 | **APPLE, INC. (AAPL) CLOSE** |

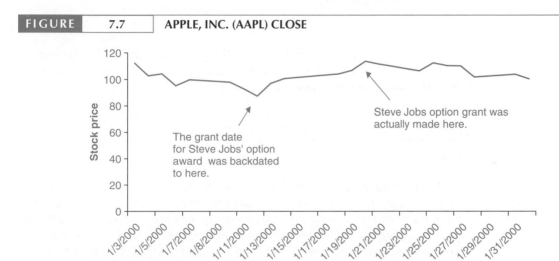

is above the exercise price), Steve Jobs had an immediate gain of $167,500,000. This should have been reported as taxable income by Jobs and as a compensation expense by Apple. Most often, options are not granted in the money and become tax-deferred compensation for the executive and a non-reportable expense for the company. Apple's former general counsel, Nancy Heinen, and former CFO Fred Anderson were accused of orchestrating and covering up backdating practices. The SEC settled with both executives, who resigned from Apple. Steve Jobs, CEO of Apple, was exonerated when an investigation showed that he never exercised his backdated options. Apple had to restate earnings for 2001 through 2006 by a total of $84 million after tax, including $4 million and $7 million in fiscal years 2006 and 2005, to reflect stock-based compensation expenses for the backdated options. At the time, earnings were already over $6 billion, so the restatement had a limited impact on the stock price.

OPTION SPRING-LOADING

Option spring-loading occurs when options are granted before the release of positive information, such as higher-than-expected earnings.

Another type of abuse is **option spring-loading**. This occurs when options are granted before the release of positive information, such as higher-than-expected earnings. Figure 7.8 shows how this is done. Spring-loading again doesn't provide incentives for managers to increase stock price. It's already higher! This practice also

| FIGURE | 7.8 | **SPRING-LOADING OPTIONS** |

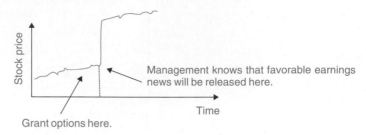

raises concerns about inside trading (see Chapter 4). Analysts need to be wary of companies that consistently appear to be "lucky" in timing their option grants via either backdating or spring-loading.

GOLDEN PARACHUTES, GOLDEN HANDCUFFS, AND GOLDEN COFFINS

Golden parachutes severance agreements that are triggered by control-related events.

Golden parachutes are severance agreements triggered by control-related events. These are typically 3 to 5 years' worth of salary that is paid out to departing executives if they lose their jobs when there is a takeover (a control-related event). Usually, any unvested option also fully vests at the time of the takeover. Some argue that these agreements unnecessarily enrich executives who are getting kicked out of their jobs for poor performance (their poor performance led to the takeover). Others argue that these agreements increase the likelihood that a beneficial takeover will occur. Incumbent managers are less likely to resist a takeover if they have a golden parachute to make their landing softer. In 2006, Mozilo's golden parachute was three times his salary of $2.9 million plus three times his prior incentive bonus of $20.5 million. Mozilo stood to make over $70 million if shareholders decided to vote him out of a job in a takeover! Golden parachutes have become more controversial during the recent financial crisis. Freddie Mac and Fannie Mae are companies that packaged and sold mortgages to investors. They were bailed out by the federal government when the housing market collapsed. In the wake of public outcry, managers' severance agreements, or golden parachutes, were rescinded.

Golden handcuffs deferred compensation agreements.

Golden handcuffs are deferred compensation agreements. A portion of the CEO's compensation is not paid out until a future date and is contingent on the CEO staying with the firm (that's where "handcuffs" comes in). These agreements can be used to ensure a CEO tenure that is consistent with increasing shareholder wealth or serve to entrench CEOs.

Golden coffins generous death benefits granted to top executives.

Golden coffins are generous death benefits granted to top executives. Some have argued they are unrelated to CEO performance and unnecessarily enrich the CEO's beneficiaries. Ethical analysts need to be wary of all these types of "golden" compensation agreements, which can indicate a board that is entrenched along with the CEO.

HORIZON PROBLEMS AND A FIRM'S LONG-RUN PROFITABILITY

Shareholders and top executives face different time horizons in their economic relationship with a firm. Shareholders have an infinite horizon. Remember that the stock value is the discounted value of a *perpetual* (forever) stream of earnings per share. CEOs have a much shorter tenure with their firms. CEOs are often appointed in middle age, and most individuals retire when they are 65 years old. CEOs are also under pressure to meet or exceed quarterly analysts' earnings expectations. Earnings manipulation is one way to pull future earnings forward. The ability to pump up earnings can reduce managers' incentives to improve the overall operating efficiency of the firm (see Chapter 6). Thus CEOs can sometimes make decisions that increase short-run profitability at the expense of long-run shareholder wealth. Shorter tenures can also reduce managers' incentives for making investments in the firm that have longer-term payoffs. Why would a CEO reduce current earnings to improve future earnings after he or she has left? When examining compensation contracts, analysts need to think about the CEO's incentives for improving shareholder wealth long after he or she has left the firm. See, for example, Mini Application 7.3. Figure 7.9 summarizes the important questions analysts need to ask when evaluating the CEO.

SHAREHOLDERS' RIGHTS AND THE TAKEOVER MARKET

Control contest a contest over the ownership control of a company.

Takeover a transfer of stock ownership control of a firm.

Target a firm that a bidder is trying to takeover stock ownership control of.

Bidder a company, investor, or group of investors that seek to acquire control of another firm.

Premium the additional amount that is offered over current market price for the stock of a firm by a bidder seeking control.

What happens when a firm's corporate governance policies fail? The market for external control can be a mechanism of last resort for shareholders. Other market participants can see that the firm will be worth more if they are calling the shots. The firm can be taken over, a new slate of directors voted in, and a new CEO hired. The key to taking over a firm is to acquire enough shares, which in turn give the bidder the majority of the votes and control over the selection of directors. Investment professionals can find themselves involved in a control transaction by either voting and/or exercising investment discretion for their clients' shares. Many different types of transactions can be used to take over a firm. Let's review some of the most common forms. But first, briefly familiarize yourself with control and takeover terminology:

- **Control contest**—a bid for control of the firm.
- **Takeover**—occurs when there is a change in control.
- **Target**—the firm being taken over.
- **Bidder**—the firm that is trying to get control.
- **Premium**—to obtain control, the bidder usually pays a higher rate (a premium) for the target's stock.

| FIGURE | 7.9 | **EVALUATING THE CEO** |

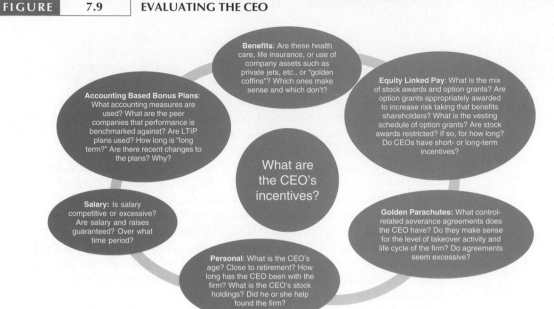

MINI APPLICATION 7.3

TEST YOURSELF

Suppose you are analyzing a firm that compensates its CEO with a mixture of salary, an annual accounting-based bonus, and stock options exercisable in five years. Suppose the board decides to keep the total level of compensation the same, but increases the dollar proportion of stock options. What do you think will happen to pay-performance sensitivity, capital investments, and stock price performance?

Hostile a bid for control of a company that is opposed by the incumbent management team of the target company.

Friendly a bid for control of a firm that is not opposed by the incumbent management team of the target company.

Hostile tender offer occurs when a bidder makes a direct appeal to the target shareholders and offers to buy their stock at a premium to market price; current or target management is opposed to the offer.

- Hostile—describes a takeover that target managers are opposed to (because they will lose their jobs).
- Friendly—describes a takeover that target managers are not opposed to.

In a **hostile tender offer**, a bidder makes a direct appeal to the target shareholders and offers to buy their stock at a premium over market price. The premium is usually 50 percent, and the number of shares sought is just over 50 percent. With just over 50 percent of the shares, the bidder has a majority of the shares and, more important, a majority of the votes. The bidder can then use those votes either to acquire the firm in a merger or to elect the bidder's board and CEO. In a merger, the board proposes terms to shareholders by which either the target firm becomes a wholly owned subsidiary of the bidder firm or the two firms become a new firm with newly issued stock. Takeover premiums of 50 percent create windfall gains for investors.

Anti-takeover amend- ments amendments to the corporate charter designed to thwart a takeover.

Anti-takeover amendments to corporate charters are designed to make a takeover more difficult and are used to entrench managers or to improve takeover terms for shareholders. Managers can agree to propose that shareholders vote to remove the amendment in exchange for a better takeover price. A **supermajor- ity amendment** requires more than a simple majority (greater than 50 percent) of votes for a merger to be approved. Between 80 and 85 percent can be required, depending on what the amendment specifies. Now the bidder has to acquire considerably more. The takeover can become too expensive, discouraging potential bidders. We have already discussed a staggered board that is broken down into classes, among which only one class goes up for election in any year. Staggered boards make it more difficult for a bidder to get control of the board. After making a sizable investment in purchasing the target shares at a premium, the bidder doesn't want to wait that long to start making changes.

Supermajority amend- ment an amendment to the corporate charter that requires more than a simple majority (greater than 50 percent) of votes for a merger to be approved.

A **poison pill** is another way to deter a bidder. Poison pills are usually preferred stock with mandatory redemption features. The preferred stock can be redeemed for a generous cash payout, triggered by a control-related event such as when an investor acquires 20 percent or more of a firm's stock (the Williams Act requires that once an investor hits the 20 percent threshold, he or she must make a formal tender offer to acquire any more stock). The cash payout by the target firm can reduce the firm's attractiveness to the bidder. The bidder may have been counting on the target's cash balances to help finance the takeover. Hence, the bidder may be successful in taking over the firm but must swallow a poison pill to do so.

Poison pill usually describes preferred stock with mandatory redemption features whereby redemption is triggered by a control-related event.

Fair price amend- ment amendment to the corporate charter providing a formula to determine a minimum price that the bidder must offer for the firm.

Firms can also have a **fair price amendment**. This provision provides a formula determining a minimum price that a bidder must offer for a firm. The formula can often specify a premium based on a market price that is calculated during a period when the price is likely to be already higher in anticipation of a takeover premium. In effect, the bidder has to pay an *even* higher premium. Again, this type of amendment is designed to make a takeover more expensive and to discourage potential bidders. Analysts need to be aware of all of these amendments and assess how they can improve or decrease shareholder wealth. Figure 7.10 shows how shareholder rights can be weakened and provides steps to strengthen them.

Corporate governance indices have been developed to attempt to capture all the different dimensions of shareholder rights, board characteristics, and directors' and officers' compensation. A common one is the GIM index (developed by Gompers, Ishii, and Metrick, 2003). This index checks for the existence of 24 corporate governance rules including classified or staggered boards, golden parachutes, cumulative voting, supermajority amendments, classes of shares with unequal voting rights, fair price amendments, and poison pills. Another index is the Corporate Governance Quotient (CGQ), developed by Institutional Shareholder Services (ISS—now part of RiskMetrics Group), which looks at 63 different measures including not only anti-takeover amendments but also board and compensation characteristics. The CGQ is reported for individual stocks on www.finance.yahoo.com. While these indices can be useful in making investment recommendations, competent and diligent analysts also do their own research (see Chapter 5).

FIGURE	7.10	SHAREHOLDER VOTING AND RIGHTS

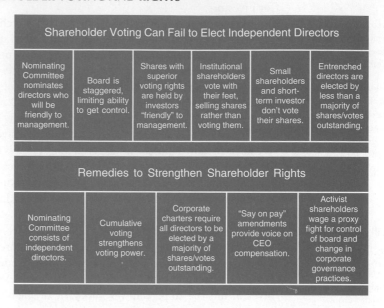

Shareholder Voting Can Fail to Elect Independent Directors

Nominating Committee nominates directors who will be friendly to management.	Board is staggered, limiting ability to get control.	Shares with superior voting rights are held by investors "friendly" to management.	Institutional shareholders vote with their feet, selling shares rather than voting them.	Small shareholders and short-term investor don't vote their shares.	Entrenched directors are elected by less than a majority of shares/votes outstanding.

Remedies to Strengthen Shareholder Rights

Nominating Committee consists of independent directors.	Cumulative voting strengthens voting power.	Corporate charters require all directors to be elected by a majority of shares/votes outstanding.	"Say on pay" amendments provide voice on CEO compensation.	Activist shareholders wage a proxy fight for control of board and change in corporate governance practices.

MINI APPLICATION 7.4

WARNING SIGNS OF WEAK CORPORATE GOVERNANCE AT COUNTRYWIDE FINANCIAL CORPORATION

- The board was staggered, increasing board and CEO entrenchment.
- The board was large (e.g., 14 directors), too large to effectively monitor management.
- The CEO was also chairman of the board and thus exerted undue influence over board decisions.
- Directors were too busy—many nonmanagement directors had three or four directorships.
- Many nonmanagement directors had lengthy tenures, thus compromising their independence from the CEO.
- The CEO had a generous golden parachute worth over $70 million if the firm was taken over and the CEO was ousted.
- The Compensation Committee met 29 times, more than any other board committee, before approving a large increase in the directors' and the CEO's compensation *just before* the company's collapse.
- Three nonmanagement directors resigned during the year before the collapse—not a good sign.
- CEO compensation was a short-term bonus based on most recent annual accounting performance, and all stock options were exercisable.

CONCLUSION: SHAREHOLDERS' RIGHTS AND CONFLICTS

Corporate governance serves to ensure that managers act in shareholders' best interests. Besides selling their shares, the only other mechanism that allows shareholders a say in how the firm is run is exercising the voting power attached to their shares; they get to vote in nonexecutive directors who are charged with monitoring managers and setting compensation. Investment professionals are often charged with voting proxies for their clients and need to consider their vote and ramifications for shareholder wealth.

Compensation should be structured to align managers' incentives with shareholders' interests. The nominating process and various other conflicts can compromise the independence of directors. When internal corporate governance mechanisms fail, the takeover market can act as a disciplining mechanism of last resort. The effectiveness of the takeover market in turn depends on shareholders' rights—that is, whether there are anti-takeover amendments that insulate managers.

Proxy statements provide the source of information for investment analysts to evaluate the effectiveness of the firm's corporate governance practices. Information about the directors, as well as details of the top management team's compensation contacts, is included. It is the analyst's job to examine this information with an eye toward identifying potential conflicts and choosing investments that are most likely to be profitable. The chapter began by looking at Countrywide Financial Corporation as an example of the ethical lapses in the most recent financial crisis of 2008–2009. Mini Application 7.4 lists some of the warning signs that Countrywide was headed for trouble. After reading this chapter (and because we know what happened at Countrywide), these warning signs should be obvious to you. An analyst armed with an understanding of corporate governance can make wise investment recommendations to investors, and be more ethical in both fulfilling his obligations to investors and society. One day you, too, could find yourself characterized as one of the "brave" analysts mentioned at the beginning of the chapter.

TERMS

corporate governance	compensation committee	proxy fight
adjustable rate mortgages (ARMs)	audit committee	dissident
	nominating committee	activist shareholders
pay-option mortgages	annual retainer fee	13D form
staggered board	per meeting fees	13G form
proxy statements	stock awards	blockholder
inside directors	stock option grants	superior voting rights
outside directors	beneficially owned stock	cumulative voting
gray directors	entrenched	"say on pay" amendments
professional directors	incumbents	vote with their feet

pay-performance
  sensitivity
accounting-based bonuses
long-term incentive plans
  (LTIPs)
clawback provisions
restricted stock
stock appreciation
  rights/phantom stock
stock options

vesting
option backdating
option spring-loading
golden parachutes
golden handcuffs
golden coffins
control contest
takeover
target
bidder

premium
hostile
friendly
hostile tender offer
anti-takeover
  amendments
supermajority
  amendment
poison pill
fair price amendment

REVIEW QUESTIONS

1. Describe the function of the board of directors in publicly held corporations.

2. Explain the process by which directors are elected to the board. Which types of voting rights strengthen the process? Which ones weaken it?

3. Identify potential conflicts and pressures in the nominating process for nonexecutive board members.

4. Identify at least three characteristics that nonexecutive directors should possess that attest to their competence and independence.

5. Describe how nonexecutive directors are compensated and how compensation is related to independence.

6. How can accounting bonuses be an effective means to align managers' incentives with shareholders'? Why isn't stock-based compensation sufficient?

7. Explain the role of stock options in creating incentives for executives.

8. Explain the practice of backdating options, and state why this practice is unethical.

9. How might the practice of granting golden parachutes to executives be in shareholders' interests?

10. Explain the horizon problem and the role it plays in conflicts between managers and shareholders.

11. Explain the role the takeover market plays in disciplining managers.

12. How does a staggered board make a takeover more difficult?

13. What is a proxy fight? Given the costs of a proxy fight, why would activist shareholders wage these as part of an investment strategy?

14. What is a poison pill, and why does this strategy discourage a takeover?

15. Why should analysts be aware of anti-takeover amendments? Provide a scenario where such amendments would lead to a sell recommendation and one with a buy.

CRITICAL THINKING QUESTIONS

1. At the beginning of the chapter, we considered the importance of context in evaluating a firm's corporate governance practices. Suppose you are analyzing a firm that has five board members: three of the members are executives with the firm, and the CEO is the chairman of the board. This is a board where insiders dominate; and at first blush, we

could conclude that this is evidence of weak corporate governance. What is a scenario where this board structure makes sense? What other measures, either governance or financial, would you look for to conclude that this board structure is effective?

2. You are analyzing a pharmaceutical company and its stock. Pharmaceutical firms' success depends on the ability to created new patented drugs. For the firm you are analyzing, you notice that the CEO and several key top executives are over age 65. What concerns would this create for a potential long-term investor in this stock, if any? What would you look for in terms of either compensation or financial performance measures that would either reinforce your concerns or alleviate them?

3. Suppose you work as an analyst for a firm that makes only short-term investments in stocks (i.e., your average holdings are nine months or less). Even if your firm is eligible to vote proxies, it often doesn't own the stock after the votes are cast. With this type of investing strategy, does a firm's corporate governance matter? Why or why not?

4. While analyzing the stock for a particular firm, you notice that the firm has changed the peer companies it will use in benchmarking its accounting performance and, subsequently, the CEO's accounting-based bonus. The proxy statement provides only vague language in discussing the change. What else would you want to know, and what research would you do to decide whether the change improves the incentives for the CEO or is a means for self-enrichment at the shareholders' expense?

5. Widget Manufacturing, a firm you have been following in the last few years, has suffered losses. In its most recent proxy statement, the firm discusses changes in strategy designed to improve performance; and in fact, in the last year, the firm has shown a small profit. However, you also know that during this year, three independent directors who are CEOs at other firms have announced their resignations from the Widget board because they are busy. How would you evaluate this change in the board relative to the firm's future prospects? Provide a scenario in which these resignations are consistent with a buy recommendation and one in which they are consistent with a sell.

APPLIED STUDENT PROJECT

You can do your own analysis of a firm's corporate governance practices. Select a publicly traded company (and you can select two more peer companies if desired) and obtain the firm's proxy statement via SEC filings of form 14As (www.sec.gov). Using the issues discussed in this chapter, judge the effectiveness of the board. Here are some questions you might answer: What is the percentage of outside directors on the board? Are there any whose independence might be compromised? Does committee membership seem effective? Does board size seem right? Are the directors appropriately compensated? Do directors have strong ownership interests? Is the board staggered? Is there cumulative voting? What about executive compensation—is it correctly structured? Is it the right amount? Does it seem consistent with the firm's financial performance? Finally, judge the role the firm's corporate governance practices play in your investment decision: buy, sell, or hold. Support your recommendations in a two- to three-page written report.

RECOMMENDED CASES

1. Case 8—Former CEO of NYSE: Grasso's Pay Package
2. Case 11—Qwest Communications International: Accounting Fraud and Overstated Revenues

3. Case 16—Merrill Lynch and Bank of America Merger: Bonuses Paid to Merrill Employees—Excessive Compensation?

4. Case 19—WorldCom: Capitalizing Operating Expenses; an Unethical Accounting Practice

5. Case 26—Enron: A Case of Extreme Hubris

6. Case 27—UnitedHealth: Backdating Stock Options

REFERENCES AND SUGGESTED READING

Adams, John. "DoJ's Open Season on Subprime." *US Banker* (October 2008), 14.

Aikin, Blaine F. "A Duty to Monitor Proxy Voting: Investment Managers Are Obligated to Vote in the Best Interests of Shareholders." *Investment News* (May 12, 2008).

Anonymous. "SEC Begins Formal Probe of Countrywide." *Wall Street Journal*, 9 August 2008, B4.

Armey, Dick. "The Fan/Fred Bailout Is a Scandal." *Wall Street Journal*, 25 July 2008: A.15.

Atanassov, Julian, and E. Han Kim. "Labor and Corporate Governance: International Evidence from Restructuring Decisions." *Journal of Finance* 64, no. 1 (2009): 341–374.

Begley, Joy, and Gerald A. Fetham. "An Empirical Examination of the Relation between Debt Contracts and Management Incentives." *Journal of Accounting & Economics* 27, no. 2 (1999): 229–60.

Bruck, Connie. "Angelo's Ashes: The Man Who Became the Face of the Financial Crisis." *The New Yorker*, June 29, 2009.

Burr, Barry B. "Proxy Votes Reveal Varied Approaches." *Pensions & Investments* (March 9, 2009), 6–7.

Burrows, Peter, with Lorraine Woellert. "Is Steve Jobs Untouchable?" *Business Week* (January 15, 2007), 28.

CFA Institute. *The Corporate Governance of Listed Companies: A Manual for Investors.* CFA Institute, 2005.

Coffin, Bill. "When the Golden Parachute Rips." *Risk Management* 55, no. 2 (2008): 27.

Coles, J. L., N. D. Daniel, and L. Naveen. "Boards: Does One Size Fit All?" *Journal of Financial Economics* 87, no. 2 (2008): 329–356.

Comment, Robert, and G. William Schwert. "Poison or Placebo? Evidence on the Deterrence and Wealth Effects of Modern Antitakeover Measures." *Journal of Financial Economics* 39, no. 1 (1995): 3–44.

Cremers, K. J. Martin, and Vinay B. Nair. "Governance Mechanisms and Equity Prices." *Journal of Finance* 60, no. 6 (2005): 2859–94.

Cremers, K. J. Martin, Vinay B. Nair, and Chenyang Wei. "Governance Mechanisms and Bond Prices." *Review of Financial Studies* 20, no. 5 (2007): 1359–89.

Dallas, George. *Governance and Risk.* New York: McGraw-Hill, 2004.

Dewally, Michaël, and Sarah W. Peck. "Upheaval in the Boardroom: Outside Director Public Resignations, Motivations, and Consequences." *Journal of Corporate Finance* 16, no. 1 (2010): 38–52.

Evans, Jocelyn D., and Frank Hefner. "Business Ethics and the Decision to Adopt Golden Parachute Contracts: Empirical Evidence of Concern for All Stakeholders." *Journal of Business Ethics* 86, no. 1 (2009): 65–79.

Fich, Eliezer M. "Can Corporate Governance Save Distressed Firms from Bankruptcy? An Empirical Analysis." *Review of Quantitative Finance and Accounting* 30, no. 2 (2008): 225–52.

Goldfarb, Zachary A. "SEC Moves to Make Companies More Accountable to Shareholders." *Washington Post*, 2 July 2009, A14.

Gompers, Paul, Joy Ishii, and Andrew Metrick. "Corporate Governance and Equity Prices." *Quarterly Journal of Economics* 118, no. 1 (2003): 107–56.

Grover, Ronald. "Icahn Is on the Attack," *Business Week* (March 9, 2009), 32.

Hagerty, James R. "Crisis on Wall Street: Regulator Plans to Bar Big Severance." *Wall Street Journal*, 15 September 2008, A19.

Hagerty, James R., and John D. McKinnon. "Fannie Mae to Pay $400 Million to Settle Probe; Accord with Ofheo, SEC to Include Harsh Report on Lapses in Accounting." *Wall Street Journal*, 23 May 2006, A3.

Iwata, Edward. "SEC, Apple's Former Lawyer Settle; Will Pay $2.2M over Backdating Case That Involved CEO Jobs." *USA Today*, 15 August 2008, B3.

Julien, Rick, and Larry Rieger. "The Missing Link in Corporate Governance." *Risk Management* 50, no. 4 (2003): 32–35.

Kedrosky, Paul. "Why Are Analysts So Screwy About Sells?" (August 16, 2007), http://seekingalpha.com/article/44633-countrywide-financial-vtb-group-why-are-analysts-so-screwy-about-sells.

Krugman, Paul. "Enron's Second Coming?" *New York Times*, 1 October 2007, 25.

Meckling, William H., and Michael C. Jensen. "Theory of the Firm: Managerial Behavior, Agency Costs and Ownership Structure," *The Journal of Financial Economics* 3, no. 4 (1976): 305–360.

Morgenson, Gretchen. "The Owners Who Can't Hire or Fire," *New York Times*, 14 October 2007, 1.

Norris, Floyd. "Rethinking Risk's Role In Bosses' Pay," *New York Times*, 12 October 2007, 1.

Pouder, Richard, and R. Stephen Cantrell. "The Influence of Corporate Governance on Investor Reactions to Layoff Announcements." *Journal of Managerial Issues*, 11, no. 4 (1999): 475–92.

Rose, Jacob M. "Corporate Directors and Social Responsibility: Ethics versus Shareholder Value." *Journal of Business Ethics*, 73, no. 3 (2007): 319–32.

Sherry, Kristina. "House Panel OKs 'Say on Pay' Bill." *Los Angeles Times*, 29 July 2009, 2.

Shleifer, Andrei, and Robert W. Vishny. "A Survey of Corporate Governance." *Journal of Finance* 52, no. 2 (1997): 737–84.

Streitfeld, David, and Gretchen Morgenson. "Building Flawed American Dreams." *New York Times*, 19 October 2008, 1.

APPENDIX: REVIEW OF STOCK OPTIONS

A stock option is the right to buy a stock at a prespecified price, the exercise price, at a prespecified date, the exercise or maturity date, in the future. If it turns out that the exercise price is greater than the stock price on the exercise date, then the holder

EXAMPLE A7.1
HOW OPTIONS WORK

Stock Price Higher than Exercise Price

Exercise price	$50
Stock price on expiration	$75
Exercise your option?	Yes
Gain	$25

Stock Price Lower than Exercise Price

Exercise price	$50
Stock price on expiration	$25
Exercise your option?	No
Gain	0

can choose *not* to buy the stock. That's why it's called an option; you are not forced to buy the stock. Suppose the exercise price is $100 and the stock is currently trading at $90. Why would you exercise your option and buy the stock at $100 when you can buy it on the open market for $90? You wouldn't—and you wouldn't have to, with an option. See Example A7.1 which provides another example.

Options are more valuable as stock prices become more uncertain or volatile. An increase in volatility increases the dispersion of stock prices. There is a higher probability of a future stock price that is both much lower and much higher than the exercise price. What happens if the stock price turns out to be not just a little lower than the exercise price, but a lot lower because the price is more volatile? Does it matter? Remember that if the stock price falls below the exercise price, the holder of the option does not have to buy the stock. Once the stock price goes below the exercise price—whether a little below or a lot below—the holder won't exercise the option anyway.

What about the upside? Now an increase in volatility increases the probability of an even higher stock price above the exercise price. The value of the option is the difference in the stock price and the exercise price. The bigger this difference is, the more valuable the payoff. An increase in volatility increases the chances of getting a higher stock price at the exercise price and a bigger payoff.

So, in sum, volatility doesn't make the downside worse and only improves the upside. And on net, volatility makes options worth more.

CHAPTER 8

Socially Responsible Investing

Learning Objectives

After reading this chapter, students should be able to:

- Knowledgeably discuss stakeholder theory.
- Delineate a variety of social issues that investment professionals might consider when making an investment.
- Understand in theory how positive and negative social issue screens work and the difficulties of putting them into practice.
- Describe SRI indices and KLD 400 long-run return performance.
- Explain how shareholder advocacy works and can be effective.
- Describe the role of divestment in supporting human rights agendas.
- Recognize the special role pension funds, foundations, and university endowments have in socially responsible investing.
- Identify the role of microfinance lending and community investing in helping the poor.
- Understand the goal of Islamic finance.

CHAPTER OUTLINE

- Introduction: Directing Financial Capital to Benefit Society
- Stakeholder Theory
- Positive and Negative Screens
- Socially Responsible Mutual Funds

- Performance: Can You Do Well by Doing Good?

- Shareholder Advocacy

- Divestment

- The Special Role of Foundations, University Endowments, and Pension Funds

- Community Investing and Microfinance Lending

- Islamic Finance

- Conclusion: Obstacles to Doing Well while Doing Good

INTRODUCTION: DIRECTING FINANCIAL CAPITAL TO BENEFIT SOCIETY

Investment professionals play a powerful role in directing capital to activities that can benefit society. *Ethical* professionals are cognizant of their larger role in society. **Socially responsible investing** (SRI) is a type of investing that takes into account not only the risk-return performance but also the societal and ethical scope of an investment. SRI can assess whether a firm protects the environment or pollutes it; treats its employees equitably or misuses them; creates safe, valuable, and sustainable products and services for its customers or products and services that are unsafe, of poor quality, and unnecessary; treats its suppliers fairly or takes advantage of them; contributes to the surrounding community or remains insular; and respects basic human rights of international citizens or exploits countries with weaker protective laws. SRI can also encompass direct investments that support social and humanitarian causes, for example, providing capital for economic development or entrepreneurs in impoverished communities. However, unlike strictly charitable contributions, these investments earn returns so investors can "do well by doing good."

Incorporating social responsibility into investment analysis, recommendations, and decisions is difficult. There is no bright line separating irresponsible corporations from responsible ones. Publicly held corporations are complex organizations; rarely are they "all bad" or "all good." Some investors may judge a firm's overall business practices as responsible, while others may judge them as irresponsible. Consider, for example, Exxon Mobil Corporation (see Mini Application 8.1). Further, individuals can differ about whether any particular business practice is socially responsible or irresponsible. Dean Foods Company, for instance, makes and sells ice cream. Some investors may believe that making and selling ice cream is an innocuous business, while other investors concerned about societal health issues may believe ice cream is an inherently dangerous and irresponsible product.

Socially responsible investing (SRI) seeking to make investments that benefit society, for example investing in the stock of companies that don't pollute.

Exxon provides an example of how different investors can have different views on whether a company is socially responsible.

Some investors could argue that Exxon is inherently a socially irresponsible company. Most of its revenues come from oil production—a primary source of greenhouse gas emissions, which are partially responsible for climate change or global warming.

Other investors may view Exxon as a socially responsible company. It has projects under way to explore the development of alternative energy sources and has supported research into carbon sequestration and renewable energy resources.

Given the difficulties in deciding which business practices and corporations are socially responsible or irresponsible, you should not be surprised to learn that studies that look at the relation between social responsibility and risk-return performance yield mixed results (see references at the end of this chapter for some of these studies). Critics of socially responsible investing claim that it restricts the investment opportunity set or creates other costs, which in turn reduce risk-return performance. Cynics claim that social responsibility is a meaningless public relations device used by corporations and mutual funds to attract socially responsible consumers and investors. Proponents of socially responsible investing claim that not only is making these investments the right thing to do, but in the long run responsible companies will earn better returns as their practices are rewarded by society and investors alike.

The lack of consensus on SRI doesn't mean that professionals should throw up their hands and walk away from considering the societal impact of investment decisions. First, social responsibility may be important to your clients. For example, some clients do not want to invest in tobacco stocks. You have a fiduciary duty to develop a mutually agreeable investment policy statement (IPS) that integrates this criterion into how you manage such clients' accounts. It is, after all, *their* money (see Chapter 2). Second, the possibility of socially irresponsible behavior can be a real risk factor for an investment. A product recall, strike, Environmental Protection Agency (EPA) fines, lawsuits, and bad publicity are all events that can drive down the price of a stock. Even if the direct costs associated with these events are small, they can create reputation risks for companies and damage profitability. Social responsibility does not always have to be at odds with fiduciary duty or maximizing risk-adjusted returns. Recently the investment industry has coined the term **environmental, social, and governance (ESG)**, which captures a broader definition of corporate responsibility that includes both SRI (this chapter) and corporate governance (Chapter 7). The creation of this term reflects the investment industry's acknowledgement that these factors are becoming increasingly important in investment decisions.

Environmental, social, and governance (ESG) a term that describes important social policies or factors in an investment decision.

Merck & Co., Inc., a pharmaceutical company, provides an example of the relation between social responsibility and return performance. In 2004, Merck recalled and stopped manufacturing one of its most profitable painkilling drugs, Vioxx, after a study completed in August 2004 showed that Vioxx significantly

FIGURE	8.1	**MERCK & CO., INC. (MRK) STOCK PRICE IMPACT OF VIOXX/DRUG RECALL AND LAWSUITS**

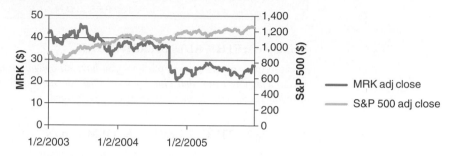

Source: www.finance.yahoo.com.

increased the risk of heart attack and stroke. In the following years, investigations showed that Merck knew of the risks and failed to fully disclose them to the Food and Drug Administration (FDA) and that Merck used ghost writers for studies published in academic journals, where the study would be written by the company first and an academic author second. The academic authors' support of Merck's studies gave them credence and respectability. The company paid $4.85 billion to settle personal injury lawsuits. As Figure 8.1 shows, the scandal took a toll on the stock price. Shareholders also sued management for providing "false and misleading" information to investors. Both patients *and* shareholders were hurt by Merck's irresponsible actions.

Could an analyst have seen this coming? Maybe. While the FDA approved the drug in 1999, in 2000 additional studies designed to approve other uses of Vioxx showed that Vioxx caused a slight increase in the risk of heart attack and stroke. The company's 10-K Filing of December 12, 2003 reported a delay in a Japanese regulatory authority's approval of Vioxx for distribution in Japan and the request for additional studies. These could have been warning signs of further trouble with the drug.

A company caught up in a more recent recall has been Toyota, an auto maker. Over the last decade, Toyota had gained market share and strong customer loyalty based on the reliability of its cars. But in 2009 reports of sudden acceleration of its cars emerged, threatening Toyota's reputation. How Toyota fixes the defect as well as acknowledges the problem will determine whether Toyota will regain its reputation for product quality, market share, profitability, and shareholder returns. You might want to follow up on this case.

Which of our four fundamental principles of investment ethics that we introduced in Chapter 1 apply to SRI? Principle 3, Responsible Investing, directly applies, but so do Principles 1, 2, and 4. It is important to gather *information* and make sure you *understand* the possible risks associated with "bad" corporate behavior before recommending an investment. Society trusts that investment professionals don't support investments in activities that, overall, harm society.

Investors implement SRI in a variety of ways. They create screens that include or exclude securities based on the issuing corporation's business practices, use their

FUNDAMENTAL PRINCIPLES OF INVESTMENT ETHICS FOR PROFESSIONALS

Principle 1: ETHICAL UNDERSTANDING

Because investments are complicated, *you have an obligation not to knowingly engage in an investment transaction that either you or others do not sufficiently understand. This includes knowing the underlying source of returns or fees charged.*

Principle 2: ETHICAL USE OF INFORMATION

Because investments are information driven, *you have an obligation to ensure that you and others have access to relevant information and that you or others do not misuse or distort information in the investment transaction.*

Principle 3: RESPONSIBLE INVESTING

Because investments provide financial resources to others, *you have an obligation to ensure that you do not knowingly make or recommend investments that support activities that harm others.*

Principle 4: TRUST AND FAIRNESS

Because you are dealing with others' money either directly or indirectly, *you have an obligation not to abuse the trust all others have either explicitly or implicitly placed in you to treat them fairly.*

---

voting power as shareholders to influence corporate decision making, or make direct investments to support social causes. But first let's identify some of the broad categories of social issues that should be considered when investing.

STAKEHOLDER THEORY

Stakeholder theory a theory that firms should maximize the welfare of all groups that are affected by the firm's policies—employees, customers, suppliers, communities, and so on.

The traditional business view of a corporation is that it exists to maximize shareholder wealth. Some have argued that if corporations maximize the wealth of shareholders, shareholders can in turn use that wealth to support activities that have social benefits (Friedman 1970). Others have argued that many groups are affected by the firm's policies: employees, customers, suppliers, and communities. **Stakeholder theory** says that all of these groups are stakeholders in the corporation, and firms should maximize the welfare of all of them (Freeman 1994). Figure 8.2 provides a list of all the firm's major stakeholders.

Yet another view is that there is no conflict between shareholders' and other parties' interests. The welfare of others is an important part of maximizing shareholder wealth in the long run. For example, if management decides to save costs by producing unsafe products, the company is likely to lose future sales and be sued by consumers. As a result, shareholder wealth will suffer. Management should make safe

| FIGURE | 8.2 | **THE FIRM'S STAKEHOLDERS** |

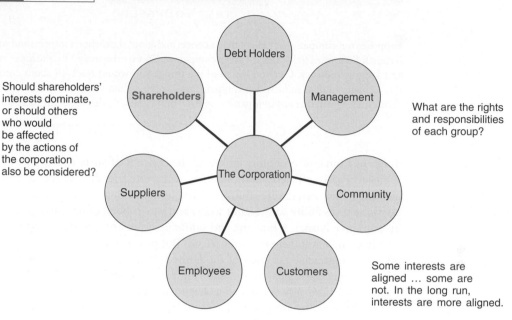

Should shareholders' interests dominate, or should others who would be affected by the actions of the corporation also be considered?

What are the rights and responsibilities of each group?

Some interests are aligned … some are not. In the long run, interests are more aligned.

products that benefit consumers *and* shareholders. To make *informed* investment decisions, analysts should research corporate policies toward other stakeholders. Mistreatment or negligent treatment of other stakeholders can potentially lead to litigation, increased regulation, boycotts, and other unpleasant results. These are potential costs and political risks for corporations. Minimizing them is *prudent* and can increase returns to shareholders. To make *ethical* investment decisions, analysts should consider the impact of corporations' actions on all social groups. Ethics dictates that actions should not harm others. **Prudent** motivations assert that corporations should take ethical actions because it makes good business sense. Ethics asserts that corporations should take ethical actions because it is the "right thing to do," regardless of the business consequences.

At this point, it might be helpful to clarify some terms. Some individuals make a distinction between "business ethics" and "corporate social responsibility (CSR)." Sometimes there is confusion about whether these two phrases refer to two different sets of behaviors. Ethics are rules based on moral standards that guide conduct toward others. Social responsibility encompasses business practices that benefit society as a whole. Doesn't being ethical imply you are socially responsible, and vice versa? What do you think?

Finally, the discussion of social responsibility brings into the discussion the debate between efficiency and equity. Recall from your economics class that **efficiency**, and in particular Pareto efficiency, strives to achieve distribution of wealth such that no one can be made better off without making someone else worse off. This concept is

Prudent describes the situation when corporations take "ethical" actions because it makes good business sense.

Efficiency an economics term describing a state where the distribution of wealth is such that no one can be made better off without making someone else worse off.

MINI APPLICATION 8.2

TEST YOURSELF

Suppose your company has a client that is concerned about the carbon footprint and wants to tilt its portfolio toward only stocks of green companies. You are the analyst for the hotel, restaurant, and lodging industry. Can you list all of the things you would research about companies in this industry to determine which companies are greener than others? To get you started, how about finding whether any companies use only biodegradable detergent for their laundry?

Equity the concept of fairness in economic distribution; to each according to his needs.

different from equity. Equity embraces the concept of fairness. Suppose society has achieved Pareto efficiency. Now one person, your friend, is suddenly and through no fault of her own in dire straits (lost her home through natural disaster, suffered a permanent disability so she can't work, and was robbed of her savings by a crooked investment advisor). A humane and *equitable* system of resource distribution would take from others to help out your friend. But now we have made these others worse off. The progressive tax code of the United States supports the concept of equity. Wealthier tax payers pay more, allowing for a redistribution of wealth to support public goods and services as well as less fortunate citizens—your friend. Ethics and social responsibility are about fairness and the treatment of others.

In the next section, we briefly review some of the issues other stakeholders might have about a firm's practices and activities. In reading this section, you will note that we suggest how addressing these issues *might* benefit shareholders. Be aware that there is a paucity of rigorous, large-sample, empirical studies that link shareholder returns to different corporate practices. However, as an ethical analyst looking at an *individual* security, you should consider the *possible* impact of the company's policies on others and in turn on shareholder returns. This process doesn't have to be markedly different from what a traditional fundamental analyst does in judging whether a firm's sales growth will generate future shareholder returns. Just as there are differences in opinion about the efficacy of a particular business model (think of buy versus sell, for instance), there can be differences in opinion about social responsibility and returns (see Chapter 5). In this chapter, we merely suggest how these issues could be considered by an ethical analyst.

ENVIRONMENT

Socially responsible companies are careful not to damage the environment. These firms use clean energy, recycle, prevent pollution, and are careful to limit carbon emissions. In turn, they are less likely to face fines and regulatory sanctions, thus leaving more profits for shareholders. Mini Application 8.2 gives you an opportunity to think about the environmental issues for a specific industry.

EMPLOYEES

Corporations should provide a safe and healthy working environment for their employees. Proponents of social justice also advocate that employers provide health-care and retirement benefits (fair CEO compensation can be another issue—see Chapter 7). Employee involvement in policy making and opportunities for profit sharing or share ownership are other signs that employees are valued. Following and supporting labor laws in areas of civil rights and sexual harassment is important as well. Treating employees beneficially may increase profits for shareholders because employees who are treated well are likely to be more productive. If a company has a reputation for being a good place to work, it is likely to incur lower recruiting and turnover costs.

PRODUCTS AND SERVICES

Firms that produce products and services that are safe, of good quality, priced fairly, and sold using ethical and truthful marketing practices are more likely to be able to sustain sales growth in the long run. Sales growth can increase profits and returns to shareholders.

SUPPLIERS

Socially responsible and ethical firms should not attempt to use purchasing power to negotiate unfair terms. Developing fair contracts with suppliers in the long run may lead to more efficiency and innovation in both products and services. And again, the result is more profit and returns for shareholders.

COMMUNITY

Corporations that are viewed as "good citizens" provide support for community activities through charitable giving and employee volunteer programs. Communities look for corporate support in a multitude of areas—the arts, education, crime reduction, affordable housing, and transportation. Corporations in turn create attractive communities for their employees to live in, which can potentially reduce recruiting costs. Warm community relations can also lead to increased public funding for infrastructure, for example, highway access, that can bring about expansion at a lower cost. Good community relations that lower costs can increase shareholder returns.

HUMAN RIGHTS

Socially responsible companies respect the rights of employees outside the United States. They support working conditions using similar standards in the United States, even if they are not required to by local law. Employees should earn a living wage—one that provides for the basic needs for food and shelter. Firms that are "good" international citizens may face less recrimination from local countries or U.S. citizens and in turn sustain profits from overseas operations.

Sweatshops manufacturing companies, to save money, have working conditions that are dangerous and workers have little to no rights or say in their working conditions.

The use of **sweatshops** in clothing manufacturing is an ongoing human rights problem. *Sweatshop* is a term we use to characterize working conditions that are dangerous and firms that give workers little to no rights or say in their working conditions. Companies use sweatshops to reduce labor costs. However, when discovered and publicized, the company that has sweatshops can suffer image problems and lower sales.

In the mid 1990s, Kathy Lee Gifford, a famous television personality, came under fire for sweatshop conditions in a factory in Honduras that made a clothing line for Wal-Mart using her name. She subsequently became active in ending sweatshop practices at Wal-Mart and other companies.

SUSTAINABILITY

Responsible corporations seek to develop products and use production processes that will sustain rather than deplete available natural resources. These are business practices that may, in the long run, benefit future generations of shareholders.

There are, of course, laws in all these areas that provide legal constraints on firms' behavior (see Figure 8.3). Investors who care about the social responsibility of firms impose an even higher set of standards. But there may be costs for companies to pursue socially responsible policies. These costs in turn may cut into profits and returns to shareholders.

How do analysts take all of these issues into account? As with any other type of research on companies and the securities they issue, this information must be gathered and integrated into the analyst's recommendation and/or performance forecasts. Information about companies' practices can be found in a variety of sources. "Management's Discussion and Analysis of Financial Condition and Results of Operations" (Item 7, required in a firm's annual 10-K SEC filing) discusses ongoing litigation. News releases and 8-K SEC filings are another source. Analysts should also have a clear understanding of the regulatory and corporate responsibility issues that face the industry in which the companies they are researching operate. Different industries face different risks; for example, oil companies face greater environmental risks than, say, a media company with no print products. Trade journals and other sources are useful here. Analysts can also use research generated by companies that specialize in evaluating the social responsibility of corporations, for example, KLD Global Socrates. Next we discuss different ways in which analysts' research on SRI is typically implemented.

A word of caution here: You must be careful as an analyst not to bring your own biases about corporations and corporate behavior into your recommendations (see

---

FIGURE **8.3** **LAWS AND REGULATIONS DESIGNED TO PROTECT OTHER STAKEHOLDERS**

Maximize shareholder profits *subject to legal constraints.*

- Consumer Product Safety Commission
- National Labor Relations Act
- Equal Pay Act
- Civil Rights Act
- Age Discrimination in Employment Act
- Clean Air Act and Clear Water Act

Chapter 5). If you are working directly with a client who is concerned about SRI, sit down with your client and develop an investment policy statement (IPS; see Chapter 2) that outlines how the *client*—not you—wants to define SRI. If you are setting SRI policies as a firm, you need to do your best to develop a well-documented set of criteria so that your investors fully understand your SRI process (see Chapter 2).

POSITIVE AND NEGATIVE SCREENS

Positive screens selection of investment opportunities based on desirable social responsibility characteristics.

Negative screens the use of social characteristics that exclude corporations and their securities as investment candidates.

From your investments course, you are probably already familiar with the technique of screening. Analysts develop screens that securities must pass to be considered for investment. Some commonly used screens are price to earnings (P/E) ratios, price momentum, earnings growth, and liquidity. SRI also uses a screening methodology. Investment professionals start by deciding on activities that are important to them and their clients and then they select or screen corporations based on these characteristics. These are known as **positive screens**. SRI investors also use **negative screens**. Here investors choose characteristics that *exclude* corporations and their securities as investment candidates. For a long time, negative screening was the most common type of SRI because it served two purposes for socially conscious investors. First, by *not* holding the stock, investors are not supporting a company whose business practices they disagree with. Second, investors hope to "punish" the company by reducing the number of investors interested in buying the company's securities. The efficacy of this second mechanism is questionable. Capital markets are large and fluid. If one investor is unwilling to hold a stock, there is likely to be another one who is. However, negative publicity from being on shareholders' "bad corporations" lists may be another way to punish these corporations economically.

Creating SRI screens can be difficult. Rarely are firms "all good" or "all bad." Analysts develop effective screens by using measurable characteristics. For example, a screen might require companies to have no history of product recalls, to provide employee health and retirement benefits, and have no history of EPA sanctions and fines. Investors may also have to prioritize their concerns. It may be too difficult to identify a sufficient number of investments if screens include too many desired and undesired characteristics. Important characteristics must be well articulated in the investment policy statement used by either clients or SRI funds (see Chapter 2). A further complication with developing screens is that different investors may judge the same company's behavior differently. Like beauty, the definition of "socially responsible" can be subjective. For example, some investors view the production of genetically altered foods as harmful. Others believe such alterations can increase food production and help eliminate worldwide hunger.

Sin stocks stock of companies that are in the following businesses: alcohol, gambling, tobacco, and adult entertainment.

Another issue is a corporation's involvement in a particular business. Some may view *any* involvement in certain types of businesses objectionable, and other investors may find certain business activities (versus practices) objectionable. These are usually alcohol, gambling, tobacco, and adult entertainment. These stocks are known as **sin stocks**. Other investors, for moral reasons, can oppose investments in military companies and nuclear power.

Socially Responsible Mutual Funds

The idea of choosing investments based on companies' business practices started in the 1920s with churches and the temperance movement. These religious organizations sought to avoid sin stocks. Socially responsible investing became popular in the 1970s as endowments, foundations, and universities sought ways to integrate social objectives with the need to earn returns. Mutual funds have evolved to take into account investors' preferences to hold only stocks that meet criteria for social responsibility. These funds seek to provide not only investments that address societal concerns but also good, risk-adjusted returns. There is a growing interest in SRI funds: the latest report from the Social Investment Forum states that as of 2007, SRI assets account for $2.71 trillion of $25.1 trillion of assets under management.

Some of the best-known SRI mutual funds are provided by Pax World investments (founded in 1971); Calvert Investments (founded in 1976); Citizens Funds (founded in 1982); and Domini Social Investments (founded in 1990). These firms provide mutual funds that have a variety of screens, both positive and negative, on issues regarding employees, environment, community, sustainability, alcohol, gambling, tobacco, adult entertainment, military companies, and nuclear power.

More focused funds, such as green and antiterrorist funds, are also available. An example of a green fund is the Winslow Green Growth Fund. This fund seeks to invest in companies with clean operations and companies in businesses involving renewable energy and organic foods, among other SRI criteria. The Roosevelt Anti-Terror Multi-Cap Fund used a negative screen for the stock of companies that do business in terrorist countries such as Iran, Syria, Sudan, and North Korea.

Performance: Can You Do Well by Doing Good?

One objection to SRI investing is that it generates lower risk-adjusted returns. Most studies that have evaluated the risk-return performance of SRI and/or the use of screens report either no effect or some positive effect. Some studies report the use of screens can increase volatility and reduce returns. For example, sin stocks tend to sell products that have inelastic demand (i.e., tobacco) and as a result provide strong returns; excluding them can then lead to lower portfolio returns.

The FTSE KLD 400 Social Index (KLD400) formerly known as the Domini 400 Social Index (DSI 400), a stock index consisting of 400 socially responsible companies.

In the 1990s, KLD Research & Analytics, Inc. developed a socially responsible index called the **The FTSE KLD 400 Social Index (KLD400)** (formerly known as the Domini 400 Social Index). The KLD 400 index consists of 400 companies—250 chosen from the S&P 500, 100 that are not part of the S&P 500 and are mid cap companies, and 50 that are small cap companies. All of these are "exemplary" companies. They are not involved in businesses related to alcohol, tobacco, gambling, nuclear power, firearms, and weapons-related defense contracting. They have a good record in the areas of community relations, diversity, employee relations, environmental stewardship, human rights, product safety and quality, and corporate governance. From May 1990 to August 2009, the DSI 400 monthly returns on average earned 0.25

percent more than the S&P 500; the monthly Sharpe ratio was 10.78 percent for the KLD400 versus 5.58 percent for the S&P 500 (the Sharpe ratio was calculated using a one-year Treasury constant maturity rate; see Chapter 3 if you need a review of the Sharpe ratio). This is at least one measure that suggests that you *can* "do well by doing good." Other commonly used indexes are the Calvert Social Index and the Citizen's Index. These indexes vary in their criteria to include or exclude companies based on their socially responsibility. Some critics of these indexes suggest that the companies they contain are not significantly more socially responsible than companies included in other, more conventional indexes. While there is significant overlap, studies have shown that on average, companies in the SRI indexes are more socially responsible on a variety of criteria.

Evaluating SRI mutual funds' risk-return performance is no different from doing so for more traditional mutual funds. Within a particular conventional asset class—for example, small cap growth—there is a large number of mutual funds with different risk-return performance histories as well as different costs. This is also true regarding SRI funds. To illustrate, consider two funds that are green—the Winslow Green Growth Fund mentioned above and Green Century Equity fund. Figure 8.4 shows that these two funds performed differently. Between May 2001 and August 2009, the Sharpe ratio for the Winslow Green Fund was 1.82 percent, while for the Green Century Equity fund it was −4.92 percent. You may be wondering why anyone would invest in a fund with a negative Sharpe ratio. For comparative purposes, the Sharpe ratio for the S&P500 was −7.04 percent during this same period. Both poor performances were driven by the precipitous market downturn in 2008. Costs of the funds are also important; as of 2009, the net expense ratio for the Winslow Green Growth Fund was 1.45 percent and the Green Century Equity Fund was 0.95 percent. Besides risk-return performance, these funds also differ on the average market capitalization of the equities they hold and the extent of bonds held in the fund. Just as with selecting any fund, all of these factors need to be considered (see Chapter 2).

FIGURE	8.4	PERFORMANCE OF TWO GREEN FUNDS: GREEN CENTURY EQUITY FUND (GECQX) AND WINSLOW GREEN GROWTH FUND (WGGFX)

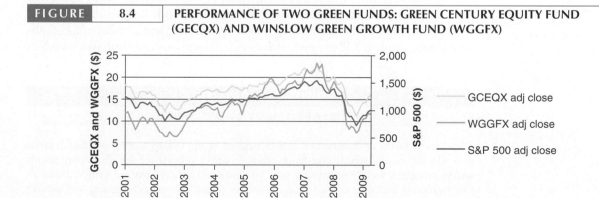

Source: www.finance.yahoo.com.

SHAREHOLDER ADVOCACY

As discussed above, one goal of negative screening is to punish a company's bad behavior by making its access to capital more difficult. Another way is for shareholders to engage with the management of badly behaving companies and work with them for positive change. Here socially responsible investors buy the stock of companies that are *not* socially responsible. This is the opposite of using a negative screen. By becoming a shareholder, investors have a voice via the proxy process. As we learned in Chapter 7, shareholders of common stock typically have one vote per share. The proxy process allows shareholders to express their preferences via their votes (see Chapter 7). Advocates of this type of SRI argue that engaging companies in dialogue is more beneficial than eschewing stock ownership in irresponsible firms. Mini Application 8.3 provides an example of how shareholder advocacy can work to bring about change.

The proxy process allows investors to elect a director who may advocate for socially responsible policies. Investors also can propose **shareholder resolutions** to management, which can be voted on during the annual shareholders' meeting as part of the proxy process (see Chapter 7). Socially responsible investors can propose resolutions regarding treatment of unions, employee benefits, community involvement, and board diversity, to name a few. Mini Application 8.4 shows a shareholder resolution for Chevron Corporation's annual meeting. Because they can be lengthy, the full resolution is not included here, but it should give you a good idea of what such resolutions look like.

Corporate charters vary, but often if the resolution doesn't meet a minimum number of votes, shareholders must withdraw the resolution from any further consideration. If it does meet the vote threshold, the sponsors can resubmit for a vote the following year. Shareholder resolutions rarely pass. However, they can serve two purposes. First, the resolution can open the door to further dialogue with management. Second, the resolution can create publicity, which pressures the corporation to change its practices.

Various shareholder advocacy groups seek to coordinate the voting of socially conscious shareholders. The **Interfaith Center on Corporate Responsibility (ICCR)** is one such group. This organization is over 30 years old and consists of 275 faith-based institutions. ICCR proposes shareholder resolutions and then asks members

Shareholder resolutions resolutions to the corporate charter, proposed by shareholders, that can be voted on during the annual shareholders meeting as part of the proxy process.

Interfaith Center on Corporate Responsibility (ICCR) a faith-based organization that proposes shareholder resolutions on social issues and coordinates voting among shareholder groups.

MINI APPLICATION 8.3
SHAREHOLDER ADVOCACY

The General Board of Pension and Health Benefits of the United Methodist Church holds over $16 billion in assets. It uses its investing power to provide for the plan's participants and to invest in a socially responsible way. To illustrate, the board worked with McDonald's Corporation to improve the working conditions of tomato harvesters by getting McDonald's to agree to pay an additional penny per pound of tomatoes harvested. This amounted to a raise of about 75% for tomato harvesters.

STOCKHOLDER PROPOSAL ON THE PROPOSAL TO REPORT ON HOST COUNTRY ENVIRONMENTAL LAWS (Item 9 on the proxy form) WHEREAS Chevron is "committed to excellence in everything" it does and aims "to be admired for world-class performance" in protecting people and the environment. (The Chevron Way) Our company's policy places the highest priority on the safety of its staff, community members and the environment where it operates. Corporate Policy 530 "commits Chevron to comply with the spirit and letter of all environmental, health and safety laws and regulations, regardless of the degree of enforcement." (Chevron Business and Ethics Code) However, our company operates in 180 countries including developing countries of Africa, Asia and Latin America where environmental regimes may be less protective of human health and the environment than in North American and European countries where Chevron operates. . .our company has repeatedly been singled out for practices that allegedly have caused environmental damage and harmed the health and welfare of local communities. . . .

RESOLVED: The shareholders request that the Board prepare a report by November 2007, prepared at reasonable cost and omitting proprietary information, on the policies and procedures that guide Chevron's assessment of the adequacy of host country laws and regulations with respect to their adequacy to protect human health, the environment and our company's reputation. Supporting Statement A commitment to abide by the highest environmental standards wherever Chevron operates would further our company's goal of being recognized for environmental excellence, and enhance the measurement and reporting of our company's environmental performance.

Source: Chevron Corporation, Proxy Statement, filed April 25, 2007, page 48.

---

of its groups to actively vote for the resolution. The purpose of these organizations is to increase the voting power of socially conscious investors.

Shareholder advocacy has several advantages over a screening approach to SRI. By using engagement, investors do not have to sacrifice returns while pursuing a social agenda. Also, they do not have to create screening criteria. Developing criteria can require additional research into a firm's business practices (beyond those used to assess future profitability). It can also be difficult to develop criteria that can be efficiently implemented. Advocates have argued that shareholder status provides a means for engaging with management, which may be more effective in creating change. The disadvantage of shareholder advocacy is the time necessary to engage with corporations; however, investors who are social activists rarely consider this to be a burden.

Divestment

Divestment occurs when shareholders sell a firm's shares and advocates that other shareholders do the same.

Another way that investors can pursue a social agenda is through divestment. **Divestment** occurs when shareholders sell a firm's shares and advocate that other shareholders do the same. The hope is that selling pressure will cause a decline in the firm's stock price. This decline in turn will cause the firm to change its business practices. While this may seem similar to a negative SRI screen, it differs in that shareholders sell shares they currently hold rather than never buying shares to begin with. This action is the source of the term *divestment*.

Divestment was first used in the 1970s, as part of the political movement to end the practice of apartheid in South America. Apartheid was a practice of racial segregation that severely limited the rights of black citizens during the years 1948 to 1994. Many colleges and universities, as well as pension funds and endowments, participated in this movement. Criteria for divestment varied across institutions. Criteria for business dealings with South Africa were broad. For example, The Coca-Cola Company could be subject to divestment because it sold soda in South Africa. It has been difficult to determine the return impact of this divestment movement. Institutions chose to divest different companies based on different criteria. However, the movement of divestment became part of the negative publicity surrounding apartheid. This publicity, along with other political mechanisms, contributed to the ending of apartheid.

Divestment that is broad based can potentially hurt the people it is designed to help. For example, deciding to divest *all* companies that have any business dealings in South Africa or with its government could have caused companies to cease supplying the South African population with food and medicine, thus further harming the people already suffering under apartheid.

A more recent divestment movement involves Sudan and the genocide in Darfur. Supporters of this movement seek to restrict the Sudanese government's access to financial resources and military supplies used in perpetuating this genocide. This recent divestment movement is different from the earlier one in South Africa. Here a political group, the Save Darfur Coalition, has organized and developed a list of companies that have been determined to be either directly providing financial resources to the Sudanese government by purchasing natural resources from Sudan or supplying the government with military supplies. Sudan has oil reserves, and 70–80 percent of the revenues from sale of these reserves support military spending. The model of limiting the number of companies targeted for divestment is known as **targeted divestment.**

Targeted divestment a model of limiting the number of companies targeted for divestment.

The idea behind targeted divestment is to minimize the cost of selling stocks out of portfolios as well as to minimize the impact on returns. At the same time, by choosing the securities of companies that are directly supporting genocide, the divestment can have the maximum benefit in saving lives. The model also calls for several months of engagement with the firms on the list to convince them to stop business transactions with the Sudanese government before selling the stock. Thus the tools of shareholder advocacy as well as selling pressure are put to work.

Many states have been approached to pass state laws requiring state pension funds to divest in order to help end genocide. Many pension funds have lobbied against these laws. They argue that adopting such a policy violates their fiduciary duty to maximize returns to beneficiaries. Implementing the screening process has administrative costs. Further, there are concerns about increases in tracking error for asset managers. Remember that tracking error shows how returns in the portfolio vary from the benchmark (see Chapter 3). Some have argued, however, that with a relatively small number of stocks on the targeted list, the tracking error is not significant. As a result, several states have adopted legislation requiring state pension funds to divest.

THE SPECIAL ROLE OF FOUNDATIONS, UNIVERSITY ENDOWMENTS, AND PENSION FUNDS

As we noted earlier, state pension funds are in a different class than other investments. While private investors have been called upon to divest, no state laws have been proposed to limit private investment. Foundations and endowments are also viewed differently. Usually a foundation or endowment is set up to support activities that benefit society. The returns on their investments provide financial resources to support their goals. Let's take a closer look at how foundations operate.

FOUNDATIONS

Some have argued that foundations should seek to earn the highest return on their investments so that they have the maximum amount of income to support their activities. But should a foundation that supports antismoking education invest in the stock of a company that makes tobacco products? Altria Group, Inc. sells cigarettes; *and* as Figure 8.5 shows, this firm has earned high returns for its shareholders. Some

---

| FIGURE | 8.5 | DO YOU SACRIFICE RETURNS FOR SRI? RETURNS FROM MAKING CIGARETTES: ALTRIA GROUP, INC. (MO) STOCK PRICES, JANUARY 1998–JANUARY 2009 |

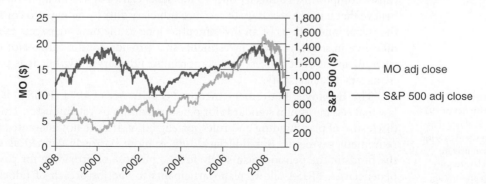

Source: www.finance.yahoo.com.

could argue that a foundation's refusal to hold Altria's stock would have negligible impact on the firm's stock. Maybe it makes sense to earn returns by holding the stock and then using those returns to fight Altria's business. Others have argued that, as a matter of principle, foundations should not own stocks of businesses that are not socially responsible. Here the message becomes more important than the economic consequences. The ability of foundations and endowments to earn good returns by investing in companies that meet their socially responsible criteria is known as the **double bottom line.**

Double bottom line to earn returns by investing in companies that meet their socially responsible criteria.

UNIVERSITY ENDOWMENTS

University endowments can also be subject to pressures to support social causes. Economically, the return on an endowment is used to support student education. However, students have argued that the endowment should support the mission of the university along with other activities on campus. If that mission includes support of social causes, then the endowment should be managed under those same constraints. Many universities were involved in the divestment movement in the 1970s to eliminate apartheid in South Africa and, more recently, in the targeted divestment movement to end genocide in Darfur.

PENSION FUNDS

State pension funds also tend to be treated differently from other funds. These funds are taxpayer supported and often politically pressured to use their funds for other purposes. We have already seen one example of divestment for Darfur. Another example is asking the fund managers to purchase a controlling block of stock to help a local company fend off a hostile takeover attempt so as to save area jobs. State laws can be enacted to require certain investments or divestments. For example, law can be passed requiring a fund to divest holdings in tobacco stocks. As seen in the Altria example, this action can eliminate the opportunity of holding stocks that earn good returns. Some have argued that using state pension funds for social causes compromises fiduciary duty to the beneficiaries by sacrificing returns. Others believe that it is not necessary to sacrifice fiduciary duty by taking into consideration the social implications of an investment as long as the fund managers exercise due diligence in selecting social investments that provide good returns. Not only does such an investment process not compromise fiduciary duty, but it *is* part of the managers' fiduciary duty.

Employee Retirement Income Security Act of 1974 (ERISA) a federal law that sets minimum standards for pension plans in private industry. This law requires disclosure of plan funding and rules for eligibility.

The **Employee Retirement Income Security Act of 1974 (ERISA)** is a federal law that sets minimum standards for pension plans in private industry. This requires disclosure of plan funding and rules for eligibility. It does not guarantee or specify retirement payments. But fiduciary duty is more narrowly defined as managing the funds of the pension plan solely for the purpose of providing for payments to beneficiaries. ERISA allows plan participants to sue for breach of fiduciary duty. Private plans tend not to pursue social agendas.

COMMUNITY INVESTMENT AND MICROFINANCE LENDING

Microfinance lending the practice of lending small amounts of money to the very poor to help them start a business so they can earn a living wage.

Grameen Bank a bank started in 1976 by an economics professor among a group of villagers in Bangladesh; members of the group monitor and support the borrowers and ensure that the loan is paid back. Once the loan is repaid, another loan can be made to another member of the group.

Microfinance lending is a practice of lending small amounts of money to the very poor to help them start a business to earn a living wage. Most of these businesses are run by women and are textile and farming based. This lending practice began with the **Grameen Bank**. This bank was started in 1976 by an economics professor, Muhammad Yunus, when he set up a bank among a group of villagers in Bangladesh. The members of the group monitor and support the borrowers and ensure that each loan is paid back. Once a loan is repaid, another loan can be made to another member of the group. Since that time, many charitable organizations and foundations have come to appreciate the power that microfinance lending has to alleviate poverty. Many of these organizations include microfinance lending in their investment activities.

In addition, charitable foundations have made investments in communities by providing capital for affordable housing, neighborhood transformation projects, and small-scale entrepreneurs. These foundations hope to recover their capital and earn a modest return. This in turn will allow them to continue to help improve communities. However, because they are primarily charitable organizations, they can risk their capital. The financial resources provided become equivalent to a charitable donation when they are not paid back.

Some organizations have sought to leverage the amount of capital they are willing to risk. They evaluate projects based on recovery of principal plus a market-adjusted return. The basic principles of capital structure are followed to finance a project: some of the financing is debt and some equity. Debt holders face less risk because most of the risk of the project is transferred to equity holders. These organizations take the money that normally would be used as a charitable contribution and turn it into equity; it has the least seniority and the greatest risk. But with the equity, they can then issue debt instruments that are creditworthy and expected to earn a good return for their investors. Further, the debt is usually issued for commercial projects where there is good collateral. The use of contributions as equity allows these organizations to leverage the contributions, and they can generate more financial resources to support worthy causes. Again, if they lose the equity capital, it turns into the equivalent of a charitable donation. Figure 8.6 shows how nonprofits can leverage charitable donations by turning them into equity.

Global Partnerships Microfinance fund exemplifies this financing strategy. The fund is set up with four tranches or slices of the deal's risk—senior debt, subordinated debt, junior subordinated debt, and equity. The tranches with seniority above equity are given default protection. The fund provides microfinance to people living in poverty in Latin America, including women and the rural poor. One family was helped when the fund provided the resources to purchase one cow that, through profits from dairy farming to buy more cows as well as breeding, eventually led to a herd of 38 cows. The loan was repaid, and the family was able to provide health care and education for its children.

| FIGURE | 8.6 | **HOW TO LEVERAGE FOUNDATION FINANCIAL RESOURCES TO GAIN MORE CAPITAL** |

Community Capital Management illustrates another way investors can make direct SRI investments. This company is an investment manager of a fixed-income fund. The fund invests in municipal and other government agency bonds that fund economic development, for example, bonds for multifamily low-income housing. The Isaiah Funds organization is set up to issue senior and subordinated debt instruments to support rebuilding in the U.S. Gulf Coast region in the aftermath of Hurricane Katrina. Rather than merely soliciting charitable donations, these organizations seek to offer attractive returns for socially conscious investors.

ISLAMIC FINANCE

Islamic finance financial instruments and transactions designed to allow religiously observant Muslims access to financial markets.

Usury another term for interest established in the Middle Ages; a term used in the Qur'an.

Islamic finance is a special type of ethical investing. The Qur'an (or more popularly, the Koran) prohibits the earning or charging of interest. Charging or earning interest is viewed as **usury**. During the Middle Ages, usury became known as charging excessive interest on loans. Thus the Qur'an's prohibition on charging interest is rooted in ethical treatment of all parties in transactions. We know of course that the ability to earn interest or returns is critical in investments. Islamic finance seeks to design financial instruments to allow religiously observant Muslims access to capital. Underlying these practices is the principle that contracts are open and fair (i.e., ethical).

To be considered ethical, transactions must occur at fully disclosed and agreed upon prices. Often transactions are set up as sale and leaseback agreements, deferred payment sales, cost plus pricing, and profit sharing. A board consisting of Muslim scholars, a **Shariah Board**, views financial contracts to ensure that they comply with the teachings of the Qur'an.

Shariah Board a board consisting of Muslim scholars who review financial contracts to ensure they are compliant with the Qur'an (Koran).

Let's look at mortgages. Traditional mortgages are structured as a principal amount borrowed and interest charged. Monthly mortgage payments include both principal and interest. Observant Muslims cannot pay interest. Instead, the monthly

MINI APPLICATION 8.5

ISLAMIC FINANCE

Sukuks government issued bonds that are structured like securitized leases to avoid paying interest and thus comply with the Qur'an's restrictions on paying interest.

Malaysia has developed an interbank money system for Islamic bonds. The government issues bonds called **sukuks**. These are like securitized leases. They are securitized with underlying assets, that is, state-owned buildings. Payments to holders are lease revenue, not interest payments. Thus these financial instruments are structured to avoid paying interest.

payment is created as an installment payment on the purchase of the house. The price for the house is negotiated to reflect interest charged, but interest is not explicitly paid in the monthly payments. The price for the house is fully disclosed, and the transaction is freely entered into by the buyer. Often Islamic banks are set up as a purchasing and selling intermediary between the seller of the house and the new homeowner. Mini Application 8.5 provides another example of Islamic finance. Islamic finance is an industry that seeks to create financial instruments, such as the mortgage just described, that are consistent with the teachings of the Qur'an. The market for Islamic finance is large; estimates are from $500 billion to $1 trillion. The Dow Jones Islamic market index and the FTSE Global Islamic Index Series are Islamic-based indexes.

CONCLUSION: OBSTACLES TO DOING WELL WHILE DOING GOOD

Being an ethical investment professional means providing the best returns for your clients while also refraining from directing capital into activities that create social harm and instead investing capital in those activities that benefit society. Socially responsible investing (SRI) creates an intersection between investment, and its goal of returns, and public policy. Public policy issues are fraught with political agendas and beliefs. Navigating the agendas and beliefs is not as easy as simply calculating a return.

SRI may be an inherently difficult goal to achieve. First, people have competing beliefs about which activities benefit and which hurt society. Second, it is difficult to find corporations that are completely "good" or completely "bad," so that investors may need to compromise their ideals. Third, investors may have to compromise returns in exchange for pursuing social agendas. This creates difficulties for fund managers charged with fiduciary duty to earn the best returns for their clients. Finally, additional costs can be imposed by further researching and characterizing the social responsibility of corporations and creating screens.

Others have argued that socially responsible investments in the long run earn returns *at least* as good as a broader-based set of investments. Further incorporating social responsibility into investment criteria is not at odds with fiduciary duty and may even be part of fiduciary duty. Irresponsible companies face greater risks for future declines in financial performance. As an investment professional, you will need to clarify these goals with your clients in a well-articulated investment policy statement (see Chapter 2). Shareholder advocacy, community lending, microfinance lending, and Islamic finance are other means of allowing investors to pursue ethical and societal goals. These activities and types of investments do not conflict with goals to maximize returns. Ethical investment professionals seek to serve investors *and* society.

TERMS

socially responsible investing (SRI)

environmental, social, and governance (ESG)

stakeholder theory

prudent

efficiency

equity

sweatshops

positive screens

negative screens

sin stocks

The FTSE KLD 400 Social Index (KLD400)

shareholder resolutions

Interfaith Center on Corporate Responsibility (ICCR)

divestment

targeted divestment

double bottom line

Employee Retirement Income Security Act of 1974 (ERISA)

microfinance lending

Grameen Bank

Islamic finance

usury

Shariah Board

sukuks

REVIEW QUESTIONS

1. Define *SRI*.
2. Explain stakeholder theory. How can stakeholder theory be reconciled with a theory that says a firm's sole purpose is to maximize shareholder wealth?
3. List and explain at least four issues that an investor would consider when deciding whether a corporation is socially responsible.
4. Discuss the ways in which firms can treat employees well, and explain why "good" treatment of employees might be beneficial to shareholders. When would good treatment of employees be at odds with maximizing shareholder returns?
5. What are the potential costs of being socially responsible to a firm? How can these costs affect shareholder returns?
6. Explain how negative and positive screens work in SRI.
7. List three problems with creating SRI screens.
8. What are sin stocks?
9. What are three indexes available to monitor the risk and return characteristics of SRI?
10. How do the risk-return characteristics of SRI compare with traditional investing?
11. Explain how targeted divestment varies from more traditional divestment movements.
12. Explain how the Grameen Bank works.
13. Discuss how microfinance lending and community investing can help alleviate poverty.
14. What is Islamic finance?
15. What is a Shariah Board?

CRITICAL THINKING QUESTIONS

1. Oftentimes, a distinction is made between social or corporate responsibility and ethics. How would *you* define each term? How would you distinguish between the two?

2. Many critics of SRI claim that it conflicts with fiduciary duty. The implicit assumption is that fiduciary duty means maximizing risk-adjusted returns and precludes the use of clients' and/or beneficiaries' monies to pursue other agendas. There are different definitions of fiduciary duty.

   The ERISA definition is consistent with a "returns only" approach.

   > The primary responsibility of fiduciaries is to run the plan solely in the interest of participants and beneficiaries and for the exclusive purpose of providing benefits and paying plan expenses. Fiduciaries must act prudently and must diversify the plan's investments in order to minimize the risk of large losses. In addition, they must follow the terms of plan documents to the extent that the plan terms are consistent with ERISA. They also must avoid conflicts of interest. In other words, they may not engage in transactions on behalf of the plan that benefit parties related to the plan, such as other fiduciaries, services providers, or the plan sponsor.
   > [See http://www.dol.gov/dol/topic/health-plans/fiduciaryresp.htm.]

   Otherwise, fiduciary duty is one that is legally imposed via the contract with the client. For example, if an individual client requests that no investments be made in sin stocks, via the investment policy statement (see Chapter 2) and the associated legal contract for engagement of the managers' services, then these investments must be avoided as part of the manager's fiduciary duty.

   Finally, state laws and codes can define *fiduciary duty* beyond the scope of "returns only." Wisconsin has the following code governing its pension fund for retirement payments for state employees:

   > The investment board shall attempt to invest in organizations which adhere to prevailing local and national laws and generally accepted standards of conduct in their affairs. The board recognizes that in many countries customs, laws and their enforcement may vary from the basic human rights concepts and freedoms prevailing in the United States. The board believes, however, that an organization, in whatever country it does business, can have a positive influence in support of basic human rights through its conduct in dealing with employees, clients and governments. Therefore, the investment board will seek investments in organizations which respect basic human rights and will encourage managements to respect basic human rights of their employees and clientele in any country, because such conduct is conducive to long run success. [See http://www.legis.state.wi.us/rsb/code/ib/ib002.pdf.]

   How would you implement such a code? What types of screens would you use? What type of quantitative measures would you use to balance the goals of the fund to pay retirement benefits to beneficiaries but at the same time make investments that respect basic human rights? These issues are much more complex than can be answered in a single question, but try to sketch out how you would begin to tackle the problem.

3. You are deciding which stock to include in a client's portfolio. You need to add a soft drink manufacturer and are trying to decide between the stock of The Coca-Cola Company

or Pepsico, Inc. You use KLD Global Socrates to evaluate the social responsibility of each company. Both companies have environmental issues with using water, a scarce resource, and polluting with plastic bottles and waste water created during manufacturing. They also produce a product with health issues (i.e., sugary sodas). But both have made strides to limit marketing their product to children and limiting adverse impacts on the environment through such programs as recycling. Coke, however, is judged to have done less than its industry peers and earns a lower grade than Pepsi. As of the end of 2009, KLD assigns an overall grade of BBB to Pepsi but only BB to Coke. Over the past 10 years, the monthly return (standard deviation) of Coke has been 0.35 percent (5.76 percent), and that of Pepsi has been 0.78 (5.15 percent). Do you think the stock price performance is related to the KLD ratings? Why or why not? What other measures would you need to make your case?

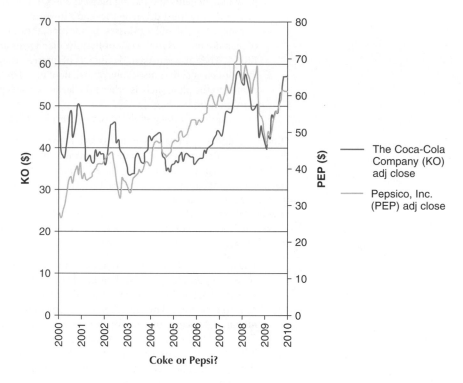

4. One argument made against SRI using negative screens is the "slippery slope." Once you decide that you are going to exclude some companies based on social criteria, where do you stop? An investor may soon find herself with very few companies that are deemed socially responsible enough to invest in. Consider one criteria—worker safety. Worker safety can be measured by examining OSHA violations and the severity of these violations (i.e., repeated and willful violations versus nonserious violations). Discuss how you would create a metric to screen for companies that care about worker safety within a particular industry. How would you balance creating these screens with providing a sufficiently large enough pool of securities to invest in? Does it matter?

5. You are an analyst evaluating two stocks in the apparel and footwear industry, Nike Inc. and Abercrombie & Fitch Co. Again you use KLD Global Socrates to evaluate

the social responsibility of each company. The retail industry is plagued by issues with respect to working conditions. In the 1990s Nike was attacked by various groups for poor working conditions and use of child labor in non-U.S. manufacturing facilities and subsequently took steps to improve conditions and eliminate exploitive employment practices. Abercrombie has been accused of failing to pay overtime and has more than its share of discrimination lawsuits. Overall, as of the end of 2009, KLD gives an AA to Nike, but only a B to Abercrombie. Nonetheless, over the past 10 years, the monthly return for Abercrombie has been 1.73 percent but for Nike only 1.39 percent. Does this mean that being socially responsible doesn't matter? How would you resolve these contradictory findings? To answer this question, what other financial measures would you want to have and why?

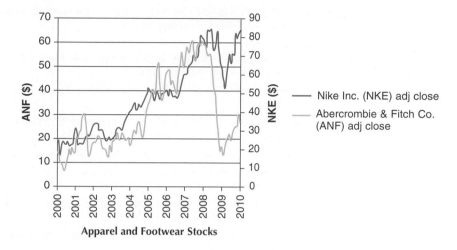

Apparel and Footwear Stocks

APPLIED STUDENT PROJECT

You can do three different projects. First, use the Internet to find the returns of a socially responsible mutual fund and compare the risk and return characteristics of this fund to a conventional index, for example, the S&P 500 (return history available on www.yahoo.finance.com). Second, attempt to devise socially responsible criteria and develop a method for implementing the criteria as either a positive or negative screen. Third, select a firm and evaluate whether its business practices are socially responsible. This last project requires you to explore your own ethical values. The results of each of these three projects can be presented in a professionally written report of two to three pages.

RECOMMENDED CASES

1. Case 26—Enron: A Case of Extreme Hubris
2. Case 28—First Cash Financial Services: Payday Loans and Return
3. Case 29—Johnson & Johnson and the Tylenol Scare: Did Recall Hurt or Help Shareholders?
4. Case 30—Infrastructure Funds: An SRI Investment?

REFERENCES AND SUGGESTED READING

Ahern, Geoffrey. "Implementing Environmental Sustainability in Ten Multinationals." *Corporate Finance Review* 13, no. 6 (2009): 27–31.

CFA Institute. *Environmental, Social, and Governance Factors at Listed Companies: A Manual for Investors.* Charlottesville, VA: The CFA Institute, 2008.

Conte, Michael A., and Douglas Kruse. "ESOPs and Profit-Sharing Plans: Do They Link Employee Pay to Company Performance?" *Financial Management* 20, no. 4 (1991): 91–100.

"Corporate News: *Vioxx* Securities Case against *Merck* Is Reinstated by Appeals Court." *Wall Street Journal*, 10 September 2008, B3.

Domini, Amy. *Socially Responsible Investing: Making a Difference and Making Money.* Chicago: Dearborn Trade Publishing, 2001.

Edwards, Ed, and Ajay Samant. "Investing with a Conscience: An Evaluation of the Risk-Adjusted Performance of Socially Responsible Mutual Funds." *Mid-American Journal of Business* 18, no. 1 (2003): 51–61.

Freeman, Edward R. "The Politics of Stakeholder Theory." *Business Ethics Quarterly* 4 (1994): 409–21.

Friedman, Milton. "The Social Responsibility of Business Is to Increase Profits." *New York Times Magazine*, 13 September 1970, 32–33, 122–26.

Flynn, Stuart. "An Islamic Capitalism." *International Financial Law Review* (July 2008): 44–45.

Grable, John E. "Profitable Socially Responsible Investing? An Institutional Investor's Guide." *Journal of Personal Finance* 4, no. 3 (2005): 109–13.

Guerad, John B. Jr. "Is There a Cost to Being Socially Responsible in Investing?" *Journal of Investing* 6, no. 2 (1997): 11–18.

Harris, Gardiner. "Merck Shares Sink on Worries over Vioxx." *Wall Street Journal*, 1 May 2000, B13.

Hellsten, Sirkku, and Chris Mallin. "Are 'Ethical' or 'Socially Responsible' Investments Socially Responsible?" *Journal of Business Ethics* 66 (2006): 393–406.

Jack, Andrew. "Vioxx Report Hits at Merck," *Financial Times*, 16 April 2008, 21.

Johnson, Richard A., and Daniel W. Greening. "The Effects of Corporate Governance and Institutional Ownership Types on Corporate Social Performance." *Academy of Management Journal* 42, no. 5 (1999): 564–77.

Julien, Rick, and Larry Rieger. "The Missing Link in Corporate Governance." *Risk Management* (April 2003): 32–35.

Kurtz, Lloyd. "No Effect, or No Net Effect? Studies on Socially Responsible Investing." *Journal of Investing* 6, no. 4 (1997): 37–50.

Rehbein, Kathleen, Sandra Waddock, and Samuel B. Graves. "Understanding Shareholder Activism: Which Corporations Are Targeted?" *Business Society* 43 (2004): 239–67.

Reyes, Mario G., and Terrance Grieb. "The External Performance of Socially-Responsible Mutual Funds," *American Business Review* 16, no. 1 (1998): 1–8.

Rivoli, Pietra. "Making a Difference or Making a Statement? Finance Research and Socially Responsible Investment." *Business Ethics Quarterly* 13, no. 3 (2003): 271–87.

Rodrigo, Pablo, and Daniel Arenas. "Do Employees Care about CSR Programs? A Typology of Employees According to Their Attitudes," *Journal of Business Ethics* 83, no. 2 (208): 265–83.

Rubin, Neil. "The Challenge of Socially Responsible Investments." *CPA Journal* 78, no. 7 (2008): 52–55.

Sethi, S. Prakash. "Investing in Socially Responsible Companies Is a Must for Public Pension Funds—Because There Is No Better Alternative." *Journal of Business Ethics* 56 (2005): 99–129.

Statman, Mier. "Socially Responsible Indexes." *Journal of Portfolio Management* 32, no. 3 (2006): 100–12.

The Social Investment Forum. *2007 Report on Socially Responsible Investing Trends in the United States.* www.socialinvest.org.

Zimmerman, Martin. "Huge Recall a New Blow to Toyota's Reputation." *Los Angeles Times*, 26 November 2009, 1.

CHAPTER

9

Cases

These "mini" cases represent a subset of the many that have been discussed by my students over the several years I have taught the Investment Management, Society, and Ethics course at Marquette University.

The information gathered about these cases is publicly available. As a result, most of them involve illegal behavior either alleged or proven in a court of law. Most illegal behavior by its nature is unethical. Thus you should focus on the motivations behind the unethical behavior, who is hurt, and the context and conditions that may have contributed to the behavior.

LIST OF CASES

Case 1—UBS and Morgan Stanley: An Elaborate Insider Trading Scheme

Case 2—Emulex and Mark Jakob: Market Manipulation with False Information

Case 3—Fidelity Traders and Gifts from Jefferies: Soliciting Brokerage from Traders

Case 4—Heartland Advisors and Bond Funds: Misrepresentation of Bond Values

Case 5—A. G. Edwards and Variable Annuities: An Inappropriate Investment

Case 6—Charles Hintz and Sanford Bernstein: Analysts' Conflicts with Personal Holdings

Case 7—Nicholas Cosmo and Agape World Inc.: A Ponzi Scheme

Case 8—Former CEO of NYSE: Grasso's Pay Package

Case 9—Nick Leeson and Barings Bank: Rogue Trader

Case 10—Kellogg's "Matched" and "Washed" Trades: Tax Avoidance or Market Manipulation?

Case 1 UBS and Morgan Stanley: An Elaborate Insider Trading Scheme

Executives at UBS and Morgan Stanley were involved in an elaborate insider trading scheme from 2001 to 2006.

Mitchel Guttenburg was the institutional services director at UBS. He owed $25,000 to his friend Erik Franklin, a trader at Bear Stearns. Guttenburg agreed to pay back Franklin by informing him when UBS research analysts were going to change their stock ratings. Guttenburg had immediate access to this information because he was a member of the UBS research advisory board. Guttenburg gave Franklin the information by sending secret codes in text messages using disposable cell phones. Eventually, Guttenburg participated in the profits generated by the scheme. Another trader at Bear Stearns, Robert Babcock, noticed Franklin's trading success and began to follow his trades. Babcock then became part of the scheme. Profits were split in cash to avoid leaving a paper trail.

Guttenburg decided to sell his information to traders at other firms. One was David Tavdy at Assent, LLC. As at Bear Stearns, other traders at Assent began to notice Tavdy's success. David Glass, another trader at Assent, paid two members of Assent's IT department, McKeever and Childs, to access Tavdy's computer so that he could mirror Tavdy's trades. McKeever and Childs then blackmailed Tavdy and Glass and got $150,000 in exchange for their silence.

At Morgan Stanley, Randi Collotta, an attorney in the compliance department, revealed information about upcoming mergers and acquisitions to her husband, Christopher Collotta, and the couple's stock broker, Marc Jurman. Jurman tipped off Babcock, who in turn tipped off Franklin.

The SEC discovered the scheme as the result of investigating unusual trading activity in the stock of Catellus Development (a Morgan Stanley client) in the account of Erik Franklin's father-in-law.

DISCUSSION QUESTIONS

1. Who is hurt by insider trading? Is this a victimless crime?

2. Why do you think so many individuals decided to join the scheme when they discovered it rather than blow the whistle?

3. What do you think UBS could have done to prevent Guttenberg's passing along changes in analysts' recommendations to others?

4. What do you think about Randi Collotta's behavior? Was her behavior *more* unethical because she was a lawyer in the compliance department?

REFERENCES

Anderson, J., and M. de la Merced. "13 Accused of Insider Trading on Wall Street." *International Herald Tribune*, 2 March 2007.

Moyer, L. "Helter-Skelter on Wall Street." *Forbes*, 1 March 2007.

Securities and Exchange Commission. Press Release: "SEC Charges 14 in Wall Street Insider Trading Ring," 1 March 2007.

Smith, R., K. Scannell, and P. Davies. "A 'Brazen' Insider Scheme Revealed: Illegal-Trading Charges Leveled Against 13; Friends' Debt Goes Sour." *Wall Street Journal*, 2 March 2007.

CASE 2 EMULEX AND MARK JAKOB: MARKET MANIPULATION WITH FALSE INFORMATION

In August of 2001, Mark Jakob was a 23-year-old student at El Camino Community College in California. He had no background in investments. He worked part-time at Internet Wire, a company that distributed press releases on the Internet. The same day that Jakob left his job at Internet Wire, he shorted 3,000 shares of Emulex, another Internet company. By shorting the stock, Jakob was betting that the stock price would decline. However, the price increased; within a week, Jakob had $97,000 in losses. After market closing, Jacob sent an e-mail to Internet Wire under the guise of a public relations firm stating that Emulex was under investigation by the SEC for faulty accounting practices, were restating their earnings, and their CEO was resigning.

Bloomberg and the Dow Jones news services reported these "rumors" to be valid. At the market open, Emulex stock plummeted from $113 to $43 (a 62 percent decline), costing the company nearly $2.45 billion of its market value. Later that day, Jakob closed out his short position and made more than $54,700. He then purchased 3,500 shares. The following day, after the company dispelled the rumors, he sold these shares and made a total of $187,000.

Authorities quickly traced the e-mails back to El Camino College and, using the trades in Emulex, located Jakob as the source of the rumors. Convicted of securities and mail fraud, Jakob was sentenced to 44 months in prison, had to forfeit his profits, and was forced to pay over $103,000 in penalties for his illegal actions.

DISCUSSION QUESTIONS

1. Does Jakob's age and background in investments play a role in his culpability?
2. What responsibility do you believe that the newswire services, Bloomberg and Dow Jones, had in the scheme?
3. What is the ethical difference between what Jakob did and posting opinions about various stocks on blogs and Internet chat rooms?
4. If the rumor had been ignored by the market, would this change your view of Jakob's actions?

REFERENCES

Becton, Neal, and Robert O'Harrow Jr. "Arrest Made in Emulex Hoax." *Washington Post*, 1 September 2000.

Richtmyer, Richard. "FBI Nabs Emulex Suspect." CNNmoney.com (August 31, 2000).

Securities and Exchange Commission. "SEC vs. Mark S. Jakob." Litigation Release No. 17094 (August 8, 2001).

CASE 3 FIDELITY TRADERS AND GIFTS FROM JEFFERIES: SOLICITING BROKERAGE FROM TRADERS

In 2002, Jefferies & Co., a midsized New York brokerage firm, hired Kevin Quinn to acquire more business from larger traders. Fidelity had over $1 trillion in assets, and as a result the company generated large trading volume. Quinn was from the Boston area, where Fidelity was headquartered, and in a position to cultivate business. Quinn claims he was given permission to entertain traders and give them gifts. Quinn spent more than $2 million between 2002 and 2004 on Fidelity executives and traders. Gifts included trips to Las Vegas and Miami, tickets to Wimbledon and the Super Bowl, concert tickets, thousands of dollars' worth of wine, and golf outings. Peter Lynch, a top executive at the firm, received theater tickets worth $3,600. Some of the other gifts given are listed below.

Gifts to Fidelity Traders and Executives

Wimbledon tickets and travel	$89,000
Super Bowl party	$125,000
Bottles of Chateau Petrus wine for two traders ($625 each)	$10,000
Trip to Las Vegas (including hotel room at Bellagio: $5,000/night)	$47,000
Trip to Florida for a Fidelity trader and family	$93,000
Tickets to *Hairspray*	$3,600
Trip to Virgin Islands	$46,000
Trip to Los Angeles	$70,000
Trip to Miami for bachelor party	$75,000
Golf outing	$225,000
Golf outing	$120,000
Pass to Boston Pops	$25,000
Trip to Florida	$61,000
Concert tickets—Justin Timberlake, Christina Aguilera, Carlos Santana	
DVD players ($1,000 each)	

Between 2002 and 2005, Fidelity traders increased their use of Jefferies' brokers for trading. Fidelity ranked brokers by the commissions they paid them. Jefferies' rank rose from 50th to 15th. Over two years, commissions from Fidelity to Jefferies increased by $30 million. The National Association of Securities Dealers restricts any gifts to a maximum of $100. Fidelity paid a fine and fired the traders involved.

DISCUSSION QUESTIONS

1. Who is hurt by the gifts? Why prevent giving them?
2. If Quinn was told to entertain traders at Fidelity, is his behavior unethical?

3. If the traders accepted *unsolicited* gifts, is their behavior wrong?

4. Was it okay for executives, but not traders, to receive gifts?

REFERENCES

Craig, Susanne, and John Hechinger. "Entertaining Excess: Fishing for Fidelity Business, One Firm Employed Lavish Bait; Mr. Quinn of Jefferies Plied Traders with Wine, Travel and Luxury Golf Outings; FBI to Question Party Dwarf." *Wall Street Journal*, 11 August 2005.

Kerber, Ross. "N.Y. Firm Courted Fidelity Traders with $2M in Gifts: To Pay $10M to Settle Claims." *Boston Globe*, 5 December 2006.

Syre, Stephen. "Jefferies' Shopping List." *Boston Globe*, 5 December 2006.

CASE 4 HEARTLAND ADVISORS AND BOND FUNDS: MISREPRESENTATION OF BOND VALUES

Heartland Advisors is an investment firm that offered bond funds. Investors could purchase or redeem their shares at a net asset value (NAV) determined by the prices of the bonds in the fund. The SEC alleged that the managers knew that the bonds' value was at a significant discount to the carrying value currently used. Thus bond redemptions forced managers to sell some of the bonds in the fund. The sale, in turn, forced the fund managers to reprice some of the bonds.

Additional redemptions occurred, and in fall 2000, two of Heartland Advisors' high-yield municipal funds lost approximately $93 million in value. One fund, Heartland's High-Yield Municipal Bond, lost approximately 70 percent; a related fund, the Short Duration High-Yield Muni Fund, lost over 40 percent. Further, the fund managers for both funds were accused of investing more than 15 percent of the funds in illiquid securities in violation of the investing agreement. The funds were so illiquid that Heartland Advisors had to borrow money to meet investors' redemptions.

Heartland Advisors had used FT Interactive Data, an independent pricing service, to price the funds. The SEC claimed that FT Interactive had colluded with Heartland in the mispricing.

Before Heartland repriced the funds, several of Heartland's advisors sold off their shares in the funds. Greg Winston, a portfolio manager of the funds, sold off all of his shares and informed his family to do the same. Two other Heartland Advisors executives, Jilaine Bauer (the company's general counsel) and Kenneth Della (Heartland's treasurer), liquidated their shares in the funds. Della liquidated his father's shares as well. William Nasgovitz, Heartland's CEO and president, was also accused of tipping off his friend and client, Raymond Krueger, to sell his shares before the drastic devaluation in September of 2000.

Heartland Advisors' accounting firm, PricewaterhouseCoopers, faced allegations that it failed to adequately audit the two Heartland funds.

DISCUSSION QUESTIONS

1. Which investors were hurt by transacting at the mispriced NAV? Which investors benefited? Why?
2. Why do you think FT Interactive Data went along with the mispricing?
3. What responsibility did PricewaterhouseCoopers have in ferreting out the mispricing?
4. Why was the selling of shares in the funds by managers unethical?

REFERENCES

Gallagher, Kathleen. "Judge to Decide on Heartland Settlement," *Milwaukee Journal Sentinel*, 29 June 2004.

Gores, Paul. "Heartland, SEC Settle Suit: Investment Firm to Pay $3.5 Million over Big Markdowns in Bond Funds." *Milwaukee Journal Sentinel*, 29 January 2008.

_____."Lawsuits Pile Up against Heartland," *Milwaukee Journal Sentinel*, 30 November 2000.

Lank, Avrum D. "Lawyers Seek 30% of Settlement: Accounting Firm for Heartland Advisors Agreed to Pay $8.25 Million." *Milwaukee Journal Sentinel*, 7 March 2006.

Securities and Exchange Commission. "SEC Levels Fraud Charges against Heartland Advisors, Inc., 12 Company Officials and Others for Misrepresentations, Mispricing and Insider Trading in Two High Yield Bond Funds." Press Release (December 11, 2003).

CASE 5 A. G. EDWARDS AND VARIABLE ANNUITIES: AN INAPPROPRIATE INVESTMENT

Variable annuities combine a life insurance policy with a tax-deferred retirement investment. Different options are usually made available to the investor for the retirement investment portion (i.e., a selection of mutual funds). The insurance policy guarantees payout of the retirement invested principal in the event of death. Variable annuities often carry high fees, both to set them up and to exit from them. Variable annuities are appropriate if the investor has reached the maximum allowable contributions to IRAs and 401(k) and is looking for another tax-deferred means to save for retirement, and the investor wants a death benefit for his or her heirs.

In 1999, Kathleen Mitton was a retiree who invested in a variable annuity. She had worked for 14 years at a public utility in California, the San Onofre Nuclear Geography Station. During that time, she had accumulated $384,210 in an IRA account. Her financial advisor was Michael Fangman at A. G. Edwards & Sons, and he advised her to put the entire amount into a variable annuity. At the time, Mitton had an adult son and no other heirs. She did not need the life insurance portion of the annuity. The exit fees started at 7 percent and declined to 0 percent over seven years.

Two years later, Mitton decided to get out of the annuity. As part of the annuity, she was invested in American Funds, which had not done well. It was then that she learned that her advisor received 6.75 percent of her initial investment as a commission and that she would have to pay a 6 percent exit fee to receive her funds. Mitton ended up paying fees of approximately $50,000, substantially reducing the $384,210 that she had originally accumulated for retirement.

DISCUSSION QUESTIONS

1. If Fangman had disclosed the fees, would his recommendation to Mitton have been ethical?
2. What responsibility did Mitton have to be informed about the terms of the annuity?
3. What obligations did A. G. Edwards have in monitoring the sale of the annuity?
4. Under what situations would an annuity be an appropriate investment?

REFERENCES

Blankfeld Schultz, Karen, and Joshua Lipton. "Guaranteed Income with Strings Attached." *Forbes* (September 9, 2008).

Geer, Carolyn. "The Great Annuity Rip-off." *Forbes* (February 9, 1998).

Weinberg, Neil. "*Shelter Skelter.*" *Forbes* (December 12, 2005). Forbes.com *2006 Investment Guide.*

CASE 6 CHARLES HINTZ AND SANFORD BERNSTEIN: ANALYSTS' CONFLICTS WITH PERSONAL HOLDINGS

In 2000, Charles Hintz was hired by Sanford Bernstein as an equity analyst covering the financial services industry. Hintz also held stocks and options in a personal domestic trust fund, including the securities of some of the companies he covered in his research.

In 2004, Hintz had a large holding of Lehman Brothers stock and expiring options from Morgan Stanley. The Lehman Brothers stock and Morgan Stanley options were earned as part of his compensation while working at those companies. Hintz sought to sell the securities despite his positive ratings on both stocks. He had a rating of "outperform" on Morgan Stanley and "market perform" on Lehman.

Hintz consulted Sanford Bernstein's compliance department to find a way to maintain his positive coverage and sell his stocks. Sanford Bernstein requested an exemption from NASD to allow the transactions. The firm claimed that Hintz needed the proceeds from the sale of Lehman to pay the cost of exercising the expiring Morgan Stanley options. Bernstein claimed the situation was unusual and warranted a waiver.

The exemption request was denied. Sanford Bernstein temporarily terminated Hintz's coverage so that he could sell the securities and then resumed coverage. Bernstein and Hintz disclosed this plan to investors on December 23, 2004. Hintz proceeded with the termination of coverage and subsequent sale of securities from December 2004 to February 2005. After the sale, he resumed coverage on the two stocks.

On February 8, 2006, NASD fined Charles B. Hintz and Sanford Bernstein $200,000 and $350,000, respectively, the largest fine for this type of incident that the NASD had ever assessed.

DISCUSSION QUESTIONS

1. Was the NASD correct in fining Hintz and Bernstein?
2. Did Hintz have a conflict with his ratings and his actions?
3. Was there another alternative set of actions that Hintz could have taken with respect to selling his securities in 2004?
4. What policies could Bernstein enact to avoid these situations in the future?

REFERENCES

Anderson, Jenny. "Analyst Is Fined in Conflict-of-Interest." *New York Times*, 9 February 2006.

Shell, Adam. "Bernstein, Analyst Fined over Personal Trades." *USA Today*, 9 February 2006.

CASE 7 NICHOLAS COSMO AND AGAPE WORLD INC.: A PONZI SCHEME

In 1999 Nicholas Cosmo was indicted on charges of mail fraud related to a stock investment scheme. While in prison, he founded Agape World Inc. in Hauppauge, New York, as a commercial bridge lender. Agape was not managing money or selling securities, nor was it registered as a licensed bank.

Cosmo's fund was designed to invest clients' money in bridge loans on the promise of healthy returns. The bridge loans were to be made to good-credit, quality businesses willing to pay a high interest rate for ready access to capital. As in most Ponzi schemes, new investors' money was paid out to old investors redeeming their investments along with a return. In 2008, a total of $370 million was invested by 1,500 investors. Most of these investors were blue-collar, working families.

Some of the investors' money was lent to a few commercial borrowers to retain some semblance of legitimacy. Ten million dollars were issued in loans. Cosmo also paid hefty commissions to brokers for providing new investors ($55 million total). Finally, some of the investors' money was invested in commodity futures markets. Eighty million dollars was lost in these investments.

DISCUSSION QUESTIONS

1. Cosmo's advertised investment scheme was different from just investing in stocks. Why do you think he choose investing in bridge loans to scam investors?
2. What do you think Cosmo's motives were? Was this a scheme designed to be illegal to begin with?
3. Why you think Cosmo invested in commodities futures markets?
4. Who was hurt by Cosmo's actions? What responsibility do investors have in being duped in Ponzi schemes? Any?

REFERENCES

Amon, Michael. "Agape Got Fed Help with Loans: U.S. Small Business Administration Backed 2 Loans for Investment Firm Now Accused of Running $370M Scam." *Newsday* (March 1, 2009).

Maier, Thomas. "U.S. Panel Sues Cosmo: Suspected Swindler Used Tens of Millions for Unauthorized Futures Trading, Says Commodity Agency." *Newsday* (January 29, 2009).

Wayne, Leslie. "The Mini-Madoffs." *New York Times*, 1 March 2009.

CASE 8 FORMER CEO OF NYSE: GRASSO'S PAY PACKAGE

Richard Grasso joined the New York Stock Exchange (NYSE) in 1968 as a clerk and worked his way up to the executive in charge of listings and then to chairman in 1995. In 2003 he was forced to leave the exchange after earning $187.5 million as chief executive officer.

Subsequently the New York state's attorney general, Eliot Spitzer, sued Grasso to return his pay. Spitzer argued that Grasso's pay was excessive and a breach of fiduciary duty.

The board of directors that approved the pay package included many Wall Street executives such as Henry Paulson, then the head of Goldman Sachs Group Inc. and subsequently U.S. Treasury secretary; Larry Fink, CEO of BlackRock Inc., a private equity firm; and Richard S. Fuld Jr., former CEO of Lehman Brothers Holdings Inc.

The NYSE board had a compensation committee. Ken Langone was the chair of the compensation committee from 1999 until a few months before Mr. Grasso left the exchange. H. Carl McCall became the new chair of the compensation committee in June 2003 and claimed that the committee did not receive detailed information about the compensation. McCall recommended that the full board approve the pay package. Even though board members claimed they were shocked by the size of the package, they approved it anyway. In 2008, the courts ruled that Grasso could keep his pay.

DISCUSSION QUESTIONS

1. Do you think Grasso's pay was excessive and that he should have been forced to return some of his compensation?
2. Was the board ethical in approving the pay package?
3. Who do you think was hurt by Grasso's compensation? Was there any benefit to parties other than Grasso?
4. What role do you think the turnover in the chair's position of the compensation committee played in the subsequent approval of the pay package?

REFERENCES

Der Hovanesia, Mara. "Ringing the Bell on Wall Street: How Dick Grasso Thrived—and Overreached—as Chairman of the New York Stock Exchange." *Business Week* (December 17, 2007), 82.

Lucchetti, Aaron. "Grasso Wins Court Fight, Can Keep NYSE Pay." *Wall Street Journal*, 2 July 2008.

Lucchetti, Aaron, and Paul Davies. "Will Grasso Get His Pay, After All?" *Wall Street Journal*, 9 May 2007.

McDonald, Ian. "Grasso Pay Package 'Shocked' Board." *Wall Street Journal*, 28 April 2006.

CASE 9 NICK LEESON AND BARINGS BANK: ROGUE TRADER

Nick Leeson began his employment with Barings Bank in the 1990s, working in the back office. The back office provides administrative support and includes confirming trades, handling trade settlements, and ensuring regulatory compliance. Shortly afterward he was promoted and asked to open an office in Singapore and assemble a team to engage in arbitrage trading between the Singapore and Osaka futures exchanges. This strategy involved buying contracts in one market while selling the same number of contracts at a higher price in the second market. Because this approach didn't involve outright, open positions, Barings executives saw it as low risk. In addition to trading, Leeson was also in charge of the back office in Singapore.

An inexperienced trader incurred a loss by executing a client's order incorrectly. Leeson hid this loss by placing it in an error account known as the five eights account. (Accounts needed five digits, per the firm's naming convention; he chose the number eight because it is lucky in Chinese culture.) Leeson hoped he would be lucky and be able to trade out of the loss and never have to report it.

Leeson soon began trading in Nikkei futures and Japanese government bond futures on the Singapore International Monetary Exchange (SIMEX) and Osaka Securities Exchange. For his bet to pay off, he needed simultaneous increases in both Japanese stock prices and Japanese interest rates. Instead, the opposite happened and Leeson incurred substantial losses. His losses, small at first, soon began to grow as he took riskier and riskier positions to try to correct the situation. He continued to conceal his losses by placing them in the five eights account. But his losses created margin calls from the exchanges and substantial cash requests to the London office. Yet, since he was hiding his losses, his office was reporting high profits and he continued to get the cash he needed.

By February 1995, Leeson's open positions had unrealized losses of nearly $1 billion. After fleeing Singapore, Leeson was caught and sentenced to 6.5 years for fraud. Meanwhile, Barings Bank management, left to sort out the aftermath, soon discovered that the losses amounted to more than the company's net worth. In the end, ING (a Dutch financial firm) bought Barings for one British pound.

DISCUSSION QUESTIONS

1. Leeson's unauthorized trading was intended to cover another employee's error. Does this matter in how you judge his actions?
2. What steps should Barings have taken to prevent Leeson's actions?
3. What red flags suggested that Leeson was not running a profitable office?
4. What conflicts did Barings have in turning a blind eye to Leeson's trading?

REFERENCES

"Barings Scandal: Inside Account. Review of *Rogue Trader* and *The Collapse of Barings*." *The Economist* (February 1996).

Reserve Bank of Australia. "Implications of the Barings Collapse for Bank Supervisors." *Reserve Bank of Australia Bulletin* (November 1995): 1–5.

Soper, R. M. "Promoting Confidence and Stability in Financial Markets: Capitalizing on the Downfall of Barings." *Duke Journal of Comparative and International Law* 7 (1997): 651–70.

Stevenson, R. W. "Markets Shaken as a British Bank Takes a Big Loss." *New York Times*, 27 February 1995.

CASE 10 KELLOGG'S "MATCHED" AND "WASHED" TRADES: TAX AVOIDANCE OR MARKET MANIPULATION?

Peter R. Kellogg was the former head of Wall Street's top market maker, Spear, Leeds & Kellogg. He sold Spear, Leeds to Goldman Sachs for $3.5 billion in 2000. Kellogg was charged by the National Association of Securities Dealers (NASD) with committing fraudulent "matched" and "washed" trades in August of 2003. Washed trades are trades of securities without a real change in ownership of the securities trades. Matched trades are trades to buy or sell securities that are entered with knowledge that a matching trade on the opposite side has been or will be entered. These charges were the result of a two-week period in which Kellogg's personal accounts and business entities conducted transactions that resulted in little change in ownership of stock but caused abnormal market activity. In addition, these actions allowed his corporations to account for gains that market prices would not have supported. The transactions created tax exemptions. The NASD reversed these charges 9 months later because they deemed the buying and selling of the securities to be solely for tax purposes—a legal activity.

Kellogg, a registered broker-dealer, owned four companies: Equity Holding Inc., IAT Reinsurance Syndicate, MMK Reinsurance, and MCM Inc. MMK Reinsurance was a unit of IAT. Through these companies, he engaged in two distinct series of transactions.

In the first transaction, Equity Holding Inc. sold 700,000 shares of Thoratec Corp. to IAT Reinsurance Syndicate. Kellogg did not use market prices for the transactions, but rather set the price of Thoratec at $18 a share, $1 over the market price. As a result, Equity Holding Inc. had a reported tax loss. IAT showed a gain. But IAT was held in trust for Kellogg's children and the gains were tax exempt. Shortly after, IAT sold 1,000,000 shares back to Equity. This created an increase in holding of only 300,000 shares by Equity. But there was no change in substantive ownership, because Kellogg owned both companies.

In the second transaction, IAT sold 500,000 shares of Thoratec to Kellogg's personal account and 500,000 shares to MMK Reinsurance, a unit of IAT. In total, 1,000,000 shares of Thoratec stocks were transferred from IAT into two separate accounts. Again, shortly after, both Kellogg and MMK sold 500,000 shares of Thoratec respectively back to IAT. As a result, there was no change of ownership in Thoratec. The trades from these two transactions accounted for 54 to 84 percent of the daily volume in Thoratec stock.

DISCUSSION QUESTIONS

1. What do you think Kellogg's intentions were in making the trades? If a trader doesn't intend to manipulate the market by trading, but his or her actions result in false market information, is the trading activity still unethical? Does your judgment about whether the activity is ethical depend on the trader's professional background?
2. Under what conditions do you think trading for tax purposes is ethical? Unethical?

3. Do you think reporting the transaction at prices other than the market prices was ethical?
4. Who might have been hurt by Kellogg's actions?

REFERENCES

"NASD Dismisses Trading Complaint against Peter Kellogg." *Wall Street Journal*, 9 August 2004.

Novack, Janet. "Are You a Chump." *Forbes Magazine* (January 29, 2007).

Smith, Randall. "Deals & Deal Makers: Kellogg, Ex-Spear Leeds Partner, Faces NASD Fraud Accusations." *Wall Street Journal*, 6 November 2003.

CASE 11 QWEST COMMUNICATIONS INTERNATIONAL: ACCOUNTING FRAUD AND OVERSTATED REVENUES

Qwest was one of many telecommunications companies in the late 1990s that appeared to experienced phenomenal growth in revenues and profits. From 1999 to 2001, the company overstated revenues and profits. Qwest posted revenue from the one-time sale of capacity of its fiber-optic network as recurring revenue.

Qwest changed auditors from Arthur Andersen to KPMG in the wake of the Enron scandal. KPMG completed an audit that Arthur Andersen was unable to finish because Andersen was caught up in the Enron scandal. The audit revealed accounting irregularities.

In the summer of 2001, a Morgan Stanley telecom analyst, Simon Flannery, pointed out that certain swap transactions among fiber-optic network operators or "rights of use" distorted revenues. He estimated that Qwest's revenues would have grown by only 7.5 percent instead of the 12.2 percent rate if these one-time revenues were excluded. Further, Flannery pointed out that there was a physical limit to capacity that could be sold. Thus revenue growth from these swap agreements was not likely to be sustainable.

Joseph P. Nacchio, Qwest's CEO, earned $101.9 million in pay in 2001, which included a long-term incentive plan payment of $24.4 million based on an increase in the value of Qwest.

In June 2002, Nacchio was forced to resign as the SEC investigated the firm for accounting irregularities that would soon lead to a charge of financial fraud. The company later restated revenue $2.49 billion lower for 2000 and 2001, resulting in losses for those years. Nacchio was also charged with insider trading on his sales of Qwest stock.

DISCUSSION QUESTIONS

1. What role do you think Qwest's type of business played in its managers' ability to perpetuate the accounting fraud?
2. Why do you think the earlier report from the Morgan Stanley analyst did not immediately trigger an investigation from the SEC?
3. What role do you think the auditors played in perpetuating the fraud?
4. What role do you think Nacchio's compensation played in the fraud? Did the board have any culpability?

REFERENCES

Berman, Dennis K. "Qwest Is Spending Top Dollar to Defend Accounting Practices." *Wall Street Journal*, 10 March 2003.

Etzel, Barbara. "Early Warning on Telecom Swaps: Morgan Stanley Analyst Tried to Warn Investors Last Year; Who Listened?" *Investment Dealers' Digest* (March 4, 2002).

Roney, Maya. "It Paid to Cheat." *Forbes* (May 9, 2005), 134.

CASE 12 REFCO: MISREPRESENTATION AND HIDDEN DEBT

Refco, once the largest broker on the Chicago Mercantile Exchange, was managing $4 billion for over 200,000 clients. Refco stock was sold in an initial public offering (IPO) in the summer of 2005. The IPO raised $583 million. Phillip Bennett was the CEO and retained majority ownership after the IPO.

A newly appointed controller, Peter F. James, noticed irregularities in financial reports for the quarter. There was $430 million of off-balance-sheet debt.

The debt was held by a subsidiary managed by Bennett, Global Securities. Refco claimed the debt had been repaid. However, federal authorities discovered that Bennett had still owed as much as $545 million.

From 2002 to 2005, Bennett hid debt within his clients' accounts. Refco had several different business units running underneath it that offered various financial services. The group that Bennett ran was called Refco Global Holdings Inc. Customers incurred trading losses, which they were unable to cover. These losses should have been written off. But write-offs would have hurt reported results. Bennett transferred these losses from client accounts into the company he controlled.

For example, on February 23, 2005, Bennett loaned a client $335 million. On the same day, the customer then turned around and loaned Bennett's Global Holdings $335 million. According to the SEC charge, the customer was guaranteed to make money on the loan because he or she lent the money to Bennett's company at a higher rate than it paid to Refco.

Refco said that during its process of going public, an external auditor found "two significant deficiencies in our internal controls over financial reporting," including a "lack of formalized procedures for closing our books."

When the fraud was revealed, the stock price collapsed and the company filed for Chapter 11. Along with Bennett, former Refco president Tone Grant was charged with securities fraud and conspiracy in January 2007.

DISCUSSION QUESTIONS

1. What do you think Bennett's motives were?
2. Who was hurt by Bennett's actions?
3. Why do you think James was the first to discover the fraud? Why didn't other accountants who worked for the firm detect the fraud earlier?
4. Would there ever be any business basis to allow customers to make loans at favorable interest rates?

REFERENCES

Atlas, Riva, and Jonathan Glater. "Mystery at Refco: How Could Such a Huge Debt Stay Hidden?" *New York Times*, 24 October 2005.

Bray, Chad, "Former Refco President Is Added to Fraud Case." *Wall Street Journal*, 17 January 2007.

Glater, Jonathon. "Mystery at Refco." *New York Times*, 24 October 2005.

Solomon, Deborah, and Michael Schroeder. "How Refco Fell Through Regulatory Cracks." *Wall Street Journal*, 18 October 2005.

CASE 13 SALOMON BROTHERS AND TREASURIES: CORNERING THE MARKET

In 1991, Salomon Brothers, a prominent Wall Street trading firm, participated in the treasury security market of $2.3 trillion. In the treasury auctions of December, February, April, and May, Salomon's traders had acquired a position of around 85 percent in Treasury notes (T-bills). This exceeded the 35 percent position limit set by the SEC and allowed Salomon traders to corner the market. As a result, the value of T-bills increased by $254 million and Salomon and the traders made millions of dollars.

Salomon traders exceeded the SEC limits by placing multiple bids, one in Salomon's name and others in unauthorized clients' names. Traders also placed orders in customers' accounts when they exceeded their 35 percent limit. Later, they bought back portions of the auction. Paul Mozer, the managing director of Government Securities, alerted top executives of the illegal activities. John Gutfreund, CEO, Thomas Strauss, president, and John Meriwether, vice chairman, admitted to knowing of the illegal activities since April 1991 but did not take proper actions until July of that year. Each of the three executives later resigned. The firm was fined $290 million. Later, the SEC fined Gutfreund $100,000 and he was barred from serving as a chief executive of any brokerage firms in the future.

DISCUSSION QUESTIONS

1. Could Salomon's executives have done anything to prevent the traders' actions?
2. Who was hurt by these actions of Salomon's traders?
3. Did the Treasury Department have any responsibility to prevent Salomon from cornering the market?
4. What do you think motivated the traders?

REFERENCES

Eichenwald, Kurt. "Salomon's 2 Top Officers to Resign Amid Scandal." *New York Times*, 17 August 1991.

Norris, Floyd. "Ex-Salomon Chief's Costly Battle." *New York Times*, 19 August 1994.

CASE 14 MERRILL LYNCH AND THE INTERNET BOOM: ANALYSTS' CONFLICTS

In the late 1990s, the stock of companies rose and fell dramatically in what has become known as the Internet and telecom bubble. In the aftermath, Eliot Spitzer, the New York state attorney general, began an investigation that lasted for months and uncovered many abuses. At Merrill Lynch, analysts gave more buy than sell recommendations. Analysts' compensation was tied to investment banking revenues. The more revenue generated by the investment bankers, the higher the analysts' compensation.

One Internet analyst, Henry Blodget, disparaged many stocks privately in e-mails that he had publicly recommended as buys. Blodget put one stock, InfoSpace, on Merrill Lynch's "favored fifteen" list. However, in e-mails Blodget called the stock nothing more than a powder keg and a piece of junk. The stock price plummeted from $132.00 in March 2000 to $1.46 in April 2002.

Blodget also sent numerous e-mails suggesting that Merrill Lynch was giving buy recommendations to companies so as to receive investment banking deals. However, not all analysts changed their ratings to earn investment banking business. John Olson, an energy analyst, covered Enron in 1998 and assigned a neutral recommendation to the company. Enron executives were furious, and they threatened to take away their investment banking business (ranging from $100 million to $200 million a year). Olson did not change his rating. After 35 years of being an energy analyst, Olson was fired.

In the aftermath of Spitzer's investigation, Merrill Lynch agreed to pay a $100 million fine as well as reform the way the company did business. For example, to prevent conflict of interests among analysts, the analysts and investment bankers at Merrill Lynch are evaluated separately from each other. Merrill Lynch claimed that it would disclose whether or not it has received investment banking business from a company in the research reports. Also, the company agreed to prohibit investment bankers from giving their input to analysts as well as to create a new committee that would review all recommendations.

DISCUSSION QUESTIONS

1. What conflicts did analysts face in making their recommendations?
2. How do you think John Olson's firing affected other analysts at Merrill Lynch?
3. Should an analyst provide a public buy recommendation while privately believing otherwise? Why or why not?
4. Should investors do their own research before relying on an analyst's recommendation?

REFERENCES

Gasparino, Charles. "New York Attorney General Turns Up Heat on Wall Street." *Wall Street Journal*, 10 April 2002.

Valdmanis, T. "Spitzer: Merrill Analyst Pitched Stock He Called 'Junk.'" *USA Today*, 4 April 2002.

CASE 15 JOHN MANGAN AND SHORT SELLING: INSIDER TRADING

John Mangan was a broker at Friedman, Billings, Ramsey Group Inc. In 2001 he learned that Friedman, Billings, Ramsey was planning a private investment offering in a public entity (PIPE) for CompuDyne Corporation. PIPEs are used to reduce the costs of equity financing. The investment banking firm does not need to market the stock with a road show (in which the investment bankers and management of the firm visit large cities to market stock to institutional investors). In addition, there are less regulatory issues with the Securities and Exchange Commission.

PIPEs usually work well for small to medium-sized public companies, which often have a hard time accessing more traditional forms of equity financing. CompuDyne was a relatively small company. As with any form of equity financing, the issuance of new equity has the potential to dilute existing equity.

In the fall of 2001, Mangan bet that CompuDyne's stock would fall in value when the PIPE was publicly announced. Before the announcement, he short-sold CompuDyne stock and made almost $179,000. Short selling occurs when borrowed securities are sold, betting that the stock price will fall. A profit is made when an equal number of shares are bought at the lower price to replace the borrowed shares. Mangan shared the profits from this transaction with his business partner, Hugh McColl III. Mangan used McColl's account to make the trades.

DISCUSSION QUESTIONS

1. Who was hurt by Mangan's short-selling trades?
2. Could anyone benefit from Mangan's actions?
3. What steps should Friedman, Billings, Ramsey Group have taken to prevent Mangan's trades?
4. If Mangan made the trades on the behalf of his clients, would that ameliorate the unethical nature of his actions?

REFERENCES

Burns, Judith, "FBR Settles Insider-Trading Suit," *Wall Street Journal*, 21 December 2006.

"Friedman, Billings Ramsey Group: Broker-Dealer Unit FBR Offers to Settle SEC, NASD Charges," *Wall Street Journal*, 27 April 2005.

Horowitz, Jed, "Moving the Market: Ex-Broker at FBR Faces Civil Case Tied To PIPE Deal," *Wall Street Journal*, 29 December 2006.

CASE 16 MERRILL LYNCH AND BANK OF AMERICA MERGER: BONUSES PAID TO MERRILL EMPLOYEES—EXCESSIVE COMPENSATION?

Bank of America agreed to merge with Merrill Lynch in fall 2008. The merger was to be completed early in 2009 and was prompted by huge losses sustained by Merrill. The company had suffered losses in mortgage-backed securities (MBS) and collateralized debt obligations (CDOs). These securities were bundles of loans. Bundling was assumed to minimize the risk of these securities. When home prices collapsed and defaults increased, the value of these securities dropped dramatically. The merger was intended to bail out Merrill Lynch and create opportunities for Bank of America to expand through an acquisition. Merrill was bought for $50 billion, a 70 percent premium over the market value of Merrill at the time of the agreement with Bank of America.

Merrill's policy was to pay out bonuses in January. Because of the merger, bonuses instead were paid out in early December before the firm's year-end results were available. About $3.6 billion in total was paid out to the top 200 employees. John Thain, the CEO of Merrill Lynch, was paid a $10 million bonus. The bonuses were based on a formula that provided for a bonus pool that was 41 percent smaller than the pool for the prior year. In the prior year, Merrill's share price had fallen by 65 percent.

Subsequent year-end results showed fourth-quarter losses of $13.8 billion. These losses were not known either at the time of merger or when the bonuses were paid out. In addition, there was some concern that traders may have mismarked their books to earn bonuses.

For example, a Merrill currency trader in London, Alexis Stenfors, earned a bonus on a trading profit of $120 million. While Stenfors was on vacation, Bank of America risk officers discovered irregularities in his trading accounts, which showed substantial losses. Stenfors was also investigated by British regulators.

After the award of bonuses, Merrill Lynch traders also marked down trades on some credit default swaps by several hundred millions of dollars. Credit default swaps are insurance policies issued on bonds. If the originator of the bond defaults, the issuer of the credit default swap agrees to make up the loss. A premium is charged for the swap, as with an insurance premium. In fall 2008, the market for these instruments had become illiquid and the write-downs were based on a bond index.

DISCUSSION QUESTIONS

1. In the context of both the merger and Merrill Lynch's shareholder losses, do you think the bonus payments were fair? Why or why not?
2. Was the payout of the bonuses in December, before fourth-quarter results were known, ethical?
3. Do you think subsequent write-downs of trades reflect that the original trades were recorded unethically?

4. What obligations did Bank of America executives have toward its own shareholders in the payment of bonuses and disclosure of losses at Merrill?

REFERENCES

Carney, John. "Bank of America's Ken Lewis Reluctantly Gives Up Bonus." *Wall Street Journal*, 6 January 2009.

Craig, Susanne, and Aaron Lucchetti, "Does Merrill Lynch CEO John Thain Deserve a Multi-Million Dollar Bonus?" *Wall Street Journal*, 9 December 2008.

Farrell, Greg. "Thain's Bonus." *The Financial Times Limited* (December 9, 2008).

Grocer, Stephen. "Afternoon Reading: The Thain Blame Game." *Wall Street Journal*, 8 December 2008.

Newmark, Evan. "Mean Street: Why Merrill Lynch's John Thain Deserves a Bonus." *Wall Street Journal*, 8 December 2008.

Story, Louise. "Cuomo Says Merrill Deceived Congress on Bonuses." *New York Times*, 12 March 2009.

Story, Louise, and Eric Dash. "Undisclosed Losses at Merrill Lynch Lead to a Trading Inquiry." *New York Times*, 5 March 2009.

CASE 17 CANARY CAPITAL PARTNERS LLC: MUTUAL FUND ABUSES

Edward Stern at Canary Capital Partners LLC, a hedge fund, oversaw a partnership with as many as 30 mutual fund companies—including Bank of America, Security Trust Company, Bank One, Janus Capital, and Strong Capital Management—to engage in late trading and market timing.

Mutual funds are priced once daily at 4:00 p.m. EST after markets close. This price, known as the net asset value (NAV), will be the fund's price the following day. Allowing some investors to transact after hours, but before the new NAV is determined, is known as late trading. Investors can purchase (or sell) at the stale price, knowing that the following day the NAV will be higher (or lower) and thereby guarantee a profit. Market timing occurs when investors are allowed to transact during the day at the prior day's NAV, thus taking advantage of information that will change the new NAV after the close.

Some mutual funds do not have enough time during the day to fulfill all their trade requests, so they fulfill these trade requests after hours.

The mutual funds permitted Canary's trading practices as long as Canary kept other assets with the investment management portion of the mutual fund firms. Canary kept millions of dollars of assets invested with the funds and also generated substantial brokerage commissions through trading.

DISCUSSION QUESTIONS

1. Who is hurt by late trading and market timing?
2. What were the mutual fund's motives for allowing such trading?
3. Why do you think Canary Partners pursued market timing and late trading as an investment strategy? How is this similar or dissimilar to other investment strategies that hedge funds typically pursue?
4. Are there ever any ethical reasons to allow for late trading or market timing?

REFERENCES

"Hedge Fund to Settle Case with N.J. for $10M; Allegations against Canary Capital Included Improper Trading." Associated Press, 18 January 2006.

Smith, Randall, and Tom Lauricella, "Regulators Probe Roles of 2 Banks in Fund Scandal." *Wall Street Journal*, 9 January 2004.

Weinberg, Ari. "Eliot Spitzer Finds His Canary." Forbes.com (September 3, 2003).

CASE 18 JÉRÔME KERVIEL AND SOCIÉTÉ GÉNÉRALE: ROGUE TRADER

Société Générale was one of the largest financial companies in France. In early 2008 it was discovered that a junior-level trader, Jérôme Kerviel, had executed $7.2 billion of unauthorized trades on a stock index future.

In 2000, Kerviel was hired in an IT position in the compliance department—also known as the back office. He was promoted to a junior-level trader in 2005. Kerviel was assigned to arbitrage equity derivatives. He earned a €60,000 bonus in 2006 in addition to his €72,000 salary. He expected to earn €600,000 in 2007.

Kerviel went outside his authority to make much larger trades, exceeding his risk limits. He hid these trades from his superiors. When asked about questionable trades, he'd say it was a mistake and immediately close out his position.

After office hours, Kerviel may have hacked into the computer systems and eliminated controls that would have blocked or flagged his risky trades. He bypassed as many as six internal security checks and firewalls. He simulated e-mails and used computers without authorization to take risky positions on futures. He also hid risky positions by offsetting one trade with another. Kerviel was allowed to enter his own trades, further allowing him to hide his unauthorized positions.

By early 2008, Kerviel had €1.4 billion in hidden trading profits. Then the market turned against him and he was caught trading beyond his authority. Kerviel was quoted as saying, "It's impossible to generate such large profits with small positions, which leads me to say that when I'm in the black, my superiors closed their eyes about the methods and volumes committed."

The bank lost €4.9 billion in closing out Kerviel's positions. Some analysts speculated that the Société Générale's frantic efforts to unwind this situation over several days, before going public, may have contributed to the volatility that rattled European markets at the time.

DISCUSSION QUESTIONS

1. What controls should the company have had in place to prevent Kerviel's actions?
2. Do you think the company allowed the unauthorized trades to continue because they were profitable? Was Kerviel a scapegoat?
3. What were Kerviel's motives for taking the risky positions?
4. Who was hurt by Kerviel's actions?

REFERENCES

Daneshku, Scheherazade. "SocGen Turns Corner but Hurdles Remain." *Financial Times* (January 16, 2009).

Hawser, Anita. "Desperate Measures." *Global Finance* (February 2009), 31–34.

Pignal, Stanley. "Rogues Gallery; It Is a Year since the Société Générale Trader Jerome Kerviel Made the News by Taking Unauthorized Positions Totaling—EUR50bn—or Twice the Bank's Capital; But He Is Only the Most Recent in an Expensive Line of Rogue Traders." *Financial Times* (January 24, 2009).

CASE 19 WORLDCOM: CAPITALIZING OPERATING EXPENSES; AN UNETHICAL ACCOUNTING PRACTICE

WorldCom was a telecom company in the late 1990s that experienced strong growth in profits. The company was frequently raising capital to finance expansion. Subsequently WorldCom disclosed that it had $3.8 billion in operating expenses that had been improperly accounted for, inflating the company's profits in 2001 and part of 2002. Scott Sullivan, the CFO, and Bernard J. Ebbers, the CEO, were fired.

Sullivan used two methods to inflate earnings. First, he took line costs, or interconnection expenses with other telecommunications companies, and capitalized them. This allowed these expenses to be moved from the income statement to the balance sheet. Second, he inflated revenues by recording revenue from "corporate unallocated revenue accounts."

Ebbers used his WorldCom stock to finance other personal activities. When the stock price of WorldCom declined, he needed additional cash for financing. At his request, the board made a personal loan to him of $400 million.

During this time, Jack Grubman was a telecom analyst who remained bullish on WorldCom despite growing evidence of poor performance. Grubman's favorable ratings were tied to his ability to secure investment banking business for his employers. In the subsequent investigation by Elliot Spitzer, then attorney general for New York, e-mail messages suggested that Grubman upgraded his rating on AT&T stock to help his employer, Citigroup, get a piece of AT&T's spin-off of its wireless division. In exchange, Grubman asked Sandy Weill, CEO of Citibank, for help in getting his children into an exclusive preschool.

Cynthia Cooper was the internal auditor at WorldCom who uncovered the fraud. Initially when she encountered the accounting irregularities, she brought them to the attention of the CFO, Sullivan. But she encountered resistance. She then expressed her concerns to Max Bobbitt, chairman of the board's audit committee. After some delay, Bobbitt brought Cooper's concerns to KPMG LLP, the company's current outside auditing firm.

WorldCom executives and the company were charged and convicted of accounting fraud in a civil lawsuit brought by the Securities and Exchange Commission.

DISCUSSION QUESTIONS

1. What do you think Sullivan's motivations were for perpetrating and perpetuating the financial fraud?
2. Do you think the board's delay in responding to Cooper's concerns would be justified? If so, under what conditions?
3. What role do you think the board and Ebbers had in facilitating the fraud?
4. What do you think of Cooper's actions? Grubman's? What does this say about personal interests versus "doing the right thing?" What does this say about personal integrity?

REFERENCES

Cooper, Cynthia. *Extraordinary Circumstances: The Journey of a Corporate Whistleblower.* Hoboken, NJ: John Wiley & Sons, 2008.

Loades-Carter, Jonathan. "Ebbers Bailed after Denying Fraud Charges in WorldCom Scandal." *Financial Times* (September 4, 2003).

Pulliam, Susan, Jared Sandberg, and Dan Morse. "Prosecutors Gain Key Witness in Criminal Probe of WorldCom." *Wall Street Journal*, 3 July 2002.

Whalen, Christopher. "Opening the Books." *Barron's* (January 19, 2004).

CASE 20 THE SQUAWK BOX: FRONT RUNNING

A squawk box is a device that allows many wire houses to share confidential information about potential orders to individuals on the sales desk. Any information transferred through the use of a squawk box is proprietary (i.e., is not to be shared outside the firm).

In 2002 John J. Amore, at A. B. Watley Inc., introduced a scheme to improve the firm's trading profitability. Through the use of a squawk box, Watley traders would listen in on customer orders from other, larger brokerage houses and then trade according to the anticipated market impact of the future large customer orders. The intent was to buy (or sell) securities at a low (or high) price and then sell (or buy) them after their value increased (or decreased) as a result of large buy (or sell) orders. In this way, the traders were "front running" ahead of client orders at other brokerage firms.

Amore enacted his scheme with three brokers: David Ghysels from Lehman Brothers, Kenneth Mahaffy from Merrill Lynch, and Timothy O'Connell from Merrill Lynch. The three brokers left their phones next to their squawk boxes with an open line to day traders at A. B. Watley Inc. Many times, the phone lines were left open for the entire day. The Watley day traders then listened for large customer orders that would potentially move market prices. The day traders then traded ahead of the client orders, hoping to profit from subsequent price moves.

To take advantage of the squawk box scheme, A. B. Watley Inc. top executives authorized the transformation of Watley into a proprietary day-trading firm. Kevin Leonard collected cash from the Watley traders to pay the brokers for access to their squawk boxes. The Watley traders also compensated the brokers by placing commission-generating trades through their desks.

The SEC found more than 400 instances of the Watley day traders using this trading scheme. It is estimated that the traders made gross profits in excess of $675,000.

DISCUSSION QUESTIONS

1. How would the clients who placed the large orders be hurt by the actions of the traders at Watley?
2. Did the traders at Watley have a fiduciary duty to the clients at the other brokerage firms?
3. Suppose a broker spoke to a trader at Watley and accidentally left the phone off the hook near a squawk box. Is this just as unethical as intentionally leaving the phone off the hook? Why or why not?
4. What role did the top executives have in perpetrating and perpetuating the scheme? What could they have done to prevent it?

REFERENCES

Bray, Chad. "Moving the Market: Mixed Verdicts, Mistrial in 'Squawk Box' Case." *Wall Street Journal*, 11 May 2007.

————."Two Discussing Pleas in 'Squawk-Box' Case." *Wall Street Journal*, 19 August 2008.

Lucchetti, Aaron. "Moving the Market: Ex-NYSE Floor Clerk Sentenced to Prison in 'Squawk Box' Case." *Wall Street Journal*, 25 April 2006.

CASE 21 MORGAN STANLEY: BROKERAGE COMMISSIONS AND BROKERAGE ABUSES

In the early 2000s, Morgan Stanley received fees from mutual funds that did business with Morgan Stanley in exchange for preferred marketing of their funds. This was known as the Partners Program.

Mutual funds that paid these higher fees could have their funds designated as preferred. These fees took the form of higher brokerage commissions paid to Morgan Stanley. In turn, Morgan Stanley increased the compensation to individual representatives and branch managers for sales of the preferred mutual funds shares coming from the companies that were paying the higher fees.

Morgan Stanley also offered Class B shares of certain of its own proprietary mutual funds. For sales of $100,000 or more of these shares, the company charged higher fees at the point of sale. These higher fees were not disclosed. Morgan Stanley sales representatives also received higher commissions for selling these shares.

Morgan Stanley did not disclose the source and amount of any remuneration received from third parties in connection with a securities transaction. Morgan Stanley sales representatives also did not disclose the higher commissions they received on sales of the preferred shares.

DISCUSSION QUESTIONS

1. Why do brokers have a duty to disclose their commissions on mutual funds they sell?
2. Under what conditions is it ethical to accept fees to market mutual fund products? Under what conditions would it be unethical?
3. When is it ethical for brokers to earn higher commissions on one mutual fund product versus others? When is it unethical?
4. What was Morgan Stanley's motivation for engaging in these practices?

REFERENCES

Borrus, Amy. "The Hubbub over 'Soft Dollars.'" *Business Week* (July 14, 2003).

Securities and Exchange Commission. "SEC Charges Morgan Stanley with Inadequate Disclosure in Mutual Fund Sales." Press Release (November 13, 2003).

Weinberg, Ari. "Morgan Stanley's Red Velvet Line." *Forbes* (November 17, 2003).

CASE 22 BRIAN HUNTER AND AMARANTH ADVISORS: MARKET MANIPULATION OF NATURAL GAS?

Brian Hunter was a trader for the hedge fund Amaranth. He was also president of Amaranth Advisors, a Calgary-based subsidiary that specialized in the natural gas market. In 2005, his trades generated over $1 billion in profits for his fund, and he earned himself a $100 million bonus. Hunter ran the energy trading desk and took long positions during this time, when the Gulf Coast was hit by strong hurricanes that drove energy prices upward.

In 2006, the U.S. Commodities Futures Trading Commission (CFTC) accused Hunter of trying to manipulate the price of natural gas futures. Hunter attempted to manipulate prices by buying large quantities of gas futures contracts and then selling them in the specific time window used to determine the settlement price of the contract. The settlement price for a futures contract is determined by the weighted average trades during the last 30 minutes of trading on the settlement date.

Hunter also had a separate short position on 19,000 gas contracts. Hunter hoped that by selling the long contracts, he could cause the price to fall below the short price. He could then make a large profit when he closed out the short position at the lower price. Hunter bought contracts before the closing date of April 26, 2006, and amassed 3,000 long gas futures. Before the trading day on the 26th, Hunter gave specific instructions to floor traders to wait until the last eight minutes of the settlement period to sell off 2,000 contracts.

In August 2006, the market moved against Hunter's long gas contract position, and he was forced to sell the contracts at a loss to meet a margin call. Amaranth lost $6.8 billion and subsequently collapsed.

DISCUSSION QUESTIONS

1. What role do you think Hunter's success in 2005 played in his trading strategy in 2006?
2. Besides Amaranth and its investors, who else could have been hurt by Hunter's actions? Who do you think was helped? If Hunter's strategy had worked, could his actions be viewed as ethical regarding his clients?
3. Could an argument be made that Hunter was employing an ethical trading strategy no matter who it was meant to benefit?
4. Why do you think Hunter's strategy failed?

REFERENCES

McLean, Bethany. "The Man Who Lost $6 Billion." *Fortune* (July 8, 2008).

Seeley, Tina. "Amaranth Tried to Manipulate Gas Prices, CFTC Says." *Bloomberg* (July 25, 2007).

Sorkin, Andrew Ross. "Amaranth Letter Puts Blame on J.P. Morgan." *New York Times*, 15 November 2007.

CASE 23 THE BAYOU GROUP: FALSE REPORTING

In 1996, Samuel Israel III and Daniel Marino founded the Bayou Group, a small institutional hedge fund. Bayou had little difficulty raising funds, since during the 1990s hedge funds became increasingly popular with investors. However, in the first year Bayou had large trading losses. To keep client deposits flowing in despite negative returns, Israel removed 1996 numbers from the Bayou record book and cited an inception year of 1997 in client literature.

At the end of 1997, Marino devised a scheme to cover the past year's trading losses to continue to attract new investors. The Bayou fund placed trades through Bayou Securities. The commissions from trading volume would be credited to the Bayou fund. In 1998, Israel and Marino also set up a fictitious accounting firm, Richmond Fairfield Associates, to provide "audited" statements for Bayou. In 2003, Bayou reported a false gain of over $25 million against actual losses of $49 million. In 2002, Bayou reported returns in excess of 10 percent; during the same year, the S&P 500 lost more than 30 percent. Based on this record, Bayou was able to attract an additional $125 million in new investor funds. Bayou continued the deception for five more years. In 2008, Bayou Group reported a gain of 17.55 percent despite having lost an estimated $300 million.

Authorities began their investigation into Bayou Group when redemption checks mailed from Bayou began to bounce. Hundreds of attempts to contact Bayou's management failed, until a suicide note of Marino's was found and both Israel and Marino turned themselves in. Upon being apprehended by authorities, they pleaded guilty to investment advisor fraud, mail fraud, and conspiracy. Both were sentenced to 20 years in prison.

DISCUSSION QUESTIONS

1. Did advertising Bayou as a hedge fund contribute to Israel and Marino's ability to commit fraud? Why or why not?
2. What responsibility, if any, did investors have in becoming victims of fraud?
3. What market conditions might be needed to perpetuate a fraud of this type? And what conditions would cause the fraud to unravel?
4. What role does organizational structure—that is, minimizing the number of roles assumed by the same individuals or organizations—play in ensuring ethical investing practices?

REFERENCES

Anderson, Jenny. "2 at Hedge Fund Emerge to Plead Guilty to Fraud." *New York Times*, 30 September 2005.

"Hedge Fund Founder Admits Guilt in Fraud." *New York Times*, 15 December 2006.

Morgenson, Gretchen, Jenny Anderson, Geraldine Fabrikant, and Riva D. Atlas. "What Really Happened at Bayou." *New York Times*, 17 September 2005.

CASE 24 MORGAN STANLEY: ANALYST'S COVERAGE AND INVESTMENT BANKING BUSINESS

From roughly 1999 to 2002, Morgan Stanley failed to disclose payments it made to *other* investment banks for favorable research coverage of Morgan Stanley's investment banking clients and potential clients. Morgan Stanley also compensated its own analysts based on investment banking fees. Morgan Stanley used the promise of research coverage to win IPO and secondary offering deals. Issuers sought research coverage to improve the market and pricing for newly issued securities.

The pitch books (marketing materials provided to clients) Morgan Stanley used to win investment banking business suggested that analysts would provide favorable research coverage to the potential client. In these pitch books, Morgan Stanley identified a specific analyst's rating history in a particular sector. The company also provided mock research reports showing favorable coverage to potential clients. Morgan Stanley analysts almost never used the underperform rating; in 1999, only 3 of the 1,033 stocks covered were given that rating.

Research analysts were compensated based on their contributions to investment banking fees. The company kept records of each analyst's contribution to investment banking revenues. Analysts also performed self-evaluations covering their contributions to investment banking revenues. An analyst's contribution to investment banking activities was the largest factor in determining annual bonuses.

Morgan Stanley paid portions of its underwriting fees to other broker-dealers who agreed to pick up research coverage on Morgan Stanley's banking clients. Morgan Stanley did not make certain that these broker-dealers disclosed these payments in their research reports, nor did Morgan Stanley disclose that these payments were made for research in offering documents or elsewhere.

DISCUSSION QUESTIONS

1. Does the relatively small number of stocks given the underperform rating necessarily mean that analysts biased their ratings upward?

2. What role would Morgan Stanley's compensation scheme play in potentially causing bias in its analysts' coverage?

3. Do you think that the independence of analysts at other investment banks was compromised by payments from Morgan Stanley? Why or why not? Why do you think Morgan Stanley did not disclose these payments?

4. Do you think that Morgan's Stanley's business practices with respect to analyst coverage will benefit or hurt Morgan Stanley's business in the long run? In the short run?

REFERENCES

Securities and Exchange Commission. "Morgan Stanley & Co. Incorporated: Lit. Rel. No. 18117/April 28, 2003."

Smith, Randall, Susanne Craig, and Deborah Solomon. "Wall Street Firms to Pay $1.4 Billion to End Inquiry—Record Payment Settles Conflict-of-Interest Charges; Dozens of New Examples." *Wall Street Journal*, 29 April 2003.

CASE 25 BERNIE MADOFF: THE LARGEST PONZI SCHEME IN HISTORY?

In late 2008, Bernard Madoff, through his firm Bernard L. Madoff Investment Securities, LLC, was reported to have perpetuated a Ponzi scheme of more than $60 billion—one of the largest in history. Madoff was able to pay off old clients with fresh money from new clients. When the financial crisis in the fall of 2008 hit, old clients were taking their money out of Madoff's firm faster than he could find new clients. The scheme unraveled.

Madoff graduated from Hofstra University of Long Island in the 1960s and set up a small trading firm with money he had earned as a lifeguard. Madoff's trading volume grew, and he subsequently started an investment firm. By 1989, his trading volume had grown to over 5 percent of the New York Stock Exchange volume. In 1990, he became the nonexecutive chairman of the NASDAQ market.

Madoff was able to attract clients because of the consistent returns his funds offered. Despite market conditions, he was always able to earn returns of 8–10 percent for his clients. He also solicited clients through his country club memberships and involvement in various charities. He often claimed that his funds were closed, but he would open them up for a particularly eager investor as a special favor. Besides individual investors, Madoff also managed money for many charitable trusts. The Elie Wiesel Foundation, named after the Holocaust survivor, Elie Wiesel, had $15 million invested with Madoff. Many hedge fund managers, notably The Fairfield Greenwich Group, invested with Madoff. These hedge fund managers earned fees on their clients' money invested with Madoff.

As part of due diligence, money managers meet with fund managers to understand their investment strategy. Many who considered investing with Madoff found his explanations lacking and subsequently declined to invest. Madoff claimed that he used a combination of market timing and options trading to generate returns. His return record showed consistent returns regardless of market conditions. Harry Markopolos, a security industry executive in 2002, contacted the SEC because he was concerned that Madoff was running a Ponzi scheme. Others didn't believe Madoff's strategy was generating his returns, but thought they were coming from front running via his trading firm. It is rumored that these investors believed Madoff's returns were real, but illegal, and invested with him anyway.

Statements to some clients did not show actual trades and were difficult to understand. Other statements showed trades that could not have occurred at the prices recorded. For example, one client's statement showed that Microsoft stock was purchased at $21.81 on a day that Microsoft never traded above $21.00. Clients received hard copies of statements that were produced on an old IBM computer. Clients did not have online access to account information.

Madoff's firm was audited by a three-person firm, Friehling & Horowitz. Madoff had used this firm for over 20 years. Under the Sarbanes-Oxley Act of 2002, Madoff's firm was not required to be subjected to auditor oversight.

DISCUSSION QUESTIONS

1. Before December 2008, what were the red flags indicating that Madoff was possibly running a Ponzi scheme?
2. What is the culpability of investors in perpetuating the scheme? Does it make a difference whether the investor was an individual, a trustee, or a money manager? Where are the conflicts?
3. What was the SEC's role in perpetuating the scheme?
4. What role, if any, did the new accounting oversight rules under Sarbanes-Oxley 2002 or the SEC play in perpetuating the fraud?

REFERENCES

Gaffen, David. "Investment Advisors Face More Oversight." *Wall Street Journal*, 28 January 2009.

Healy, B. "Madoff Might Not Have Made Any Trades." *Boston Globe*, 15 January 2009.

Lauricella, Tom, Amir Efrati, and Aaron Lucchetti. "Painting the Scene of Madoff's Operation." *Wall Street Journal*, 26 January 2009.

CASE 26 ENRON: A CASE OF EXTREME HUBRIS

In the late 1990s, Enron Corporation was an energy-trading company riding the telecom and Internet stock market boom. The company's stock seemed to be unable to go anywhere but up. In 2001, Enron filed for bankruptcy in a wave of scandals costing thousands of employees their jobs and investors millions of dollars. Kenneth Lay, Jeff Skilling, and Andrew Fastow were top executives; they prided themselves on their intellect, innovation, and competitive spirit.

Enron, with the approval of its auditor, Arthur Andersen, used "creative" accounting practices that inflated earnings. First, the company used special-purpose entities to remove debt from Enron's books and inflate profits—the so-called raptors (see the discussion in Chapter 6). Second, Enron used mark-to-market accounting. This strategy allowed the company to book expected future revenue from current projects. For example, the estimated sales on an oil well based on proven reserves and estimated oil prices could be used to book the entire value of the oil well at the time of purchase. There is nothing illegal about mark-to-market accounting. However, Enron stretched the limits, most famously booking revenue from a power plant built in India that never went online or was started up.

John Olson, an energy analyst with Merrill Lynch, questioned Enron's reported profits. When he downgraded Enron, Enron executives threatened to withdraw lucrative investment banking business from Merrill Lynch. Olson was fired and replaced with an analyst who upgraded Enron.

Enron's energy traders made real profits but largely through market manipulation. They would arrange for blackouts by asking managers of local utilities to shut down power grids in California and then sell power back to California at elevated prices.

Enron had a competitive culture using a "rank and yank" employee evaluation system. Employees had to rank each other, but top executives demanded that 10–15 percent of the lowest-ranked employees needed to be fired each year, regardless of performance. Employees were rewarded with Enron stock and strongly encouraged to continue holding stock even as it was falling. Yet, top executives sold their stock during this time and made millions of dollars.

In 2000, Enron's board had 14 directors. Twelve of these were nonemployee positions. Jeff Skilling served as president and CEO, succeeding Kenneth Lay, who remained on the board as its chairman. Nonemployee directors received on average $79,107 in fees. Enron required half of these fees to be deferred into a phantom stock account; many directors had close to a quarter million dollars, and in many cases even more, in these accounts. In 2000, the year before filing for bankruptcy, Kenneth Lay earned $11.95 million in cash and stock.

DISCUSSION QUESTIONS

1. What role do you think the board and the pervasive use of stock-based compensation had in Enron's downfall? Conventional wisdom is that stock-based compensation is an effective mechanism for aligning management and shareholder interests. What do you think went wrong at Enron?

2. What do you think of Enron's policies in energy trading? Who was hurt by the company's trading practices?

3. Why do you think Olson didn't believe Enron's reported accounting income? As an analyst, what would you have investigated in Enron's accounting results that would have suggested something wasn't right? Do you think that Olson and other analysts had any ethical obligation to sound a louder warning bell on Enron? Who do they owe an ethical obligation to?

4. What do you think of Enron's competitive culture? Do you think this contributed to unethical practices? When can a competitive culture lead to ethical behavior? Unethical behavior?

REFERENCES

Brody, Richard G., D. Jordan Lowe, and Kurt Pany. "Could $51 Million Be Immaterial when Enron Reports Income of $105 Million?" *Accounting Horizons* 17, no. 2 (2003): 153–60.

McLean, Bethany, and Peter Elkind. *The Smartest Guys in the Room: The Amazing Rise and Scandalous Fall of Enron.* New York: Penguin Group, 2003.

Mokhiber, Russell. "Enron Prosecutions." *Multinational Monitor* 24, no. 11 (2003): 30.

Securities and Exchange Commission. *Enron Corporation, Proxy Statement—Schedule* 14A. Filing Date: May 1, 2001.

CASE 27 UNITEDHEALTH: BACKDATING STOCK OPTIONS

William McGuire was the CEO of UnitedHealth Group Inc. for 15 years during the time that the company experienced phenomenal growth. In 2006 it was revealed that he repeatedly approved stock options, to himself and other top executives, that were backdated to earlier dates when the stock price was lower (see Chapter 7). The result was to grant options that were in the money, and it created gains of millions of dollars for these executives.

McGuire also engaged in accounting and tax fraud when signing these documents. Backdated options are legal as long as taxes are paid by executives on their gains and corporate income is reduced to reflect the extra compensation expense. The SEC accused UnitedHealth of over $1 billion worth of hidden compensation created by backdating the options grants. The company was forced to restate $1.13 billion of earnings over a 12-year period to reflect the extra compensation paid but not reported.

McGuire and David J. Lubben (general counsel) were forced to resign and pay fines in a settlement with the SEC. McGuire forfeited over $620 million in compensation, giving back the largest amount of compensation at the time. Over his entire career as CEO, he earned a total of $800 million in stock options and $530 million in other compensation. McGuire received $1.1 billion in severance pay when he resigned in 2006; it was one of the largest golden parachutes in history. During McGuire's tenure, the stock price rose from less than $1 to over $50 per share.

UnitedHealth was not alone in the practice of backdating stock options. The SEC investigated 140 companies that engaged in the practice, and more than 80 officers and directors lost their jobs as a result of the scandal.

DISCUSSION QUESTIONS

1. Who is hurt when firms backdate stock options? Because McGuire increased the stock price during his tenure, did he deserve to receive the in-the-money options created by the backdating?
2. Because other companies also habitually engaged in backdating, does this make the practice acceptable? Why or why not?
3. Because McGuire voluntarily gave back some of the compensation he earned by backdating, does this act influence how you judge his character? Why or why not?
4. What do you think of McGuire's severance pay? Was the board right in granting him the pay?

REFERENCES

Coffin, Bill. "When the Golden Parachute Rips." *Risk Management* (February 1, 2008), 27.

Fuhramans, Vanessa, and James Bandler. "Ex-CEO Forfeits $620 Million in Options Case." *Wall Street Journal*, 7 December 2007, A1.

Iwata, Edward. "UnitedHealth, Ex-CEO Settle Options Case." *USA Today*, 7 December 2007, 4B.

Shwiff, Kathy. "Corporate News: UnitedHealth Settles SEC Options Suit." *Wall Street Journal*, 23 December 2008, B2.

CASE 28 FIRST CASH FINANCIAL SERVICES: PAYDAY LOANS AND RETURN

First Cash Financial Services, Inc. is a company that operates pawn shops in the United States and Mexico and also offers payday loans. Pawn shops allow customers to pawn personal items such as jewelry or electronics and get cash loans. They can then retrieve the items by paying back the loan with interest. Payday loans allow customers to get cash advances against paychecks, again by paying interest.

Payday lenders have come under attack because of the high interest rates they charge. For example, a payday lender might charge $15 for a two-week $100 advance loan. This would result in an interest charge of $390 per year for a $100 loan, or an interest rate of 3,900 percent! Payday lenders also are attacked for failing to fully disclose the interest they charge. But the $15 fee may not sound like much to someone who really needs the money.

Others support payday lenders. Some consumers might not have sufficient credit history to give them access to conventional forms of credit. Other consumers might be suspicious of other, more conventional lending financial institutions. Proponents of payday loans and pawn shops argue these are better alternatives than dealing with loan sharks who can introduce criminality and violence into lending.

Below is the stock price history for First Cash Financial Services (FCFS). The graph shows that FCFS stock has earned good returns for its investors. During the time shown, FCFS stock earned an 812 percent return while the market earned 246 percent.

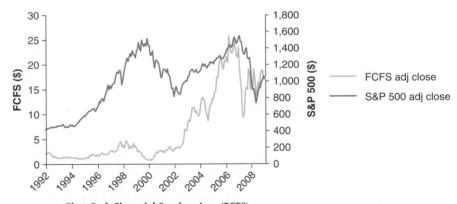

First Cash Financial Services Inc. (FCFS)
Source: www.finance.yahoo.com.

DISCUSSION QUESTIONS

1. Do you think payday loans and pawn shops are socially responsible businesses? Why or why not? Who is helped by these businesses? Who is hurt?

2. What do you think is the underlying source of returns for the stock of First Cash? Does the source matter?

3. What do you think about the interest charged for payday loans? Do you think it is fair?

4. What are some potential risks that a company such as First Cash faces? How would you take these into account in analyzing the stock?

REFERENCES

Anonymous. "Center for Responsible Lending; Annual Percentage Rate: An Apples-to-Apples Consumer Tool." *Marketing Weekly News*, 11 July 2009, 179.

Fernholz, Tim. "When Creditors Are Predators," *The American Prospect* (August 10, 2009), A20–A23.

Securities and Exchange Commission. *First Cash Financial Services, Inc., Form 10-K*. Filing Date: December 31, 2008.

CASE 29 JOHNSON & JOHNSON AND THE TYLENOL SCARE: DID RECALL HURT OR HELP SHAREHOLDERS?

Johnson & Johnson is a company that makes home health-care products. Toward the end of September 1982, seven people in the Chicago area died after taking Tylenol extra-strength capsules that had been contaminated with cyanide. Within days the company recalled 31 million bottles of Tylenol capsules, and the CEO went on a massive campaign to inform the public. The company offered a $2.50 coupon for each package of Tylenol recalled. The total cost of the recall (including coupons, public relations, and so forth) was $50 million or $0.27 earnings per share (EPS), driving EPS down to $2.25; without the recall it would have been $2.52. Following the recall, Johnson & Johnson introduced tamper-resistant packaging. Later, the company took capsules off the market and replaced them with caplets, which are more difficult to tamper with. Many other companies followed Johnson & Johnson's lead, using both tamper-resistant packaging and caplets.

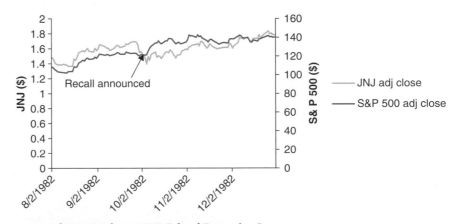

Johnson & Johnson (JNJ) Tylenol Tampering Case
Source: www.finance.yahoo.com.

DISCUSSION QUESTIONS

1. Given the cost to shareholders in both stock price decline and EPS, do you think the company made the right choice in protecting consumers? Did it put consumers' interests ahead of shareholders' interests?

2. Given that the company had no involvement in the poisonings, did they have any responsibility by not preventing the tampering?

3. Do you think the company's lead in preventing future product tampering by introducing tamper-resistant packaging and caplets had any benefit for shareholders?

4. Because of Johnson & Johnson's actions, would you consider recommending the company's stock for inclusion in an SRI portfolio? What else would you want to know about the company's products and practices?

REFERENCES

Johnson & Johnson. Annual Report to Shareholders, Securities and Exchange Commission, January 2, 1983.

_____. Annual Report to Shareholders, Securities and Exchange Commission, January 1, 1984.

Moore, Oliver. "For Companies, Surviving a Recall Crisis Takes Forthrightness." (Canada) *Globe and Mail*, 26 August 2008, A9.

Yang, Jia Lynn. "Getting a Handle on a Scandal." *Fortune* (May 8, 2007), 26.

CASE 30 INFRASTRUCTURE FUNDS: AN SRI INVESTMENT?

Infrastructure funds allow for private investments in public assets. Some of these public assets are bridges, tollways, seaports, oil pipelines, gas pipelines, electricity distribution, water distribution, alternative energy (wind power), and airports. An initial investment is made to purchase the asset, and the investor agrees to service the asset in exchange for the revenues generated. For example, if an investor owns a wind farm, the investor is responsible for maintaining the wind turbines but gets to keep the revenues from the electricity generated and sold.

The United States has aging highways, bridges, water systems, and other infrastructure that badly needs to be replaced. Infrastructure funds can help cash-strapped municipalities through the creation of private and public partnerships. Further cash flows from tolls and utilities are considered to be long term and have low risk. Thus these funds would make good investment vehicles for public pension plans that have been hard-hit by the stock market crash of 2008. The "asset" cash flows would match well with the "liability" cash flows, which are payments to retirees that will be made long into the future. Because infrastructure funds provide financial resources to benefit society, they could be considered as socially responsible. Critics of these funds are wary of private ownership of public assets. They are concerned that private owners may choose profits over service and safety.

Infrastructure funds are valued using discounted cash-flow methods, based on forecasted cash flows that are developed by the manager of the funds. Managers of these funds can earn fees on asset value and/or asset returns. Many of these funds are closed-end or private funds, limiting liquidity. Because of the steady cash flow of the assets, they tend to have high amounts of leverage—typically 50–70 percent of asset value. Many investors are eager to get into these funds, and several have been recently launched. Macquarie Group is one of the oldest infrastructure firms originated in Australia. In 2007, it launched an exchange-traded fund (ETF). An ETF acts like an indexed fund. Below is the performance of the ETF relative to the market.

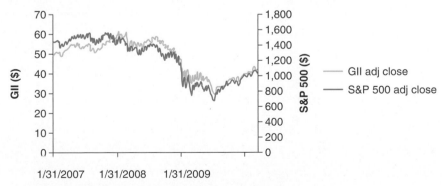

SPDR FTSE/Macquarie Global Infra 100 (GII) Performance
Source: www.finance.yahoo.com.

DISCUSSION QUESTIONS

1. Do you think an infrastructure should be considered a socially responsible investing (SRI) investment? Why or why not? What would you take into consideration when selecting a particular fund for SRI?

2. What risks do you think infrastructure funds pose to investors?

3. Are there issues with respect to reporting performance of these funds? What types of questions would you ask before making an investment?

4. Who do you think is potentially helped by these funds? Who is hurt?

REFERENCES

Bor, Michael. "Framing the Infrastructure Market." *Mergers & Acquisitions Report* (July 6, 2009), 32.

Jacobius, Arleen. "Bye-Bye Buyout; Hello Infrastructure." *Pensions & Investments* (June 1, 2009), 2–3.

Lindsay, Bill, and Joe Bel Bruno. "International Finance: Macquarie Purchases Fox-Pitt as Model Dims." *Wall Street Journal*, 1 October 2009, C2.

Merrion, Paul. "Is Midway Deal Losing Altitude? Declining Traffic, Credit Turmoil Could Erode Value of Privatization." *Crain's Chicago Business* (July 21, 2008).

Stephan, Robert B. "What Needs to Be Done about the Nation's Infrastructure?" *Washington Times*, 22 March 2009, M13.

Glossary

13D form—SEC disclosure form required when an investor or an investor group acquires 5 percent or more of the firm's shares and intends to influence or change control of the firm.

13G form—when an investor or an investor group acquires 5 percent or more of the firm's shares outstanding in the ordinary course of business, they must use this form to file quarterly with the SEC.

401(k)—an account that allows investors to save and invest for retirement without having to pay taxes on a certain allowed portion of income invested or any returns earned by the investments until they withdraw the money during retirement.

A

abnormal return—the extra return beyond the expected risk-adjusted market return.

ABSs—*see* asset-backed securities.

accounting—a system that provides financial information about a firm through the vehicles of the balance sheet, the statement of cash flows, and the income statement.

accounting-based bonuses—bonuses tied to meeting ex ante goals of accounting performance—earnings, sales, return on assets, and so on.

accruals—accounting measure created to adjust for a mismatch between when the economic substance of the transaction has occurred and is recorded and when the cash changes hands.

active managers—managers who actively pick and choose investments within a particular investment strategy and seek to offer a better return relative to a prespecified benchmark.

activist shareholders—shareholders who seek to increase investment returns by pressuring the firm to change its operating strategy and corporate governance practices.

adjustable rate mortgages (ARMs)—refers to mortgages where the interest adjusts periodically over the life of the loan.

agency theory—this is a theory that explains the incentives and contractual solutions when a principal hires an agent to act on his or her behalf, and the agent's incentives are not perfectly aligned with the principal's.

agent—someone who is hired to work on behalf of another (the principal); *see* agency theory.

agreement—an arrangement formed between a client and financial advisor on investments and financial goals per CFP.

allocation of initial public offerings—occurs when shares of an initial public offering (IPO) are allocated to investors.

alpha—extra return that is the economic profit from investing; often depicted as alpha in the following equation: $E(R_i) = \alpha_i + R_f + \beta_i[E(R_m) - R_f]$.

anchoring—occurs when analysts hold on to a past reference point, even though there is no longer any rational basis for that point.

annual holding period return—the geometric mean of returns earned over the period measured.

annual retainer fee—fee paid to nonexecutive directors of corporate boards.

annuity—a constant or variable-period cash flow paid out for a fixed length of time.

anti-takeover amendments—amendments to the corporate charter designed to thwart a takeover.

arbitrage pricing theory (APT)—a theory that explains the expected return of an investment based on its sensitivity to various economic factors: $E(R_i) = R_f + \beta_{ij}\Sigma_{j=1 \text{ to } n}F_{jl}$; where R = return on an individual security, i; F_j = the jth factor, usually macroeconomic measures, such as change in GDP and inflation; and β is beta, the risk measure for the jth factor and the individual security, i.

ARMs—*see* adjustable rate mortgages.

arrogance—excessive pride or belief in oneself.

asset-backed securities (ABSs)—pools of securities that are backed by assets such as auto loans or credit cards.

assets under management—the total dollar amount invested by all clients by an investment management firm.

audit committee—a board committee charged with hiring the external auditor and overseeing the internal audit controls of the firm.

average return—created by averaging past returns; *see also* expected return.

B

balance sheet method of measuring accruals—the use of changes in various balance sheet amounts to measure the accrual component of net income.

basis point (bp)—1/100th of a percentage point.

behavioral finance—an area of finance that seeks to explain the behavior of markets via psychological principles.

benchmark—the measure against which the portfolio manager is compared.

beneficially owned stock—stock in which the holder has either a direct or indirect ownership or voting interest.

beneficiaries—individuals who receive the benefit; beneficiaries are often retirees, employees (in an employee stock option plan, or ESOP), charitable recipients, and heirs.

Beneish (1999) model—a model developed by Messod D. Beneish to detect accounting earnings manipulation.

best execution—using the trading process to the overall benefit of your client.

biased forecast—occurs when an earnings forecast systematically inflates the earnings upward or downward.

bidder—a company, investor, or group of investors that seek to acquire control of another firm.

big bath—occurs when firms make large write-downs or charge-offs to earnings.

blockholder—an investor who has 5 percent or more ownership of the shares outstanding in a firm.

bond—economic incentive to ensure that an agent will work on the principal's behalf; *see* agency theory.

bp—*see* basis point.

buy-side analyst—describes analysts who provide their recommendations to portfolio managers

C

capital asset pricing model (CAPM)—describes the risk-return relation: $R_{p \text{ or } i} = R_f + \beta_{p \text{ or } i} \times (R_m - R_f)$, where R = return on a portfolio, p, or individual security, i; R_m = return on the market; R_f =risk-free return; and β is beta, the risk measure for the portfolio, p, or individual security, i.

cash-flow method of measuring accruals—the use of operating cash flows to measure the accrual component of net income.

CDO—*see* collateralized debt obligation.

CDS—*see* credit default swap.

Certified Financial Planner (CFP)—a designation oriented toward financial planners. Certification as a CFP® is encouraged to indicate ethical standards and competence among the members.

channel stuffing—practice whereby managers ship products they know will be returned so that they can book revenues.

Chartered Financial Analyst (CFA)—a designation oriented toward analysts, portfolio, and active money managers. Certification as a CFA® is encouraged to indicate ethical standards and competence among the members.

cherry-pick—to use any selection process that selects the best accounts in creating the fund's composite reported performance.

Chinese wall—firm policies and procedures to prevent sharing of information between the investment banking and investment management division of the same firm. *See also* firewall.

churning—occurs when a broker excessively buys and sells securities in a client's account to generate commissions for her- or himself.

clawback provisions—compensation that must be returned if it turns out it was based on faulty financial reports.

collateralized debt obligation (CDO)—a security that is created from a portfolio of debt obligations. Different "pieces" or tranches of the promised cash flows in the portfolio are then sold off. The underlying collateral is corporate assets used in the original debt obligation.

commissions—fees earned by making an investment or trade on behalf of a client.

compensation committee—a board committee that sets the compensation of the CEO and other top executives.

competent—having adequate abilities.

confidential voting—proxy voting that is confidential and not disclosed to management.

control contest—a contest over the ownership control of a company.

cookie jar reserves—reserve accounts created in anticipation of future liabilities and/or expenses.

corporate governance—a set of internal mechanisms and policies designed to ensure that officers fulfill their fiduciary duty to shareholders.

credit default swap (CDS)—a security that provides for insurance against a bond default.

cumulative voting—a voting practice that allows shareholders to cast all their votes for one particular director nominee.

D

DEF 14A—materials sent to shareholders on the financial performance, executive compensation, board composition, and major shareholder ownership as well as biographical information about the directors that are nominated by the firm and subject to a proxy vote by shareholders.

diligent—the quality of carrying out professional investment tasks with care.

directed brokerage—occurs when clients direct their investment advisor to use a particular broker when making trades on behalf of their account.

discretionary accruals—accounting accruals that occur because of the accounting choices made by management; *also called* unexpected accruals.

dissidents—a shareholder or shareholder group that criticizes the current slate of director nominees and offers an alternative slate.

divestment—occurs when shareholders sell a firm's shares and advocates that other shareholders do the same.

double bottom line—to earn returns by investing in companies that meet their socially responsible criteria.

E

earnings accuracy—a measure of how accurate forecasted earnings are relative to actual reported earnings.

earnings informativeness—the ability of earnings to convey information about the true economic profitability of a firm.

earnings persistence—how long earnings are expected to persist in the future.

earnings quality—how informative earnings are.

earnings response coefficient (ERC)—the estimate of regression coefficient between the unexpected stock price reaction to the earnings surprise.

earnings smoothing—managing earnings via discretionary accruals to eliminate period-to-period volatility.

ECN—*see* electronic communications network.

effective spread—the difference between the price of the actual transaction and the amount halfway between the quoted spread.

efficiency—an economics term describing a state where the distribution of wealth is such that no one can be made better off without making someone else worse off.

efficient market hypothesis—a hypothesis that on average all securities prices reflect all relevant publicly available information.

electronic communications network (ECN)—networks that allow brokers to trade directly with each other—electronically—and eliminate the need for a market maker.

Employee Retirement Income Security Act (ERISA)—a federal law that sets minimum standards for pension plans in private industry. This law requires disclosure of plan funding and rules for eligibility.

entrenched—refers to directors and executives who become secure enough that they do not fear being replaced for doing a poor job.

environmental, social, and governance (ESG)—a term that describes important social policies or factors in an investment decision.

equity—the concept of fairness in economic distribution; to each according to his needs.

ERC—*see* earnings response coefficient.

ERISA—*see* Employee Retirement Income Security Act.

ESG—*see* environmental, social, and governance.

ETFs—*see* exchange-traded funds.

ethics—standards for determining right or wrong behavior toward others in a particular context.

ex ante—before the fact.

exchange-traded funds (ETFs)—investment funds that trade on an exchange throughout the day and usually track an index.

ex post—after the fact.

expected return—return that is most likely to occur; the average or mean return.

F

fair price amendment—amendment to the corporate charter providing a formula to determine a minimum price that the bidder must offer for the firm.

Fama-French three-factor model—a model that determines the expected return of security based on the formula: $E(R_i) = R_f + \beta_i[E(R_m) - R_f] + s_i$ (relative book-to-market measure) + h_i (relative market capitalization measure) where R = return on an individual security, i; R_m = return on the market; R_f = risk-free return; and β is beta, the risk measure for the individual security, i.

fiduciary—a person who is entrusted to act in the interests of another.

fiduciary duty—a duty that is owed to others when placed in a position of trust.

Financial Industry Regulatory Authority (FINRA)—a nonprofit organization with the legal authority to enforce securities rules and regulations among its members, who are primarily brokers and traders.

firewall—firm policies and procedures to prevent the sharing of information between the investment banking and investment management division of the same firm. *See also* Chinese wall.

forecast earnings accuracy—measured by looking at the absolute value of the magnitude of deviation between the analysts' forecast and the actual earnings numbers.

forecast errors—the difference between actual earnings and forecasted earnings.

forecasters—analysts who forecast earnings.

Form 10-K—filing with SEC; firm's annual financial statements.

Form 10-Q—filing with SEC; firm's quarterly financial statements.

Form 8-K—filing with SEC; firm's significant events and news releases.

Form ADV—filing with SEC required of investment advisors that manage $25 million or more.

Form S-1—filing with SEC for issuers to register securities.

Forms 3, 4, and 5—filing with SEC to disclose stock ownership; form 3 is the initial filing, form 4 is for changes in filings, and form 5 is for insiders.

friendly—a bid for control of a firm that is not opposed by the incumbent management team of the target company; *see also* hostile.

front running—the practice of placing an order ahead of the trade of another investor.

FTSE KLD 400 Social Index (KLD400)—formerly known as the Domini 400 Social Index (DSI 400), a stock index consisting of 400 socially responsible companies; *see also* KLD400.

fundamental analysts—analysts who research companies' financial statements within an industry and look at economic trends to help forecast trends that affect the future profitability of a company.

G

Global Investment Performance Standards (GIPS)— guidelines for reporting performance developed by the Chartered Financial Accounting (CFA) Institute.

golden coffins—generous death benefits granted to top executives.

golden handcuffs—deferred compensation agreements.

golden parachutes—severance agreements that are triggered by control-related events.

Grameen Bank—a bank started in 1976 by an economics professor among a group of villagers in Bangladesh; members of the group monitor and support the borrowers and ensure that the loan is paid back. Once the loan is repaid, another loan can be made to another member of the group.

gray directors—directors who are nonexecutives and might have ties to executives.

greed—desire to have more than one deserves.

gross of fees—investment returns before management fees. *See also* net of fees.

H

hedge funds—an investment fund open only to financial qualified investors that may invest in non-traditional investments and proprietary trading strategies, some of which might seek to hedge risks.

herding—occurs when people "flock" together and mimic each others' behavior.

heuristics—rules of thumb.

high-speed flash trading—the ability to "flash" customer orders to traders for a few seconds before they are distributed to the market.

holding period return—a holding period return is calculated by dividing the capital gain and any investment income earned during the period by the original investment amount.

hostile—a bid for control of a company that is opposed by the incumbent management team of the target company; *see also* friendly.

hostile tender offer—occurs when a bidder makes a direct appeal to the target shareholders and offers to buy their stock at a premium to market price; current or target management is opposed to the offer.

hubris—overconfidence in oneself.

hybrid analysis—the practice of using a combination of both statistical analysis and fundamental analysis.

I

IBG YBG—*see* "I'll be gone; you'll be gone."

ICCR—*see* the Interfaith Center on Corporate Responsibility.

"I'll be gone; you'll be gone" (IBG YBG)—phrase used to characterized the lack of accountability of parties to financial transactions.

incumbents—these are current nonmanagement directors and top executives that the current board nominates for re-election to the board.

index funds—a fund that actively trades during the day and is designed to mimic the returns of an index, for example, the S&P 500 index.

information asymmetry—occurs when one party has better information than another.

information disclosure—information that is disclosed to investors in various required filings by the Securities and Exchange Commission.

informed investor—investor who has better information than other investors, whether it involves illegal inside information or superior analysis.

initial public offering (IPO)—the first time that a firm's securities, usually stock, are offered to the investing public. *See also* allocation of initial public offerings.

inside directors—directors who are management or have obvious affiliations with management.

insider information—confidential information that, if made public, is likely to have a material impact on the securities value.

insider trading—insiders as well as others that trade on insider information.

Interfaith Center on Corporate Responsibility (ICCR)—a faith-based organization that proposes shareholder resolutions on social issues and coordinates voting among shareholder groups.

intermediaries—firms or individuals who act to bring other parties (i.e., issuers and investors) together in an investment transaction.

internalization—using the company's own trading desk to fulfill orders.

investment performance—various risk and return measures of an investment.

investment policy statement (IPS)—written documentation of your client's investment goals as well as the compensation agreement between you and your client.

Investor Advisors Act and the Investment Company Act of 1940—under these acts, firms or individual professionals who seek to be compensated for advising on investments and in aggregate manage $25 million or more are required to register with the SEC and provide information about the nature of their business, their business and education and criminal background, and financial statements of the sole proprietorship or firm; advisors and investment companies must follow rules regarding record keeping and custody of client accounts and funds, disclosure of fees and commissions, and advertising.

investors—parties who seek to invest money or capital in order to earn a return.

IPO—*see* initial public offering; *see also* allocation of initial public offerings.

IPS—*see* investment policy statement.

Islamic finance—financial instruments and transactions designed to allow religiously observant Muslims access to financial markets.

issuers—corporations or other entities that issue securities in exchange for capital.

J

Jensen's alpha—*see* alpha.

Jones (1991) model—a widely known model of expected or normal accruals developed by Jennifer J. Jones and reported in an 1991 article in *Journal of Accounting Research*.

K

KLD400—*see* FTSE KLD 400 Social Index (KLD400).

Kantian ethics—an ethical philosophy; espouses that the ends never justify the means and that people are never to be used as the means to an end, but that the ethical treatment of individuals is an end in itself.

L

late trading—the practice of allowing investors to purchase a share of a mutual fund at that day's net asset value (NAV) after the market has closed but before markets have opened the next day.

leverage—the borrowing of cash to increase the size of a client's portfolio; also, the use of debt.

leveraged buyout—a transaction financed with high amounts of debt or leverage whereby all of the public shareholders are bought out.

limit order—an order that specifies the price at which the trade can occur.

liquidity—the ability to freely buy and sell securities.

long-term incentive plans (LTIPs)—incentive plans that are based on comparative accounting performance beyond that in the current year.

M

manage earnings—managers make accounting choices that change the accrual component of reported earnings.

mandate—amount of money to be invested in a particular asset class, fund, or firm.

market makers—intermediaries in financial markets who act as middle men between buyers and sellers. *See also* specialists.

market manipulation—the use of trading or rumors to mislead other market participants about the value of a security.

market order—an order that can be fulfilled at whatever price is available in the market.

market timing—trading in or out of a mutual fund at the previous day's net asset value (NAV) to take advantage of the difference in timing of public announcements across different markets and the calculation of NAV.

market timing strategies—relies on the ability to predict whether different asset markets, i.e., the stock or the bond market, will do better and then reallocate investments across these markets.

MBS—*see* mortgage-backed security.

microfinance lending—the practice of lending small amounts of money to the very poor to help them start a business so they can earn a living wage.

monitor—to watch over or oversee.

moral hazard—occurs when parties do not fully bear the costs of their risk-taking behavior. As a result, they take more risks than they would otherwise.

mortgage-backed securities (MBS)—securities that are created from a portfolio or a pool of mortgages; investor receives income from the securities from the interest and principal repayments on the underlying mortgages.

mosaic theory—the idea that securities researchers can take pieces of public information and, through analysis, assemble the pieces to reveal an accurate forecast of future value.

mutual fund—a fund that invests in several securities and allows investors to purchase shares in the fund to achieve diversification at a low price; *see also* net asset value (NAV).

N

NAV—*see* net asset value.

negative screens—the use of social characteristics that exclude corporations and their securities as investment candidates.

net asset value (NAV)—price of mutual fund shares determined by taking the total market value of securities in the fund minus the total liabilities of the fund divided by the number of shares.

net income—reported accounting earnings of a company or entity.

net of fees—investment returns minus management fees. *See also* gross of fees.

nominating committee—a board committee that nominates new directors to the board.

nondiscretionary accruals—accruals that occur due to past choices of accounting method coupled with the underlying economic activity of the firm and not due to the discretion of management.

normal or expected accruals—*see* nondiscretionary accruals.

normal return—a return that is what you would expect to earn, given the risk of an investment.

O

option backdating—use of hindsight to change the grant date or exercise price to be on the date of the lowest stock price of the year.

option spring-loading—occurs when options are granted before the release of positive information, such as higher-than-expected earnings.

outside directors—directors who are nonexecutive and have no obvious affiliations with management.

overconfidence—having an irrational belief in one's self and one's ability to make superior investment recommendations or earnings forecasts; displaying hubris, or arrogance.

overreaction—an exaggerated reaction to an event; stock price that moves either too high or too low in response to new information.

P

passive managers—investment managers who do not seek to actively trade investments or select superior investments to save transactions costs; *see also* index funds *and* ETFs.

pay-performance sensitivity—a measure of how total executive compensation changes with changes in shareholder wealth or stock value.

payment for order flow—occurs when brokers reduce costs of trading to increase the number of trades.

pay-option mortgages—mortgages that allow borrowers to defer interest and principal payments by adding these deferred payments on to the principal already owed.

PCAOB—*see* Public Company Accounting Oversight Board.

per meeting fees—fees paid to nonexecutive directors for attendance at board or committee meetings.

phantom stock—rather than awarding stock, the firm agrees to pay out the difference in share value that has accumulated over a set period of time.

pickers—investment professionals who make investment recommendations, buy, sell, or hold, or "pick" stocks that will be "winners" or "losers."

poison pill—usually describes preferred stock with mandatory redemption features whereby redemption is triggered by a control-related event.

Ponzi scheme—a fraudulent scheme whereby old investors' returns are paid out of funds raised by new investors.

positive screens—selection of investment opportunities based on desirable social responsibility characteristics.

premium—the additional amount that is offered over current market price for the stock of a firm by a bidder seeking control.

present value of growth opportunities (PVGO)—this is present value of all positive net present projects (those that earn a return higher than the cost of capital) that is reflected in the stock price today.

principal—a party who hires another party, the agent, to work on her or his behalf; *see* agency theory.

private information—the superior ability to interpret information or the ability to formulate a "better" belief about the pricing implications of the information.

professional directors—individuals who have retired from their primary profession but are serving as board directors.

pro rata basis—system by which each client account receives an amount in proportion to the size of that account.

proxy fight—a fight over the proxies to elect directors.

proxy statements, or form 14A filings—materials sent to shareholders to disclose the financial performance, executive compensation, board composition, and major shareholder ownership as well as biographical information about the directors that are nominated by the firm and subject to a proxy vote by shareholders.

prudent—describes the situation when corporations take "ethical" actions because it makes good business sense.

Public Company Accounting Oversight Board (PCAOB)—governmental body established by the Sarbanes-Oxley Act of 2002 to oversee and enforce new laws imposed on auditors.

Public Company Accounting Reform and Investor Protection Act of 2002—*see* Sarbanes-Oxley Act of 2002.

pump-and-dump scheme—a tactic designed to artificially increase the price of the stock before selling it.

PVGO—*see* present value of growth opportunities.

Q

quantitative analysts—analysts who use statistical and mathematical techniques applied to large data sets in looking for systematic mispricing of securities.

R

rating agencies—these are agencies, for example, Moody's, that rate the investment safety of various securities, most often the credit safety of debt securities.

realized and unrealized capital gains and losses—changes in price are known as capital gains or capital losses. Capital gains or losses are realized when the security is sold; otherwise, they are unrealized.

regret aversion—taking actions to avoid losses or making mistakes.

Regulation Fair Disclosure (FD)—a rule requiring that conference calls be made publicly available.

residual loss—the loss that occurs because of the inability to enforce all contracts perfectly.

restricted stock—stock that is awarded but whose transfer of ownership is restricted for a certain period of time.

return uncertainty—the uncertainty of the future return or price of a security; *see also* standard deviation.

Rule 10b-5—rule preventing the manipulation of markets either through deceitful trading or use of information (i.e., rumors or inside information).

S

salary—cash amount of compensation paid on an annual basis.

Sarbanes-Oxley Act of 2002—this act (also known as SOX, and as the Public Company Accounting Reform and Investor Protection Act of 2002) was designed to enforce greater accountability for corporate executives for financial statements, more fully disclose compensation contracts and other payments made to executives, and eliminate conflicts of interest between accounting firms and the corporations that they audited. It also established the Public Company Accounting Oversight Board (PCAOB) to oversee and enforce new laws imposed on auditors.

"say on pay" amendments—corporate charter amendments that allow shareholders to provide advisory voting on the approval of CEO compensation.

Securities and Exchange Commission (SEC)—a federal organization that oversees the enforcement of securities laws and information disclosure.

Securities Exchange Acts of 1933 and 1934—established the Securities and Exchange Commission (SEC), new securities laws regulating markets, and filing disclosures including audited financial statements.

self-reversing accruals—when an accrual amount accrues more revenue (less expense) earlier it must accrue less revenue (more expense) later so that the total amount accrued doesn't exceed the total amount of the transaction.

sell side—investment banking firms that sell securities or provide brokerage, trading, for clients.

sell-side analyst—describes analysts who work for companies with investment banking business.

shareholder resolutions—resolutions to the corporate charter, proposed by shareholders, that can be voted on during the annual shareholders meeting as part of the proxy process.

Shariah Board—a board consisting of Muslim scholars who review financial contracts to ensure they are compliant with the Qur'an (Koran).

Sharpe measure—a measure of how well the portfolio is performing relative to risk measured by standard deviation: $S_p = (R_p - R_f)/\text{var } R_p$.

short sales—involves selling a stock you don't own by borrowing one from a broker in the hopes that stock price will decline.

sin stocks—stock of companies that are in the following businesses: alcohol, gambling, tobacco, and adult entertainment.

SIVs—*see* structured investment vehicles.

socially responsible investing (SRI)—seeking to make investments that benefit society, for example investing in the stock of companies that don't pollute.

soft dollars—brokerage commissions generated that can be used for the purchase of services and equipment.

SOX—*see* Sarbanes-Oxley Act of 2002.

special-purpose entity (SPE)—research and other products and services that are paid using trading commissions.

specialists—professionals and/or companies with the role of fulfilling all orders for particular stocks that trade on the New York and American Stock Exchange. On the NASDAQ, these professionals are called market makers. *See also* market makers.

SRI—*see* socially responsible investing.

staggered board—refers to a board that is divided into classes, and only one class of directors is eligible for election in any given year.

stakeholder theory—a theory that firms should maximize the welfare of all groups that are affected by the firm's policies—employees, customers, suppliers, communities, and so on.

standard deviation—total volatility or likely fluctuations of security or portfolio: $(\text{var } (R_i))^{1/2} = ([\Sigma i = 0 \text{ to } n(R_i - E(R_i))^2]/(n - 1))^{1/2}$.

standardized unexpected earnings surprises (SUES)—the difference between actual and forecasted earnings divided by a standard error term from the forecasting model.

star analysts—analysts who are top rated by various financial publications and have the ability to move stock prices with their investment recommendations.

stock appreciation rights—*see* phantom stock.

stock awards—stock-based compensation essential to managers' incentives. There are many types of stock awards.

stock option; stock option grants—the right to buy a stock at a prespecified price, the exercise price, at a prespecified date, the exercise or maturity date, in the future.

stop-loss order—a trade order that specifies a price below (sell) or above (buy) which the order is not to be executed.

structured investment vehicles (SIVs)—a class of securities that are created out of pools or a portfolio of debt obligations that are then sliced into different "pieces" or tranches of the promised cash flows in the portfolio and sold off.

style boxes—these boxes were developed by Morningstar, an independent investment research firm, to allow equity investors and managers to capture both a size (market capitalization) and value-growth continuum for equity investments.

style drift—this is when an investment manager selects securities that move away from the original investment strategy or "style" originally specified by the client; *see also* style boxes.

SUES—*see* standardized unexpected earnings surprises.

sukuks—these are government issued bonds that are structured like securitized leases to avoid paying interest and thus comply with the Qur'an's restrictions on paying interest.

superior voting rights—a class of stock with more than one vote per share.

supermajority amendment—an amendment to the corporate charter that requires more than a simple majority (greater than 50 percent) of votes for a merger to be approved.

surrender charges—charges for withdrawing from an account, usually with annuities.

sweatshops—manufacturing companies, to save money, have working conditions that are dangerous and workers have little to no rights or say in their working conditions.

T

takeover—a transfer of stock ownership control of a firm; *see also* hostile, control contest, *and* hostile tender offer.

target—a firm that a bidder is trying to take over stock ownership control of.

targeted divestment—a model of limiting the number of companies targeted for divestment.

thinly traded—describes securities for which there is not much trading volume.

third-party research—original research that can be purchased from companies such as Standard & Poor's, Bloomberg, or Dow Jones.

tippee—a friend, acquaintance, or anybody else who gets inside information from a corporate fiduciary or another reliable source.

tracking error—a measure of how well the manager is tracking the benchmark; the standard deviation between the return on the portfolio and the return on the benchmark.

Treynor Measure Information Ratio—a measure of how well the portfolio is performing relative to market risk; $T_p = (R_p - R_f)/\beta_p$.

trustee—a fiduciary who acts in the interest of the beneficiaries. *See also* beneficiaries.

two-and-twenty fee structure—this is a fee structure commonly used by hedge funds where management fees are two percent of the dollar amount in the client's account and twenty percent of returns earned in excess of a pre-specified benchmark.

U

unexpected accruals—*see* discretionary accruals.

usury—another term for interest established in the Middle Ages; a term used in the Qur'an.

utilitarian ethics—an ethical philosophy whereby the "end justifies the means"; where the pursuit of self-interest maximizes the benefits to society as a whole.

V

value at risk (VaR)—a measure that tells investors the probability of the dollar amount they can potentially lose during any given period.

vesting—the point at which granted benefits such as stock awards or contributions to retirement plans can be kept by the employees even after leaving the firm.

vote with their feet—occurs when institutional investors disagree with management proposals or director nominees; they sell their shares rather than vote no.

window dressing—the practice by mutual funds of investing in stocks that have done particularly well during the quarter toward the end of the quarter; this is done to give the impression that managers can pick "winners."

Index

F

Fair price amendment, 183
Fair treatment of clients, 43–45
Fairness, 17–18, 51
Fama-French three-factor model (FF), 88
Federal deposit insurance corporation (FDIC), 24
Federal Reserve (FED), 24
Fees, 36–37
    12b-1 fees, 37
    mutual fund, 36
    schedule of management fees, 37
    trailer fees, 37
Fidelity investments and gifts from traders, 39
Fiduciary duty, 17
    of investment professionals, 26–52
        agency versus, 30–32
        efficient markets hypothesis, 28
        Hedge funds, 28
        market timing strategy, 28
        return uncertainty, 28
        role of laws, regulations, and professional
          standards, 32
        tech bubble, 29
Finance committee, 170
Financial Industry Regulatory Authority (FINRA),
    23–24, 32
Financial scandals, *See* Scandals
Firewalls, 98–99, *See also* Chinese walls
First in, first out (FIFO) method, 143
Forecast errors, 119–120
Forecasters, 114, 118–122
Foundations, social role of, 207–208
Friendly tender offer, 182
Front running, 100
FTSE KLD 400 Social Index (KLD400), 202
Fundamental analysts, 117
Future performance, predicting, 58

G

13G form, 174
Generally accepted accounting principles (GAAP), 138
GIM index, 183
Global Investment Performance Standards (GIPS), 56
Golden coffins, 180–181
Golden handcuffs, 180–181
Golden parachutes, 180–181
Grameen Bank, 209
Gray directors, 166

Greed, 18
Green Century Equity Fund (GECQX), 202–203
Gross of fees, 66

H

Hedge funds, 28
Heller, Edwin, 167
Herding, 126–127
    market sentiment and, 126
Heuristics, 127
Hidden debt, 148–149
Hidden risks, 71–73
    leverage, 71–72
    liquidity, 73
    short selling, 72–73
High-speed flash trading, 100–101
Historical risk, time periods, 59–61
    asset-backed securities (ABS), 61
    collateralized debt obligations (CDOs), 61
    mortgage-backed securities (MBSs), 61
    picking benchmarks, 62–66, *See also* Benchmarks,
      picking
    structured investment vehicles (SIVs), 60
    window dressing, 61
Holding period return, 58
Horizon problems, 181
Hostile tender offer, 182
Human rights, 199–200
Hybrid analysis, 117–118

I

IBG YBG (I'll be gone; you'll be gone), 27
Identification of clients, 43–45
Illegal insider trading, 92
Incentives, executive compensation, 174–178
Incumbents, 173
Index fund, 62
Influential publications, 97
Information, 13, 86–110
    advantages from stale prices, 101–105
    asymmetry, 91
    disclosure, SEC, 10
    informed investor, 87
    ratio, 84
Information, ethical use of, 16–17, 86–110, *See also*
  Insider information, trading on
    determination, 89
      accessibility, 89